Frommer's

W9-DDQ-371

Beijing
4th Edition

by Graeme Smith

Here's what the critics say about Frommer's:

"Amazingly easy to use. Very portable, very complete."

—*Booklist*

"Detailed, accurate, and easy-to-read information for all price ranges."
—*Glamour Magazine*

"Hotel information is close to encyclopedic."

—*Des Moines Sunday Register*

"Frommer's Guides have a way of giving you a real feel for a place."
—*Knight Ridder Newspapers*

WILEY

Wiley Publishing, Inc.

About the Author

Graeme Smith has lived in China on and off for the past 17 years. He studied at Beijing and Tsinghua Universities, but attributes his fluency in Mandarin to an incurable love of Chinese soap operas. Graeme is currently a researcher at the Contemporary China Centre of the Australian National University, which gives him a wonderful excuse to spend time with rice farmers and work on poverty alleviation projects in Huoshan County, Anhui (www.cedpa.org.cn).

Published by:

Wiley Publishing, Inc.

111 River St.
Hoboken, NJ 07030-5774

ISBN-13: 978-0-471-76990-3
ISBN-10: 0-471-76990-8

Editor: Caroline Sieg
Production Editor: Eric T. Schroeder
Cartographer: Nick Trotter *(Special thanks to Tim Lohnes)*
Photo Editor: Richard Fox
Production by Wiley Indianapolis Composition Services

Front cover photo: Beijing: Woman in traditional dress talking on cell phone.
Back cover photo: People cycling to work

For information on our other products and services or to obtain technical support, please contact our Customer Care Department within the U.S. at 800/762-2974, outside the U.S. at 317/572-3993 or fax 317/572-4002.

Wiley also publishes its books in a variety of electronic formats. Some content that appears in print may not be available in electronic formats.

Manufactured in the United States of America

5 4 3 2 1

Contents

List of Maps

An Invitation to the Reader

In researching this book, we discovered many wonderful places—hotels, restaurants, shops, and more. We're sure you'll find others. Please tell us about them, so we can share the information with your fellow travelers in upcoming editions. If you were disappointed with a recommendation, we'd love to know that, too. Please write to:

Frommer's Beijing, 4th Edition
Wiley Publishing, Inc. • 111 River St. • Hoboken, NJ 07030-5774

An Additional Note

Please be advised that travel information is subject to change at any time—and this is especially true of prices. We therefore suggest that you write or call ahead for confirmation when making your travel plans. The authors, editors, and publisher cannot be held responsible for the experiences of readers while traveling. Your safety is important to us, however, so we encourage you to stay alert and be aware of your surroundings. Keep a close eye on cameras, purses, and wallets, all favorite targets of thieves and pickpockets.

Other Great Guides for Your Trip:

Frommer's China

Frommer's China: The 50 Most Memorable Trips

Frommer's Shanghai

Frommer's Hong Kong

Suzy Gershman's Born to Shop Hong Kong, Beijing & Shanghai

Frommer's Star Ratings, Icons & Abbreviations

Every hotel, restaurant, and attraction listing in this guide has been ranked for quality, value, service, amenities, and special features using a **star-rating system.** In country, state, and regional guides, we also rate towns and regions to help you narrow down your choices and budget your time accordingly. Hotels and restaurants are rated on a scale of zero (recommended) to three stars (exceptional). Attractions, shopping, nightlife, towns, and regions are rated according to the following scale: zero stars (recommended), one star (highly recommended), two stars (very highly recommended), and three stars (must-see).

In addition to the star-rating system, we also use **eight feature icons** that point you to the great deals, in-the-know advice, and unique experiences that separate travelers from tourists. Throughout the book, look for:

Finds	Special finds—those places only insiders know about
Fun Fact	Fun facts—details that make travelers more informed and their trips more fun
Kids	Best bets for kids and advice for the whole family
Moments	Special moments—those experiences that memories are made of
Overrated	Places or experiences not worth your time or money
Tips	Insider tips—great ways to save time and money
Value	Great values—where to get the best deals
Warning	Warning—traveler's advisories are usually in effect

The following **abbreviations** are used for credit cards:

AE	American Express	DISC	Discover	V	Visa
DC	Diners Club	MC	MasterCard		

Frommers.com

Now that you have the guidebook to a great trip, visit our website at **www.frommers.com** for travel information on more than 3,000 destinations. With features updated regularly, we give you instant access to the most current trip-planning information available. At Frommers.com, you'll also find the best prices on airfares, accommodations, and car rentals—and you can even book travel online through our travel booking partners. At Frommers.com, you'll also find the following:

- Online updates to our most popular guidebooks
- Vacation sweepstakes and contest giveaways
- Newsletter highlighting the hottest travel trends
- Online travel message boards with featured travel discussions

What's New in Běijīng

If there's one thing that remains constant in Běijīng, it's that nothing remains the same. Returning visitors cry, "Where am I? And what have you done with the *real* Běijīng?" Blame the imminent Olympics for the current accelerated rate of change. Go NOW.

GETTING TO KNOW BĚIJĪNG

Traffic has worsened considerably. Measures have been taken to improve the situation, including the removal of the tolls from the Fifth Ring Road, and a hefty fine for drivers who run red lights. But with nearly a thousand new cars hitting the streets every day, gridlock is the norm. Those arriving by air will find a new bus route following the East Third Ring Road via Liàngmǎ Qiáo (near the Kempinski Hotel) to Fāngzhuāng in the south. The fare is still ¥16 ($2). The Sixth Ring Road will be finished by the time you arrive, although you'll have little reason to use it.

There are now 19 brand new Z (*zhídá;* direct) trains connecting with other cities, which depart at night and arrive early the following morning. All compartments are very clean, and staff is noticeably more enthusiastic than on other services. TV screens have been installed in soft-sleeper compartments.

The metro has the new light-rail **Line 8,** which extends **Line 1** further east. Proper machine-readable tickets were promised, but not delivered, but the involvement of the Hong Kong–based MTR Corporation in the construction of the north-south **Line 4** (due for completion in 2008) suggests that fumbling around with paper tickets will soon be in the past. Metro **Line 5,** which will run past the east side of the Temple of Heaven, up to Dōng Dān, Dōng Sì, Lama Temple and further north to the east side of Yàyùn Cūn (Asian Games Village), is projected to open in late 2006.

Vast new rail/metro/light-rail/bus interchanges are under construction at Dōng Zhí Mén and Xī Zhí Mén. Dedicated bus lanes have opened, and should help ease traffic congestion. Road-widening schemes have commenced in the once-charming Dà Zhàlán area, and a proposal to widen Déshèng Mén Nèi Dàjiē will see a 50m-wide (164-ft.) road plow through the middle of Běijīng's finest remaining *hútòng.* A Belgian member of BOGOC (Běijīng Olympic Games organizing committee), presumably commenting from his limousine, has identified *bicycles* as the root of Běijīng's traffic woes, and proposed banning them from the city center.

WHERE TO STAY

Competition is heating up in the **five-star** market with the arrival of several familiar names from the West, and more of the top-rank Asian brands. New arrivals include the excellent **Holiday Inn Central Plaza,** offering great value for money in the south of town, and the less spectacular **Crowne Plaza Park View Wǔzhōu,** appealingly located in Yàyùn Cūn, home to the capital's best new Chinese restaurants. Many upscale properties are due to open during the life of this book, including Park Hyatt,

Westin, Four Seasons, Ritz-Carlton, and a new Marco Polo in Yàyùn Cūn.

Rooms at the **Hilton Běijīng** are much improved after a substantial top-to-bottom refurbishment, and a major makeover at the centrally located **Crowne Plaza Hotel** should be finished when you arrive. **The Peninsula Palace Běijīng** recently completed a 5-year renovation program, and is now our pick for the best address in Běijīng, offering many in-room facilities (free WiFi, plasma TVs, and so on) that are simply unavailable at other hotels.

Converted *hútòng* courtyards *(sìhéyuàn)* are still the most interesting mid-range options. **Héjìng Fǔ Bīnguǎn,** home to the Qiánlóng emperor's third daughter, completed renovations of its spectacular courtyard rooms in 2003, but is yet to decide on whether to rent them to the public or to hand them over to a well-connected official.

Budget options in Běijīng were once restricted to a cluster of dire hotels on the South Third Ring Road. The arrival of Youth Hostel International has changed that. Simple but clean lodgings are now ubiquitous, but demand for rooms is such that it is now advisable to book ahead, using **www.hostelworld.com**. The best of several new YHAs is the **City Central Youth Hostel,** located directly opposite Běijīng Railway Station. We've uncovered inexpensive courtyard accommodation at **Zhōnggòng Běijīng Shì Wěi Bàn Jīguān Zhāodàisuǒ,** a friendly hostel that formerly housed Běijīng's mayor, the shady Wú Dé.

At the other end of the scale, we must mention the **Howard Johnson Paragon Hotel,** where a few years under local management has seen a well-run mid-range hotel transform into a sleazy dive. See chapter 5.

WHERE TO DINE   Turn to our list of specialty dishes in appendix A, and point to the Chinese characters for the dish. It's as easy as that.

Sìchuān cuisine still reigns supreme in the capital, as you'll find at **Málà Yòuhuò,** where locals queue down the street, even on a Monday night. Some of the capital's most authentic cuisine is to be found at restaurants which cater to government officials from different provinces and cities, as no expense is spared to ensure that the cadres obtain authentic ingredients. We introduce **Chuān Jīng Bàn Cāntīng** (Sìchuān) and the **Yúnténg Bīnguǎn** (Yúnnán). You'd never guess it from reading the expatriate magazines, but the center of gravity in Běijīng dining has shifted away from the tired neon of Cháoyáng's embassy areas. The focus now is on both the **Back Lakes area (Shíchà Hǎi),** where stylish decor accompanies—and frequently overshadows—the food, and the **Asian Games Village** area **(Yàyùn Cūn),** home to the city's best new Chinese restaurants. The beloved string of 24-hour restaurants known as **Ghost Street** has largely been reduced to bite-size pieces by the wrecking ball, although a few establishments on its western end still survive. **Starbucks** continues to take over Běijīng, although its coffee is a good deal better than the battery acid served up in some outlets in the U.S. It now faces competition from a handful of cafes that have mastered the bean, notably **Tasty Taste** in Sān Lǐ Tún. See chapter 6.

EXPLORING BĚIJĪNG   Several major sites have introduced seasonal pricing with higher prices from April to October and lower prices from November to March.

Some newly renovated sections of the **Forbidden City** formerly closed to the public have reopened. These include the **Wǔyīng Diàn (Hall of Valiance and Heroism)** and the **Jiànfú Gōng Huāyuán (Garden of the Palace of**

Building Happiness) in the western section of the palace. In the northeast of the palace, the magnificent private theater of the Qiánlóng emperor, **Juànqín Zhāi**, will open in late 2006. Do not miss it. The **Lìdài Dìwáng Miào (Temple for Emperors of Past Dynasties)**, where the emperors of the Míng and the Qīng came to pay homage to their forebears, has reopened to the public after decades of neglect. The whole of **Prince Gōng's Mansion** should be open to the public by 2008, more than 2 decades after the current tenants were provided with funds to relocate. If you have an interest in Buddhist art, take the chance to visit **Fǎhǎi Sì** in the far west of town, as there are rumors that it may be closed to protect the stunning frescoes. A second eunuch museum is due to open south of the Summer Palace, at the **Lìmǎ Guāndì Miào.** In the name of the Olympics, the automobile, or just naked greed, the destruction of the city's charming *hútòng* has been continuing apace. See what you can, because it probably won't be there next time you visit. See chapter 7.

BĚIJĪNG STROLLS   We introduce a new stroll, far from the pedicab tours, which takes you along narrow, temple-lined lanes; to the former residences of two of China's most influential artists and a local wet market; you have the chance to meet bonsai and Peking opera aficionados and drink tea in a former concubine's residence. See chapter 8.

SHOPPING   The future of Běijīng's largest money-losing **Friendship Store** looks doubtful, although one announcement of its demise has already proven premature. The renowned **Silk Market** has been moved indoors, but is now a feeble copy of **Sān Lǐ Tún Yǎxiù Fúzhuāng Shìchǎng,** located in the old Kylin Plaza building. Preferable to both is **Rì Tán Shāngwù Lóu** where you'll find more than 70 shops stocking high-quality women's clothing, footwear, and accessories. See chapter 9.

BĚIJĪNG AFTER DARK   Despite government attempts to nudge nightlife in the direction of Cháoyáng Park, where it is less likely to disturb residents, Běijīng's bars and clubs have instead proliferated all over the city. The greatest explosion has again been in and around the **Back Lakes,** where bright green beer signs and the thump of dance music increasingly confuse the senses, otherwise lulled into vulnerability by the pleasant scenery. One bar that rises above the neon is **Bed,** perfect for a mojita on a summer's evening. Many of Běijīng's best bars are now surprisingly found inside hotels, most notably **Centro** in the Kerry Centre, the **Red Moon Bar** in the Grand Hyatt, and **Cloud Nine Bar** in the Shangri-La Hotel. The wrecker's ball and a shifty landlord spelled the end for the **No Name Bar** and **Treelounge,** respectively, though the void was quickly filled by **Babyface, Destination,** and Běijīng's finest live music venue, **Yú Gōng Yí Shān.** See chapter 10.

AROUND BĚIJĪNG   The Great Wall finally boasts respectable lodgings, allowing you to appreciate its ancient ramparts at sunset and sunrise. If expense is no object, treat yourself to the **Red Capital Ranch,** a boutique resort styled after a Manchurian hunting lodge, set in a river valley near **Mùtiányù.** Those on a budget will find adequate lodgings at the friendly **Sīmǎtái Youth Hostel.** See chapter 11.

1

The Best of Běijīng

If you can see only one city in China, it should be Běijīng, because many of the capital's "bests" are also China's "bests." We've included the obvious, but also the offbeat experiences that reflect the city far better than any list of tourist sites, as impressive as those sites are. We give you the best of the splurge hotels, but also the best moderately priced hotels—prices far more in keeping with the real Chinese economy. We give you the most unforgettable dining experiences, plus the best things to do for free (or almost). If imitation is the highest form of flattery, then our competitors have flattered us highly. But they'll always be a few steps behind . . .

1 The Most Unforgettable Běijīng Experiences

- **Dining & Drinking around the Back Lakes:** The combination of peaceful man-made lakes, many of the city's best bars and restaurants, and several pockets of rambling lanes called *hútòng* keep foreign residents coming back here despite the growing crowds. Dine with a view of the lakes (or arrange to eat on a private traditional boat), take a post-meal stroll through the less explored lanes, and find your way back to the lakes to sip gin-and-tonics as lights from nearby courtyard mansions flicker on the water. See "Back Lakes & Dōng Chéng" (p. 87) for recommended restaurants, and see chapter 10 for recommended bars.

- **Enjoying a Moment of Quiet at the Museum of Ancient Architecture:** Standing just west of the Temple of Heaven on grounds once nearly as extensive as those of its neighbor, the Altar of Agriculture is largely overlooked. So is its excellent museum, in halls with a grandeur to match those at the heart of the Forbidden City,

but receiving fewer than one ten-thousandth of the visitors. See p. 138.

- **Investigating the Northeast Corner of the Forbidden City:** Away from the main north-south axis on which the former palace's grander halls stand, there's a more human scale similar to that of the rapidly disappearing *hútòng* beyond the palace's walls, although with much greater luxury. Venturing so far from the main arteries, is well worth the effort for such treasures like the ornate theater building where the Empress Dowager Cíxǐ watched her favorite operas on demand, and the well in which she ended the life of her nephew's favorite concubine. See p. 124.

- **Rubbing Shoulders with Monks at Běijīng Temples:** Among the capital's temples that have once again become genuine places of worship as well as tourist attractions, the **Yōnghé Gōng** (p. 135) has an active and approachable community of Tibetan monks (although under careful scrutiny by the authorities), while leafy **Fǎyuán Sì** (p. 132) houses amicable Chinese Buddhist monks in Běijīng's most venerable temple. **Báiyún Guàn** (p. 131) is the Daoist alternative, where blue-frocked monks wear their hair in the rarely seen traditional manner—long and tied in a bun at the top of the head.

- **Bargaining for Fakes:** At **Pānjiāyuán Jiùhuò Shìchǎng,** the first asking prices for foreigners are at least 10 to 15 times those asked of Chinese, but this weekend market has the city's best selection of bric-a-brac, including row upon crowded row of calligraphy, jewelry, ceramics, teapots, ethnic clothing, Buddha statues, paper lanterns, Cultural Revolution memorabilia, army belts, little wooden boxes, Míng- and Qīng-style furniture, old pipes, opium scales, painted human skulls, and more conventional souvenirs. A similar, but more intimate market at **Bàoguó Sì Wénhuà Gōngyìpǐn Shìchǎng** is set in the grounds of an ancient temple, and is open all week long. Bargaining fun can also be had at **Yǎxiù Fúzhuāng Shìchǎng,** a hunting ground for souvenirs and gifts including kites, calligraphy materials, army surplus gear, tea sets, and farmer's paintings from Xī'ān. The basement and the first two floors house a predictable but comprehensive collection of imitation and pilfered brand-name clothing, shoes, and luggage. Starting prices are increasingly imaginative, however. See p. 167 for all three markets.

- **Haggling for Tea at Mǎlián Dào:** If you're serious about tea, this is the only place to go. Mǎlián Dào may not have all the tea in China, but it does have over a mile of shops hawking tea leaves and their paraphernalia. Most shops are run by the extended families of tea growers from Fújiàn and Zhèjiāng provinces, and you may

rate this friendly street the highlight of your visit. See p. 179.

- **Attending Běijīng Opera at the Zhèngyǐcí Xìlóu:** The Zhèngyǐcí, last of a handful of theaters that supported Běijīng Opera from its beginnings, only occasionally hosts performances and is under constant threat of permanent closure. But the scarcity of performances only makes the experience of watching the colorful operas in this intimate, traditionally decorated space all the more precious. *Tip:* Ask your hotel staff to call and ask about performance schedules and tickets. See p. 183.

- **Unwinding at a Traditional Teahouse:** Several quiet teahouses offer you the chance to remove yourself temporarily from the tourist rush. The teahouse in the **Sānwèi Bookstore** (p. 171) offers live traditional music with its bottomless cups of jasmine. For a little extra, the **Purple Vine Tea House** (p. 191) near the Forbidden City and **The Teahouse of Family Fù** (p. 192) in the Back Lakes area brew your Oolong (Wūlóng) in the Chinese version of the tea ceremony. All three teahouses are furnished with replica Míng dynasty tables and chairs and make ideal spots for reading, writing, or doing absolutely nothing.

- **Seeing a Band at Yúgōng Yíshān:** The owners of the now defunct Loup Chante have created what Běijīng lacked for years: an atmospheric venue showcasing an eclectic range of musical styles, from Mongolian mouth music to acid jazz. It's stuffy, smoky, difficult to find, and run by serious and talented musicians. See appendix A for more about Běijīng music.

- **Hiking along the Great Wall from Jīn Shān Lǐng to Sīmǎtái:** Visitors are scarce at Jīn Shān Lǐng, although the Wall runs in a continuous ribbon along a high ridge, several kilometers visible at a time. Strike out eastwards to Sīmǎtái and you'll quickly reach unrestored and crumbling sections of considerable charisma. Views sweep across a sea of blossoms in spring and rich reds and golds in autumn. See p. 199.

• **Taking a Trip to Qīng Dōng Líng:** The Eastern Qīng Tombs offer more

to the visitor than the better-known Míng Tombs, but see a fraction of the visitors. Undeniably difficult to reach, the effort is rewarded many times over by the Qiánlóng emperor's breathtakingly beautiful tomb chamber, Yù Líng, and a drop-dead funny photo exhibit of the much-maligned dowager empress Cíxǐ. See p. 202.

2 The Best Splurge Hotels

• **The Peninsula Palace Běijīng** (Jīnyú Hútòng 8; ✆ **1866/382-8388** or 010/8516-2888). Glowing after a 4-year renovation program, the Peninsula is still the only hotel in mainland China which will send a Rolls-Royce to collect you from the airport. There's free wireless Internet in all rooms, huge plasma-screen televisions, and bedside controls for just about every function in the entire room. They also boast the most thorough staff training program: Everyone from the bell boy to the business center staff is at the top of their game. See p. 65.

• **Red Capital Residence** (Dōngsì Liù Tiáo 9; ✆ **010/8403-5308**). This boutique hotel has only five rooms, all decorated with gorgeous Art Deco

furniture salvaged by its owner from the Zhōngnánhǎi government compound. Cool slate floors, Máo-inspired kitsch, and a peaceful traditional courtyard complete the picture. The secluded concubines' quarters are the two most romantic rooms in the capital. See p. 68.

• **St. Regis Běijīng** (Jiànguó Mén Wài Dàjiē 21; ✆ **010/6460–6688**). Nothing comes close to the personalized service offered at the St. Regis, where an impeccably trained butler attends to every need, from posting a parcel to pressing your pants. At the end of the day, you can take your pick of unwinding in the luxurious spa, the cozy Press Club Bar, or the deep tub in your marvelously appointed bathroom. See p. 71.

3 The Best Moderately Priced Hotels

• **City Central Youth Hostel** (Běijīng Zhàn Qián Jiē 1; ✆ **010/6525-8066**): The railway station area finally boasts a well-run, affordable hotel. Explicitly modeled on Sydney's Central YHA, this hostel set in the old post office building has simply furnished rooms with spotless bathrooms and free in-room broadband for just ¥268 ($33). See p. 74.

• **Far East Youth Hostel** (Tiěshù Xié Jiē 113; ✆ **010/6301-8811,** ext.

3118): The best budget option in Běijīng is located at the center of one of the city's most interesting *hútòng* neighborhoods, only a 10-minute walk from both the Hépíng Mén and Qián Mén metro stops. It has clean, nicely renovated three-star rooms at unbeatable rates (¥200/$25 with a little bargaining). See p. 76.

• **Fēiyīng Bīnguǎn** (Xuānwǔ Mén XīDàjiē 10; ✆ **010/6317-1116**): The most "hotel-like" branch of Youth

Hostelling International in Běijīng. Dorms have in-room bathroom and brand-new floors, and beds are only ¥60 ($7.50). See p. 76.

4 The Most Unforgettable Dining Experiences

- **Dào Jiā Cháng** (Guāngxī Mén Běilǐ 20; ⓒ **010/6422-1078**): Loud as any street market, with service like a hurricane, this inexpensive eatery offers the most memorable experience of the capital's native cuisine, from shouted welcome to final belch. See p. 98.

- **Kèjiā Cài** (Southeast bank of Qián Hǎi; ⓒ **010/6404-2259**): There are fancier places to eat in Běijīng, but none can top the Hakka minority food of this charming establishment. Literally every item on the menu sings with flavor. The paper-wrapped fish is culinary Nirvana. Add a charming location, delightful decor, and reasonable prices. See p. 90.

- **Kǒng Yǐjǐ Jiǔlóu** (Northwest bank of Hòu Hǎi; ⓒ **010/6618-4917**): This crowded restaurant is decorated with the trappings of Chinese scholarship and named for the scholar-bum protagonist of a Lǔ Xùn short story. It specializes in the delicate and delicious Huáiyáng dishes of northern Zhèjiāng, the author's place of origin, as well as the birthplace of "yellow wine" which impaired his character's career. See p. 91.

- **RBL** (Dōng'ān Mén Dàjiē 53; ⓒ **010/6522-1389**): Newly opened RBL oozes chic simplicity, and is the closest the capital comes to a serious upscale dining adventure. Aside from the excellent Japanese-inspired cuisine, there's an adventurous wine list and superb cocktails. Round off the occasion by taking in a world-class live jazz performance in the attached subterranean bar, Icehouse. See p. 86 and 186, respectively.

5 The Best Things to Do for Free (or Almost)

- **Go Bohemian at Factory 798:** We left Factory 798 out of the previous edition, reasoning that an ad hoc gathering of performance artists, painters, and sculptors in a former military complex wasn't something the regime would tolerate. We were wrong. Market rents are now charged, so don't expect to pick up a bargain, but there's no need to make a purchase: The Dàshānzi art district makes for a thoroughly enjoyable afternoon of gallery and cafe hopping. See p. 140.

- **Pay Your Respects to the Chairman:** While Jung Chang's *Máo: The Untold Story* subjects the Great Helmsman to a Cultural Revolution–style denunciation, you'll find no trace of such disrespect inside **Chairman Máo's Mausoleum,** set to the south side of Tiān'ān Mén Square. While there are souvenir vendors, this is far from the kitsch experience you may expect. See p. 110.

- **Exercise with Octogenarians:** At the break of dawn each day, retired Beijingers flock to numerous local parks. Aside from *tàijíquán* and ballroom dancing, you may spy master calligraphers practicing their art with oversize sponge-tipped brushes, or amateur troupes performing Běijīng Opera or revolutionary airs from the 1950s. See section 6 of chapter 7, "Parks & Gardens."

2

Planning Your Trip to Běijīng

Visiting China isn't as hard as you think it is. If you can manage Paris by yourself without speaking French, you can manage Běijīng without Mandarin. Tens of thousands of visitors travel in China independently each year, making arrangements as they go and without more than a guidebook and phrase book to help them. You can certainly arrange various levels of assistance, either on arrival or from home, but you can also travel just as freely as you would elsewhere, perhaps using agents to get your tickets and picking up the odd day tour.

But whether you plan to travel at random, with a pre-booked route, or with a fully escorted tour, it's *vital* that you read this chapter carefully in order to understand how the way you travel, even in many other developing nations, doesn't apply here. Much supposed wisdom on China travel is far from wise, what's good advice in the rest of the world is often the worst advice in China, and without absorbing what's below, some of the rest of this guide may seem inscrutable.

So put down your preconceptions, and read on . . .

1 Visitor Information

NATIONAL TOURIST OFFICES

The mainland travel industry is, in general, a quagmire of deception that provides no truly reliable information either within China or via its overseas operations. The branches of the China National Tourism Administration in foreign countries are called **China National Tourist Offices.** Nominally nonprofit, they used to be little more than agents for the state-owned China International Travel Service (CITS), but they now offer links to a variety of operators. Don't expect them to be accurate about even the most basic visa or

---

Tips Before you go

Offset the greenhouse gas emissions generated by your air travel. There are a number of organizations that do this by purchasing "greenhouse credits" on your behalf. The credits cancel out those generated by your flights. They do this by investing in projects that prevent greenhouse gases entering the atmosphere, such as clean energy (wind power, solar power, and energy efficiency projects) or planting trees to absorb greenhouse gases. For more information, visit www.climatefriendly.com, www.climatecare.co.uk, or www.futureforests.com.

Consider planning domestic travel within China by train or bus: You'll see far more of rural China (the life of 70% of the Chinese, which differs hugely from urban China), and your travels will emit far less carbon dioxide than air travel.

China

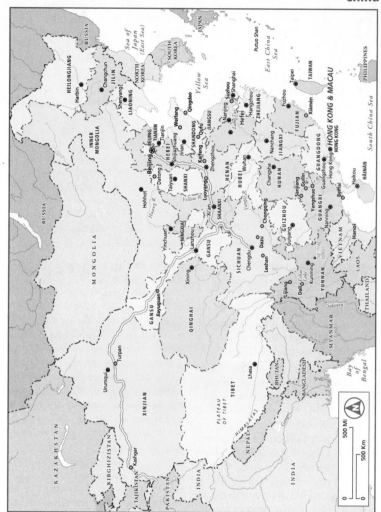

Customs regulations, and don't expect them to update their websites, which sometimes give conflicting information and can't even get the names of tour operators right.

Tourist offices are in the following locations:

- In the **United States:** 350 Fifth Ave., Suite 6413, Empire State Building, New York, NY 10118 (© **212/760-8218/8807/4002;** fax 212/760-8809; ny@cnta.gov.cn); 600 W. Broadway, Suite 320, Glendale, CA 91204 (© **818/545-7505;** fax 828/545-7506; la@cnta.gov.cn).

- In **Canada:** 480 University Ave., Suite 806, Toronto, ONT M5G 1V2

(© **416/599-6636;** fax 416/599-6382; www.tourismchina-ca.com).

- In the **U.K.:** 71 Warwick Rd., London SW5 9HB (© **020-7373-0888;** fax 020-7370-9989; london@cnta gov.cn).
- In **Australia:** Level 19, 44 Market St., Sydney, NSW 2000 (© **02/9299-4057;** fax 02/9290-1958; sydney@ cnta.gov.cn).

BĚIJĪNG ONLINE

Be cautious of official sources of information and unofficial Chinese-run sources alike, especially if they also offer travel services. Canadian-owned but Běijīng-based *Xiànzài* (www.xianzai.com) offers a weekly e-mail newsletter with hotel, restaurant, and airfare advertising (often including special offers only publicized locally), and a diary of events. The site also offers an assortment of other newsletters with information on travel in China.

Amateurish expat magazines, such as *that's Beijing* (www.thatsbj.com) and *Time Out,* have a certain amount of Běijīng news, information about what's on, and new restaurant reviews online, along with modest features on Běijīng life.

For an ad- and spam-free general discussion of any Běijīng (or other China) travel issues not covered in this book, subscribe to the e-mail discussion list *The Oriental-List.* To subscribe, send a blank e-mail to subscribe-oriental-list@ datasinica.com.

2 Entry Requirements & Customs

ENTRY REQUIREMENTS

PASSPORT   Visitors must have a valid **passport** with at least 6 months' validity and two blank pages remaining (you *may* get away with just one blank page).

VISAS   All visitors to **mainland China** (as opposed to Special Administrative Regions of Hong Kong and Macau) must acquire a visa in advance. Visa applications typically take 3 to 5 working days to process, although this can be shortened to as little as 1 day if you apply in person and pay extra fees. "L" (tourist) visas are valid for between 1 and 3 months. Usually 1 month is granted unless you request more, which you may or may not get according to events in China at the time. Double-entry tourist visas are also available. It varies, but typically your visit must *begin* within 90 days of the date of issue.

You should apply for a visa in person at your nearest **consulate,** although it's possible to obtain Chinese visas in other countries while you're on an extended trip. To apply for a visa, you must complete an **application form,** which can be downloaded from many consular websites or acquired by mail. Visas are valid for the whole country, although some small areas require an extra permit from the local police. Temporary restrictions, sometimes for years at a time, may be placed on areas where there is unrest, and a further permit may be required to enter them. In general, do not mention Tibet or Xīnjiāng on your visa application, or it may be turned down flat.

Some consulates request that you show them an airline ticket, itinerary, or proof of sufficient funds, or they claim to issue visas only to those traveling in groups (while happily carrying on business with individuals who have none of the supporting documentation). Such guidelines provide consulates with a face-saving excuse for refusing a visa should there be unrest or political difficulties, or should Tibet or Xīnjiāng appear on the application.

One **passport photograph** is required per adult, as well as for any child traveling on a parent's passport.

A complete list of all Chinese embassies and consulates, including addresses and contact information, can be found at the Chinese foreign ministry's website: www.fmprc.gov.cn/eng (or various mirror sites around the world). Click on "Missions Overseas." Many consulates (including all those in the U.S. and Canada) will only accept applications in person; applications by post or courier must go through an agent, which charges additional fees. Contacting some embassies can be very difficult: Many telephone systems are automated, and reaching a human can be next to impossible; faxes and e-mails usually don't receive a reply; and websites are often out of date.

What follows are visa fees and requirements for some countries:

- **United States:** Single-entry visas are US$50; double-entry US$75. Visit www.china-embassy.org, which has links to all U.S. consular sites and a downloadable application form. Applications must be delivered and collected by hand, or sent via a visa agency.
- **Canada:** Single-entry visas are C$50; double-entry C$75. Visit www.chinaembassycanada.org for an application form. Applications must be delivered and collected by hand, or sent via a visa agency.
- **United Kingdom:** Single-entry visas are £30; double-entry £45. There's a supplementary charge of £20 for each package dealt with by mail. Visit www.chinese-embassy.org.uk for an application.
- **Australia:** Single-entry visas are A$30; double-entry A$45. Add A$10 per package dealt with by mail or courier, and a pre-paid return envelope. Visit www.chinaembassy.org.au for an application.
- **New Zealand:** Single-entry visas are NZ$60; double-entry NZ$90. Add NZ$15 per package dealt with by mail or courier, and a pre-paid return envelope. Visit www.chinaembassy.org.nz or www.chinaconsulate.org.nz for an application.

Note: The visa **fees** quoted above for each country are the current rates for *nationals of that country,* and can change at any time. In addition to the visa fees quoted, there may be supplementary fees for postage. Payment must always be in cash or by money order.

VISA EXTENSIONS Single-entry tourist visas may be extended once for a maximum of 30 days at the PSB Exit/Entry Division offices in most cities. The office in Běijīng (📞 **010/8401-5292**) is on the south side of the eastern North Second Ring Road, just east of the Lama Temple metro stop (Mon–Sat 8:30am–4:30pm). Applications take 4 working days to process. Bring your passport and two passport photos (these can be taken at the office for ¥30/$4). Extension fees vary by nationality: U.S. citizens pay ¥414 ($52), U.K. citizens ¥469 ($59), Canadians and Australians ¥160 ($20).

GETTING A VISA IN HONG KONG Nationals of most developed nations do not require a visa to enter Hong Kong, and visas for mainland China are more easily obtainable there than anywhere else.

The cheapest tourist visas are available at the **Visa Office of the PRC,** 7th floor, Lower Block, China Resources Building, 26 Harbour Rd., Wanchai (📞 **852/3413-2424;** www.fmcoprc.gov.hk; Mon–Fri 9am–12pm and 2–5pm). Here a single-entry tourist visa costs HK$390 ($50) for U.S. citizens, HK$450 ($58) for citizens of the U.K., and HK$150 (US$19) for Canadians and Australians. Same-day service costs an extra HK$250 (US$32). For urgent departures, or 6-month "F" *(fǎngwèn)* visas, go to **Grand Profit International Travel Agency,** 705AA, 7th Floor, New East

Ocean Centre, 9 Science Museum Rd., Tsimshatsui (about a 15-min. walk east of Nathan Rd.; © **852/2723-3288**).

CUSTOMS
WHAT YOU CAN BRING INTO CHINA
In general terms, you can bring anything into China for personal use that you plan to take back with you, with the usual exceptions of arms and drugs, or plant materials, animals, and foods from diseased areas. There are no problems with cameras or video recorders, GPS equipment, laptops, or any other standard electronic equipment. Two unusual prohibitions are "old/used garments" and "printed matter, magnetic media, films, or photographs which are deemed to be detrimental to the political, economic, cultural and moral interests of China," as the regulations put it. Large quantities of religious literature, overtly political materials, or books on Tibet might cause you difficulties but, in general, small amounts of personal reading matter in non-Chinese languages do not present problems. Customs officers are for the most part easygoing, and foreign visitors are rarely searched. Customs declaration forms have now vanished from all major points of entry, but if you are importing more than US$5,000 in cash, you should declare it, or theoretically you could face difficulties at the time of departure—although, again, this is highly unlikely.

WHAT YOU CAN TAKE HOME FROM CHINA
An official seal must be attached to any item created between 1795 and 1949 that is taken out of China; older items cannot be exported. But, in fact, you are highly unlikely to find any genuine antiques, so this is moot (however, a genuine antiques dealer would know how to obtain the seal).

3 Money

CURRENCY
Although for most destinations it's usually a good idea to exchange at least some money before you leave home so you can avoid the less-favorable rates at airport currency-exchange desks, mainland China is different. RMB yuán are not easily obtainable overseas, and rates are worse when they can be found.

There is no legal private money-changing in mainland China. Nationwide outlets offer the same rates on a daily basis. You can exchange currency at the airport when you arrive, at larger branches of the Bank of China, at a bank desk in your hotel, or at major department stores. Shops that offer to exchange money at other than formal Bank of China exchange counters do so illegally, and are known for rate shenanigans and passing fake bills, which are fairly common. *Do not deal with black market money-changers.*

Keep receipts when you exchange money, and you can **reconvert** excess ¥RMB into hard currency when you leave China, although sometimes not more than half the total sum for which you can produce receipts, and sometimes these receipts must be not more than 3 months old.

Hotel exchange desks will only change money for their guests but are open very long hours, 7 days a week. **Banking hours** vary from branch to branch but are limited on Saturday, and banks are closed on Sunday. For more information, see "Banks, Currency Exchanges & ATMs" in the "Fast Facts: Běijīng" section of chapter 4.

YUÁN NOTES There are notes for ¥100, ¥50, ¥20, ¥10, ¥5, ¥2, and ¥1, which also appears as a coin. The word *yuán* is rarely spoken, and sums are referred to as *kuài qián,* "pieces of

Exchange Rates: the Yuán, the Dollar, the Pound & the "Crawling Peg"

In a bid to avert a trade war with the U.S., China allowed a 2% appreciation of the yuán in 2005. It is no longer pegged solely to the U.S. dollar, but rather a basket of currencies, in an arrangement known as a "crawling peg." The U.S. dollar has recently been trading around ¥8.09, the pound sterling at ¥14.88, and the euro at ¥10.06. For this edition, we have taken ¥8 to the U.S. dollar as an approximate conversion, as major appreciation of the yuán seems unlikely. The latest rates can be found at www.xe.com/ucc.

money," usually shortened to just *kuài*. *Sān kuài* is ¥3. Notes carry Arabic numerals as well as numbers in Chinese characters, so there's no fear of confusion. The next unit down, the *jiǎo* (¥0.10), is spoken of as the *máo*. There are notes of a smaller size for ¥0.50, ¥0.20, and ¥0.10, as well as coins for these values. The smallest and almost worthless unit is the *fēn* (both written and spoken), or cent. Unbelievably, when you change money you may be given tiny notes or lightweight coins for ¥0.05, ¥0.02, and ¥0.01, but this is the only time you'll see them except in the bowls of beggars or donation boxes in temples. The most useful note is the ¥10 ($1.25), so keep a good stock. Street stalls, convenience stores, and taxis are often unhappy to receive ¥100 ($13) notes.

ATMS

There are many ATMs in China, but with few exceptions, only a selection of Bank of China machines accept foreign cards. Check the back of your ATM card for the logos of the **Cirrus** (www.master card.com), **PLUS** (www.visa.com), and **Aeon** (www.americanexpress.com) systems, and then contact the relevant company for a list of working ATM locations in Běijīng, which is fairly well served. The capital also has one branch each of Citibank and the Hongkong and Shànghǎi Bank, whose machines take just

about any card ever invented. Bank of China machines have a limit of ¥2,500 ($310) per transaction, but they often allow a second transaction the same day. *Note:* If you have memorized you PIN as a word, be sure to learn it as a number.

TRAVELER'S CHECKS

Traveler's checks are only accepted at selected branches of the Bank of China, at foreign exchange desks in hotels, and at the exchange desks of some department stores. In bigger bank branches, checks in any hard currency and from any major company are welcome, but at department-store exchange desks, currencies of the larger economies are preferred. You can exchange U.S. dollars in cash at most branches of almost any Chinese bank, so even if you plan to bring checks, having a few U.S. dollars in cash (in good condition) for emergencies is a good idea. Checks attract a marginally better exchange rate than cash, but the .75% commission on checks makes the result slightly worse (worse still if you paid commission when buying them).

CREDIT CARDS

Although Visa and MasterCard signs abound, credit cards are of limited use—in many cases only the Chinese versions of the cards are accepted. You can use foreign cards at most hotels, but they are accepted only at relatively upmarket

What Things Cost in Běijīng	Yen ¥	U.S.$	U.K.£
Taxi from airport to city center (use meter!)	64.00-96.00	8.00–12.00	4.30–6.50
Up to 4km (2½ miles) by taxi	10.00	1.25	0.67
Metro ride	3.00	0.38	0.20
Local telephone call	0.48	0.06	0.03
Hearty bowl of beef noodles at a basic restaurant	4.80	0.60	0.32
Regular coffee at Starbucks	12.00	1.50	0.81
McDonald's set meal for one	18.00	2.25	1.21
Tasty dinner for two at a simple homestyle restaurant	30.00	3.75	2.02
Dinner for two in restaurants around foreigner-frequented bar areas	100.00	12.50	6.72
Dinner for two in top hotel restaurants	640.00	80.00	43.00
Bottle of beer at an ordinary restaurant or store	3.00	0.38	0.20
Bottle of beer in a foreigner-frequented bar district	30.00	3.80	2.04
Admission to the Forbidden City	60.00	7.50	4.32
Admission to the Lama Temple	24.00	3.00	1.61

restaurants outside hotels, and at those souvenir shops where you are paying well over the odds—in fact, if a shop accepts foreign credit cards, you might consider looking elsewhere.

You can also obtain cash advances on your MasterCard, Visa, Diners Club, or Amex cards at major branches of the Bank of China, with a minimum withdrawal of ¥1,200 ($150) and 4% commission, plus whatever your card issuer charges you—this expensive way to withdraw cash only makes sense for emergencies. If you do plan to use your card while in China, it's a good idea to call your issuer in advance to let them know that you'll do so.

EMERGENCY CASH American Express runs an **emergency check cashing system,** which allows you to use one of your own checks or a counter check (more expensively) to draw money in the currency of your choice from selected banks. Consult American Express for a list of participating banks before leaving home.

You can also have money wired from **Western Union** (✆ **800/325-6000;** www.westernunion.com) to you at many post offices and branches of the Agricultural Bank of China across China, including 49 in Běijīng. Western Union charges a 0.5% service fee. You must present valid ID to pick up the cash at the Western Union office.

4 When to Go

The biggest factor in your calculations on when to visit Běijīng should be the movement of domestic tourists, who during the longer public holidays take to the road in tens or even hundreds of millions, filling transportation, booking out hotels, and turning even the quieter tourist sights into litter-strewn bedlam.

PEAK TRAVEL SEASONS Chinese New Year (Spring Festival) Like many Chinese festivals, this one operates on the lunar calendar. Solar equivalents for the next few years are January 29, 2006; February 18, 2007; and February 7, 2008. The effects of this holiday are felt from 2 weeks before the date until 2 weeks after, when anyone who's away from home attempts to get back, including an estimated 150 million migrant workers. If you are flying from overseas to Bĕijīng, this won't affect you, but a land approach may be difficult, except in the few days immediately surrounding the holiday. Banks, as well as smaller restaurants and businesses, may be shut for a week. But main attractions are mostly open.

Labor Day & National Day In a policy known as "holiday economics," the May 1 and October 1 holidays have now been expanded to 7 days each (including 1 weekend—most people are expected to work through the weekend prior to the holiday in exchange for 2 weekdays, which are added to the official 3 days of holiday). These two holidays now mark the beginning and end of the domestic travel season, and mark the twin peaks of leisure travel, with the remainder of May, early June, and September also busy. The exact dates of each holiday are not announced until around 2 weeks before each takes place.

CLIMATE For the best weather, visit Bĕijīng in September or October when warm, dry, sunny days with clear skies and pleasantly cool evenings are the norm. The second best time is spring, late March to mid-May, when winds blow away the pollution but also sometimes bring clouds of scouring sand for a day or two, turning the sky a livid yellow. Winters can be bitter, but the city is much improved visually under a fresh blanket of snow: The gaudy colors of the Forbidden City's palaces are emphasized, as is the Great Wall's bleakness. Summers are humid and hot, but air-conditioning makes them tolerable. The number of foreign visitors is high during summer, but the Chinese themselves mostly wait until the weather cools before traveling.

Bĕijīng's Average Temperatures & Rainfall

	Jan	Feb	Mar	Apr	May	June	July	Aug	Sept	Oct	Nov	Dec
Temp. (°F)	26	31	43	57	68	76	79	77	69	57	41	30
Temp. (°C)	-3	-1	6	14	20	24	26	25	21	14	5	-1
Days of Rain	2.1	3.1	4.5	5.1	6.4	9.7	14.5	14.1	6.9	5.0	3.6	1.6

HOLIDAYS A few years ago the Chinese were finally granted a 2-day weekend, but while offices close, shops, restaurants, post offices, transportation, and sights all operate the same services 7 days a week. Most sights, shops, and restaurants are open on public holidays, too, but offices and anything government-related close for as much time as possible. Although China switched to the Gregorian calendar in 1911, some public holidays (and many festivals—see the following "Bĕijīng Calendar of Events") are on a lunar cycle, with solar dates varying from year to year. Holidays are **New Year's Day** (Jan 1), **Spring Festival** (Chinese New Year's day and the following 2 days—see "Peak Travel Seasons" above, for exact dates in coming years), **Labor Day** (May 1 plus up to 4 more weekdays and a weekend), **National Day** (Oct 1 plus extra days, as for Labor Day).

BĔIJĪNG CALENDAR OF EVENTS

Festivals are more family affairs in Bĕijīng, which doesn't have much of a calendar of public events compared with some other parts of China.

Winter

Spring Festival (Chūn Jié), or Chinese New Year, is still the occasion for large lion dances and other celebrations in Chinatowns worldwide, but in mainland China it's mainly a time for everyone to return to his or her ancestral home and feast. Fireworks are now banned in Běijīng, however. Temple fairs have been revived in Běijīng but are mostly fairly low-key shopping opportunities without much of the color or professional entertainers of old. But in the countryside, there's been a gradual revival of stilt-walking and masked processions. New Year is on the day of the first new moon after January 21, and can be no later than February 20.

Lantern Festival (Dēng Jié) perhaps reached its peak in the late Qīng dynasty, when temples, stores, and other public places were hung with fantastically shaped and decorated lanterns. Many people paraded through the streets with lightweight lanterns in the shapes of fish, sheep, or other animals, and hung others, often decorated with riddles, outside their houses. There are modest signs of a revival. This festival always falls 15 days after Spring Festival.

Spring

Tomb-Sweeping Festival (Qīngmíng), frequently observed in Chinese communities overseas, and more often in rural areas of China, as a family outing on a free day near the festival date. It's a day for honoring ancestors by visiting and tidying their gravesites, and making offerings of snacks and alcohol, which often turns into a picnic. April 5.

Autumn

The last remnant of the **Mid-Autumn Festival (Tuányuán Jié),** except among literary-minded students, is the giving and eating of *yuèbing* (moon cakes), circular pies with sweet and extremely fattening fillings. Traditionally it's a time to sit and read poetry under the full moon, but pollution has made the moon largely invisible. Takes place the 15th day of the 8th lunar month (usually Sept).

National Day itself is for avoiding Tiān'ān Mén Square, especially if the government considers the anniversary important enough for one of its military parades, when the square may be blocked to you anyway. October 1.

5 Travel Insurance

Check your existing insurance policies and credit card coverage before you buy travel insurance. You may already be covered for lost luggage, cancelled tickets, or medical expenses. The cost of travel insurance varies widely, depending on the cost and length of your trip, your age, your health, and the type of trip you're taking.

TRIP-CANCELLATION INSURANCE Trip-cancellation insurance helps you get your money back if you have to back out of a trip, if you have to go home early, or if your travel supplier goes bankrupt. Allowable reasons for cancellation can range from sickness to natural disasters to a government department declaring your destination unsafe for travel. Insurers usually won't cover vague fears, though, and in 2003 travelers were not given refunds for SARS-related cancellations.

MEDICAL INSURANCE For China, purchase travel insurance that includes an air ambulance or scheduled airline repatriation. Be clear on the terms and conditions—is repatriation limited to life-threatening illnesses, for instance? While there are advanced facilities staffed by foreign doctors in Běijīng, regular Chinese hospitals are to be avoided. They may charge you a substantial bill, which you must pay in cash before you're allowed to leave. If this happens to you, you'll have to wait until you return home to submit your claim, so make sure you have adequate proof of payment.

LOST-LUGGAGE INSURANCE On U.S. domestic flights, checked baggage is covered up to $2,800 per ticketed passenger. On international flights (including U.S. portions of international trips), baggage is limited to approximately $9.07 per pound, up to approximately $635 per checked bag. If you plan to check items more valuable than the standard liability, see if your valuables are covered by your homeowner's policy, or get baggage insurance as part of your comprehensive travel-insurance package. Read the policy carefully—some valuables are effectively uninsurable, and others have such high excess charges that the insurance is not worth buying.

If your luggage is lost, immediately file a lost-luggage claim at the airport. For most airlines, you must report delayed, damaged, or lost baggage within 4 hours of arrival. The airlines are required to deliver luggage, once found, directly to your house or destination free of charge, although don't expect that necessarily to work with domestic Chinese airlines.

6 Health & Safety

STAYING HEALTHY
GREATEST RISKS
The greatest risk to the enjoyment of a holiday in China is one of **stomach upsets** or more serious illnesses arising from low hygiene standards. Keep your hands frequently washed and away from your mouth. Only eat freshly cooked hot food, and fruit you can peel yourself—avoid touching the part to be eaten once it's been peeled. Drink only boiled or bottled water. *Never* drink from the tap. Use bottled water for brushing your teeth.

The second most common cause of discomfort is the **upper respiratory tract infection, common cold,** or similar symptoms, often mistaken for cold or flu, which is caused by **heavy pollution.** Many standard Western remedies or sources of relief (and occasionally fake versions of these) are available over the counter, but bring a supply of whatever you are used to. If you have sensitive eyes, you may wish to bring an eye bath and solution.

If you regularly take a nonprescription medication, bring a plentiful supply with you and don't rely on finding it in China. Feminine hygiene products such as panty-liners are widely available in Běijīng, but tampons are not.

GENERAL AVAILABILITY OF HEALTHCARE
See "Fast Facts: Běijīng" in chapter 4 for a list of reliable (and very expensive) clinics with up-to-date equipment and English-speaking foreign-trained doctors. Should you begin to feel unwell in China, your first contact should be your hotel reception. Many major hotels have doctors on staff who will give a first diagnosis and treatment for minor problems, and who will be aware of the best places to send foreigners for further treatment.

Be very cautious about what is prescribed for you. Doctors are poorly paid, and many earn kickbacks from pharmaceutical companies for prescribing expensive medicines. Antibiotics are handed out like candy; indeed, dangerous and powerful drugs of all kinds can be bought over the counter at pharmacies. In general, the best policy is to stay as far away from Chinese healthcare as possible.

BEFORE YOU LEAVE
Plan well ahead. If you intend merely to visit Běijīng, you may not need to bother

with some of the inoculations listed below, but take *expert* advice (not website hearsay) on the latest situation. Some inoculations are expensive, some need multiple shots separated by a month or two, and some should not be given at the same time as others. So start work on this 3 or 4 months before your trip.

For the latest information on infectious diseases and travel risks, and particularly on the constantly changing situation with malaria, consult the World Heath Organization (www.who.int) and the Centers for Disease Control in Atlanta (www.cdc.gov). Note that family doctors are rarely up to date on vaccination requirements, so when looking for advice at home, consult a specialist travel clinic.

To begin with, your standard inoculations, typically for **polio, diphtheria,** and **tetanus,** should be up to date. You may also need inoculations against **typhoid fever, meningococcal meningitis, cholera, hepatitis A and B,** and **Japanese B encephalitis.** If you will be arriving in mainland China from a country with **yellow fever,** you may be asked for proof of vaccination, although border health inspections are cursory at best. See also advice on **malaria,** below.

WHILE YOU ARE THERE

Mosquito-borne **malaria** comes in various forms, and you may need to take two different prophylactic drugs, depending upon the time you travel, whether you venture into rural areas, and where you go. You must begin to take these drugs 1 week *before* you enter an affected area and *for 4 weeks after you leave it, sometimes longer.* For a visit to Běijīng and other major cities only, prophylaxis is usually unnecessary.

Standard precautions should be taken against exposure to **strong summer sun.** Its brightness may be dimmed by Běijīng's pollution, but the sun's power to burn is undiminished.

The Chinese are phenomenally ignorant about **sexually transmitted diseases,** which are rife. As with the respiratory disease SARS, the government denied there was any AIDS problem in China until it grew too large to be contained. Estimates of the spread of infection are still highly conservative. Condoms, including Western brands, which should be your first choice, are widely available in Běijīng.

STAYING SAFE

China is one of Asia's safest destinations. As anywhere else, though, you should be cautious of theft in places such as crowded markets, popular tourist sites, bus and railway stations, and airports. Take standard precautions against pickpockets (distribute your valuables around your person and wear a money belt inside your clothes). The main danger of walking the ill-lit streets at night is of falling down an uncovered manhole. There's no need to be concerned about dressing down or not flashing valuables—it's automatically assumed that all foreigners, even the scruffiest backpackers, are astonishingly rich.

Visitors should be cautious of various **scams,** especially in areas of high tourist traffic, and of Chinese who approach and say in English, "Hello friend! Welcome to China!" or something similar. Scam artists who want to practice their English and suggest moving to some local haunt may leave you with a bill which has two zeros more than it should, and with trouble should you decline to pay. "Art students" are a pest, approaching you with a story about raising funds for a show overseas, but in fact enticing you into a shop where you will be lied to extravagantly about the authenticity, uniqueness, originality, and true cost of various paintings you will be pressured into buying. The man who is foolish enough to accept an invitation from pretty girls to sing karaoke deserves all the hot water in which he will find himself, up to being forced by large, well-muscled gentlemen to visit an ATM and withdraw large sums to pay for services not actually provided.

If you are a **victim of theft,** make a police report (go to the same addresses given for visa extensions earlier in this chapter; you are most likely to find an English-speaking policeman there). But don't expect sympathy, cooperation, or action. The purpose is to get a theft report to give to your insurers for compensation.

Harassment of **solo female travelers** is very rare, but slightly more likely if the traveler appears to be of Chinese descent.

Traffic is a major hazard for the cautious and incautious alike. In mainland China, driving is on the right, at least occasionally. The rules of the road are routinely ignored for the one overriding rule, "I'm bigger than you so get out of my way," and pedestrians are at the bottom of the pecking order. Cyclists come along the sidewalk, and cars mount it right in front of you and park across your path as if you don't exist. Cyclists go in both directions along the bike lane at the side of the road, which is also invaded by cars looking to mount the sidewalk to park. The edges of the main road also usually have cyclists going in both directions. The vehicle drivers are gladiators, competing for any way to move into space ahead, constantly changing lanes and crossing each other's paths. Pedestrians are like matadors pausing between lanes as cars sweep by to either side of them. Pedestrians often edge out into traffic together, causing cars to swerve away from them, often into the paths of oncoming vehicles, until one lane of traffic parts and flows to either side, and the process is repeated for the next lane.

DEALING WITH DISCRIMINATION

In mainland China, in casual encounters, non-Chinese are treated as something between a cute pet and a bull in a china shop, and sometimes with pitying condescension because they are too stupid to speak Chinese. At sights, Chinese tourists from out of town may ask to have their picture taken with you, which will be fun to show friends in their foreigner-free hometowns. ("Look! Here's me with the Elephant Man!") Unless you are of Chinese descent, your foreignness is constantly thrust in your face with catcalls of *"lǎowài,"* a not particularly courteous term for foreigner, and a bit like shouting "Chinky" at a Chinese you encounter at home. Mocking, and usually falsetto, calls of "Helloooooo" are not greetings but are similar to saying "Pretty Polly!" to a parrot. Whether acknowledged or not (and all this is best ignored), these calls are usually followed by giggles. But there's little other overt discrimination, other than persistent overcharging wherever it can possibly be arranged. In general, however, once some sort of communication is established, foreigners get better treatment from Chinese, both officials and the general public, than the Chinese give each other. People with darker skin do have a harder time than whites, but those who do not speak Mandarin will probably not notice.

7 Specialized Travel Resources

TRAVELERS WITH DISABILITIES

China is not a good choice for travelers with disabilities. If you do choose to come here, travel with a specialist group (although such tours to China are rare) or with someone fully familiar with your particular needs. The Chinese hide people with disabilities, who are rarely seen unless reduced to begging, when they may even be subjected to taunting (although this won't happen to foreigners).

China is difficult for those with limited mobility. The sidewalks are very uneven, and public buildings, sights, and hotels almost always have stairs with no alternative ramps. In theory, some major hotels in the largest cities have wheelchair accessible rooms, but rarely are they properly executed. Metro stations do not have lifts, and any escalators usually run up only.

GAY & LESBIAN TRAVELERS

Homosexuality was only removed from an official list of mental illnesses in 2001, but the situation (while still grim) has improved in recent years. Běijīng has a few gay bars of note, and the expatriate magazine *Time Out* recently broke the longstanding taboo against using the words "gay" and "lesbian." **The International Gay & Lesbian Travel Association (IGLTA)** (℃ **800/448-8550** or 954/776-2626; www.iglta.org) lists three gay-friendly organizations dealing with inbound visitors to China. See p. 185 for a description of the gradually improving scene.

SENIOR TRAVEL

There are no special arrangements or discounts for seniors in China, with the exception that some foreign brand-name hotels may offer senior rates if you book in advance (although you'll usually beat those prices simply by showing up in person, if there are rooms available).

FAMILY TRAVEL

Běijīng is not the place to make your first experiment in traveling with small children, although it's a better choice that anywhere else in China. Your biggest challenges will be the lack of services or entertainment aimed at children, the lack of familiar foods outside the bigger hotels and fast-food chains (unless your children have been brought up with Chinese food), and hygiene.

Some children find Chinese strangers a little too hands-on, and may tire of forced encounters (and photo sessions) with Chinese children met on the street. But the Chinese put their children firmly first, and stand up on buses while the young ones sit.

China is grubby at best, and for children who still have a tendency to put their hands in their mouths, constant vigilance will be necessary, or constant toilet visits the result. Older children should be instructed on frequent hand-washing and special caution with food.

Some familiar Western brands of disposable diapers, along with familiar creams and lotions, are available in Běijīng.

China accepts children traveling on a parent's **passport,** although the child's photo must be submitted along with the parent's when a visa application is made.

Běijīng **hotels** generally don't charge for children 12 and under who share a room with their parents. Almost all hotels will add a bed, turning a double room into a triple, for an extra ¥80 to ¥100 ($10–$13), which you can often bargain down.

Although **babysitting** services are not uncommon in the best hotels (the Sino-foreign joint-ventures with familiar names, in particular), in most cases the babysitters will speak very little English or none at all, will have no qualifications in child care, and will simply be members of the housekeeping staff.

All **restaurants** welcome children, but outside the Western fast-food outlets, some Chinese copies of those, and major hotels, don't expect high chairs or special equipment except very occasionally. The general Chinese eating method of ordering several dishes to share will at least allow your child to order whatever he or she deems acceptable (although it will not taste the same in any two restaurants), while allowing you to try new dishes at each meal.

Although Chinese food in Běijīng is different from (and mostly vastly superior to) Chinese food served in the West, it would still be wise to acclimatize children as much as possible before leaving by making trips to the local Chinese restaurant. In many cases only chopsticks will be available, so consider taking forks and spoons with you to China. You can now find McDonald's (complete with play areas), KFC, and Pizza Hut in Běijīng, and almost all hotels of four stars or up have coffee shops which deliver poor attempts at Western standards.

Keep in mind that although Western cooking is available at many excellent Běijīng restaurants, authenticity comes at a price. Cheap bakeries, however, often sell buttery cakes and close relatives of the muffin containing raisins and chopped walnuts.

In general, **attractions** for children are few, and exploring temples may quickly pall. Success here will depend upon your ability to provide amusement from nothing, and the sensitivity of your antennae to what captures your child's imagination.

Discounts for children on travel tickets and entrance fees are based on height, not age. There are variations, but typically children below 1.1m (3 ft., 7 in.) enter free and travel free if they do not occupy a seat on trains and buses. Children between 1.1m and 1.4m (4 ft., 2 in.) pay half price. Many ticket offices have marks on the wall at the relevant heights so that staff can quickly determine the appropriate price.

STUDENT TRAVEL

There are no particular benefits or discounts available to foreign students traveling in China unless they are registered at Chinese educational institutions (and then not many).

8 Planning Your Trip Online

SURFING FOR AIRFARES

The "big three" online travel agencies, **Expedia.com**, **Travelocity.com**, and **Orbitz.com**, sell most of the air tickets bought on the Internet. (Canadian travelers should try Expedia.ca and Travelocity.ca; U.K. residents try Expedia.co.uk and Opodo.co.uk.) Also remember to check **airline websites** for Web-only specials. For the websites of airlines that fly to and from your destination, go to section 10, "Getting There," in this chapter.

Do *not* buy China domestic travel online from English-language sites, as the markups are horrendous.

SURFING FOR HOTELS

Booking hotel rooms online in China is not a good idea, unless money is no object or you absolutely must stay at a specific hotel at a very busy time of the year. There are no online services offering Chinese hotel rooms at discounts lower than you can get for yourself, whatever they may tell you. There is a case to be made for booking the first couple of nights of your stay at a joint-venture hotel, as major international hotel chains have their best *published* rate online, but do not book far in advance.

9 The 21st-Century Traveler

INTERNET ACCESS AWAY FROM HOME

Despite highly publicized clamp-downs on cybercafes, monitoring of traffic, and blocking of websites, China remains one of the easiest countries in the world in which to get online.

Online Traveler's Toolbox

- **ATM Locators:** Visa ATM Locator (www.visa.com) gives locations of PLUS ATMs worldwide; MasterCard ATM Locator (www.mastercard.com) provides locations of Cirrus ATMs worldwide.
- **Online Chinese Tools** (www.mandarintools.com) has dictionaries for Mac and Windows users, Chinese calendars for conversions between the solar and lunar calendars (on which most Chinese festivals are based), and more.
- **China Pulse** (www.chinapulse.com/wifi) provides listings of restaurants, cafes, and hotels in Bĕijīng that have wireless Internet access. Choose "Browse Hotspot Listings" and click on the entries to find out what network is available, and whether there's a charge involved.
- **The Oriental-List** is a noncommercial mailing list dedicated solely to the discussion of travel in China. This spam-free list, moderated to stay on-topic, offers swift answers to just about any China travel question not already dealt with in these pages. To subscribe, send a blank e-mail to subscribe-oriental-list@datasinica.com.
- **Travel Warnings** are available at: http://travel.state.gov, www.fco.gov.uk/travel, www.voyage.gc.ca, and www.smartraveller.gov.au.
- **Universal Currency Converter** (www.xe.com/ucc) posts the latest exchange rates of any currency against the ¥RMB.
- **Weatherbase** (www.weatherbase.com) gives month-by-month averages for temperature and rainfall for individual cities in China.
- **Xianzai.com** (www.xianzai.com) provides free entertainment listings for Bĕijīng and other Chinese cities, as well as special offers from China for hotels and air tickets.
- **Zhongwen.com** (www.zhongwen.com), an online dictionary, looks up English and Chinese and provides explanations of Chinese etymology using a system of family trees.

WITHOUT YOUR OWN COMPUTER

In central Bĕijīng, government clampdowns have significantly reduced the number of Internet cafes *(wǎng bā)*. Those still in operation tend to charge from ¥4 to ¥20 (50¢–$2.50) per hour. For a list of locations, see "Fast Facts: Bĕijīng" in chapter 4. Also keep your eyes open for the *wǎngbā* characters; see appendix B.

Many media websites, and those with financial information or any data whatsoever on China which disagrees with the Party line, are blocked from mainland China, as are even some search engines.

WITH YOUR OWN COMPUTER

Don't bother looking for a local access number for your ISP in Bĕijīng. You can connect by using the number 95962 and making the account name and password both 263. Speeds vary but are usually fine for checking e-mail directly, although variable for checking mail via a Web interface. The service is paid for through a tiny increment in the low cost of a local phone call.

Mainland China uses the standard U.S.-style RJ11 telephone jack also used as the port for laptops worldwide. Cables with RJ11 jacks at both ends can be picked up for around ¥8 ($1) in Běijīng department stores and electrical shops. Standard electrical voltage across China is 220v, 50Hz, which most laptops can handle, but North American users in particular should check. For power socket information see "Fast Facts: Běijīng" in chapter 4.

Those with on-board Ethernet can take advantage of broadband services, which are sometimes free in major hotels. Ethernet cables are often provided but it's best to bring your own. Many cafes and hotels in Běijīng offer wireless connectivity in public areas, and at least one (the Peninsula Palace) offers free wireless access in all guest rooms.

USING A CELLPHONE IN CHINA

All Europeans, most Australians, and many North Americans use GSM (Global System for Mobiles). But while everyone else can take a regular GSM phone to China, North Americans, who operate on a different frequency, need a more expensive tri-band model.

International roaming charges can be horrendously expensive. Buying a pre-paid chip in China with a new number is far cheaper. You may need to call up your cellular operator to "unlock" your phone in order to use it with a local provider.

For Běijīng, **buying a phone** is the best option. Last year's now unfashionable model can be bought, with chip and ¥100 ($13) of pre-paid airtime, for about ¥800 ($100); you pay less if a Chinese model is chosen. Europeans taking their GSM phones, and North Americans with tri-band phones, can buy chips (quán-qiútōng) for about ¥100 ($13). Recharge cards (shénzhōuxíng kǎ) are available at post offices and mobile-phone shops. Calling rates are low, although those receiving calls pay part of the cost.

10 Getting There

BY PLANE

On direct, nonstop flights, China's own international airlines always offer rates slightly lower than those of foreign carriers. Cabin staff try to be helpful but are never quite sure how. Air China only recently suffered its first and only fatal accident and should not be confused with China Airlines from Táiwān, at quite the other end of the scale. **Departure tax** is now included in the price of your ticket.

FROM NORTH AMERICA Among North American airlines, **Air Canada** (www.aircanada.com), **Northwest Airlines** (www.nwa.com) (via Tokyo), and **United Airlines** (www.ual.com) fly to Běijīng.

Japan Airlines (www.jal.co.jp) flies via Tokyo to Běijīng, as does **All Nippon Airways** (www.ana.co.jp). **Korean Air** (www.koreanair.com) and **Asiana Airlines** (us.flyasiana.com) fly via Seoul.

FROM THE UNITED KINGDOM British Airways (www.britishairways.com) flies to Běijīng. Fares with **KLM Royal Dutch Airlines** (www.klm.com) via Amsterdam, **Lufthansa** (www.lufthansa.com) via Frankfurt, or **Finnair** (www.finnair.com) via Helsinki, can often be considerably cheaper. Fares with eastern European airlines such as **Tarom Romanian Air Transport** (www.tarom.ro) via Bucharest, and **Aeroflot** (www.aeroflot.com) via Moscow, or with Asian airlines such as **Pakistan International Airlines** (www.piac.com.pk) via Islamabad or Karachi, **Malaysia Airlines** (www.mas.com.my) via Kuala Lumpur, or **Singapore Airlines** (www.singaporeair.com) via Singapore, can be cheaper still. There are even more creative routes via Ethiopia or the Gulf States.

FROM AUSTRALASIA Sydney is served by **China Eastern, Air China,** and **Qantas** (www.qantas.com.au) to Běijīng and Shànghǎi, and by **Air China** and **China Southern** to Guǎngzhōu, where you can catch a connecting flight to Běijīng. **Air New Zealand** (www.airnew zealand.com) flies to Shànghǎi, and there are possible indirect routes with **Philippine Airlines** (www.pal.com.ph) via Manila, **Malaysian Airlines** (www.malaysiaairlines.com.my) via Kuala Lumpur, and Vietnam Airlines (www.vietnamairlines.com) via Ho Chi Minh City. Hong Kong's **Cathay Pacific** (www.cathaypacific.com) flies directly from six Australian cities and Auckland.

BY ROAD

Foreign visitors are not permitted to drive their own vehicles into China, unless arrangements are made far in advance with a state-recognized travel agency for a specific itinerary. The agency will provide a guide who will travel in your vehicle, or in a second vehicle with a driver, and make sure you stick to the planned route. You will have to cover all the (marked-up) costs of guide, driver, and extra vehicle if needed, and of Chinese plates for your vehicle. The agency will book and over-charge you for all your hotels and for as many excursions as it can. Forget it.

BY TRAIN

From Hung Hom station in Kowloon (Hong Kong), expresses run directly to Běijīng's West Station on alternate days (see www.kcrc.com for schedules and fares). From Moscow there are weekly trains via Ulaan Baatar in Mongolia to Běijīng, and weekly via a more easterly route directly to Harbin in China's north-east and down to the capital. There's also a separate weekly run from Ulaan Baatar to Běijīng. Trains run twice-weekly from Hanoi in Vietnam to Běijīng West via Guìlín. There's also a service between Běijīng and Pyongyang in North Korea, but you'll only be on that if you've joined an organized tour.

BY SHIP

There are ferry connections from Incheon in South Korea (english.tour2korea.com) and from Shimonoseki and Kobe in Japan (www.celkobe.co.jp) to Tiānjīn, a couple of hours from Běijīng.

11 Packages for the Independent Traveler

For many destinations around the world, buying an unescorted package tour of pre-booked flights, internal travel, and hotels is a way of tapping into lower prices than you can obtain by buying each individual element yourself. China, as in so many other ways, is different.

Since China re-opened to foreign tourism in the early 1980s, all foreign tour operators have been required to use official state-registered travel companies as ground handlers. All arrangements in China were usually put together by one of three companies, China International Travel Service (CITS), China Travel Service (CTS), or China Youth Travel Service (CYTS). Controls are now loosening, foreign tour companies are now allowed some limited activities in China, and the range of possible Chinese partners has increased, but in effect, CITS and the like are the only companies with nationwide networks of offices, and most foreign tour companies still turn to them. They work out the schedule at the highest possible prices and send the cost to the foreign package company, which then adds its own administration charges and profit margins, and hands the resulting quote to you. You can get the same price yourself by dealing with CITS (which has many offices overseas) directly. But if things go wrong, you will be unlikely to obtain any compensation whatsoever. If you book through a tour operator in your home country, you can expect to obtain funds and compensation if this becomes necessary.

Other than convenience, there's little benefit and a great deal of unnecessary cost in buying a package. You'll get better prices by organizing things yourself as you go along.

Warning: Never book directly over the Web with a China-based travel service or "private" tour guide. Many are not licensed to do business with foreigners, many individuals have not been licensed as guides, and both will hugely over-charge and frequently mislead you (in the most charming way possible).

If money is no object, then start with the list of tour companies in the next section, nearly all of whom will arrange indi-vidual package tours (particularly Abercrombie and Kent, and Steppes East). Or you can contact the China National Tourist Offices (see section 1 in this chapter) to find properly registered Chinese agencies who can help you.

12 Escorted General-Interest Tours

Escorted tours are structured group tours with a group leader. The price usually includes everything from airfare to hotels, meals, tours, admission costs, and local transportation, but not usually domestic or international departure taxes. Almost all include a visit to Běijīng, but very few tackle Běijīng alone, or in any depth. For that you'll need to ask the companies below to organize an independent tour for you (but you'd be better off just to jump on a plane and be completely at lib-erty once you arrive).

Again, due to the distorted nature of the Chinese industry, escorted tours do not usually represent savings, but rather a significant increase in costs over what you can arrange for yourself. Foreign tour companies are for now required to work with state-owned ground handlers, although some book as much as they can directly or work discreetly with private operators they trust. But even as markets become more open, most arrangements will continue to be made with the official state operators, if only for convenience. Please read the brochures skeptically (one man's "scenic splendor" is another's "heavily polluted"), and carefully read the advice in this section.

As with package tours (see previous section), the arrangements within China itself are managed by a handful of local companies, whose cupidity often induces them to lead both you and your tour company astray. Various costs, which should be in the tour fee, can appear as extras; itineraries are altered to suit the pocket of the local operator; and there are all sorts of shenanigans to separate the hapless tourist from extra cash at every turn, usually at whatever point the tour staff appear to be most helpful. (The driver has bottles of water for sale on the bus each day? You're paying three times the shop price.)

EVALUATING TOURS

When choosing a tour company for China you must, of course, consider cost, what's included, the itinerary, the likely age and interests of other tour group members, physical ability required, and the payment and cancellation policies, as you would for any other destination. But you should also investigate:

Shopping Stops These are the bane of any tour in China, designed to line the pockets of tour guides, drivers, and some-times the ground handling company itself. A stop at the Great Wall may be limited to only an hour so as to allow an hour at a cloisonné factory. The better foreign tour operators design their own itineraries and have instituted strict contractual controls to keep these stops to a minimum, but they are often unable to do away with them altogether, and tour guides will introduce extra stops whenever they think they can get away with it. Other companies, particularly those companies that do not specialize in China, just take the package from the Chinese ground handler, put it together with flights, and pass it on uncritically. At shopping stops, you should never ask or accept your tour guide's advice on what is the "right price." You are shopping in the wrong place to start with, where prices will often be 10 to 15 times higher than they should be. Your driver gets a tip, and your guide gets 40% of sales. The "discount" card you are given marks you for yet higher initial prices and tells the seller to which guide commission is owed. So ask your tour company how many of these stops are included, and simply sit out those you cannot avoid.

Tipping   There is *no* tipping in mainland China. If your tour company advises you to bring payments for guides and drivers, costs that should be included in your total tour cost are being passed on to you through the back door. Ask what the company's tipping policy is and add that sum to the tour price to make true comparisons. Some tour guides are making as much as *400 times* what an ordinary factory worker or shop assistant makes, mostly through kickbacks from sights, restaurants, and shops, all at your expense, and from misguided tipping. Some tour operators say that if they cut out the shopping stops, then they have to find other ways to cover the tour guides' income or there'll be no tour guide. Shopping-free trips are nearly always accompanied by a higher price or a higher tip recommendation (which is the same thing). The guides are doing so well that now, in many cases, rather than receive a salary from the ground-handling company, they have to

pay for the privilege of fleecing you. The best tour companies know how China works, make what arrangements they find unavoidable, and leave you out of it. A middle path is to put a small sum from each tour member into a central kitty and disburse tips as needed, but only for truly exceptional service and at a proper local scale which short-time visitors from developed nations are incapable of assessing. Foreign tour leaders can be tipped according to the customs of their country of origin, and most companies issue guidelines for this.

Guides   Mainland guides rarely know what they are talking about, although they won't miss a beat while answering your questions. What they will have on the tip of their tongue is an impressive array of unverifiable statistics, amusing little stories of dubious authenticity, and a detailed knowledge of the official history of a place which may bear only the faintest resemblance to the truth. Their main concerns are to tell foreigners what they want to hear, and to impress them with the greatness of China. So you may be told that the Great Wall can be seen from outer space (silly), that China has 5,000 years of culture (what does this actually mean?), and that one million people worked on building the Forbidden City (it was only 100,000 on last year's trip). Guides are short-changed by China's shoddy and politically distorted education system, and also tend to put the potential profit from the relationship first.

Ask your tour company if it will be sending a guide and/or tour manager from home to accompany the trip and to supplement local guides. This is worth paying more for, as this person's presence ensures a smoother trip and more authoritative information.

TOUR COMPANIES
Between them, the following tour companies (a tiny selection of what's available) serve just about all budgets and

interests. The companies are from the United States, Canada, China, the United Kingdom, and Australia, but many have representatives around the globe. Plus you can often just buy the ground portion of the trip and fly in from wherever you like.

- **Abercrombie and Kent** (U.S.): Top-of-the-range small group tours, with the very best accommodation and transport. © 800/554-7016; fax 630/954-3324; www.abercrombiekent.com (U.S.). © 08450/700610; fax 08450/700607; www.abercrombiekent.co.uk (U.K.). © 1300/851-800; www.abercrombiekent.com.au (Australia). © 0800/441-638 (New Zealand).

- **Academic Travel Abroad** (U.S.): Tours in China for The Smithsonian (educational, cultural) and National Geographic Expeditions (natural history, soft adventure). © 877/338-8687; fax 202/633-9250; smithsonian journeys.org. © 888/966-8687; fax 202/342-0317; www.nationalgeo graphic.org/ngexpeditions.

- **Adventure Center** (U.S.): Small group tours aimed at those who are usually independent travelers; one tour includes the Eastern Qīng Tombs and walking on several stretches of the Great Wall. © 800/228-8747 (U.S.). © 888/456-3522 (Canada). For representatives in Australia and New Zealand, see www.adventurecenter.com.

- **China Focus** (U.S.): Larger groups at budget prices, but with additional costs to cover extras. © 800/868-7244 or 415/788-8660; fax 415/788-8665; www.chinafocustravel.com.

- **Elderhostel** (U.S.): Educational tours for seniors. © 877/426-8056; www.elderhostel.org.

- **Gecko's Adventures** (Australia): Down-to-earth budget tours for small group tours of 20- to 40-year-olds, using smaller guesthouses, local restaurants, and public transport. © 03/9662-2700; fax 03/9662-2422; www.geckosadventures.com.

- **Intrepid Travel** (Australia): Slightly more adventurous tours with small groups, following itineraries that are a deft mix of popular destinations and the less-visited. One trip includes 4 days of trekking on the Great Wall. © 613/9478-2626; fax 613/9419-4426; www.intrepidtravel.com (Australia). © 877/448-1616 (U.S).

- **Laurus Travel** (Canada): Small group tours from a Vancouver-based China-only specialist, run by a former CITS guide. © 877/507-1177 or 604/438-7718; fax 694/438-7715; www.laurustravel.com.

- **Monkey Business** (China): Běijīng-based outfit specializing in organizing onward travel on the Trans-Siberian express. © 010/6591-6519; fax 010/6591-6517; www.monkeyshrine.com.

- **Pacific Delight** (U.S.): A large variety of mainstream trips for a wide range of different group sizes, with endless permutations for different time scales and budgets. Watch for extra costs. © 800/221-7179; www.pacificdelighttours.com.

- **Peregrine Adventures** (Australia): Small group trips with good quality centrally located accommodation; includes visits to private houses and smaller restaurants frequented by local people and, possibly, walks and bike rides. © 613/9663-8611; fax 613/9663-8618; www.peregrine adventures.com (Australia). © 800/227-8747 (U.S.).

- **R. Crusoe & Son** (U.S.): Small group tours include extras such as a visit to areas of the Forbidden City usually closed to the public. © 800/585-8555; fax 312/980-8100; www.rcrusoe.com.

- **Ritz Tours** (U.S.): Groups range in size from 10 to 40 people, and ages range widely; parents often bring children. Ritz is the foremost U.S. tour operator to China in terms of volume. ℂ 800/900-2446; www.ritz tours.com.

- **Steppes East** (U.K.): Tours organized to very high standards. Its itineraries are merely suggestions that can be adapted to your specifications. ℂ 01285/651010; fax 01285/ 885888; www.steppeseast.co.uk.

13 Recommended Books

The best single-volume introduction to the people of China and their world is **Jasper Becker**'s *The Chinese* (John Murray, 2000). Longtime resident of Běijīng and former Běijīng bureau chief for the *South China Morning Post,* Becker delivers an immensely readable account of how the Chinese got to be who they are today; their pre-occupations, thoughts, and fears; and the ludicrous posturings of their leaders.

Old Běijīng can now only be found in literature. The origins of many Western fantasies of the capital, then called Khanbalik, lie in the ghost-written work of **Marco Polo,** *The Travels of Marco Polo.* Dover Publications' two-volume reprint (1993) of the Yule-Cordier edition is a splendid read (although only part of Polo's time was spent in Běijīng) because of its entertaining introduction and footnotes by famous explorers attempting to follow his route. **Ray Huang**'s ironically titled *1587, A Year of No Significance* (Yale University Press, 1982) is an account of the Míng dynasty in decline; written in the first person, it paints a compelling picture of the well-intentioned Wànlì emperor trapped by a vast, impersonal bureaucracy. The parallels with the present regime are striking. **Lord Macartney**'s *An Embassy to China* (J. L. Cranmer-Byng [Ed.], Longman, 1962) gives a detailed account of Qīng China and particularly Běijīng at the end of the 18th century. This should be compulsory reading for modern businesspeople, as it prefigures WTO negotiations and the expectations of what will arise from them.

Macartney's prediction that the Chinese would all soon be using forks and spoons is particularly relevant. **Hugh Trevor-Roper**'s *Hermit of Peking* (Eland Press, 1976), part history, part detective story, uncovers the life of Sir Edmund Backhouse, resident of Běijīng from the end of the Qīng dynasty into the Republic, who knew everyone in the city at the beginning of the century, and who deceived them all, along with a generation of China scholars, with his fake diary of a Manchu official at the time of the Boxer Rebellion. A serviceably translated bilingual edition of **Lǎo Shě**'s *Teahouse* (Chinese University Press, 2004) succinctly captures the flavor of life in Běijīng during the first half of the 20th century. The helplessness of the characters in the face of political movements is both moving and prophetic. **John Blofeld**'s *City of Lingering Splendour: A Frank Account of Old Peking's Exotic Pleasures* (Shambala, 1961) describes the seamier side of Běijīng in the 1930s, by someone who took frank enjoyment in its pleasures, including adventures in "the lanes of flowers and willows"—the Qián Mén brothel quarter. In the same period, **George Kates,** an American, lived more decorously in the style of a Chinese gentleman-scholar in an old courtyard house of the kind now rapidly vanishing, and gives a sensitive and very appealing portrait of the city in *The Years That Were Fat* (Harper, 1955; reprinted by Oxford University Press, 1988). **Ann Bridge,** the wife of a British diplomat in Běijīng, wrote novels of life in the capital's Legation Quarter in the 1930s (cocktail parties, horse racing, problems with servants, love affairs—spicy stuff in its day, and best-selling, if now largely forgotten). *Peking Picnic* (Chatto and Windus, 1932; reprinted Virago, 1989) features a disastrous trip to the outlying temples of Tánzhè Sì and Jiètái Sì (but one well worth undertaking yourself). *The Ginger Griffin* (Chatto and Windus, 1934; reprinted by Oxford University Press, 1985) offers the adventures of a young woman newly arrived in the city who attends the horse races, and has a happier ending.

David Kidd, another American, lived in Běijīng for a few years before and shortly after the Communist victory of 1949, and gives an account of the beginning of the city's destruction in *Peking Story* (Eland Press, 1988; originally *All the Emperor's Horses,* John Murray, 1961). Perhaps the best example of the "hooligan literature" of the late 1980s is *Please Don't Call Me Human* (No Exit Press, 2000) by **Wáng Shuò.** There's little plot to speak of, but it's a devastating and surreal parody of Chinese nationalism, all the more poignant as the Olympics draw near. *Black Hands of Beijing* (John Wiley Inc., 1993), by **George Black and Robin Munro,** is the most balanced and least hysterical account of the Tiān'ān Mén protests of 1989, putting them in the context of other, better-planned movements for social change, all of which suffered in the fallout from the chaotic student demonstrations and their bloody suppression. Only one of **Tim Clissold**'s tales in *Mr. China* (Constable & Robinson, 2004) is set in Běijīng, and the naivety of the author is at times breathtaking, but his account of setting up joint-ventures from the mid-1990s onwards is frank testimony that should be read by anyone considering doing business in China.

Chris Elder's *Old Peking: City of the Ruler of the World* (Oxford University Press, 1997) is a compendium of comments on the city from a wide range of literary and historical sources, sorted by topic. For those intent on digging out the last remains of the capitals' ancient architecture, **Susan Naquin**'s magisterial *Peking Temples and City Life, 1400–1900* (University of California Press, 2000) gives a scholarly yet readable background to many buildings now open to the public and many now long vanished. **Frances Wood**'s *Forbidden City* (British Museum Press, 2005) is a short and thoroughly entertaining introduction to Běijīng's main attraction.

3

Suggested Itineraries

Seeing Běijīng in a day? You must be kidding. It is technically possible to see the big names—the **Forbidden City, Temple of Heaven, Summer Palace,** and **Great Wall**—in as little as 3 days, but you'll need at least a week to get any sort of feel for the city. People spend years here and still fail to see everything they should.

But if a day is all you have, we want to help you make the most of it by providing a ready-made itinerary that allows you to have a satisfying trip.

We've left the Great Wall out of the itineraries below, as it requires a full day in itself, or better yet, an overnight stay to allow for spectacular late afternoon and early morning photography (see chapter 11 for details). The traffic in Běijīng means that the only sensible way to tour the city is to tackle the sights in groups. We take you to the central sights on the first day, the north of town on the following day and to the less-visited south of town on the third day.

1 The Best of Běijīng in 1 Day

Fortunately for the harried tourist, when the Mongol founders laid down the Běijīng (then Khanbalik) city grid, it was on a north-south axis, making navigation straightforward, and grouping the key landmarks in a central location. The main downside, for which Kublai Khan cannot be blamed, is that there are few dining options en route, so we recommend that you either eat a hearty breakfast at your hotel, or take a picnic (p. 94). Tài Miào and Běihǎi Park are both fine picnic spots. *Start: Metro to Qián Mén (208, exit A).*

❶ **Chairman Máo's Mausoleum (Máo Zhǔxí Jìniàn Guǎn)** ✦
Built on the site of Dà Qīng Mén (Great Qīng Gate) this hastily constructed building is unimpressive in itself, but what makes this site compelling is the genuine reverence of local visitors for The Great Helmsman. A memorable 15 minutes of people watching. *Note:* The Mausoleum is closed Sundays. See p. 110.

Immediately north of the Mausoleum lies:

❷ **Tiān'ān Mén Square (Tiān'ān Mén Guǎngchǎng)** ✦
Set on the site of the former Imperial Way, the broad square is also a recent

creation, dating from the 1950s when Máo, encouraged by his Soviet advisors, ordered the clearing away of the old government ministries. There were plans to "press down" the "feudal" Forbidden City by surrounding it with high-rise buildings and smokestacks, but the fledgling republic lacked the resources to carry out the plan.

To your left looms the **Great Hall of the People,** to your right is the **National Museum,** neither worth a visit if you're pressed for time. Impressive in its vastness, there's little to do in the Square unless you plan to cut short your tour by unfurling a protest banner. See p. 105.

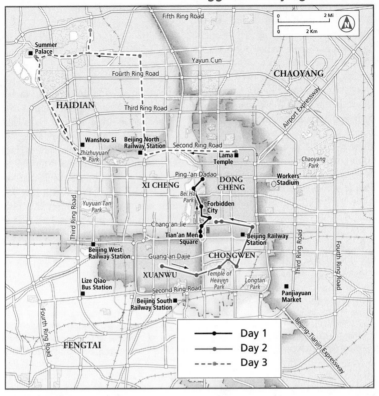

Day 1
Day 2
Day 3

Walk north, taking the underpass to:

❸ Tiān'ān Mén (Gate of Heavenly Peace)

Climb to the dais above Mao's portrait for a view south along the former Imperial Way. Beyond **Qián Mén** (Front Gate) you may spy the newly reconstructed **Yǒngdìng Mén.** It's not in the same spot as the original, but it is one of the first steps in a plan to revamp the north-south axis. A boulevard connecting to Olympic Park in the north of town is underway, with input from Albert Speer, Jr., who also happens to be the son of Hitler's personal architect.

A less traditional structure is apparent to your right: the **National Theater** resembles a UFO that made an emergency landing in a pond. See p. 122.

Head east to:

❹ Tài Miào 🐾🐾

Nearly all visitors head immediately north to the main entrance to the Forbidden City. Resist the pull of the throng and take the time to explore Tài Miào—adjacent to and just east of the main entrance—you'll be rewarded with halls every bit as impressive as those inside the Forbidden City, but with a handful of visitors.

The Chinese countryside is dotted with ancestral halls, often the finest structure in the village. Most were converted to schools after the revolution, although some now are reverting to their original usage. There's little chance of that happening at this imperial equivalent, where emperors would worship their forbears at New Year, each of the four seasons, and on their birthday. See p. 134.

Turn left as you exit, you'll soon reach:

⑤ Forbidden City (Gù Gōng) ⚑⚑⚑

The majority of visitors to Běijīng's main attraction rent their audio tour and rush through the central route without ducking into the eastern and western axes. This is a mistake. While narrator Roger Moore is droll, the most charming and intriguing parts of the Forbidden City are located away from the main tourist route. Allow at least 3 hours, and do not miss newly opened sights, particularly the **Wǔyīng Diàn** (west side) and **Juànqín Zhāi** (northeast side). See p. 120.

TAKE A BREAK
There's something so overwhelmingly naughty about the **Starbucks** Empire penetrating to the once-sacred heart of China that I can never resist stopping here for a latte with all the trimmings. Located east of the entrance to the Inner Court, their cause is also strengthened by other food outlets serving utterly diabolical fare.
East of Qianqing Men. (✆ 010/8511-7520).

If you wish to gain an aerial view of the Forbidden City, proceed to Jīng Shān Gōngyuán (p. 136), immediately opposite the north entrance to the Forbidden City. If time is short, head west to:

⑥ Běi Hǎi Gōngyuán (Běi Hǎi Park) ⚑

After all the grandeur you've just sampled, you'll find that this park, set around a lake carved out in the 12th century, provides a welcome change. On the south side of the park, **Qióng Dǎo,** an islet topped by a white dagoba built to commemorate the visit of the first Dalai Lama to the capital, is worth a quick look.

The north side of the park is more interesting, so catch a boat from the islet to the opposite side of the lake. Don't miss **Dàcí Zhēnrǔ Bǎo Diàn;** this Buddhist hall is one of the most impressive structures in Běijīng. See p. 135.

Emerging from the north of the park, turn right and cross at the first set of lights. Head back in the direction you came before turning right. Follow the southeast bank of Qián Hǎi to the finest Chinese restaurant in Běijīng.

TAKE A BREAK
There is no finer spot to spend the evening in the capital than the Back Lakes area, and there is no finer purveyor of Chinese food than **Kèjiā Cài,** a chic Hakka restaurant. On the southeast bank of Qián Hǎi (✆ 010/6404-2259). See p. 90. After your meal, pleasant walking awaits in the surrounding *hútòng* (small lanes), or seek out one of the many bars and Back Lakes restaurants we recommend in chapter 6, and put your feet up.

2 The Best of Běijīng in 2 Days

If you've survived "The Best of Běijīng in 1 Day," you'll find your second full-day tour takes in a different part of Běijīng. Today we'll take you in the footsteps of the notorious Empress Dowager, Cíxǐ. *Start: Lama Temple/Yōnghé Gōng metro stop (215, exit B).*

❶ Yōnghé Gōng (Lama Temple) ⚑⚑⚑

During the Qīng dynasty, the official religion of China was, unlikely as it seems, Tibetan Buddhism. However, in Běijīng, Buddhism was very much a religion for the rulers. Many emperors styled

themselves as reincarnations of Bodhisattvas (beings who have delayed nirvana in order to help others), and Cíxǐ was known as "the old Buddha."

Head for the rear hall, which houses a marvelous **statue of Maitreya** (the future Buddha). See p. 135.

Walk west to:

② **Guó Zǐ Jiàn and Kǒng Miào** ⊛

Cíxǐ was also an enthusiastic defender of the Confucian tradition, and fought to preserve the imperial examination system, which was managed by the all-powerful Guó Zǐ Jiàn (the Directorate of Education). It's a quiet spot now, except when university entrance examinations are held. See p. 132.

You can easily cover both sites in half an hour. Duck into **Shèngtáng Xuān** ⊛ (① 010/8404-7179; p. 180), a Manchurian toy store diagonally opposite.

Return to the metro, and change to Line 13 to reach Wǔdàokǒu metro stop (1304).

TAKE A BREAK
Before Starbucks decided the market was ripe for its first venture in China, **Sculpting in Time (Diāokè Shíguāng)**, a tiny cafe next to Peking University, was the city's only oasis for coffee lovers. It has since spawned a host of imitators, and has four branches; this is the largest. Try the carbonara, as well as delicious chocolate brownies. (Chéngfǔ Lù Huáqīng Jiāyuán 12 Lóu 1 [just west of metro]; ① 010/8286-7025). See p. 191.

The afternoon holds plenty of walking, so be sure you're well fed before heading on.

Hop in a taxi, or take bus 743 to Tiān'ān Mén Square :

Walk north, taking the underpass to:

③ **Tiān'ān Mén (Gate of Heavenly Peace)**

Climb to the dais above Máo's portrait for a view south along the former Imperial Way. Beyond **Qián Mén** ("Front Gate") you may spy the newly-reconstructed city gate, **Yǒngdìng Mén** . It's not in the same spot as the original, but it is one of the first steps in a plan to revamp the north-south axis. A boulevard connecting to

Olympic Park in the north of town is underway, with input from Albert Speer Jr., who also happens to be the son of Hitler's personal architect.

A less traditional structure is apparent to your right: the **National Theater** resembles a UFO that made an emergency landing in a pond. See p. 122.

④ **Yuán Míng Yuán** ⊛

If pushed for time, just visit the northeast side of the park, which is home to the remnants of the **Xī Yáng Lóu (Western Mansions)**. These buildings were razed by British and French forces a year before Cíxǐ rose to Empress Dowager status. They featured spectacular fountains and housed magnificent European art, but it could have been worse—the Anglo-French forces considered destroying the Forbidden City. See p. 137.

If you're feeling peckish, north of the Dōng Mén (East Gate) you'll find the magnificently decorated **Mima Cafe** (p. 192).

Hop in a cab to reach the east entrance (Dōng Gōng Mén) of:

⑤ **Summer Palace (Yí Hé Yuán)** ⊛⊛⊛

Later in her rule, Cíxǐ spent a considerable amount of time in this watery imperial playground, even setting up her own photographic studio. Modeled on Hángzhōu's West Lake, the complex was ransacked by foreign troops in 1860 and 1900, and restored under Cíxǐ's orders, on the first occasion with funds earmarked for the navy. The lake is the gem of the palace: Escape the crowds for an hour or so by hiring a boat, or in winter, a pair of skates. On land, allow 3 hours for a cursory look around.

Proceed to the south exit to join a rusty "imperial yacht." See p. 128.

After about half an hour, you'll spot what appears to be a temple on your left. Hop off to visit:

⑥ Wànshòu Sì ✿
The Empress Dowager would break up her journey from the Forbidden City to the Summer Palace with a stopover here, and after all the ground you've covered,

this smallish temple makes a pleasant change. Just to the east is **Zǐzhú Yuàn Gōngyuán (Purple Bamboo Park),** a delightful spot to watch the sun go down. See p. 134.

3 The Best of Běijīng in 3 Days

Having traveled north in the footsteps of the Empress Dowager, your next day takes you south for a dose of religion and ritual. Commence in a tiny Buddhist monastery, follow the emperors in an entreaty for the harvest, bargain for pearls and silk, search for ill omens at an ancient observatory, and then settle in for a martini and a magnificent sunset. **Start:** *Xuānwǔ Mén metro (206, exit D1).*

① Fǎyuán Sì (Source of Dharma Temple)
The gates of this tranquil monastery open at 8:30am, so early risers should duck into the back lanes to explore the surrounding *hútòng* neighborhood. The monastery is the most venerable in Běijīng, and the neighborhood also has an agreeable air of antiquity. The government says this area is "protected," so visit it before they send in the bulldozers. *Note:* Temple closed on Wednesdays. See p. 132.

Take a short cab ride east to:
② Gǔdài Jiànzhù Bówùguǎn (Museum of Ancient Architecture) ✿✿
Following prayers for a good harvest at the Temple of Heaven, the emperor and his officials would chance their arm at farming here: the emperor sowing rice, while his officials planted a coarser grain, millet. It is now a compelling museum housed in buildings as magnificent as those in the Forbidden City. Allow at least an hour. See p. 138.

Walk east to find the west gate of:
③ Temple of Heaven (Tiān Tán Gōngyuán) ✿✿✿
Běijīng's most emblematic building, the **Hall of Prayer for Good Harvests (Qínián Diàn)** is said to be closed for renovations until October 2006. If it is

closed when you visit, just purchase park admission, rather than the more expensive all-inclusive ticket *(lián piào).* The park is vast, and perfect for a quick picnic. See p. 125.

Two hours are required for a look around the extensive grounds, by which time you'll be ready for a hearty bowl of noodles.

> **TAKE A BREAK**
> Departing Tiān Tán via the east gate, turn left and walk north to find **Lǎo Běijīng Zhájiàng Miàn Dàwáng,** a cheap but clean Běijīng diner next to a pedestrian overpass. No English is spoken here, so turn to appendix A to order traditional Běijīng fare, such as the signature *zhájiàng miàn* (wheat noodles with black bean mince) or pungent *má dòufu* (mashed soybean). Lunch ends abruptly at 2pm. (Chóngwén Mén Wài Dàjiē 29; ✆ 010/ 6705-6705).

After lunch, it's time to shop. Just around the corner is:
④ Yuánlóng Silk ✿
Tour groups descend on Yuánlóng at noon, so aim to arrive slightly later. On the third floor you'll find a staggering array of silk fabric, only surpassed by the fabric wholesalers in Zhèjiāng Cūn, south of the Third Ring Road. You'll need

2 days to spare to have a suit or *qípáo* made up. See p. 179.

Cross the pedestrian overpass and turn right (south) and follow your nose to:

❺ Hóng Qiáo Shìchǎng ⚝

The knockoff merchandise here is cheaper than Yǎxiù, but generally of poorer quality. Footwear and luggage are your best choices, but the real value is in the pearls on the third and fourth floors, and the toys in the seldom-visited **toy market** *(wánjù shìchǎng)*, behind the main building. If you're feeling weighed down by all your purchases, there's a post office on the fourth floor.

By 2007 there will be a metro stop (Tiān Tán Dōng Mén) outside. Take the metro to Jiànguó Mén (120/211, exit C). Before then, take a cab for the short ride north to:

❻ Ancient Observatory (Gǔ Guānxiàng Tái)

The Ancient Observatory (p. 139) admits the last visitors at 4:30pm, so if time is tight, head straight to **Wángfǔjǐng Dìjiē** (below). The observatory offers a fascinating insight into early interactions between European (usually Jesuits) scientists and the Chinese court.

Ride the subway two stops west to:

❼ Wángfǔjǐng Dìjiē

In contrast to today's first destination, this pedestrian mall is "new China," the side the regime is desperate for you to see. Those with weary legs may wish to duck into **Oriental Plaza** for coffee and air-conditioned comfort, while the energetic can sample part of our Walking Tour of Wángfǔjǐng (p. 157).

Be sure to reach your final destination before sunset.

TAKE A BREAK
With nothing but air between you and the Forbidden City, the rooftop bar **Palace View Bar (Guān Jǐng Jiǔbā)** ⚝⚝ offers a magical spot to view Běijīng's pollution-enhanced sunset. Open May through September. In the Grand Hotel (✆ 010/6513-7788, ext. 458). See p. 189.

4

Getting to Know Běijīng

Since the 1920s, guidebook writers have complained that as quickly as they can write about one of Běijīng's historic buildings, it is pulled down.

Today we face the same problem with bars, clubs, and restaurants, whose lifetimes seem even shorter than the Chinese government's swiftness to suppress dissent. Whole streets and city blocks are often bludgeoned into oblivion almost overnight.

Historic buildings, other than ordinary housing, are not the problem. To be sure, some ancient temple buildings, long hidden by more modern construction, are demolished if the developer beats the culture cadres to the punch or induces them to look the other way. But others are emerging from roles as residences, offices, and storehouses spruced up to attract the tourist *yuán*. The choices of what to do and see in a city already packed with pleasures increase all the time.

This chapter deals with everything you need to know to get yourself around Běijīng, a city better supplied with taxis and public transport than almost any counterpart in Europe. Běijīng's layout is simple; navigation is mainly by landmark, and the only confusion lies in the fact that any particular landmark may well be pulled down by the time you reach the city, taking two or three of our favorite restaurants with it.

In the next few years leading up to the 2008 Olympics, the massive and chaotic transformation of the city, a process which has been hiccuping along destructively for nearly a century, will become faster and ever more feverish.

1 Orientation

ARRIVING

Běijīng's Capital Airport (Shǒudū Jīchǎng), one of three in the city but the only one to see foreigners, and which for now handles all international and nearly all domestic flights, is 25km (16 miles) northeast of the city center (*✆* **010/6457-1666,** information in Mandarin only; *✆* **010/6601-3336** domestic ticketing; *✆* **010/6601-6667** international ticketing). The new terminal building, opened in October 2000 and resembling other airports the world over, is straightforward to navigate, with a departures level stacked on top of an arrivals level.

Health declaration and **immigration forms** are usually supplied in-flight or are available as you approach the immigration counters, which typically take 10 to 15 minutes to clear on arrival. Have the forms completed and your passport ready.

There are no longer **Customs declaration forms,** and foreigners are rarely stopped. Immediately after Customs, you may be asked to put your larger bags through an **X-ray machine,** which may or may not be photo-safe.

There are signposted **money-changers** (branches of various Chinese banks, all of which can help you), ATMs accepting foreign cards (two at arrivals level and two at departures level), and even automated money-changing machines. Exchange rates are the same here as everywhere else, although this may change eventually. So exchange as much currency as you think you'll need, and try to get at least ¥100 in ¥10 notes.

TRAINS   Twice-weekly Trans-Siberian services from Moscow (one via Ulaan Baatar in Mongolia, and one via Harbin), weekly services from Ulaan Baatar only, and services from Pyongyang in North Korea (which you'll only take if on a pre-arranged tour) all arrive at **Běijīng Zhàn,** Běijīng's original main railway station, built with Soviet assistance in the late 1950s to replace one built by the British in 1901. Twice-weekly trains from Hanoi in Vietnam, and trains from Kowloon in Hong Kong which run on alternate days, arrive at the new and far larger but already disintegrating **Xī Kè Zhàn** (also known as Běijīng Xī Zhàn), the West Station. Neither station has any currency exchange facility or ATM, although there are banks and ATMs accepting foreign cards 5 minutes' walk north of Běijīng Zhàn, at Citibank next to the Běijīng International Hotel, and at the Hong Kong and Shànghǎi Bank (HSBC) on the north side of the COFCO shopping complex.

Domestic train services from Shànghǎi and most of the south, southeast, east, and northeast arrive at Běijīng Zhàn, which has its own metro station (210) on the circle line, with entrances across the forecourt to the right and left as you leave the railway station. The West Station will gain its own metro connection in a few years' time.

GETTING INTO TOWN

TAXIS   You will be pestered by **taxi** touts as soon as you emerge from Customs. *Never* go with these people. The signposted taxi rank is straight ahead and has a line that mostly works, although a few people will always try to cut in front of you. Line up at the two-lane rank, and a marshal will direct you to the next available vehicle as you reach the front of the line. Rates are clearly posted on the side of each cab. If you prefer a ¥1.60 (20¢) per-kilometer cab to a ¥2 (25¢) one, you can simply wait for it. After 15km (9 miles), rates increase by 50%, making a higher-priced taxi substantially more expensive, especially if you are heading for the far side of town. If you only want to go to the hotels (such as the Kempinski, Hilton, or Sheraton) in the Sān Yuán Qiáo area, where the Airport Expressway meets the Third Ring Road, your taxi driver may be a bit grumpy, but that's his bad luck.

In a ¥1.60 (20¢) cab, expect to pay under ¥80 ($10) to reach the eastern part of the city and around ¥100 ($13) to reach the central hotels. These estimates include the meter rate and a ¥10 ($1.25) expressway toll, which you'll see the driver pay en route. Fares to the central hotels will increase significantly if you travel during rush hours (8–9am and 3:30–7pm). For most of the day, you can reach hotels on the Third Ring Road within about 30 minutes, and central hotels in about 45 minutes—the latter trip may rise to more than an hour during rush hours. Make sure you read the box "Ten Tips for Taking Taxis Around Town," in this chapter.

Tips **Sustainable Travel**

Use public transport. Metro and bus options are listed throughout this book.
Rent or buy a bike and explore the bicycle kingdom on two wheels.
Set an example by sticking to marked paths when hiking outside Běijīng. In many areas, particularly the Great Wall, tourism is having a large impact.

Běijīng

HOTEL SHUTTLES   If you book a hotel room in advance, ask about shuttle services. Some hotels, such as the Kempinski, offer guests free transportation with a regular schedule of departures. The Peninsula Palace Hotel will send a Rolls-Royce for you, but for a fee.

AIRPORT BUSES   Air-conditioned services, run by two different companies, leave from in front of the domestic arrivals area. The Airport Shuttle Bus runs three routes; the most useful, Line A, runs 24 hours a day, departing every 15 minutes from 8am to 10pm, less frequently through the night. The fare is ¥16 ($2). Destinations include Sān Yuán Qiáo (near the Hilton and Sheraton hotels), the Dōng Zhí Mén and Dōng Sì Shí Tiáo metro stations, Běijīng Railway Station, the CAAC ticket office in Xī Dān, and Hángtiān Qiáo (near the Marriott West). Lines A, B, C, and D all pass through Sān Yuán Qiáo, but only Line A lets off passengers at a location convenient for picking up taxis to continue to other destinations. Most hotels in the center of the city can be reached by taxi for under ¥20 ($2.50) from there. The Civil Aviation Traveler Regular Bus, to the left of the exit, runs the same routes, but it also offers stops at the CAAC ticket office at the north end of Wángfǔjǐng Dàjiē.

DEPARTING BĚIJĪNG

Check with your airline for the latest advice, but for international flights make sure you are at the airport *at least* 1½ hours before departure; 1 hour for domestic flights. As you face the terminal, international departures are to the right, and domestic to the left. Departure tax for international and domestic flights is now included in the price of your ticket. Before joining lines for emigration, pick up and complete a departure card. Have your passport, departure card, and boarding card ready.

TRAVELING BEYOND BĚIJĪNG

BY PLANE   There are daily **direct flights** from Capital Airport to nearly every major Chinese city, including Shànghǎi (¥1,130/$141), Guǎngzhōu (¥1,700/$212), Xī'ān (¥1,050/$131), Chéngdū (¥1,440/$180), and Lhasa (¥2,430/$304). Prices vary widely, according to season and your bargaining skills, and may be reduced to half the amounts quoted here. Much Chinese domestic flying is done on a walk-up basis, but the best discount is never available at the airport. The aviation authority officially permits the airlines to discount to a maximum of 40% on domestic flights, but discounts of 50%, sometimes even more, are not uncommon at ticket agencies.

Tickets for domestic flights (and international flights) on Chinese airlines are best purchased through a travel agent, such as **Airtrans** (next to the Jiànguó Hotel; ✆ **010/6595-2255**), or in one of two main ticketing halls: the Aviation Building (Mínháng Dàlóu; ✆ **010/6601-7755;** fax 010/6601-7585; 24 hr.) at Xī Cháng'ān Jiē 15, just east of the Xī Dān metro station; or at the Airlines Ticketing Hall (Mínháng Yíngyè Dàtīng; ✆ **010/8402-8198;** fax 010/6401-5307; 8am–5pm), opposite the north end of Wángfǔjǐng Dàjiē at Dōng Sì Xī Dàjiē 155. Both ticketing halls accept credit cards and offer discounts similar to those of an agent. When pricing tickets, *always* shop around and *always* bargain for a discount. And don't expect agents inside major hotels to give you anything like the reductions you'll find elsewhere.

Booking from overseas via websites offering tickets for Chinese domestic flights, most of which do not appear on international ticketing systems, is *always* a mistake. You'll nearly always be charged the full price, which is generally only paid by a handful of people traveling at peak times at the last minute, and probably a booking fee, too.

Most hotels can arrange tickets for flights on **foreign airlines,** but they tend to levy hefty service fees. The airline offices themselves do not usually attempt to match the prices offered by agents, but are merely a source of the price to beat elsewhere. Special offers are often published in *Xianzai Beijing,* a weekly e-mail newsletter (www.xianzai. com), but sometimes agents undercut even these, or they bend the rules on advance booking requirements to give an advance-purchase price at the last minute.

BY TRAIN   The main railway stations are **Běijīng Railway Station (Běijīng Zhàn;** © 010/5182-1114) and **West Station (Xī Kè Zhàn;** schedule information © 010/ 5182-6253). Tickets can be purchased at these stations for any train leaving Běijīng up to 4 days in advance, and during the busiest seasons up to 10 days in advance. It is possible to buy **round-trip tickets** *(fǎnchéng piào)* to major destinations like Shànghǎi or Xī'ān up to 12 days in advance, subject to availability. There are now 19 brand new Z (direct) **trains** connecting with other cities, which depart at night and arrive early the following morning. Cities served are: Chángchūn, Chángshā, Harbin, Hángzhōu, Héféi, Nánjīng, Shànghǎi (five trains), Sūzhōu, Wǔhàn (four trains), Xī'ān, and the newly opened railway station in Yángzhōu. All compartments are spanking new, and staff is more enthusiastic than on other services. Television screens have been installed in soft-sleeper compartments, which may disturb your night's rest. Tickets for Z trains may be purchased 20 days in advance.

Satellite ticket offices *(tiělù shòupiào chù)* scattered throughout the city charge a negligible ¥5 (60¢) service fee; convenient branches are just inside the main entrance of the Sānhé Bǎihuò (department store), south of the Xīn (Sun) Dōng Ān Plaza on Wángfǔjǐng Dàjiē (9am–9pm); at the Shātān Shòupiào Chù further north at Píng'ān Dàdào 45, west of Jiāodàokǒu Nán Dàjiē (8am–6pm; © 010/6403-6803); and at the Gōngtǐ Dōng Lù Shòupiào Chù (© 010/6509-3783) in Sān Lǐ Tún, opposite and slightly south of the Workers' Stadium east gate. Tickets for all trains from Běijīng can also be booked free of charge at Běijīng South Station (Běijīng Nán Zhàn, © 010/ 6303-0031) and at Běijīng North Station (Běijīng Běi Zhàn, © 010/6223-1003), which is more conveniently located just north of the Xī Zhí Mén metro station. Ordinary travel agents without computers on the railway system will usually also handle rail-ticket bookings. The fee per ticket should be no more than ¥20 ($2.50), including delivery to your hotel, although some agencies like to take foreign visitors for a ride in more than one sense. Ticket desks in hotels may charge up to ¥50 ($6.25) per ticket. Mandarin speakers can check train times and book tickets using one of several hot lines (© 010/9510-5105, 010/5165-3050, or station numbers below).

At **Běijīng Railway Station (Běijīng Zhàn;** © 010/5182-1114), the best place to pick up tickets is the "ticket office for foreigners" inside the soft-berth waiting room on the ground floor of the main hall, in the far left corner (5:30am–11pm). Tickets for both versions of the **Trans-Siberian,** the Russian K19 via Manchuria (Sat 10:56pm) and the Chinese K3 via Mongolia (Wed 7:40am), must be purchased from the CITS international railway ticket office inside the International Hotel (Mon–Fri 8:30am–noon and 1:30–5pm, weekends 9am–noon and 1:30–4pm; © 010/6512-0507) 10 minutes' walk north of the station on Jiànguó Mén Nèi Dàjiē (metro: Dōng Dān). Both trains travel to Moscow (¥2,512/$314 soft sleeper), but only the K3 passes through Mongolia and stops in Ulaan Baatar (¥845/$105). There is a separate train, the K23, which goes to Ulaan Baatar (Sat 7:40am).

At the **West Station (Xī Kè Zhàn;** schedule information © 010/5182-6253), the best ticket outlet is not the main ticket hall but a second office inside the main building, on the second floor to the left of the elevators (signposted in English); this is also where you go to purchase tickets for the **T97 express to Kowloon/Jiǔlóng** (10:06am; 27 hr.; ¥1,028/$129 soft sleeper, ¥662/$83 hard). The West Station is also the starting point for **trains to Hanoi,** but you have to buy tickets (Thurs, Sun; ¥1,163/$145 soft sleeper only) at a "travel service" booth (9am–4:30pm; ℂ **010/ 6398-9485**) inside the Construction Bank on the east side of the station complex. The nearest **airport shuttle** stops at the Aviation Building in Xī Dān (see above), reachable by bus no. 52 from the station's east side. The taxi rank is on the second floor.

Warning: Larger baggage is X-rayed at the entrances to most Chinese railway and bus stations. Keep film in your hand baggage.

VISITOR INFORMATION

The Běijīng Tourism Administration maintains a 24-hour **tourist information hot line** at ℂ **010/6513-0828.** Staff actually speak some English, so it's unfortunate that they rarely have the answers to your questions, and simply refer you on to CITS. Hotel concierges and guest relations officers are at least close at hand, although they often have little knowledge of the city, will be reluctant to work to find the answers if they can convince you to do something else instead, and, when they do find the answer to a question, they do not note it down for the next time a guest asks. Beware of strong recommendations to visit dinner shows or other expensive entertainments, as they are often on a kickback.

You can also try the new BTA-managed **Běijīng Tourist Information Centers (Běijīng Shì Lǚyóu Zīxún Fúwù Zhōngxīn)** located in each district and all marked with the same aqua-blue signs. The most competent branch is in Cháoyáng, on Gōngtǐ Běi Lù across from the City Hotel and next to KFC (ℂ **010/6417-6627;** fax 010/6417-6656; chaoyang@bta.gov.cn; daily 9am–5pm). Free maps are available at the door, and staff can sometimes be wheedled into making phone calls. Ignore the extortionist travel service.

For the most current information on life in Běijīng, particularly restaurants and nightlife, see the intermittently accurate listings in the free English-language expat-produced monthlies *that's Beijing* or *Time Out* (largely translated from a vastly superior Chinese language magazine), available in hotel lobbies and at bars in the major drinking districts (see chapter 10 for these). Online, *City Weekend* (www.cityweekend. com.cn) manages to update its website with fair regularity. The e-mail newsletter *Xianzai Beijing* (see www.xianzai.com for more information) provides a list of each week's events, as well as special hotel, air ticket, and restaurant offers.

CITY LAYOUT & HISTORY

Modern Běijīng stands on the site of the capital founded in 1271 by the Mongols when the territory of modern-day China was merely a part of a far larger Mongol empire. Known to the Mongols as Khanbalik and to their Chinese subjects as Dà Dū or "Great Capital," it lay on a plain with limited and bitter water supplies, handy for the steppe from which the Mongols had emerged, but well away from the heartlands of the Hàn, as the main ethnic Chinese group still call themselves. When, in 1368, the Mongol Yuán dynasty was expelled, the foreigner-founded capital was abandoned for Nánjīng, the "Southern Capital." The third Míng emperor, who had formerly been in charge of resisting fresh Mongol advances from the north, returned the city to capital status in 1420, renaming it Běijīng, or "Northern Capital."

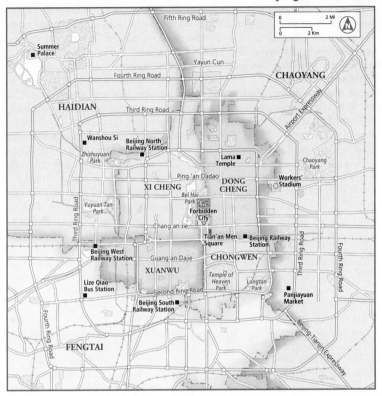

Although retaining much of the plan and grid of the Mongol founders, the emperor remodeled the city extensively, creating a secondary, broader walled extension to the south of the Mongol original. Many of the capital's major monuments date from this period, and its most extensive, the Forbidden City, right at the city's heart, is the one around which the remainder of the capital is still more or less arranged. The key ceremonial halls lie on a nearly north-south axis (actually aligned on the Pole Star), which bisects the city. Most north-south streets parallel this, and main east-west routes cross them at right angles. There are very few major streets running diagonally. The grid created was originally filled in with a maze of lanes peculiar to Běijīng and to a handful of other northern cities, called *hútòng* (both singular and plural), derived from a Mongol word. But most of these narrow streets have now been destroyed.

In 1644 the Míng dynasty was overthrown by a peasant rebellion, and the peasants were driven out shortly afterwards by invading Manchu forces from beyond the Great Wall to the northeast. China was absorbed into the Qīng empire, and foreigners ruled from Běijīng until the Qīng abdication of 1912. Including occupation by foreign forces in 1860 and from 1900 to 1901, and Japanese occupation during World War II, Běijīng has been under foreign control for more than half of its existence.

Běijīng was once a set of walls within walls. The Qīng took over the walled Forbidden City and the walled Imperial City within which it sat, and their followers took over the remainder of the northern section of the walled city. This area was known to other foreigners as the Tartar City, while the broader but separate walled section to the south of the Qián Mén (Front Gate) became the Chinese City—the Chinese quarter of Běijīng.

The enemy was now within the gates, and the outer city walls were neglected, but the Qīng built many temples and palaces, leaving the city's basic grid largely unchanged while building extensive gardens to the northwest.

With the exception of a limited number of Russians and small groups of missionaries, some of whom were allowed to erect churches, Běijīng remained free of Western influence or a Western presence until 1860, when emissaries sent to complete ratification of a treaty forced on the Qīng at the end of the Second Opium War by the British and French were put to death or imprisoned. British troops, led by Lord Elgin, torched the vast area of palaces and gardens to the northwest of the city, of which now only fragments remain at the Summer Palace and Old Summer Palace. French troops opposed razing such magnificent buildings, and were content simply to loot them.

For the first time, Western powers were allowed to station ministers in Běijīng, and accommodation was allocated to them just inside the Tartar City, east of the Qián Mén and what is now Tiān'ān Mén Square. At the end of the 19th century, resentment at the expansion of foreign influence in China led to attacks on Chinese who had converted to Christianity, destruction of railway lines and foreign property, and eventually to a siege of the Legation Quarter during which the attackers razed much of the surrounding housing, a fabulous library of ancient learning, and part of the Qián Mén. The siege was only lifted 2 months and many deaths later by the forces of eight allied powers who marched from the coast. Imperial troops, Boxers, Běijīng residents, and foreign troops indulged in an orgy of looting and destruction, which supplemented the burning of shops selling foreign goods and the destruction of churches already accomplished by the Boxers. The Legation Quarter subsequently became a further walled enclave, with many foreign banks, offices, and legation (embassy) buildings. In the early 20th century it was still the only area with paved roads and proper drainage and sewerage in an otherwise notably malodorous city.

The churches were rebuilt (and still stand), but the temples that had been collateral damage were mostly left in ruins. The Qīng were in decline, and after their fall in 1912, much else went into decline, too; ancient buildings being the victims of neglect or casual destruction. This process continued during the 1911/1912 to 1949 Republic and accelerated following the Communist Party victory and the creation of the People's Republic of China.

Signs at the Old Summer Palace and elsewhere harp on foreign destruction in 1860 and 1900, but since 1949 the Chinese themselves have almost completely demolished their city. Temples have been turned into housing, warehouses, industrial units, offices, and police stations. The slender walled space south of the Tiān'ān Mén was smashed open to create the vast expanse of the modern square, lined by hideous Soviet-influenced halls of rapidly down-at-heel grandeur. The city walls and most gate towers were pulled down to allow the construction of the Second Ring Road and the first metro line. Areas of traditional courtyard houses were pulverized for the construction of shabby six-story concrete dormitory blocks. Political campaigns against all traditional culture led to the defacing, damage, or destruction of many ancient buildings and their contents, particularly during the 1966 to 1976 Cultural Revolution.

The *hútòng*, once "numberless as the hairs on an ox," will soon be no harder to count than your fingers and toes, because China's increasing wealth has seen the government trying to turn the capital from a sleepy backwater town into a city of international standing. The broad boulevards apparently required by Marxist theory have become ever more numerous, and the last few years have seen several new routes blasted across the city. An assortment of often hideous towers representing no particular style or culture but sometimes with cheesy Chinese toppings have sprung up within the vanished city walls, dwarfing the Forbidden City and the few older buildings which remain.

The awarding of the 2008 Olympics to Běijīng has delivered the coup de grâce. Whole blocks of housing disappear every few weeks as developers, hand-in-glove with the government, expel residents. Developers race to destroy the remaining halls of ancient and largely forgotten temples before those charged with preserving them can catch up, although a few are given ham-fisted restoration and reopened to the public for a fee. A third, fourth, fifth, and now a sixth ring road have dropped like nooses around the neck of the old city center, inevitably leading to road-widening schemes through the heart of the remaining *hútòng*. Demolition of the ancient Dà Zhàlán district is well advanced, and the latest scheme is to widen Dé Shèng Mén Nèi Dàjiē into a 50m- (164-ft.-) wide road, which will plunge right through the heart of the Back Lakes area. The authorities are determined that by 2008 we should be impressed by the city's modernity, and all but the basic grid of the Yuán and Míng plan will have been swept away for shiny towers and gridlock. The most noticeable buildings will be those most alien to China—a three-venue National Grand Theatre resembling a flying saucer which has landed in a lake, under construction in the heart of the city just west of Tiān'ān Mén Square and designed by Frenchman Paul Andreu; and the vast venues for the Běijīng Olympics including the $100-million National Swimming Center.

MAIN STREETS

The main west-to-east artery of interest to visitors runs across the top of Tiān'ān Mén Square, past the Tiān'ān Mén (Gate of Heavenly Peace) itself. It changes names several times, but is most importantly Xī Cháng'ān Jiē to the west of the square, Dōng Cháng'ān Jiē to the east, then Jiànguó Mén Nèi Dàjiē until it crosses the Second Ring Road, when it becomes Jiànguó Mén Wài Dàjiē. Compass points such as *xī* (west) and *dōng* (east) turn up very frequently in street names, as do words such as *mén* (gate), *nèi* (inside), and *wài* (outside). Metro Line 1 runs under this route, passing several major hotels and shopping areas. The Xī Dān Běi Dàjiē and Wángfǔjǐng Dàjiē shopping streets run north from this route. The Second Ring Road runs around the combined outer perimeter of the old city walls they replaced, still showing the bulge of the wider Chinese City to the south and, depending on the time of day, usually provides a quicker route around the city center than going though it. Further out and quicker still, the Third Ring Road, which links with the airport expressway and routes to the Summer Palace, is the site of several major long-distance bus stations, numerous upmarket joint-venture hotels, and important restaurants. Beware the taxi driver who suggests using the Fourth or Fifth Ring Roads. Speeds on these routes are higher, but the kilometer count for getting round the city will also be significantly greater, and so will the cost.

FINDING AN ADDRESS

Maps of Běijīng are rarely accurate—the cartographers don't seem to feel it necessary to do more than sketch the main roads—and the smashing of new routes across and around the city is so rapid they can't keep up. Although some claim to issue half a dozen editions a year, the presence of *zuì xīn* or "newest" on the map cover is only an indication that the characters *zuì xīn* have been put on the cover. Bilingual maps, or maps with Romanized Chinese, tend to be less accurate to start with, and are printed less often. Regardless of this, **always buy a map,** available from vendors at all arrival points and at all bookstores, for around ¥5 (65¢). The small pages of this book cannot give you a detailed picture of any area, but the characters on the maps, map keys, and in the text of chapters 5 and 6 can be used to help you find your way around the Chinese map. The staff at your hotel can mark where you are and where you want to go, and you can compare the street-name characters with those on the road signs so you can keep track of your route. There's no question of really getting lost, and you can always flag down a cab and show the driver the characters for where you want to go. Street numbers are given in this book: odd numbers indicate the north or west side of the street, while an even-numbered residence will be on the south or east side, but otherwise no one uses them. Navigation is by street name and landmark.

NEIGHBORHOODS IN BRIEF

Citywide architectural uniformity makes the boundaries of Běijīng's official districts rather arbitrary, so we've avoided them in favor of maps showing in more detail the areas of most interest to visitors for their clusters of accommodations, restaurants, and attractions. Beyond the districts listed below, the metropolitan area stretches far into the countryside, adding perhaps another five million people to the urban population of around 10 million.

Dōng Chéng

Dōng Chéng (East City) occupies the eastern half of the city center, spreading north and east from the southwest corner of Tiān'ān Mén Square until it reaches the Second Ring Road, and occasionally spills over it. It includes the square itself, the Forbidden City, major temples such as the Yōng Hé Gōng (Lama Temple) and Confucius Temple, and the major shopping streets of Wángfǔjǐng and Dōng Dān. It's essentially the eastern half of the Qīng-era Tartar City, north of the wall separating it from the Chinese City, of which the twin towers of the Qián Mén (Front Gate) are the most significant remaining fragments.

Xī Chéng

The western half of the old Tartar City, Xī Chéng spreads farther west beyond the line of the original city wall at the Second Ring Road. It is home to

Zhōng Nán Hǎi, the off-limits central government compound otherwise known as the new Forbidden City, Běi Hǎi Gōngyuán, and the Bái Tǎ Sì (White Dagoba Temple). The Shíchà Hǎi (Back Lakes) and Dì'ān Mén area within Xī Chéng, with its string of lakes and relatively well-preserved *hútòng,* is where the last fading ghosts of (pre-1949) Old Běijīng reside. It's popular among writers, musicians, foreigners teaching in Běijīng, and other younger expatriates who haunt a collection of trendy, nameless bars and cafes at the waters' edge. Several minor sights here provide the excuse for a day's wandering.

Cháoyáng

Part urban, part suburban, Cháoyáng sprawls in a huge arc around the northeast and eastern sides of the city, housing the two main diplomatic compounds (and a third new one on the way), the Sān Lǐ Tún and Cháoyáng drinking districts, and the newly coined CBD (Central Business District) around the China World Trade Center. This is the richest district in Běijīng, the result, according to some, of the district's good *fēngshuǐ*.

The South

If Cháoyáng has Běijīng's best *fēngshuǐ*, the old Chinese City south of the Qián Mén, made up of Chóngwén (east) and Xuānwǔ (west), both enclosed by the suburban sprawl of Fēngtái to the south and southwest, has the worst. Squalid since its construction in the

Míng dynasty, this is where you'll find the city's grittiest *hútòng* and some of its best bargains on fake antiques, as well as Míng architectural jewels such as the Temple of Heaven (Tiān Tán).

Hǎidiàn and Yàyùn Cūn

Sprawling to the northwest, Hǎidiàn is the university and high-tech district, referred to hopefully in local media as "China's Silicon Valley" and home to the Summer Palace. Directly north of town is Yàyùn Cūn (Asia Games Village), home to Běijīng's best new Chinese restaurants, and site of many Olympic venues.

2 Getting Around

The major street layouts in Běijīng are often well planned: sidewalk for pedestrians, a fenced-off bike lane, two lanes for cars, another bike lane, and then sidewalk again. This is one of the benefits of the hideous boulevardization, or would be if only the inhabitants used these layouts properly. However, cars are parked on the pavement, usually at an angle so as to drive pedestrians into the bike lanes, and even pushbikes are usually parked so as to cause quite unnecessary obstruction to pedestrians. So the pedestrians are forced to get in the way of the cyclists, who are anyway going in both directions in the lanes on each side of the road, as well as along the edges of the lanes for cars, often in the wrong direction. Meanwhile, cars come along the bike lanes, also often in the wrong direction, so as to get access to the pavements and drive at a few pedestrians before parking.

Although residents quickly become inured to all this madness, and although if visitors use taxis and buses they are unlikely to get injured, they'll certainly see a few accidents and injuries. The best way to get around the city is by metro or by taxi, or often by a combination of the two.

BY METRO

The Běijīng metro system *(dìtiě)* is undergoing a process of rapid expansion, which is contributing to the traffic snarls at ground level, which make using the existing four lines (two underground, two light rail or *chéngtiě*) essential. Although other cities have involved foreign companies in the construction of up-to-date rolling stock, Běijīng seems to have stuck to a locally made product, which is slow and squeaky. And whereas other cities have switched to modern electronic gates to read your ticket, Běijīng has stuck with a paper ticket system and lots of staff to check the tickets.

Eventually there will be 15 metro and light-rail lines, but for now the system consists of the **Circle Line** (sometimes known as **Line 2**), which follows the upper portion of the Second Ring Road, cutting across under Qián Mén, effectively following the line of the Tartar City walls that were demolished to make its construction possible (the Dōngnán Jiǎolóu, home to the Red Gate Gallery, was spared because the metro takes a turn at that point). **Line 1** runs from Píngguǒ Yuán in the west, the site of Capital Iron and Steel and other heavy industry which are the sources of much of

Běijīng's throat-tickling pollution, right across town beneath Cháng'ān Jiē and its extensions to Sì Huì Dōng in the east. **Line 8** extends Line 1 into the eastern suburbs. The light-rail **Line 13** swings in a suburban loop to the north, from the Circle Line's Xī Zhí Mén to Dōng Zhí Mén stations. Several other lines, such as north-south Line 5, and one to the airport, will be completed by 2008. Stations are numbered (see Běijīng metro map), signs on platforms tell you which station is the next in each direction, and English announcements are made on trains, so navigation is not difficult.

For now, ticket booths are below ground, and a ticket costs ¥3 (35¢) for a ride anywhere from any Circle Line or Line 1 station to any other on those two lines, with free interchange. Because there's a fair bit of pushing and shoving at the ticket counters, buy a few tickets at one time (just hold up a number of fingers), but note that the two lines have different colored tickets, and you must use the right color as you start your journey. A ticket allowing you to start from or switch to Line 13, a *huànchéng piào*, is ¥5 (65¢), ¥4 (50¢) for Line 8. The system is said to be changing to machine-readable tickets, but no one can say when. The involvement of the Hong Kong–based MTR Corporation should speed things along.

Entrances are not clearly marked. Find them on maps, marked with a D (for *dìtiě*) in a circle, and look for the same sign at entrances. Escalators are up only, staircases are long, and there are no elevators. Those with limited mobility should stay on the surface.

BY TAXI

Běijīng's rapid conversion from a city for bicycles to one for cars has brought the inevitable traffic jams. Get on the road well before 7:30am to beat the rush, or forget it until about 10am. The city's arteries start to clog again about 3pm, and circulation slows to a crawl until 7:30pm. Take the metro to the point nearest your destination and jump in a cab from there.

By the time you reach Běijīng, the cheap but poorly air-conditioned **Xiàlì** rattletraps should be a thing of the past. There are now essentially two fare types available, with their per-kilometer rates posted on the side window.

The red **Fùkāng**, a Citroën joint-venture built in Wǔhàn on the Yángzǐ River, are slightly older than green or brown **Xiàndài** (Hyundai, a Běijīng-based joint venture). The Xiàndài have better air-conditioning. Both have an initial charge of ¥10 ($1.25) which includes 3km (2 miles), and each subsequent kilometer is ¥1.60 (20¢).

The **Santana** and **Jetta** are roomier vehicles built in various Volkswagen joint-ventures around China. They're similar to popular Volkswagen models in the West and are equally solid. The smaller versions have the same charges as the Fùkāng above; the larger ones charge ¥2 (25¢) per kilometer after 3km (2 miles). Occasionally, there are larger vehicles charging as much as ¥3 (35¢) per kilometer. Some of these have dodgy meters and hang around larger hotels where corrupt bellhops call them for you. Always follow the advice in the box "Ten Tips for Taking Taxis Around Town."

All taxis are metered. But on the front of the meter they also have a button, for one-way trips out of town, which is pushed regardless of the type of trip to be taken. This causes the rate per kilometer to increase by 50% after 15km (9 miles). If you are hiring the vehicle to take you somewhere, wait, and bring you back, or to run you around town all day, then you should insist that the button is not pushed. As elsewhere in the world, the meter also ticks over slowly when the vehicle is stationary or moving very slowly.

Běijīng Metro

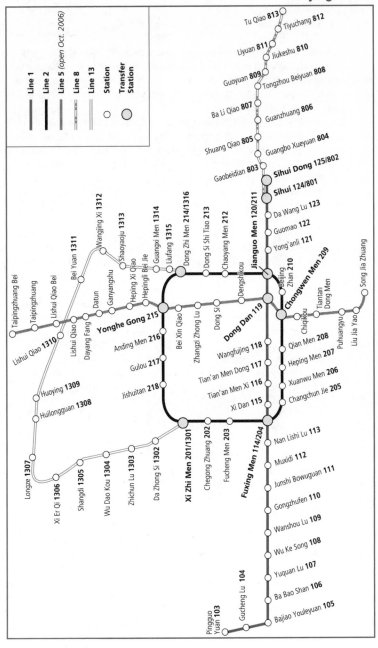

> *Tips* **Ten Tips for Taking Taxis Around Town**
>
> 1. *Never* go with a driver who approaches you at the airport (or railway stations). Leave the building and head for the rank. As with everywhere else in the world, airport taxis are the most likely to cause trouble. Drivers who approach you are usually *hēi chē*—illegal and meterless "black cabs."
> 2. Cabs waiting for business outside major tourist sights, especially those whose drivers call out to foreigners, should be avoided, as should cabs whose drivers ask you where you want to go before you even get in. Always flag down a passing cab, and nine times in ten the precautions listed here will be unnecessary.
> 3. If you're staying in an upmarket hotel, do not go with taxis called by the doorman or waiting in line outside. Even at some famous hotels, drivers pay kickbacks to the doormen to allow them to join the line on the forecourt. Some cabs are merely waiting because many guests, Chinese and foreign alike, will be out-of-town people who can be easily misled. Instead, flag down a passing cab for yourself. Take the hotel's business card to show to a taxi driver when you want to get back.
> 4. Better hotels give you a piece of paper with the taxi registration number on it as you board or alight, so that you can complain if something goes wrong. Often you won't know if it has, of course, and there's no guarantee that anything will happen if you complain to the hotel, but hang onto it anyway.
> 5. Look to see if the supervision card, usually with a photo of the driver and a telephone number, is prominently displayed, as regulations require. If it isn't, you may have problems. Choose another cab.

Taxi rates are also 30% higher between 11pm and 5am, but the meter's clock may decide that 11pm has arrived a little before your watch says so.

Consider taking taxis for **trips out of town.** Your hotel's transport department would love for you to take one of their cars for the day—and they would love to separate you from up to ¥1,200 ($150) for a trip you can bargain for yourself for ¥350 ($44), which is what most drivers take in each day. Even after overhead, this puts them well above the average Běijīng resident in income, but they often work 12 hours a day, 7 days a week to obtain it, and the vehicle often works 24 hours, with a separate driver on the night shift. They are also squeezed by the taxi companies. So a trip out of town is a welcome change, and better than spending much of the day cruising the city empty. But the rate you pay should be well under the official per-kilometer rate, and a price should be negotiated. Again, deal with drivers stopped at random and not those targeting foreigners or better hotels, and begin getting quotes the day before you want to travel. The lack of a common language need not deter you, as long as you have the characters for the name of your destination and can write down the start and return times. Prices can be negotiated using pen and paper or a calculator. ¥350 ($44) for a round-trip of around 200km (124 miles) is fine. You should also be prepared to

6. Can you clearly see the meter? If it's recessed behind the gear stick partly hidden by an artfully folded towel, for example, choose another cab.

7. Always make sure you see the meter reset. If you didn't see the flag pushed down, which shouldn't happen until you actually move off, then you may end up paying for the time the cab was in the rank. This is a particularly popular scam outside better hotels.

8. If you are by yourself, sit in the front seat. Have a map with you and look as if you know where you are going (even if you don't).

9. Rates per kilometer are clearly posted on the side of the cab and vary by vehicle type. The flag drop of ¥10 ($1.25) includes 3km (2 miles), after which the standard kilometer rate begins. But in Běijīng, after 15km (9 miles), the rate jumps by 50% if the driver has pushed the "one-way" button on the front of the meter. This button is for one-way trips out of town and usually should not be pushed, but always is. As a result, it's rarely worthwhile to have a cab wait for you and take you back.

10. Pay what's on the meter, and don't tip—the driver will insist on giving change. Always ask for a receipt *(fā piào)*. Should you leave something in a cab, there's a remarkably high success rate at getting even valuable items back if you call the number on the receipt and provide the details. You'll need the assistance of a Mandarin speaker.

pay road tolls and parking fees (probably in total no more than about ¥60/$7.50), and it's a nice gesture to buy the driver lunch.

BY BUS

Unless you are on the tightest of backpacker budgets and are traveling alone, your first choice for getting around town is the metro, your second choice is taxi, and your last resort should be the bus, although the introduction of dedicated bus lanes will make them more appealing. Most buses have conductors who'll need to know your destination in order to work out how much to charge. Sometimes fees are payable into a slot at the front of the bus with no change given. Regular buses charge a flat fare of ¥1 (10¢), while air-conditioned buses charge ¥2 (25¢) and up. Entrance and exit doors are marked with the *shàng* and *xià* characters respectively (see appendix B).

BY PEDICAB

Unless you are competent in Mandarin and obviously familiar with the city, a ride in a pedicab will always end in grief, and arguments over the agreed fare ("No! Thirty *dollars!*"). A taxi is cheaper, quicker, and less stressful, and it won't make you look like an idiot tourist.

BY BICYCLE

There used to be considerable charm in being one fish in a vast shoal of bicycles, but cycling is now ill-advised for the timid (or sensibly cautious). But enthusiasts for two-wheeled travel will certainly find that at some times of day they can get around more quickly than anyone else. Many upmarket hotels will rent you a bicycle for around ¥80 to ¥100 ($10–$13) for the day, however a *new* bike may be purchased for as little as ¥130 ($16), so if you're going to be using a bike for a few days, buying one is a better deal. Don't expect sophisticated accessories such as gears on rental bikes or bikes purchased for these prices. Flat Běijīng does not require them anyway. Budget accommodations and some bike enclosures next to metro stops charge a more appropriate ¥10 ($1.25) for the day. Check the bike's condition carefully, especially the brakes and tires. Sidewalk bicycle-repair operations are everywhere and will make repairs for a few *yuán,* if the worst comes to the worst. Always park the bike in marked and supervised enclosures, using the lock, which is built in or provided, or expect the bike to be gone when you get back. The parking fee is usually ¥0.20 (2¢).

ON FOOT

The vast width of Běijīng's boulevards make maps deceiving. Blocks are long, and everything is further away than it seems. Save your feet for getting around temples, palaces, and markets, which can be very extensive, or for the walking routes in chapter 8. Use pedestrian underpasses and footbridges wherever available, or be prepared to adopt the matador approach of the locals, letting cars sweep past you to either side as you wait for the opportunity to cross to the next lane. Traffic turning right at lights does not give way to pedestrians, nor does any other traffic unless forced to do so by large groups of people bunching up to cross the road.

BY CAR

The rule of the road is "me first," regardless of signs, traffic lights, road markings, safety considerations, or common sense, unless someone with an ability to fine or demand a bribe is watching. In general, the bigger your vehicle, the more authority you have. Maximum selfishness in the face of common sense characterizes driving in general, and there is no maneuver so ludicrous, unreasonable, or unexpected that someone will not attempt it. Residents have time to adapt—visitors do not. Our strong advice is to forget it, and take a taxi.

FAST FACTS: Běijīng

Airport See "Arriving" under "Orientation" at the beginning of this chapter.

American Express Běijīng: Room 2313-14, China World Tower 1, China World Trade Center; ✆ 010/6505-2838. After hours: U.S. hot line ✆ 001336/393-1111. Emergency card replacement: 00852/2277-1010. Stolen traveler's checks: 010800/610-0276 (toll-free).

Area Codes In mainland China, area codes begin with a zero, which must be dropped when calling China from abroad. The whole area code can be dropped when calling another number in the same area.

Babysitters Babysitting services are widely available in hotels but are usually carried out by regular members of the housekeeping staff. Don't expect special qualifications, but do expect your children to be spoiled rotten.

Banks, Currency Exchanges & ATMs Larger branches of the **Bank of China** typically exchange cash and traveler's checks on weekdays only, from 9am to 4pm, occasionally with a break for lunch (11:30am–1:30pm). Most central is the branch at the bottom of Wángfǔjǐng Dàjiē, next to the Oriental Plaza. Other useful branches include those at Fùchéng Mén Nèi Dàjiē 410; on Jiànguó Mén Wài Dàjiē, west of the Scitech Building; in the Lufthansa Center, next to the Kempinski Hotel; and in Tower 1 of the China World Trade Center. Outside the airport, Bank of China **ATMs** accepting international cards 24 hours a day are now widespread, and include those outside the Wángfǔjǐng Dàjiē branch mentioned above. Others exist further north on Wángfǔjǐng Dàjiē, outside the Xīn (Sun) Dōng Ān Plaza; on the left just inside the Pacific Century Plaza on Gōngtǐ Běi Lù east of Sān Lǐ Tún (only 9am–9pm); and adjacent to the Bank of China branch next to the Scitech Building (see above; also 24 hr.). The Citibank ATM east of the International Hotel, and the Hongkong and Shanghai Bank machine at the entrance to COFCO Plaza, roughly opposite each other on Jiànguó Mén Nèi Dàjiē, are Běijīng's most reliable. There are also six ATMs at the airport. See "Money" in chapter 2 for further details on using ATMs.

Books The best selection of English-language books in Běijīng can be found at the clearly marked **Foreign Languages Bookstore** (Wàiwén Shūdiàn; 9am–8:30pm) at Wángfǔjǐng Dàjiē 235, opposite the Xīn (Sun) Dōng Ān Plaza. Look on the right side of the first floor for China-related nonfiction, glossy *hútòng* photo books, cookbooks, the full range of Asiapac's cartoon renditions of Chinese classics, and even Frommer's guides. Cheap paperback versions of a huge chunk of the English canon, as well as a number of contemporary works, are sold on the third floor. **The Bookworm** (p. 190) in Sān Lǐ Tún carries a smaller but more daring collection of fiction, and also houses Běijīng's most intriguing library of English-language materials.

Business Hours Offices are generally open 9am to 6pm, but closed Saturday and Sunday. All shops, sights, restaurants, and transport systems offer the same service 7 days a week. Shops are typically open at least 8am to 8pm. Bank opening hours vary (see "Banks, Currency Exchanges & ATMs" above).

Car Rentals Because of the many driving hazards in Běijīng, renting a car is not recommended for visitors. Taking taxis is cheaper and easier. If you must, **Hertz** (www.hertz.net.cn) has offices inside the Lufthansa Center (✆ **010/6462-5730**) and the Jiànguó Fàndiàn (✆ **010/6595-8109**), open 9am to 7pm weekdays, 9am to 5pm on weekends. The big snag is that a Chinese driver's license and a residence permit is required, something no short-term visitor will be able to arrange. Daily rates start from ¥320 ($40) per day for Jettas and free mileage is restricted to 180km (112 miles) per day (300km/186 miles for members). Your passport, a business card, and a whopping ¥20,000 ($2500) credit card deposit are required the first time you rent a vehicle. The fleet is fairly battered (locals rent cars when learning to drive), and it's often difficult to obtain a vehicle on weekends.

Currency See "Money" in chapter 2.

Doctors & Dentists For comprehensive care, the best choice is **Běijīng United Family Hospital (Hémùjiā Yīyuàn; ℂ 010/6433-3960)** at Jiàngtái Lù (2 blocks southeast of the Holiday Inn Lido); it is open 24 hours, is staffed with foreign-trained doctors, and has a pharmacy, dental clinic, in- and out-patient care, and ambulance service. Other reputable health-service providers, both with 24-hour ambulance services, are the **International Medical Center (ℂ 010/6465-1561)**, inside the Lufthansa Center; and the **International SOS Clinic and Alarm Center (ℂ 010/6492-9111)**, in Building C of the BITIC Leasing Center.

Driving Rules "I'm bigger than you, so get out of my way," sums it up. See "By Car" above.

Drugstores Bring supplies of your favorite over-the-counter medicines with you because supplies of well-known Western brands are unreliable and some-times fake. The real thing can be found in the lobbies of international five-star hotels. Better still, branches of **Watson's** (on the first floor of Full Link Plaza at Cháoyáng Mén Wài Dàjiē 19, and in the basement of the Oriental Plaza at the bottom of Wángfǔjǐng Dàjiē 1; 10am–9pm) stock most common remedies and toiletries, mostly in the British versions. For more specific drugs, try the pharmacy in the Běijīng United Family Hospital (see "Doctors & Dentists" above).

Electricity The electricity used in all parts of China is 220 volts, alternating current (AC), 50 cycles. Most devices from North America, therefore, cannot be used without a transformer. The most common outlet takes the North American two-flat-pin plug (but not the three-pin version, or those with one pin broader than the other). Nearly as common are outlets for the two-round-pin plugs common in Europe. Outlets for the three-flat-pin (two pins at an angle) used in Australia, for instance, are also frequently seen. Most hotel rooms have all three, and indeed many outlets are designed to take all three plugs. Adapters are available for only ¥8 to ¥17 ($1–$2) in department stores. Shaver sockets are common in bathrooms of hotels from three stars upwards. British-style three-chunky-pin plugs also often occur in mainland joint-venture hotels built with Hong Kong assistance, but hotels of this caliber will have adapters available.

Embassies & Consulates Běijīng has two main embassy areas—one surrounding Rìtán Gōngyuán north of Jiànguó Mén Wài Dàjiē, and another in Sān Lǐ Tún north of Gōngtǐ Běi Lù. A third district, future home of the new U.S. Embassy, has sprouted up next to the Hilton Hotel outside the north section of the East Third Ring Road. Embassies are typically open Monday through Friday from 9am to between 4 and 5pm, with a lunch break from noon to 1:30pm. The **U.S. Embassy** is due to move in 2008, but for now it's in Rìtán at Xiùshuǐ Dōng Jiē 2 (ℂ **010/6532-3431** or, after hours, 010/6532-1910; fax 010/6532-4153). The **Canadian Embassy** is at Dōng Zhí Mén Wài Dàjiē 19 (ℂ **010/6532-3536;** bejing-cs@international.gc.ca). The **British Embassy** consular section is in Rìtán at Floor 21, North Tower, Kerry Centre, Guānghuá Lù 1 (ℂ **010/8529-6600,** ext. 3363; fax 010/8529-6081). The **Australian Embassy** is in Sān Lǐ Tún at Dōng Zhí Mén Wài

Dàjiē 21 (℡ 010/5140-4111; fax 010/6532-4605). The **New Zealand Embassy** is in Rìtán at Dōng Èr Jiē 1 (℡ 010/6532-2731, ext. 220; fax 010/6532-4317).

Emergencies No one speaks English on emergency numbers in China, although your best bet will be ℡110. Find help nearer at hand.

Etiquette & Customs **Appropriate attire:** Wear whatever you find comfortable. Some of the diaphanous or apparently spray-on dressing of younger women is more likely to surprise you than your attire will surprise them. Foreigners are stared at regardless of what they wear. Swimwear should tend towards the conservative by Western standards—shorts rather than briefs for men, swimsuits rather than bikinis for women—but not if you are using pools in deluxe hotels with plenty of foreign guests. Business attire is similar to that of the West. For most visitors, opportunities to dress up formally are few, and there are no restaurants or hotels absolutely requiring jacket or tie.

Greetings and gestures: The handshake is now used as it is in the West, although there's a tendency to hang on longer. Take business cards if you have them, as an exchange of cards almost always follows. Present yours with two hands, and then hold the one you're given with two hands. If you can speak even two words of Mandarin, you will be told that you speak very well. But even if you are fluent, this is something you should deny.

Avoiding offense: However great the provocation, do not lose your temper and shout at someone in public or cause them to experience public shame (loss of face). Even flatly contradicting someone in front of others (so he loses face) is also best avoided if harmony is to be maintained. Instead, complain calmly and privately, and directly to a superior if you wish. Punctuality is very important in China, and the traffic situation in most cities makes that difficult, so allow plenty of time.

Eating and drinking: Master the use of chopsticks before you go. Suggestions that the food is lacking in some way, made by the host, should always be greeted with firm denials. Serve yourself from main dishes using the spoon provided, then eat with chopsticks. Do not leave them sticking up out of your bowl. Your cup of tea will constantly be topped up—when you want no more, leave it full. There's a great deal of competitive drinking at banquets, which is done by the simultaneous drinking of toasts in *bái jiŭ* (Chinese spirits), to cries of *"Gān bēi!"* ("dry cup"—down in one). Avoid participation by drinking beer or mineral water instead, but if toasts of welcome are made, be sure to make one in reply. Dining tends to happen early, and at the end of the meal everyone disappears quickly. If you are invited to eat at someone's home, be sure to take off your shoes at the entrance (your host's protestations that it's not necessary are merely polite).

Holidays See "Holidays" under "When to Go" in chapter 2.

Hot Lines Hot lines and all kinds of telephone booking and information numbers are given throughout this book. But in almost no cases will English be spoken at the other end. Ask English-speaking staff at your hotel to find answers to your questions and to make any necessary calls on your behalf.

Information See "Visitor Information" earlier in this chapter.

Internet Access Internet bars in Bĕijīng are subject to numerous regulations (no one under 18, no smoking) and are restricted in number. The best bet for affordable Internet access is any of the city's various **youth hostels;** the cost is usually ¥10 ($1) per hour. There are two conveniently located Internet bars on the third floor of the Lăo Chē Zhàn (Old Train Station) shopping center next to Qián Mén. **Qiányì Wăngluò Kāfēiwū** (© 010/6705-1722) is open from 9:30am to 11pm and charges ¥20 ($2.50) per hour in a cafe setting with a full coffee menu. A simpler, nameless place next door, open from 9am to midnight, charges ¥6 (80¢) per hour. **Moko Internet Café** (**Mòkè Wăngbā;** © 010/6252-3712) on Dōng Sì Dàjiē, just south of the Dōng Sì Mosque, is open from 8am to midnight. Rates are ¥10 ($1.25) per hour downstairs, ¥4 (50¢) upstairs, or free for the first hour if you spend ¥12 ($1.50) in the cafe. The basement of East Gate Plaza, just south of Oriental Kenzo on Dōng Zhōng Jiē (metro: Dōng Zhí Mén, exit C) houses **Yúntiān Wăngluò** (© 010/6418-5815) open 8am to 10pm, ¥4 (50¢) per hour. The fastest in-room **dial-up** service is 95962 (user name and password 263). See "The 21st-Century Traveler" in chapter 2 for a full explanation.

Language English is rare in Bĕijīng, although there will be someone at your hotel who speaks at least a little. Ask him or her to help you with phone calls and bookings. Almost no information, booking, complaint, or emergency lines in Bĕijīng have anyone who speaks English.

Legal Aid If you get on the wrong side of what passes for the law in China, contact your consulate immediately.

Liquor Laws With the exception of some minor local regulations, there are no liquor laws in Bĕijīng. Alcohol can be bought in any convenience store, supermarket, restaurant, bar, hotel, or club, 7 days a week, and may be drunk anywhere you feel like drinking it. If the shop is open 24 hours, then the alcohol is available 24 hours, too. Closing times for bars and clubs vary according to demand, but typically it's all over by 3am.

Lost & Found Be sure to contact all of your credit card companies the minute you discover your wallet has been lost or stolen. Your credit card company or insurer may require a police report number or record of the loss, although many Public Security Bureaus (police stations) will be reluctant to do anything as energetic as lift a pen. Most credit card companies have an emergency toll-free number to call if your card is lost or stolen: In **mainland China,** Visa's emergency number is © 010/800-440-2911; American Express cardholders and traveler's check holders should call © 010/800-610-0277; MasterCard holders should call © 010/800-110-7309. Diners Club members should call Hong Kong at © 852/2860-1800, or call the U.S. collect at © 416/369-6313. Also see "Emergency Cash" under "Money" in chapter 2.

Mail Sending mail from China is remarkably reliable, although sending it to private addresses within China is not. Take the mail to post offices rather than use post boxes. Some larger hotels have postal services on-site. It helps if mail sent out of the country has its country of destination written in characters, but this is not essential, although hotel staff will often help. Letters and cards written in red ink will occasionally be rejected, as this carries extremely negative overtones. Costs are as follows: Overseas mail: **postcards** ¥4.20 (50¢), **letters**

under 10g (.35 oz.) ¥5.40 (70¢), **letters under 20g** (.70 oz.) ¥6.50 (80¢). EMS (**express parcels** under 500g/18 oz.): to the U.S. ¥180 to ¥240 ($23–$30); to Europe ¥220 to ¥280 ($28–$35); to Australia ¥160 to ¥210 ($20–$26). **Normal parcels** up to 1kg (2.2 lb.): to the U.S. by air ¥95 to ¥159 ($12–$20), by sea ¥20 to ¥84 ($2.50–$14); to the U.K. by air ¥77 to ¥162 ($10–$20), by sea ¥22 to ¥108 ($11–$13); to Australia by air ¥70 to ¥144 ($8.75–$18), by sea ¥15 to ¥89 ($1.90–$11). Letters and parcels can be registered for a small extra charge. Registration forms and Customs declaration forms are in Chinese and French.

Maps Purchasing city maps as you go is absolutely essential, even though few are bilingual. These are available at bus and railway stations and at airports for around ¥5 (65¢). Get your hotel staff to circle the characters for your hotel on the map, and the characters for the main sights you plan to see. You can then jump in a taxi at any point, show the driver the characters for where you want to go, and keep an eye on the route he takes.

Newspapers & Magazines Sino-foreign joint-venture hotels in the bigger cities have a selection of foreign newspapers and magazines available, but these are not otherwise on sale. The government distributes a propaganda sheet called *China Daily,* usually free at hotels. Běijīng also supports a number of self-censoring entertainment magazines usually produced by resident foreigners. Nevertheless, these do have intermittently accurate entertainment listings, as well as restaurant reviews. See "Visitor Information" earlier in this chapter.

Police Known to foreigners as the PSB (Public Security Bureau, *gōng'ān jú*), this is only one of several different bureaus in mainland China. The police (*jǐngchá*) are quite simply best avoided–honestly, they are keen to avoid doing any work. Ideally, any interaction with the police should be limited to visa extensions. If you must see them for some reason, approach your hotel for assistance first, and visit the office listed under "Visa Extensions," under "Entry Requirements & Customs" in chapter 2, where you are likely to find an English speaker of sorts.

Post Office There are numerous post offices across the city, including one a long block north of the Jiànguó Mén metro station on the east side of Jiànguó Mén Běi Dàjiē (8am–6:30pm), one inside the Landmark Tower (next to the Great Wall Sheraton), one next to the Friendship Store on Jiànguó Mén Wài Dàjiē, one on Gōngtǐ Běi Lù (opposite the Workers' Stadium), the main office on Jiànguó Mén Nèi Dàjiē on the corner of Běijīng Zhàn Kǒu leading to Běijīng Station (almost opposite the International Hotel), and the EMS Post Office (Běijīng Yóuzhèng Sùdì Jú) at the corner of Qián Mén Dōng Dàjiē and Zhèngyì Lù. There is a **FedEx** office in Oriental Plaza, Room 107, No. 1 Office Building. **DHL** has branches in the China World Center and COFCO Plaza, and **UPS-Sinotrans** has a useful branch in the Scitech Building at Jiànguó Mén Wài Dàjiē 22.

Restrooms Street-level public toilets in China are common, many detectable with the nose before they are seen. Entrance fees have been abolished in Běijīng, but someone may still try to charge you for toilet paper ¥0.20. In many cases you merely squat over a trough. So, use the standard Western equipment in your hotel room, in department stores and malls, and in branches of foreign fast-food chains. This is the principal benefit of the presence of so many branches of McDonald's.

Safety See "Health & Safety" in chapter 2.

Smoking The government of China is the world's biggest cigarette manufacturer. China is home to 20% of the world's population but 30% of the world's cigarettes. About one million people a year in China die of smoking-related illnesses. Nonsmoking tables in restaurants are almost unheard of, and NO SMOKING signs are favorite places beneath which to smoke, especially in elevators. Smokers are generally sent to the spaces between the carriages on trains, but they won't bother to go there if no one protests. Similarly on air-conditioned buses: Some people will light up to see if they can get away with it (but usually they'll be told to put it out).

Taxes Service charges mostly only appear in Sino-foreign joint-venture hotels, and range from 10% to 15%. Airport departure taxes are now included in the cost of your ticket.

Telephone The international country code for mainland China is **86.**

To call China:

1. Dial the international access code: 011 in the U.S., 00 in the U.K, for example.
2. Dial the country code: 86 for China.
3. Dial the city code, omitting the leading zero, and then dial the number. To reach Běijīng from the U.S., you would dial 011-86-10-plus the 8-digit number.

To call within China: For calls within the same city, omit the city code, which always begins with a zero when used (010 for Běijīng, 020 for Guǎngzhōu, for example). All hotel phones have direct dialing, and most have international dialing. Hotels are only allowed to add a service charge of up to 15% to the cost of the call, and even long-distance rates within China are very low. To use a public telephone you'll need an IC (integrated circuit) card *("àicēi" kǎ)* available from post offices, convenience stores, and street stalls, available in values beginning at ¥20 ($2.50) (wherever you can make out the letters "IC" among the Chinese characters). A brief local call is typically ¥0.30 to ¥0.50 (4¢–6¢). Phones show you the value remaining on the card when you insert it, and count down as you talk.

To make international calls: First dial 00 and then the country code (U.S. or Canada 1, U.K. 44, Ireland 353, Australia 61, New Zealand 64). Next dial the area or city code, omitting any leading zero, and then dial the number. For example, if you want to call the British Embassy in Washington, D.C., you would dial 00-1-202-588-7800. Forget taking access numbers for your local phone company with you—you can call internationally for a fraction of the cost by using an IP (Internet Protocol) card *(àipì kǎ),* available wherever you see the letters "IP." You should bargain to pay less than the face value of the card—as little as ¥40 ($5) for a ¥100 ($12) card from street vendors. Instructions for use are on the back, but you simply dial the access number given, choose English from the menu, and follow the instructions to dial in the number behind a scratch-off panel. Depending on where you call, ¥50 ($6) can give you an hour of talking. If using a public phone, you'll need an IC card (see above) to make the call.

In emergencies, dial 108 to negotiate a collect call, but again, you'll need help from a Mandarin speaker.

For directory assistance: Dial 114. No English is spoken, and only local numbers are available. If you want numbers for other cities, dial the city code followed by 114—a long-distance call. You can text the name of the establishment you are looking for (in English) to 85880, and for a small fee, the address will return in Chinese, ready to show to your taxi driver.

For operator assistance: Just ask for help at your hotel.

Toll-free numbers: Numbers beginning with 800 within China are toll-free, but calling a 1-800 number in the States from China is a full tariff international call, as is calling one in Hong Kong from mainland China, or vice versa.

Time Zone The whole of China is on Běijīng time—8 hours ahead of GMT (and therefore of London), 13 hours ahead of New York, 14 hours ahead of Chicago, and 16 hours ahead of Los Angeles. There's no daylight saving time (summer time), so subtract 1 hour in the summer.

Tipping In **mainland China,** as in many other countries, there is *no tipping,* despite what tour companies may tell you (although if you have a tour leader who accompanies you from home, home rules apply). Until recently, tipping was expressly forbidden, and some hotels still carry signs requesting you not to tip. Foreigners, especially those on tours, are overcharged at every turn, and it bemuses Chinese that they hand out free money in addition. Chinese never do it themselves, and indeed if a bellhop or other hotel employee hints that a tip would be welcome, he or she is likely to be fired. Waitresses may run out of restaurants after you to give you change, and all but the most corrupt of taxi drivers will insist on returning it, too. Hotel employees and taxi drivers are already far better paid than the average Chinese, and to be a tour guide is already a license to print money. In China, the listed price or the price bargained for is the price you pay, and that's that.

Water Tap water in mainland China is not drinkable, and should not even be used for brushing your teeth. Use bottled water, widely available on every street, and provided for free in all the better hotels.

Weather For daily weather forecasts, check *China Daily* or CCTV 9, China Central Television's English channel (broadcast in most hotels). There is also a weather hot line (*C* **121**); dial 6 after a minute or so for the report in English (¥3/45¢ per min.).

5

Where to Stay

There are two types of hotel in mainland China: the **Sino-foreign joint-venture** hotels with familiar brand names, and **Chinese-owned and -managed** hotels. At the four- and five-star levels (see below for details on local star ratings), the Chinese-owned and -run hotels want you to think they are on par with the joint ventures. At lower levels they can range from indescribably battered and grubby to friendly, clean, and comfortable. (*Note:* We awarded the star ratings shown at the beginning of each review in this chapter. Our 0–3 star scale does not coincide with the Chinese star-rating system.)

Your **first choice** at the four- or five-star level should be a familiar brand name, or a property from one of the Asian luxury chains. In most cases, the buildings are Chinese-owned, and the foreign part of the joint venture is the management company, which supplies worldwide marketing efforts, staff training, and senior management, while ensuring conformity with brand standards (never entirely possible; you'll generally find 90% of what you'd expect from the same brand at home).

Your **second choice** should be a wholly Chinese-owned and -run hotel with foreigners in senior management whose main purpose is to be there and make sure that things actually happen. But in both types of hotel, the general manager may have far less idea than he thinks he has of what's going on: The transport department uses hotel vehicles for private hires to make money on the side; the

human resources manager rejects applicants whose experience may be threatening and makes a good income from bribes (to ensure that the housekeeper's nephew gets a job in security, for instance); the front office manager institutes a system of fines, and pockets them himself; or the doormen charge taxis to be allowed to wait in the rank.

Entirely **Chinese-owned and -run** hotels at four- and five-star levels usually have only one thing in common with their counterparts: They charge the same (or, at least, attempt to do so); but you'll rarely get value for your money. At the four-star level and below, the best choice is almost always the newest hotel—teething troubles aside, most things will work, staff will be eager to please (if not quite sure how), rooms will be spotless, and rates can be easily bargained down, since few hotels spend any money on advertising. The aim is to find sweetly inept but willing service rather than the sour leftovers of the *tiě fànwǎn* (iron rice bowl) era of guaranteed employment, for whom everything is too much effort.

A drawback for all hoteliers is that the government requires them to employ far more people than they need, and it's nearly impossible to obtain staff with any experience in hotel work. The joint-venture hotels are the training institutions for the rest of the Chinese hotel industry, which steals their local staff as soon as possible. Lower-level hotels are run by half-understood rules, with which there's half-compliance, half the time. A hotel may have designated nonsmoking rooms, but that doesn't mean they don't have ashtrays in them.

Until recently throughout China, only hotels with **special licenses** were allowed to take foreign guests. This requirement has now vanished from Běijīng. In theory, all hotels with such licenses have at least one English speaker, usually of modest ability.

The Chinese **star-rating system** is meaningless. Nationwide, five-star ratings are awarded by a central authority, but four-star and lower ratings depend upon local standards, and both depend upon compliance with a checklist, but more crucially, with banqueting the inspectors. (Inspectors have no idea how to run a hotel anyway.) In general, Chinese hotels receive almost no maintenance after they open. There are Chinese "five-star" hotels in Běijīng which have gone a decade without proper redecoration or refurbishment. Foreign managements force the issue with building owners, but it's rare for standards to be maintained. A new three-star will usually be better than an old four-star.

Outside of joint-venture hotels, don't rely on finding **amenities;** even if we list them in this book, there's no guarantee that you'll find them fit to use. Salons, massage rooms, nightclubs, and karaoke rooms are often merely the bases for other kinds of illegal entertainment (for men). Fitness equipment may be broken and inadequately supervised, and Jacuzzis may have more rings than a sequoia, so proceed with care.

You may receive unexpected **phone calls.** If you are female, the caller may hang up without saying anything, as may be the case if you are male and answer in English. But if the caller persists and is female, and if you hear the word *ànmō* (massage), then what is being offered needs no further explanation, but a massage is only the beginning. Unplug the phone.

Almost all rooms, however basic, have the following: A telephone whose line can usually be unplugged for use in a laptop; air-conditioning, which is either central with a wall-mounted control or individual to the room with a remote control, and which may double as a heater; a television, usually with no English channels except CCTV 9 and possibly an in-house movie channel using pirated DVDs or VCDs; a thermos of boiled water or a kettle to boil your own, usually with cups (wash before using) and free bags of green tea; and an array of switches, which may not control what they say they control, found near the bed. The bathrooms have free soap and shampoo, and in better hotels a shower cap and toothbrush/toothpaste package.

Ordinary Chinese hotels usually contain a *biāozhǔn jiān*, or "standard room," which means a room with twin beds or a double bed, and with a private bathroom. In older ordinary hotels, double beds may have only recently been installed, the switches are all in the wrong place, and the room is now referred to as a *dānrén jiān* or single room. Nevertheless, two people can stay there and the price is lower than for a standard room with twin beds.

Foreign **credit cards** are increasingly likely to be accepted in three-star hotels and above, but never rely on this. Most hotels accepting foreigners will exchange foreign currency(cash) on the premises; some may not accept traveler's checks. Almost all hotels require **payment in advance,** plus a deposit *(yājīn)*, which is refundable when you leave. Some hotels add a 5% to 15% **service charge** on top of their room rates (our listings indicate where this is done).

Keep all **receipts** you are given. To get your deposit back, you may need to hand over the receipt for your key when you check out, and since staff occasionally forget to enter payments in computers or ledgers, you may need receipts to prevent yourself from being charged twice.

To **check in** you'll need your passport, and you must complete a registration form (which will be in English). Always inspect the room before checking in. You'll be asked how many nights you want to stay, and you should always say just 1, because if you say 4, you'll be asked for 4 nights' money in advance (plus a deposit), and because it may turn out that the hot water isn't hot enough, the karaoke rooms are above your head, or a building site behind the hotel starts work at 8am sharp. Once you've tried 1 night, you can pay for more.

When you **check out,** the floor staff will be called to verify that you haven't stolen anything. This step may not happen speedily, so allow extra time.

Children 12 and under stay free. Hotels will add an extra bed to your room for a small charge, which you can bargain down.

SAVING ON YOUR HOTEL ROOM

The **rack rate** is the maximum rate that a hotel charges for a room. In China these rates are nothing more than the first bid in a bargaining discussion, designed to keep the final price as high as possible. You'll almost never pay more than 90%, usually not more than 70%, frequently not more than 50%, and sometimes as little as 30% of this first asking price. To lower the cost of your room:

- **Do not book ahead.** Just show up and bargain. In China this applies to the top class joint-venture names as much as all the others. The best price is available over the counter, as long as there's room. For most of the year there are far more rooms than customers at every level. For ordinary Chinese hotels you may well pay double by booking ahead, and there's no guarantee that your reservation will be honored if someone else arrives before you, cash in hand. E-mail is almost never answered, and faxes get ignored. Chinese mostly just show up and bargain.
- **Book online.** If you want to reserve a room in a particular joint-venture hotel during a busy period, look at its website for rates. Major hotel chains operating in China often have their best *published* rate on their websites. However, these rates fluctuate constantly according to demand, and are sometimes linked to inventory systems that alter prices at frequent intervals, sometimes hourly. Prices for any time of year quoted far in advance will always look uninviting. Rates are much cheaper nearer the time, unless some major event is taking place. Ordinary hotels, if they have a website, will just quote rack rates.
- **Dial any central booking number.** Contrary to popular wisdom, as the better hotels manage their rates with increasing care, the central booking number is likely to have a rate as good as or better than the rate you can get by calling the hotel directly, and the call is usually toll-free.
- **Avoid booking through Chinese hotel agencies and websites specializing in Chinese hotels.** You'll obtain the same discount if you contact the hotels directly. In fact, you can usually beat the agency's discount because you won't be paying their markup (usually at least 10%). Many agencies have no affiliations with hotels, and simply jump on the phone to book a room as soon as they hear from you.

HOW TO CHOOSE THE LOCATION THAT'S RIGHT FOR YOU

On short visits, the best option is to stay in the **city center,** within walking distance of the Forbidden City and Tiān'ān Mén Square, on Wángfǔjǐng Dàjiē or nearby. The range of accommodation in this area—from super-luxury to rock-bottom—is unmatched.

The greatest luxury and highest standards of service can be found in **Cháoyáng,** near the two main diplomatic areas just outside the East Second Ring Road. The district's southern half, also known as the CBD (Central Business District), is filled almost exclusively with high-end hotels and is the city's glitziest shopping area. The north boasts proximity to the airport and to the dining and nightlife options of Sān Lǐ Tún.

A wide variety of mid-range and budget accommodation options are offered in the **southern districts** of Xuānwǔ (southwest) and Chóngwén (southeast). Hotels here offer convenient access to the metro line, Běijīng Railway Station, and Běijīng West Railway Station.

A district that has blossomed markedly in the past few years, the **Back Lakes (Hòu Hǎi** or **Shíchà Hǎi)** area is the most picturesque place to stay. Here you'll find interesting cafes, narrow lanes called *hútòng,* and a last glimpse of Old Běijīng.

The **western** part of the city, where most universities are located, is the least charming area in which to park your luggage, but hotels are generally cheaper and are near the Summer Palace.

1 Best Hotel Bets

- **Best Newcomer:** The Intercontinental Hotels Group usually delivers a safe, bland variety of luxury, but somehow they have produced one of Běijīng's best-designed hotels, the **Holiday Inn Central Plaza,** tucked away in the city's Muslim quarter. It has an elegant minimalist lobby, modern and comfortable furnishings in the guest rooms, rainforest showers in the bathrooms, snappy service, and fine restaurants. See p. 73.
- **Most Relaxed Atmosphere:** The low-rise **Jiànguó Hotel,** the first Sino-foreign joint-venture hotel in Běijīng, looks its age from the outside, but has kept itself up-to-date with frequent renovations inside. Its pleasantly bustling lobby has retained the loyalty of long-standing expats, who have meetings over afternoon tea while enjoying the string quartet, or turn up in droves for the Sunday morning string orchestra concert, a Běijīng institution. Some ground-floor rooms have French windows opening on to small patios alongside goldfish-stocked pools, providing a level of calm quite astonishing in such a hectic city. See p. 72.
- **Best Whiff of Old Běijīng:** The recently refurbished **Lǔsōng Yuán Bīnguǎn,** situated on the site of a former Manchu general's residence in a *hútòng* within walking distance of the Back Lakes, features bright paneled ceilings in the hallways, an inviting teahouse in the lobby, and traditionally furnished rooms that somehow avoid the museum-like feel of rooms in other similar hotels. Certain units have direct access to that most Běijīng of architectural features: the private courtyard. Grander but not yet fully renovated, the **Héjìng Fǔ Bīnguǎn,** originally the home of a Qīng emperor's daughter, will probably eclipse the Lǔsōng Yuán once work on its impressive courtyards finally finishes. See p. 69 and 68, respectively.
- **Best Hotel Garden:** The **Bamboo Garden Hotel**'s three courtyards are filled with rockeries, stands of bamboo, and other green leafiness. A traditional Chinese garden stretches away behind the otherwise modern **Shangri-La Běijīng Hotel** to its tennis courts at the rear. See p. 68 and 77, respectively.
- **Best Business Hotel:** That 90% of **China World Hotel**'s guests are there for business comes as no surprise. It's part of a vast shopping complex offering a

full-scale business center and top-notch executive floors, state-of-the-art conferencing facilities, free wireless connectivity in public areas, Běijīng's finest European restaurant, a specialist wine store, and a supermarket. It sits right above a metro stop and the east Third Ring Road. See p. 69.

- **Most Efficient Hotel:** Four-star **Traders Hotel Běijīng** deliberately markets itself to the "guerrilla traveler," with simple but well-equipped rooms, the city's snappiest service, and a generally straightforward approach as rare in Běijīng as a spring without sandstorms. Room rates are very reasonable, there's a metro stop 5 minutes' walk away, and staff members are genuinely apologetic when there's a delay in service (which there rarely is). See p. 72.

- **Best Health & Fitness Facilities:** The health club and spa at the **St. Regis Běijīng** is the capital's most luxurious by far, but the most extensive facilities, including a running track and courts for almost everything, can be found at the **Kerry Centre Hotel.** See p. 71.

- **Best Pool:** The pool at the **Grand Hyatt** is very kitsch and out of keeping with the tastefully understated modern but comfortable design of the remainder of the hotel. A small lagoon buried among mock-tropical decor beneath a ceiling of electric stars, it's worth visiting even if you have no plans to swim, and it has plenty of space if you do. See p. 65.

- **Best for Children:** The **Kerry Centre Hotel** has the largest and best supervised play area for children, handy for a wide range of sports facilities and a pool for the older ones. See p. 71.

2 Běijīng City Center, Around Wángfǔjǐng Dàjiē

VERY EXPENSIVE

Běijīng Hotel (Běijīng Fàndiàn) 北京饭店 *(Overrated)* In a city where hotels are deemed historic if open for more than a decade, it's a shame the genuinely old Běijīng Hotel is bent on maintaining a bland semblance of youth. The original French-owned Hotel de Pekin, considered among the finest hotels in prewar China, was destroyed in the Boxer Rebellion (1900) and moved to this location, at the bottom of Wángfǔjǐng Dàjiē, in 1917. It was taken over by the government after 1949 and was until the mid-1980s one of the few hotels where foreigners could stay. A recent renovation buried most reminders of the hotel's past behind an unimaginative mix of marble and glass, the lone exception being a 100-year-old Bosendorfer piano that sits forlornly in the original lobby. Rooms are spacious but offer the same lackluster luxury found in most government-affiliated high-end hotels. Many visitors still stay here for nostalgia's sake, but facilities and service don't match the hotel's five-star rating.

Dōng Cháng'ān Dàjiē 33 东长安街33号; see map p. 106. (C) 010/6513-7766. Fax 010/6523-2395. www.chinabeijing hotel.com.cn. 891 units. ¥2,656 ($332) standard room (summer discount rate around ¥1,250/$156), plus 15% service charge. AE, DC, MC, V. Metro: Wángfǔjǐng (118, exit A). **Amenities:** 4 restaurants (Imperial, Cantonese, American steakhouse, Japanese); cafe; bar; indoor pool; indoor and outdoor tennis courts; exercise room; Jacuzzi; sauna; concierge; tour desk; business center; shopping arcade; salon; 24-hr. room service; same-day dry cleaning/laundry service; executive-level rooms; currency exchange; squash courts. In room: A/C, satellite TV, dataport, minibar, hair dryer, safe.

Grand Hotel (Běijīng Guìbīn Lóu Fàndiàn) 北京贵宾楼饭店 The Grand Hotel, a separately managed 1990 addition to the west end of the Běijīng Hotel (see above), has better service than its neighbor and a pleasant central atrium with glass elevators, cascading greenery, and a handful of elaborate fountains. Decent sized rooms are elegantly outfitted with rosewood furniture; those on the west side offer clear views of the Forbidden City (within walking distance). Bathrooms have separate shower and bathtub. Rates are unreasonably inflated, however. As with the Běijīng Hotel, your money is better spent elsewhere, but do take the chance to visit the rooftop bar.

Dōng Cháng'ān Dàjiē 35 东长安街35号 (at Nán Hé Yàn); see map p. 106. ℂ 010/6513-7788. Fax 010/6513-0048. www.grandhotelbeijing.com.cn. 217 units. ¥2,300–¥2,500 ($288–$312) standard room (summer discount rate around ¥1,500/$188), plus 15% service charge. AE, DC, MC, V. Metro: Wángfǔjīng (118, exit A). **Amenities:** 4 restaurants (Cantonese, Sìchuān, Imperial, French); 2 bars; indoor pool; exercise room; Jacuzzi; sauna; concierge; tour desk; business center; shopping arcade; salon; 24-hr. room service; same-day dry cleaning/laundry service; executive-level rooms; currency exchange. In room: A/C, satellite TV, fax, dataport, free broadband, minibar, hair dryer, safe.

Grand Hyatt Běijīng (Běijīng Dōngfāng Jūnyuè Dàjiǔdiàn) 北京东方君悦大酒店 ★★
The Grand Hyatt, another Li Ka-hsing venture, has the best position: directly over the Wángfǔjīng metro station, at the foot of the capital's most famous shopping street, within walking distance of the Forbidden City. The theatrically lit, palatial lobby is a popular meeting place, with live music in the evenings and Běijīng's best chocolate shop at one end. Rooms offer signature Grand Hyatt comfort and modernity. Well-equipped bathrooms have separate shower cubicles. The vast swimming pool, buried among mock-tropical decor and a ceiling of electric stars, is very kitsch and un-Hyatt—worth visiting even if you have no plans to swim. Some of Běijīng's best restaurants—including Noble Court and Made in China (p. 86)—are scattered throughout.

Dōng Cháng'ān Jiē 东长安街1号 (within the Oriental Plaza complex at the foot of Wángfǔjīng Dàjiē); see map p. 106. ℂ 800/633-7313 in the U.S. and Canada, 0845/888-1226 in the U.K., 1800/13-1234 in Australia, 0800/44-1234 in New Zealand, or 010/8518-1234. Fax 010/8518-0000. beijing.grand.hyatt.com. 782 units. $367 standard room (summer discounts around ¥1,440 /$180), plus 15% service charge. AE, DC, MC, V. Metro: Wángfǔjīng (118, exit A). **Amenities:** 4 restaurants (Běijīng, Cantonese, Italian, International); cafe; bar; indoor resort-style pool (50m/164 ft.); children's pool; fitness center with latest equipment; Jacuzzi; sauna; airport limousine pick-up; business center; shopping arcade; 24-hr. room service; massage; jogging path; solarium. In room: A/C, satellite TV, dataport, broadband, minibar, hair dryer, safe.

The Peninsula Palace Běijīng (Wángfǔ Fàndiàn) 王府饭店 ★★★
The range of accommodation choices in Běijīng are now so vast that no hotel can claim to be the absolute best, but if a choice had to be made, it would be the Peninsula. Many in-room features—free wireless Internet, 42-inch plasma screen TVs, and silent, direct-line fax machines—are simply unavailable elsewhere. Most international hotel management agencies are forced to work with Chinese parent companies, which typically hold the majority stake and are interested in squeezing their properties, rather than investing in staff training or renovations. The Peninsula is owned by its parent company, and it shows. A 4-year renovation program was completed in March 2005, and no corner of the hotel was left untouched. Service is impeccable, and helpful touches abound: Braille on all signs; a user-friendly bedside control panel which displays the outside temperature and humidity; and tri-level mood lighting. In the exclusive shopping arcade is Jīng, one of the city's best fusion restaurants.

Jīnyú Hútòng 金鱼胡同8号 (1 block east of Wángfǔjīng Dàjiē); see map p. 106. ℂ 866/382-8388 (toll-free from U.S.) or 010/8516-2888. Fax 010/6510-6311. www.peninsula.com. 525 units. $340 standard room (summer discounts around $215), plus 15% service charge. AE, DC, MC, V. **Amenities:** 2 restaurants (Fusion, Cantonese); cafe; indoor pool; fully equipped fitness center; saunas and steam rooms; 24-hr. concierge; tour desk; Rolls-Royce and Mercedes limousines; business center; shopping arcade (with ATM and bank); Clarins Beauty Institute; 24-hr. room service; massage; babysitting; same-day dry cleaning/laundry service. In room: A/C, 42-in. plasma TV with satellite channels, silent fax, free wireless and broadband Internet, minibar, hair dryer, safe, DVD player.

EXPENSIVE

Crowne Plaza Hotel (Guójì Yìyuàn Huángguān Fàndiàn) 国际艺苑皇冠饭店

The Crowne Plaza was closed for renovations at press time, so we were unable to review the hotel for this edition. The location, north of Wángfǔjǐng mall, is ideal, and a comprehensive makeover (much-needed in this case) is never a bad thing.

Wángfǔjǐng Dàjiē 48 王府井大街48号 (corner of Dēngshì Kǒu Dàjiē); see map p. 106. ℂ 877/932-4112 in the U.S. and Canada, 1800/36-300 in Australia, 0800/80-1111 in New Zealand, 0800/917-1587 in the U.K., or 010/6513-3388. Fax 010/6513-2513. www.sixcontinentshotels.com. 358 units. $200 standard room, plus 15% service charge. AE, DC, MC, V. **Amenities:** 2 restaurants (Cantonese, Western); bar; tiny indoor pool; small health club with new equipment; underwhelming Jacuzzi, sauna, and solarium; concierge; Panda Tours desk; business center; salon; 24-hr. room service; babysitting; same-day dry cleaning/laundry service. In room: A/C, satellite plasma TV, broadband/dataport, minibar, hair dryer, iron, safe.

Wángfǔjǐng Grand (Wángfǔjǐng Dàjiǔdiàn) 王府井大酒店

At this price level, this is one of the better city-center hotels, offering views of the Forbidden City and a fresher feel than the nearby Crowne Plaza. "Deluxe" rooms, available for roughly the same rate as a standard room at the Crowne Plaza, are bright and modern, with cheap but new fixtures and cramped but nicely outfitted bathrooms. Prices are the same on both sides of the hotel; ask for a west-facing unit on one of the higher floors if you want to see the palace. The hotel's standard rooms, usually only ¥80 ($10) cheaper than rooms in deluxe class, were refurbished less recently. Go for the upgrade.

Wángfǔjǐng Dàjiē 57 王府井大街57号 (south of Cháoyáng Mén Nèi Dàjiē intersection); see map p. 106. ℂ 010/6522-1188. Fax 010/6522-3816. www.WangfujingHotel.com. 405 units. ¥2,328 ($291) superior rooms (summer discount rate around ¥830/$104), plus 15% service charge. AE, DC, MC, V. **Amenities:** 3 restaurants (Cantonese, Western, Imperial); bar; small indoor pool; exercise room with new equipment; simple sauna; concierge; tour desk; business center; salon; 24-hr. room service; same-day dry cleaning/laundry service; executive-level rooms; currency exchange. In room: A/C, satellite TV, free broadband, minibar, hair dryer, safe.

MODERATE

Cuìmíng Zhuāng Bīnguǎn 翠明庄宾馆

This sleepy little three-star, built inside a Republican-era government complex west of Wángfǔjǐng Dàjiē, is a 10-minute walk east of the Forbidden City. The structure was admirably restored in 1998 and rooms should be fitted with "Chinese-style" furniture by the time you arrive. Rooms are smallish, and the staff is friendlier than you might expect at a state-run hotel. (For history fans: The building originally housed offices of the Communist Party half of the Běipíng Military Mediation Section, a government body that maintained a cease-fire between the Communists and Nationalists so China could fight a Japanese invasion during World War II.)

Nán Hé Yàn 1 南河沿1号 (at intersection with Dōng'ān Mén Jiē); see map p. 106. ℂ 010/6513-6622. Fax 010/6526-1516. www.cuimingzhuanghotel.com.cn. 133 units. ¥600 ($75) standard room (summer discount rates around ¥480/$60). AE, DC, MC, V. **Amenities:** Restaurant (Chinese); bar; small exercise room with new equipment; business center; tour desk; laundry service; currency exchange. In room: A/C, satellite TV, fridge, safe.

Hǎoyuán Bīnguǎn 好园宾馆 ✿

Located down a lane just off one of Běijīng's trendiest shopping streets, the 19-room Hǎoyuán is among the most exclusive of the city's popular courtyard-style hotels. Red doors hung with lanterns and flanked on either side by stone lions mark the entrance. Inside is a neatly restored Qīng-era house, with a small unadorned courtyard in front and a sublime larger courtyard at the back decorated with flowers and tree-shaded, stone chess tables. Larger rooms in the rear courtyard are furnished with canopy beds and custom-made Míng reproduction furniture. A bonus for fans of Communist Party history: The house once belonged to Huà Guófēng, Party chair after Máo, who aped the Great Helmsman's coiffure but not his stature.

Shíjiā Hútòng 53 史家胡同53号 (blue sign points way on Dōng Dān Běi Dàjiē); see map p. 106. ℂ 010/6512-5557. Fax 010/6525-3179. 19 units. ¥585–¥715 ($73–$89) standard room (discounts rare, even in winter). AE, DC, MC, V. **Amenities:** Restaurant (Chinese/Western); bike rental; tour desk; laundry service; Internet access. In room: A/C, satellite TV, fridge, hair dryer.

Novotel Peace Běijīng (Běijīng Nuòfùtè Hépíng Bīnguǎn) 诺富特和平宾馆
This French-managed hotel, part of the Accor stable, has surprisingly average service, but its reasonable rates make it an affordable alternative to the Peninsula Palace across the street. "Deluxe" rooms renovated in 2002 are spacious and comfortable despite the overdone blue color scheme (probably meant to soothe); corner rooms cost the same and are even larger. Standard rooms in the older west wing were undergoing renovations at press time, and management was tight-lipped about how they would look.

Jīnyú Hútòng 3 金鱼胡同3号 (west of Dōng Sì Nán Dàjiē); see map p. 106. ℂ 0800/610–0171 or 010/6512-8833. Fax 010/6512-6863. www.accorhotels-asia.com. 337 units. ¥1,494–¥2,075 ($187–$259) standard room (summer discount rate around ¥760/$95), plus 15% service charge. AE, DC, MC, V. **Amenities:** 4 restaurants (Cantonese, Sìchuān, Korean, French/International); bar; small indoor pool; small but well-equipped exercise room; Jacuzzi; disappointing sauna; concierge; tour desk; business center; 24-hr. room service; same-day dry cleaning/laundry service; executive-level rooms; bakery; currency exchange. In room: A/C, satellite TV, dataport, minibar, hair dryer, safe, video on demand.

Tiānlún Sōnghè Jiǔdiàn 天伦松鹤酒店   *Overrated*
The three-star Sōnghè was abandoned by Accor Hotels in 1995 but has slipped surprisingly little after years under Chinese management. It still offers some of the best value for money in the Wángfǔjīng area. This place is often ignored because of its bland and somewhat battered exterior, or more because of its location opposite the better-known Crowne Plaza. However, the interior is on a par with some of the city's four-stars' interiors. Standard rooms are midsize and bright, although a bit banged up. Deluxe rooms, roughly ¥50 ($6) more per night, are larger and more comfortable, with new carpets and furniture.

Dēngshì Kǒu Dàjiē 88 灯市口大街88号 (diagonally across from Crowne Plaza); see map p. 106. ℂ 010/6513-8822. Fax 010/6513-9088. www.tianlunsonghehotel.com. 310 units. ¥950 ($119) standard room (summer discount rates around ¥600/$75), plus 15% service charge. AE, DC, MC, V. **Amenities:** 4 restaurants (Cantonese, Sìchuān, hot pot, Western); bar; small exercise room; business center; limited room service; laundry service; currency exchange. In room: AC, satellite TV, fridge, free bottled water.

INEXPENSIVE

Saga Youth Hostel (Shíjiā Guójì Qīngnián Lǚshè) 史家国际青年旅社
Opened in May 2002 in one of Běijīng's most famous *hútòng*, the Saga is the current favorite among savvy backpackers. The view west from the third-floor balcony across well-preserved old courtyard houses is a joy, especially at sunrise. To the east, alas, hastily built monstrosities are rising from the rubble of Old Běijīng. Sunnier dorm rooms on the third floor are preferable, although their proximity to the kitchen means an early night's sleep is not guaranteed. The large, clean, communal kitchen is a huge plus, and staff is incredibly helpful. Unfortunately, the cost of popularity shows in the bathrooms, which are tatty.

Shíjiā Hútòng 9 史家胡同9号 (west of intersection with Cháoyáng Mén Nán Xiǎo Jiē); see map p. 106. ℂ 010/6257-2773. Fax 010/6524-9098. www.hostelworld.com. 24 units, 12 with in-room shower. ¥180 ($22) twin; ¥60 ($7) dorm bed. No credit cards. Bus: 713 from Běijīng Zhàn [210, exit B] to Lùmǐcāng. **Amenities:** Cafe; travel service; self-service laundry; cheap Internet access; self-service kitchen; table soccer. In room: A/C, no phone.

3 Back Lakes & Dōng Chéng

EXPENSIVE

Red Capital Residence 东四六条9号 ★★   When Communist Party elders in Zhōng Nán Hǎi decided it was time to upgrade to Ikea, they were surprised to find old China hand Lawrence Brahm desperate to obtain their clapped-out furniture. Art Deco furnishings steal the show at this Cultural Revolution–themed *sìhéyuàn*, set around a tiny central courtyard which conceals a homemade bomb shelter, now converted into a somewhat claustrophobic wine bar. It may be a tad museum-like, pretentious even, but if you can't resist the chance to curl up with a book in stuffed armchairs once used by Marshal Péng Déhuái and Premier Zhōu Ēnlái, then this boutique hotel is worth the outlay. The two Concubine's Private Courtyards, fitted with ornate Qīng dynasty beds, are the most romantic rooms in the capital. Book well in advance.

Dōng Sì Liù Tiáo 9 (walk long block west from metro, turn left into Cháo Nèi Běi Xiǎo Jiē, take 4th turn on right); see map p. 106. ☎ 010/8403-5308. Fax 010/6402-7153. www.redcapitalclub.com. 5 units, shower only. $150 single room; $190 double room, plus 15% service charge. AE, DC, MC, V. Metro: Dōng Sì Shí Tiáo (213, exit D). **Amenities:** Cigar lounge; underground wine bar; laundry service. In room: A/C, satellite TV, safe.

MODERATE

Bamboo Garden Hotel (Zhú Yuán Bīnguǎn) 竹园宾馆 ★   Said to be the former residence of the infamous Qīng dynasty eunuch, Lǐ Liányīng, Bamboo Garden was the first major courtyard-style hotel in Běijīng and is among the most beautiful. It's slightly more luxurious than the Lǔsōng Yuán (see below), but with less character. Rooms border three different-size courtyards; each filled with rock gardens, clusters of bamboo, and covered corridors. Standard rooms in two multi-story buildings at opposite ends of the complex are decorated with Míng-style furniture and traditional lamps that cast pleasant shadows on the high ceilings. A restaurant looks out over the rear courtyard.

Xiǎoshí Qiáo Hútóng 24 小石桥胡同24号 (3rd hútóng on right walking south from metro stop); see map p. 106. ☎ 010/6403-2229. Fax 010/6401-2633. 44 units. ¥580–¥680 ($72–$85) standard room (discounts rare). AE, DC, MC, V. Metro: Gǔ Lóu Dàjiē (217, exit B). **Amenities:** Restaurant (Chinese); bar; concierge; travel service; business center; salon; laundry service; currency exchange. In room: A/C, satellite TV, fridge.

Héjìng Fǔ Bīnguǎn 和敬府宾馆   This elaborate imperial complex was the home of Qiánlóng's third daughter (Gùlún Héjìng), and more recently the ominously named Central Records and Investigation Committee. The spooks have moved to premises unknown, but their presence spared some of Běijīng's most spectacular courtyard buildings from the Cultural Revolution. Exquisitely carved stone statues of camels, lions, and mythical beasts dot the rear and middle courtyards. Ornate wooden carvings fitted to the walls and the huge slate-tiled bathrooms boded well, but after renovations in 2003, a decision is yet to be made on whether to rent out the rooms. Call ahead to check. Rooms on the first and second floors of the plain rear building are spacious, if a little musty. Smaller, more recently renovated rooms on the third and fourth floors contain less-scarred bathrooms and well-sprung mattresses.

Zhāng Zizhōng Lù 7 张自忠路7号 (a block west of Dōng Sì Běi Dàjiē); see map p. 106. ☎ 010/6401-7744, ext. 6001. Fax 010/8401-3570. hjf_hotel@china.com. 137 units. ¥400–¥480 ($40–$60) standard room. 30% summer discounts. AE, DC, MC, V. Metro: Dōng Sì Shí Tiáo (213; exit A). **Amenities:** Restaurant; bar; tiny exercise room; business center; laundry service; currency exchange. In room: A/C, TV.

Lǔsōng Yuán Bīnguǎn 吕松园宾馆 ★★ The Lǔsōng Yuán, set on the site of a Qīng dynasty general's residence down a quaint *hútòng* north of Píng'ān Dàdào and nicely renovated in 2001, is a thoroughly charming courtyard hotel. Smaller and more intimate than the Bamboo Garden, with more traditional rooms, it wins with the details—bright paneled ceilings in the hallways, faux rotary phones in-room, and Chinese-style wall-mounted lamps over the beds. A few rooms open directly onto quiet, semi-private courtyards, adorned with potted plants and presided over by white stone busts of "the father of modern China" (Sun Yat-sen) and "the father of modern Chinese literature" (Lǔ Xùn). A teahouse with stone floors and low-backed Míng-style chairs is next to the lobby. Avoid the airless dorms in the basement.

Bǎnchǎng Hútòng 22 板厂胡同22号 (walking north from Dì'ān Mén Dōng Dàjiē on Jiāodàokǒu Nán Dàjiē, 2nd hútòng on left); see map p. 106. (*) 010/6404-0436. Fax 010/6403-0418. www.the-silk-road.com. 59 units. ¥638 ($80) standard room (summer discounts rare, 40% discounts in winter). AE, DC, MC, V. **Amenities:** Restaurant (Chinese); laundry service; limited currency exchange; Internet access. In room: AC, TV.

INEXPENSIVE

Qílǔ Fàndiàn 齐鲁饭店 *Value* The bland, white-tiled exterior promises little, but the rooms are a pleasant surprise—freshly painted and carpeted and containing firm mattresses. Best of all, you're within sight of the delightful Shíchà Lakes area and the north gate of Běi Hǎi. The friendly staff speak little English, but are willing to try. Owned by the Women's Federation, the hotel hosts mostly business travelers. An excellent vegetarian restaurant is attached.

Dì'ān Mén Xī Dàjiē 103, Xī Chéng Qū 地安门西大街103号; see map p. 106. (*) 010/6618-0966. Fax 010/6618-0969. 126 units, 10 shower only. ¥378–¥428 ($47–$53) standard rooms. Summer discounts 20%, up to 40% in winter. AE, DC, MC, V. Bus: 810 from Jīshuǐ Tán metro to Běi Hǎi Hòu Mén. **Amenities:** 2 restaurants (Sìchuān, Vegetarian); concierge; business center; dry cleaning/laundry service. In room: A/C, TV.

Zhōnggòng Běijīng Shì Wěi Bàn Jīguān Zhāodàisuǒ 中共北京市委办机关招待所 *Finds* Normally you should give a wide berth to any venture with the words *zhōnggòng* (Chinese Communist Party) and *jīguān* (government organ) in the name, but this newly opened hotel is an exception. The impressive twin-courtyard residence formerly housed Wú Dé, the mayor of Běijīng during the Cultural Revolution, who wasn't included in the Gang of Four, but assuredly made the shortlist. Staff are surprisingly friendly, the smallish rooms are packed with amenities, and the location, in one of Běijīng's best-preserved *hútòng*, is hard to top. This is one of the few budget hotels with genuine single rooms.

Dōng Sì Liù Tiáo 71 东四六条71号; see map p. 106. (*) 010/6401-8823, ext. 8100. Fax 010/6401-8823, ext. 8200. 16 units, 13 shower only. ¥320–¥800 ($40–$100) standard room. 20%–30% summer discounts. No credit cards. **Amenities:** Restaurant; inexpensive bike rental. In room: A/C, TV, fridge, safe, washing machine.

4 Cháoyáng

VERY EXPENSIVE

China World Hotel (Zhōngguó Dàfàndiàn) 中国大饭店 ★★★ Long the city's top business hotel, China World now aims to be the best Běijīng hotel altogether. Praised for its comfort and sterling service, the hotel, managed by Shangri-La, has used its most recent face-lift to add several up-to-date luxuries, including an oxygen chamber in the health club. Refurbished standard rooms are narrow but modern, with glass-topped desks and vaguely Asian objets d'art on walls and shelves. Comfortably elegant Aria (p. 91), tucked away up a spiral staircase, serves the city's finest Continental cuisine. The attached China World shopping complex boasts upmarket boutiques, a well-stocked supermarket, an ice rink, and a specialist wine store. A metro stop connected to the shopping area means quick (15 min.) access to the city center. Even numbered rooms are preferred: south-facing rooms are sunnier and less affected by construction noise.

Jiànguó Mén Wài Dàjiē 1 建国门外大街1号 (at intersection with East Third Ring Rd.); see map p. 111. ℂ 010/6505-2266. Fax 010/6505-0828. www.shangri-la.com. 716 units. $350 standard room (discount rates down to $175), plus 15% service charge. AE, DC, MC, V. Metro: Guómào (122, exit A). **Amenities:** 4 restaurants (Chinese, European, Japanese, Asian/International) plus several more in attached mall; indoor pool (25m/82 ft.); golf simulator; 3 indoor tennis courts; full-service health club; separate spa with aromatherapy; concierge; business center; shopping complex; salon; 24-hr. room service; same-day dry cleaning/laundry service; executive-level rooms; nonsmoking rooms; currency exchange; wireless in executive rooms. In room: A/C, satellite TV, dataport, free broadband, minibar, hair dryer, safe.

Great Wall Sheraton (Cháng Chéng Fàndiàn) 长城饭店 ⭐ The Great Wall
was the city's first international five-star when it opened in 1984, and the building is starting to look it's age, but wins a star not for what it is now, but what it will be once renovations are completed. During the lifetime of this book, there will be a substantial reduction in the number of rooms, complete remodeling of the lobby (no more tawdry gold pillars), two new restaurants, and the opening of an international-level spa on the third floor. Executive floor rooms will be renovated first, and should your budget extend to it, they should be your first choice. The beautifully refurbished 21st Floor Restaurant serves first-class Sìchuān food together with commanding views of eastern Běijīng.

Běi Sān Huán 10 北三环10号 (south of Lufthansa Centre); see map p. 111. ℂ 800/810-3088 or 010/6590-5566. Fax 010/6590-5938. www.starwood.com. 1007 units. ¥1,490 ($180) standard room (summer discounts around ¥1,300/$160), plus 15% service charge. Most rates include breakfast. AE, DC, MC, V. **Amenities:** 3 restaurants (Cantonese/Sìchuān, Italian/International, French); bar; small indoor pool with sun deck; 2 outdoor tennis courts; exercise room; Jacuzzi; sauna; concierge; tour desk; business center; salon; 24-hr. room service; same-day dry cleaning/laundry service; executive-level rooms; currency exchange. In room): A/C, satellite TV, broadband, minibar, hair dryer, safe.

Hilton Běijīng (Běijīng Xīěrdùn Fàndiàn) 希尔顿饭店 ⭐ What a difference a
renovation can make. Once saddled with some of the most tired guest rooms in the capital, Hilton's newly overhauled rooms now sport attractive carpets, stylish and functional glass desks, and ultra-comfortable beds. Bathrooms have deep tubs, but there's nowhere to hang your clothes, and the wood finishing looks cheap. Major changes will occur during the life of this book, including a refit of the bathroom-tiled exterior, the opening of an atrium bar that aims to rival Centro, and two new restaurants. Louisiana, which offers quality American-Cajun fare and a long wine list, will be staying put.

Dōngfāng Lù 1, Dōng Sān Huán Běi Lù 东方路1号 (east side of North Third Ring Rd., south of Xiǎoyún Lù); see map p. 111. ℂ 800/445-8667 in the U.S. and Canada, 0800/909090 in the U.K., 1800/22-2255 in Australia, 0800/44-8002 in New Zealand, or 010/5865-5000. Fax 010/5865-5800. www.beijing.hilton.com. 375 units. $165 standard room, plus 15% service charge. AE, DC, MC, V. **Amenities:** 3 restaurants (American-Cajun, International, Asian); bar; indoor pool; small outdoor tennis court; fitness club; Jacuzzi; sauna; bike rental; concierge; tour desk; business center; salon; 24-hr. room service; massage; babysitting; same-day dry cleaning/laundry service; 2 squash courts; wheelchairs; valet. In room: A/C, satellite TV, expensive broadband, minibar, hair dryer, safe.

Kempinski Hotel (Kǎibīnsījī Fàndiàn) 凯宾斯基饭店 ⭐ The Kempinski's plain
but large and very comfortable rooms have been refurbished to a high standard. Some of the staff could do with renovation, too. Last time we visited, the coffee failed to materialize at breakfast not once, but twice. Aside from this, response time to requests is the most rapid in Běijīng (even outdoing the St. Regis) and its position in the vast

Lufthansa Centre means every facility imaginable is at hand. These include a specialist wine store, endless airline offices and ticket agents, medical and dental clinics with Western staff, eight restaurants and cafes, a supermarket, a bookshop, and a department store. Large numbers of long-staying expats from the Kempinski's well-fitted apartments help support an assortment of other Western enterprises, including Běijīng's branch of the Hard Rock Cafe. The Paulaner Bräuhaus offers top-of-the-range beers brewed on-site and hearty German dishes. The Kempi Deli has an excellent range of baked goods (half price after 9pm). Surprisingly for such a business-focused hotel, there is no wireless Internet anywhere in the hotel.

Liàngmǎ Qiáo Lù 50 亮马桥路50号 (east of North Third Ring Rd., near airport expressway junction); see map p. 111. ✆ 010/6465-3388. Fax 010/6465-3366. www.kempinski-beijing.com. 526 units. $310 standard room (discount rates around $199), plus 15% service charge. AE, DC, MC, V. **Amenities:** 7 restaurants (including Cantonese, Italian, Japanese, and German); indoor pool; outdoor tennis court; fitness center; Jacuzzi; sauna; concierge; free shuttle to airport and city center; business center; shopping complex; 24-hr. room service; same-day dry cleaning/laundry service; executive-level rooms; 6 nonsmoking floors; currency exchange; squash courts. In room: A/C, satellite TV, broadband/dataport, minibar, hair dryer, safe.

Kerry Centre Hotel (Běijīng Jiālǐ Zhōngxīn Fàndiàn) 北京嘉里中心饭店 ★★

Kids The latest addition to the Shangri-La–managed properties in the city, the Kerry Centre is also the most chic, with a clean, stylish, modern design to its warm, curvaceous, and unusually high-ceilinged rooms. Full facilities, such as shower cubicles in bathrooms, in-room air fresheners and humidifiers (a godsend in winter), and free in-room broadband Internet access, have all helped make it one of Běijīng's most successful hotels. Executive-floor rooms have luxuries such as CD players and wireless Internet access. The Kerry Centre complex has several noteworthy restaurants, including Horizon (p. 93), one of the city's best Cantonese restaurants, and the city's hottest bar, Centro. Service can be too casual, however: Reception staffs chew gum, and the concierge fails to follow up simple requests for information.

Guānghuá Lù 1 光华路1号 (on west side of Kerry Centre complex, north of Guómào metro station); see map p. 111. ✆ 010/8529-6999. Fax 010/8529-6333. www.shangri-la.com. 487 units. ¥3,000 ($375) standard room (summer discounts around ¥1,500/$188), plus 15% service charge. AE, DC, M, V. Metro: Guómào (122, exit A). **Amenities:** 2 restaurants (Cantonese, Western); bar; indoor pool (25m/82 ft.); fitness center; children's play area; concierge; tour desk; business center; shopping arcade; 24-hr. room service; same-day dry cleaning/laundry service; executive-level rooms; 5 nonsmoking floors; currency exchange; roof-top track for running and in-line skating; sun deck; indoor basketball/tennis/badminton courts. In room: A/C, satellite TV, dataport, free broadband, minibar, hair dryer, safe.

St. Regis Běijīng (Běijīng Guójì Jùlèbù Fàndiàn) 北京国际俱乐部饭店 ★★★

No hotel in Běijīng can rival the on-call personalized butler service of the St. Regis, which boasts the highest staff to guest ratio in China. Almost unnerving attention is paid to your individual needs, down to what side of the bed you sleep on for turndown service, and what fruit you take from the fruit bowl. The white marble lobby, with its towering palms and afternoon tea, is the city's most elegant and the health club is world class, with a spa drawing on waters from a mile under ground. If there's a complaint, it's the smallness of the rooms, but all are beautifully appointed with traditional Chinese furniture, Běijīng's deepest bathtubs, and a full range of extras. Danieli's on the second floor is one of the city's finest Italian restaurants, and the Press Club Bar, under renovation at press time, is a stylish, clubby watering hole.

Jiànguó Mén Wài Dàjiē 21 建国门外大街21号 (southwest of Rìtán Park); see map p. 111. ✆ 010/6460-6688. Fax 010/6460-3299. www.stregis.com/beijing. 273 units. ¥2,720 ($340) standard room (summer discount rates ¥1,600/$200), plus 15% service charge. AE, DC, MC, V. Metro: Jiànguó Mén (120/211, exit B, 1 block away). **Amenities:** 5 restaurants (Cantonese, American, Japanese, Italian, International); bar; gorgeous indoor pool (25m/82 ft.); putting green and driving area; well-equipped exercise room; spa; concierge; business center; salon; 24-hr. room service; same-day dry cleaning/laundry service; nonsmoking rooms; cigar and wine-tasting rooms; currency exchange; 24-hr. butler service; squash courts; billiards room. In room: A/C, satellite TV, broadband, minibar, hair dryer, safe, DVD player.

EXPENSIVE

Jiànguó Hotel (Jiànguó Fàndiàn) 建国饭店   This four-star property, opened in 1982, was the first joint-venture hotel in Běijīng. It's one of the few older hotels to have kept up standards with constant refurbishment and comprehensive staff training. The ground floor contains the best rooms, with French windows opening onto small patios alongside goldfish-stocked pools. Běijīng's bustle is excluded. A popular meeting place for expats and business visitors, the large lobby boasts afternoon tea, a string quartet every evening, and an orchestra during Sunday morning coffee. Justine's, Běijīng's first serious French restaurant, now faces massive competition but is still worth a visit, particularly for the set-price Sunday lunch.

Jiànguó Mén Wài Dàjiē 5 建国门外大街5号 (east of Silk Market); see map p. 111. ✆ 010/6500-2233. Fax 010/6500-2871. www.hoteljianguo.com. 469 units. ¥1,870 ($234) standard room (summer discount rates ¥1,258/$157), plus 15% service charge. AE, DC, MC, V. Metro: Yǒng'ānlǐ (121, exit B). **Amenities:** 3 restaurants (Chinese, French, International); bar; indoor pool; fitness center; Jacuzzi; sauna; concierge; tour desk; business center; shopping arcade; salon; 24-hr. room service; same-day dry cleaning/laundry service; executive-level rooms; currency exchange. In room: A/C, satellite TV, broadband/dataport, minibar, hair dryer, safe.

Traders Hotel Běijīng (Guómào Fàndiàn) 国贸饭店 ✍   The greatest advantage to staying in this efficient and well-run Shangri-La four-star hotel is access to the five-star health club facilities in the China World Hotel next door. (These two sister hotels are joined by an underground shopping center.) Otherwise, Traders is a straightforward business hotel, with slightly small and plain but nicely outfitted rooms, unobtrusive service, and easy access to the metro. The only major drawback is the tiny bathrooms, but this is compensated for by reasonably low (after-discount) room rates. The West Wing has the slightly nicer (and more expensive) rooms, renovated in 2004.

Jiànguó Mén Wài Dàjiē 1 建国门外大街1号 (behind China World Hotel); see map p. 111. ✆ 010/6505-2277. Fax 010/6505-0818. www.shangri-la.com. 570 units. ¥2,240 ($280) standard room (discount rates around ¥1,550/$194), plus 15% service charge. AE, DC, MC, V. Metro: Guómào (122). **Amenities:** 2 restaurants (Cantonese, Western); bar; small exercise room; Jacuzzi; sauna; concierge; business center; shopping complex; salon; 24-hr. room service; same-day dry cleaning/laundry service; executive-level rooms; nonsmoking rooms; currency exchange. In room: A/C, satellite TV, free broadband, minibar, hair dryer, safe.

MODERATE

Red House (Ruìxiù Bīnguǎn) 瑞秀宾馆   Located in a large, red brick building, the Red House was once the best choice for long stays, but renovations have increased the number of rooms and transformed the apartments into quite spacious hotel rooms. Rooms come with faux hardwood floor and a brand-new couch. Refitted bathrooms are shower-only. The hotel lobby contains Běijīng's most bizarre shop, the **Pyongyang Art Studio** (see chapter 9, p. 177), showcasing North Korean socialist realist art.

Chūnxiù Lù 10 春秀路10号 (1 block south of Pizza Hut on Dōng Zhí Mén Wài Dàjiē); see map p. 111. ✆ 010/6416-7810. Fax 010/6416-7600. www.redhouse.com.cn. 48 units. ¥300–¥400 ($38–$50) standard room. Rates include breakfast. AE, MC, V. **Amenities:** Free laundry service. In room: A/C, TV, fridge.

INEXPENSIVE

Gōngtǐ Youth Hostel (Gōngtǐ Qīngnián Lǔshè) 工体青年旅社 *Value*   Located inside the Workers Stadium, in the heart of the Sān Lǐ Tún bar area, this well-run YHA offers a quiet location above a three-star hotel (The Sports Inn), a view over pleasant gardens and a lake, and relatively new facilities. The fourth-floor rooms (not ideal if you have lots of luggage) are agreeably curved, and all face southeast. If you crave privacy, there are single rooms. The problems facing this YHA are common to all youth hostels in Bĕijīng: There are not enough hostels to meet demand, so they're frequently overbooked (particularly in summer); turnover is high, as other hotels poach their well-trained staff; and they rely on the state-run parent hotel for house-keeping, which often leads to messy bathrooms.

Gōngrén Tǐyùchǎng 9 Tái 工人体育场9台; see map p. 111. ☎ 010/6552-4800. Fax 010/6552-4860. 38 units, communal bathrooms/showers. Dorm beds from ¥60 ($7.50); ¥120 ($15) single room. Discounts for YHA members. No credit cards. Metro: Dōng Sì Shí Tiáo (213), exit B), 3 long blocks east. **Amenities:** Bike rental; travel service; self-service kitchen and laundry; Internet access; reading room. In room: A/C, TV, no phone.

Zhàolóng Qīngnián Lǚguǎn 兆龙青年旅馆

Whether proximity to the Sān Lǐ Tún bar area is a plus or a minus is open to question, but the Zhàolóng is a quiet alter-native to the madness of its better-known cousin, Poacher's. Most guests are Chinese backpackers or foreigners conversant in Chinese. Doors close at 1am to discourage revelers. Twins and dorms are simple and clean; neither has an in-room bathroom, but common showers are adequate. Facilities are minimal. Proximity to the East Third Ring Road means convenient bus access to all parts of town.

Gōngtǐ Bĕi Lù 2 工体北路2号 (behind Great Dragon Hotel); see map p. 111. ☎ 010/6597-2299, ext. 6111. Fax 010/6597-2288. outdoor@etang.com. 50 units. ¥160 ($20) twin; dorm beds from ¥50 ($6). AE, DC, M, V. Bus: 115 from Dōng Sì Shí Tiáo metro to Nóngzhǎnguǎn. **Amenities:** Bar; access to indoor pool and sauna; travel service; self-service laundry. In room: A/C, no phone.

5 Bĕijīng South

EXPENSIVE

Holiday Inn Central Plaza (Zhōnghuán Jiǎrì Jiǔdiàn) 中环假日酒店 ★★

Value This site was right in the middle of things during the Jīn dynasty (1122–1215), but there's nothing central about the location of this stylish hotel. However, if you're visiting Bĕijīng to be among Chinese people, rather than pampered expatriates, we strongly recommend this hotel. Intercontinental Hotels in China often present a bland, cut-price version of luxury (such as the Downtown and Lido Holiday Inns), but this Zen-like hotel is a startling exception. Credit must be given to the local designer, who has achieved the architectural Holy Grail: minimalism without cold-ness. Service is equally to the point. Set in a residential area, Bĕijīng's Muslim quarter is a short walk to the east, a lively strip of restaurants near Bàoguó Sì lie to the north, and it's also handy to both of Bĕijīng's main railway stations.

Càiyuán Jiē 1 菜园街1号; see map p. 114. ☎ 800/830-6368or 010/8397-0088. Fax 010/8355-6688. 322 units. Standard rooms ¥1,660 ($208), plus 15% service charge (summer discounts ¥803/$100 all inclusive). AE, DC, MC, V. Bus: 395 from Chángchūn Jiē metro (205; exit Á). **Amenities:** 2 restaurants (Cantonese, International); cafe; bar; indoor pool; well-equipped exercise room; yoga room; concierge; tour desk; business center; 24-hr. room service; same-day dry cleaning/laundry; executive-level rooms; currency exchange. In room: A/C, satellite TV, broadband, minibar, hair dryer, safe.

The Marco Polo (Mǎgē Bóluó Jiǔdiàn) 马哥孛罗酒店 ★ *Value*

Although not among the main clusters of foreign hotels, the Marco Polo is as close to the center of things as any of them, and is quieter and better connected than most. (The location—just south of the No. 1 Line's Xī Dān station and north of the Circle Line's Xuānwǔ Mén station—enables guests to get in and out during the worst of rush hour.) The lobby, sumptuously decorated with white marble and gold friezes, is stylish yet of a modest enough scale to suggest the atmosphere of a discreet boutique hotel. The

Finds　In the Red Lantern District

Southwest of Qián Mén, beyond the mercantile madness of Dà Zhàlán, in the *hútòng* that never dreams of pedicab-tour salvation, is where you'll find the remains of Běijīng's once-thriving brothel district, **Bā Dà Hútòng** (eight great lanes). Prior to the Communists' elimination of prostitution in the 1950s (and its rapid reemergence since the 1980s), government officials, foreign diplomats, and other men of means would come here to pay for the pleasures of "clouds and rain."

The transaction was not always lurid. The women were closer to courtesans than whores, akin to Japanese geishas, and their customers often paid simply for conversation and cultured entertainment, and popular guidebooks were published advising on the etiquette for wooing courtesans. Although the promise of another brand of entertainment always lurked in the background, and many of the women who worked south of Qián Mén were kidnapped from other provinces; nonetheless, the dynamic was not half as base as its modern counterpart's.

Many wonderful old bordellos still stand, although local tour groups are forbidden to take tourists to the area, or even mention it. Most buildings were converted into apartments or stores, but a few were restored and turned into cheap hotels. While those who can afford it will prefer to stay in a more luxurious hotel further north, travelers on a budget would be hard-pressed to find affordable accommodations with so much character.

Among the best restored of the old brothels is **Shǎnxī Xiàng Dì'èr Bīnguǎn** 陕西巷第二宾馆 (© **010/6303-4609**), at the north end of Shǎnxī Xiàng (once home to the most upmarket bordellos), a poorly marked and malodorous lane a few minutes' walk south of Dà Zhàlán. As with most buildings of its kind, it is recognizable by its multi-story height (rare in a neighborhood made up of single-floor houses) and by the glass that divides

medium-size rooms are well-appointed, although bathrooms are somewhat cramped. Café Marco features buffet or a la carte dishes from the Mediterranean, Middle East, Southeast Asia, and China in honor of the routes the great traveler took himself.

Xuānwǔ Mén Nèi Dàjiē 6 宣武门内大街6号 (south of Xī Dān metro stop); see map p. 114. © **010/6603-6688.** Fax 010/6603-1488. www.marcopolohotels.com. 296 units. ¥2,080 ($260) standard room, plus 15% service charge. Summer discounts up to 70%. AE, DC, MC, V. Metro: Xī Dān (115, exit E). **Amenities:** 2 restaurants (Cantonese, Café Marco); bar; indoor pool; fitness center; concierge; tour desk; business center; salon; 24-hr. room service; same-day dry cleaning/laundry service; executive-level rooms; currency exchange. In room: A/C, satellite TV, expensive broadband, minibar, hair dryer, safe.

MODERATE

City Central Youth Hostel (Chéngshì Qīngnián Jiǔdiàn) 城市青年酒店 *Value*

Housed in the old post office building, this newly opened hostel cum hotel has an unbeatable location directly opposite Běijīng railway station. The manager was inspired by a visit to Sydney Central YHA, and has attempted to create a replica here. Standard rooms on the fifth and sixth floor are minimalist and clean, with none of its roof, designed to let light into the central courtyard while blocking an outsider's view of the activities taking place inside. Far nicer than the late-night barber shops and karaoke parlors where Běijīng's working girls now do business, the hotel is spacious and lavishly decorated, with red columns and walls supporting colorfully painted banisters and roof beams, the latter hung with traditional lanterns. The rooms, arranged on two floors around the courtyard, are tiny and windowless, as befit their original purpose, but now have air-conditioning, TVs, and bathrooms (¥100/$12 per night). To reach the hotel, walk east from Far East Youth Hostel (see above) and turn left down the second *hútòng* on the right.

The 200-year-old **Qián Mén Chánggōng Fàndiàn** 前门长工饭店 (ⓒ 010/6303-2665), at Yīngtáo Xiéjiē 11 樱桃斜街11号, is less well maintained than the Shǎnxī Xiàng Dì'èr but closer to the city center and far grander inside. The tell-tale roof peeks over the rest of the street but the facade has been pasted over with anonymous white tile, which makes the elaborate interior more surprising. A large sign by the door describes the building's history as a "black meeting hall." Beyond is a large, high-ceilinged central courtyard surrounded by green walls with traditional red pillars and banisters. Informal cross-talk performances (a traditional Chinese form of storytelling) and chess games take place in summer. Standard rooms (¥140/$18) on the first floor are basic and have grotty bathrooms but are still livable, with air-conditioning and TV. The second floor has more luxurious rooms (¥180/$23), which are brighter and cleaner with a few pieces of traditional Chinese furniture. A gathering spot for elderly men from the neighborhood, the hotel is worth visiting for its Old Běijīng atmosphere even if you don't plan to stay overnight (see "Walking Tour 1: Liúlichǎng & Dà Zhàlán" in chapter 8). To get here, walk west along Dà Zhàlán, and take a right at the fork.

the sleaze associated with other railway hotels (such as the nearby Howard Johnson, whose rooms now sport point-and-choose menus of massage girls), and at a fraction of the expense. Ask for a room on the north side, facing away from the railway station square. Dorm rooms on the fourth floor have double-glazed windows and comfortable bunk beds, but squat toilets are a surprise for the less limber.

Běijīng Zhàn Qián Jiē 1 北京站前街1号; see map p. 114. ⓒ 010/6525-8066. Fax 010/6525-9066. www.central-hostel.com. ¥268 ($33) standard room; dorm beds from ¥60 ($7.50). Discounts on dorm beds for YHA members. AE, DC, MC, V. Metro: Běijīng Zhàn (210, exit A). **Amenities:** Bar; bike rental; tour desk; self-service laundry and kitchen; supermarket; Internet access; billiards and movie room. In room: A/C, TV, free broadband.

Harmony Hotel (Huáměilún Jiǔdiàn) 华美伦酒店   A stone's throw from Běijīng Railway Station, this small and slightly tattered three-star is ideal for those arriving late from the station or looking to catch an early train. Rooms are small for the price and renovations long overdue; however, staff is friendly, and after years of struggling to comprehend the broad accents of Intrepid Tours groups, their English is passable. "Luxury" rooms *(háohuá jiān)* are nearly double the size of standard rooms and come with bathtubs—well worth the extra ¥100 ($12). Ask for a quieter room on an upper floor facing the west side, as the railway area is predictably rowdy.

Sūzhōu Hútòng 59 苏州胡同59号 (from Běijīng Zhàn metro walk west, taking the 1st right onto Yóutōng Jiē and continuing for 100m/328 ft. northwest); see map p. 114. ℂ 010/6528-5566. Fax 010/6559-9011. 122 units. ¥756 ($94) standard room (summer discounts to ¥450/$56). AE, DC, MC, V. Metro: Běijīng Zhàn (210, exit A). **Amenities:** Restaurant (Cantonese); cafe; bike rental; concierge; tour desk; business center; same-day dry cleaning/laundry service; currency exchange. In room: A/C, TV, minibar; fridge.

INEXPENSIVE

Far East Youth Hostel (Yuǎndōng Qīngnián Lǚshè) 远东青年旅社 ℛ *Finds*
Buried deep inside one of the city's most interesting *hútòng* neighborhoods, but only a 10-minute walk from both the Hépíng Mén and Qián Mén metro stations, the Far East offers comfortable rooms at competitive rates. Even the hallways—partly adorned with faux brick and latticed, dark wood panels—are pleasant. The hostel maintains cheaper dorms behind a courtyard house across the street, but those in the main building are far better. The Far East makes a good choice even if you usually stay at midrange places.

Tiěshù Xié Jiē 113 铁树斜街 (south of Liúlichǎng); see map p. 114. ℂ 010/6301-8811, ext. 3118. Fax 010/6301-8233. 110 units. ¥298 ($37) standard room (often discounted to ¥200/$25); ¥60–¥75 ($8–$10) dorm bed. No credit cards. Metro: Hépíng Mén (207, exit C2). **Amenities:** Restaurant (Chinese); bike rental; tour desk; cheap coin-op laundry; self-catering kitchen; Internet access. In room: AC, TV, fridge.

Fēiyīng Bīnguǎn 飞鹰宾馆   The Fēiyīng became one of the top budget options in the city after completing a top-to-bottom refurbishment in 2002 and joining Youth Hostelling International. It's the most "hotel-like" YHA you'll find. Standard rooms are bright and well equipped with low, slightly hard, twin beds; bathrooms have proper tubs. Dorms are also nice with in-room bathroom and brand-new floors. The hotel's best feature is its location, just east of the Chángchūn Jiē metro stop and next to several useful bus stops.

Xuānwǔ Mén Xī Dàjiē 10 宣武门西大街10号 (down alley east of Guóhuá Market); see map p. 114. ℂ 010/6317-1116. Fax 010/6315-1165. www.hostelworld.com. 46 units. ¥180 ($22) standard room; ¥60 ($7.50) dorm bed. Discounts for YHA members. No credit cards. Metro: Chángchūn Jiē (205, exit C1). **Amenities:** Bar; travel service; self-service laundry and kitchen; Internet access; small convenience store. In room: A/C, TV.

6 Běijīng West, Hǎidiàn & Yàyùn Cūn

VERY EXPENSIVE

Crowne Plaza Park View Wǔzhōu (Wǔzhōu Huángguān Jiàrì Jiǔdiàn) 五洲皇冠假日酒店 *Kids*   From a *fēngshuǐ* perspective, the recently opened Wǔzhōu is unbeatable. It lies close to the north-south axis that runs through the Forbidden City, the invisible line that marked the temporal center of the world until it was usurped by the Greenwich Meridian. Far from the expatriate ghettos, the surrounding area has considerable appeal: Yàyùn Cūn is a (relatively) pedestrian-friendly residential area that boasts some of Běijīng's best Chinese restaurants (see chapter 6). Within the striking white edifice, you'll find a very North American brand of luxury: *USA Today* delivered to the door and the inevitable Brazilian restaurant. It's all comfortable enough, but I find it a bit bland. Little luxuries are lacking, service can be indifferent, and much of the clientele is the upmarket version of the obnoxious Man Bag Man. It's worth upgrading to a "luxury" *(háohuá)* room, as bathrooms in the "superior" *(gāojí)* rooms are a bit poky.

Běi Sì Huán Lù 4 北四环路4号 (northwest of Ānhuì Qiáo on the N. Fourth Ring Rd.); see map p. 116. © 800/ 830-2628 or 010/8498-2288. Fax 010/8499-2933. www.crowneplaza.com. 478 units. Luxury rooms ¥2,300 ($288), plus 15% service charge. AE, DC, MC, V. Bus: 803 from Āndìng Mén metro (216, exit B). **Amenities:** 3 restaurants (Cantonese, Brazilian, International); bar; indoor pool; exercise room; Jacuzzi; sauna; concierge; business center; 24-hr. room service; massage; same-day laundry/dry cleaning; executive-level rooms; currency exchange. In room: A/C, satellite TV, broadband, minibar, hair dryer, iron, safe.

Shangri-La Běijīng Hotel (Xiānggélǐlā Fàndiàn) 香格里拉饭店 ★

That Shangri-La is now one of the biggest players among foreign hotel managements in China is due perhaps to its success with staff, who provide impeccable levels of service. The hotel has expanded since its 1987 opening, and the Horizon Tower, housing an opulent Chi Spa and 140 new guest rooms, will open in late 2006. Currently, rooms are a good size and comfortably furnished, if less imaginative than rooms at other Běijīng hotels in this chain. Cafe Cha, on the first floor, offers the finest buffet breakfast in the capital. Although off by itself in the northwest, the hotel benefits from having space for a large and lush garden, easy access to the Summer Palaces and the Western Hills, and quick routes around Běijīng via the third and fourth ring roads.

Zízhú Yuàn Lù 29 紫竹院路29号 (northwest corner of Third Ring Rd.); see map p. 116. © 010/6841-2211. Fax 010/ 6841-8002. www.shangri-la.com. 528 units. ¥2,000 ($240) standard room (summer discounts ¥1,050/$131), plus 15% service charge. AE, DC, MC, V. **Amenities:** 3 restaurants (Cantonese, Japanese, International); bar; indoor pool; health club with sauna, solarium, exercise room; concierge; tour desk; business center; 24-hr. room service; same-day dry cleaning/laundry service; executive-level rooms; nonsmoking rooms; currency exchange. In room: A/C, satellite TV, free broadband and wireless Internet, minibar, hair dryer, safe.

EXPENSIVE

Běijīng Marriott West (Běijīng Jīnyù Wànháo Jiǔdiàn) 北京金域万豪酒店 ★

The first full-fledged Marriott in Běijīng, this hotel offers good value after the discount, although the location is far from the major sights. Along with the Shěnyáng Marriott (the first Marriott in China), it's among the country's most opulent hotels. The structure was an apartment building before the Marriott Group took over, so rooms are immense. Eighty percent have Jacuzzi tubs and all are furnished with sumptuous beds and overstuffed chairs. Guests have free access to the attached Bally fitness center.

Xī Sān Huán Běi Lù 98 西三环北路98号 (in Jīnyù Dàshà, at intersection with Fùchéng Lù); see map p. 116. © 010/6872-6699. Fax 010/6872-7302. www.marriotthotels.com/bjsmc. 155 units. ¥2,080 ($260) standard room (summer discount rates ¥1,090/$136), plus 15% service charge. AE, DC, MC, V. **Amenities:** Restaurant (Western); bar; health club with indoor pool; tennis courts; concierge; business center; salon; 24-hr. room service; same-day dry cleaning/laundry; executive rooms; nonsmoking rooms; bowling center; currency exchange. In room: A/C, satellite TV, dataport, minibar, hair dryer, iron, safe.

INEXPENSIVE

International Exchange Center (Wàijiāo Xuéyuàn Guójì Jiāoliú Zhōngxīn) 外交学院国际交流中心 _Finds_

This seldom-exploited international students' building on the Foreign Affairs College campus offers freshly refurbished dorm-style twins and large apartments at reasonable daily rates. The apartments have kitchens and washing machines, and regular rooms come with sparkling en suite bathrooms. There's a well-equipped self-catering kitchen on each floor, plus such amenities as Ping-Pong, Internet access, and laundry machines. Several buses pass by here.

Zhǎnlǎn Guǎn Lù 24 展览馆路24号 (in gray concrete apartment behind main campus building); see map p. 116. © 010/ 6832-3000. Fax 010/6832-2900. faciec@mx.cei.gov.cn. 170 units. ¥195 ($24) standard room (discounts for long stay). No credit cards. **Amenities:** Coin-op laundry; Internet access; self-catering kitchens. In room: A/C, satellite TV, fridge upon request.

Airport Hotels

Plenty of hotels, all with free shuttle services, are located near the airport. The most pleasant choice is the **Sino-Swiss Hotel (Guódū Dàfàndiàn)** ✪ (✆ 010/6456-5588; fax 010/6456-1588; www.sino-swisshotel.com), formerly a Mövenpick, containing large rooms with two queen-size beds for around ¥830 ($104) after discount. Guests have free access to a pleasant resort-style pool complex, and regular shuttles go the airport (10 min.) and downtown. Almost within walking distance of the airport to the south is the very basic **Air China Hotel** (Guóháng Bīnguǎn; ✆ 010/6456-3440), with standard rooms from ¥260 to ¥320 ($33–$40). Slightly nicer rooms can be had at the three-star **Blue Sky Hotel** (Lán Tiān Dàshà; ✆ 010/8048-9108), 15 minutes away in the Kōnggǎng Industrial Zone. A standard room costs ¥528 ($66). Further from the airport, in northern Cháoyáng, the **Holiday Inn Lido** (Lìdū Jiàrì Fàndiàn; ✆ 010/6437-6688; fax 010/6437-6237; http://beijing-lido.holiday-inn.com) is part of an extensive complex with foreign restaurants and shops. Standard rooms are large but tired and in dire need of refurbishment (¥1,170/$146 after discount), and the coffee served with breakfast is vile. The **Kempinski Hotel** (p. 70), on the Third Ring Road, offers free shuttle service to the airport.

6

Where to Dine

This, most people tell themselves after their first meal in Běijīng, is not Chinese food. There's none of the lemon chicken you usually get delivered from the Ho-Ho Gourmet back home, the chicken you do get still has its head, and the sauce doesn't drip from it in gelatinous clumps. The rice comes at the end of the meal unless you ask for it early—and there are no fortune cookies.

Of all the vertigo first-time visitors experience in Běijīng, the worst spins often come from eating. In the past, fear of the food kept many travelers turning to their hotels and a few free-standing "Western" eateries for sustenance. This is no longer necessary, if it ever was.

Běijīng is China's best city for gastronomes. No other Chinese city provides a greater variety of restaurants. Better standards of hygiene have erased the biggest barrier to eating out in the past, making it almost criminal to stay in your hotel. And once you get over the shock of strange flavors, most travelers find the real Chinese food astronomically better than its Western corruption.

Most restaurants in Běijīng have very short life spans, creating headaches for guidebook writers and readers. But the volatility is also what makes the city such a wonderful place to eat, as establishments that manage to stick around have generally earned the right to exist.

Běijīng has its native cuisine, but it is by no means the dominant one. While there are entire restaurants devoted to producing the city's most famous local dish, Běijīng roast duck, local diners are fickle and fond of new trends. These sweep through the city like tornadoes through Kansas. A few years ago it was Cultural Revolution nostalgia dishes, then fish and sweet sauces from Shànghǎi, then yuppified minority food from Yúnnán, and now the fiery flavors of Sìchuān hold sway. Tomorrow it will be something else. Each leaves its mark on the culinary landscape after it has passed, making it possible for visitors to sample authentic dishes from nearly every corner of the country. (For a summary of the most popular cuisines, see "The Cuisines" box below.)

The choices expand well beyond China's borders. Most of Asia and Europe are well represented at close-to-authentic levels. Italian, Russian, French, Indian, and Japanese restaurants are numerous, some of superb quality.

American fast-food outlets are ubiquitous. KFC is the most popular among locals and McDonald's is a close second. Subway, Sizzler, and even A&W are also in the mix. For sandwiches, there are several other choices: Schlotsky's Deli (in the China World Trade Center), and the Kempi Deli (inside the Kempinski Hotel).

Among sit-down options are Pizza Hut, T.G.I. Friday's, Henry J. Bean's (in the China World complex), the American-owned Outback Steakhouse, and the Běijīng Hard Rock Cafe (check *that's Beijing* for location details).

The Cuisines

China has between four and ten seminal cooking styles, depending on who you ask, but regional permutations, minority contributions, and specialty cuisines like Buddhist-influenced vegetarian and medicinal dishes push the number into the dozens. Most of these have at least passed through Běijīng since privately owned restaurants really took off in the 1980s. Below are summaries of the most consistently popular styles, as well as the cuisines du jour, which may or may not be around next time you visit:

Běijīng This ill-defined cuisine was influenced over the centuries by the different eating habits of successive rulers. Emphasis is on lamb and pork, with strong, salty, and sometimes musky flavors. Staples are heavy noodles and breads rather than rice. Jiǎozi, little morsels of meat and vegetables wrapped in dough and usually boiled, are a favorite local snack.

Cantonese The most famous Chinese cooking style, Cantonese tends to be light and crisp, with pleasing combinations of salty and sweet, elaborate presentations, and a fondness for rare animal ingredients at the high end. As with Sichuanese food, real Cantonese puts its American version to shame. It's available in swanky and proletarian permutations.

Homestyle (Jiācháng Cài) The most pervasive style in Běijīng, homestyle food consists of simplified dishes from a variety of regions, primarily Sìchuān. It is cheap, fast, and gloriously filling, with straightforward flavors that run the gamut. This is the Chinese equivalent of down-home American cooking, but far healthier and more colorful.

Huáiyáng This ancient style from the lower reaches of the Yangtze River (Cháng Jiāng) is celebrated for delicate knife work and light, slightly sweet fish dishes. Vegetarian dishes often make interesting use of fruit. The tendency here is to braise and stew rather than stir-fry.

Běijīng frequently ranks among the most expensive cities in which to dine for business travelers, according to the Corporate Travel Index and other sources of such information. While it is possible to spend a lot of money on food in the city, it is also possible to eat, and eat well, for very little. A typical dinner for two at a relatively upscale Chinese restaurant costs ¥80 to ¥140 ($10–$18), but prices can go much lower with little to no drop in quality.

Main courses in almost every non-Western restaurant are placed in the middle of the table and shared between two or more people. The "meal for two" price estimates in this chapter include two individual bowls of rice and between two and four dishes, depending on the size of the portions, which tends to decrease as prices rise.

Credit cards are generally accepted in most restaurants above the moderately priced level. Hotels frequently levy a 15% service charge, but free-standing restaurants seldom do. Tips are not given; waitresses will often come running out into the street to give your money back if you try to leave one.

Shànghǎi These richly sweet, oil-heavy dishes are no longer as trendy as they were a few years ago, but are still easy to find. Shanghainese food tends to be more expensive than fare from Sìchuān or Běijīng, but affordable Shànghǎi-style snack shops dot the city. Best are the varieties of *bāozi,* or bread dumplings.

Sìchuān The most popular of the pure cuisines in Běijīng, real Sichuanese is far more flavorful than the "Szechuan" food found in the United States. Main ingredients are vividly hot peppers, numbing black peppercorns, and garlic, as found in classics like *gōngbào jīdīng* (diced chicken with chilies and peanuts). Spicy Sìchuān-style hot pot is the city's best interactive food experience.

Southern Minority Cuisine and rare ingredients from Nàxī-dominated regions of Yúnnán Province are especially fashionable, but Hakka, Dǎi, Miáo, and other ethnic traditions are also well represented. This is some of the city's most interesting food right now, but also its most inconsistent and overpriced.

Uighur Uighur cooking is the more distinctive of Běijīng's two Muslim styles (the other being Huí), with origins in remote Xīnjiāng Province. The cuisine is heavy on lamb and chicken and is justly adored for its variety of thick noodles in spiced tomato-based sauces. Uighurs produce the city's favorite street snack: *yángròu chuàn,* roasted lamb skewers with cumin and chili powder.

Vegetarian An increasingly diverse style, the Běijīng version of vegetarian cuisine is moving away from its previous obsession with soy- and taro-based fake meat dishes. Decor and quality vary from restaurant to restaurant, but none allow smoking or booze.

Restaurants in this chapter are a mix of established favorites and newer places creative enough or just plain good enough to survive. Běijīng's enthusiasm for the wrecking ball can sometimes take down even the most venerable of eating establishments, but new worthies inevitably rise to fill the gap. Most restaurants of note, especially those that cater to foreign clientele, are located in Cháoyáng, but excellent establishments exist all over the city. The most picturesque spot to dine in Běijīng is around the Back Lakes, north of Běi Hǎi Park, an area of well-preserved *hútòng* (narrow lanes) and idyllic man-made lake promenades that is home to several of the city's most compelling eateries.

Note: For tips on dining etiquette, see "Fast Facts: Běijīng" in chapter 4. For more tips and a menu guide to the city's most popular dishes, see "Appendix A: Běijīng in Depth" on p. 207.

The price ranges in the reviews below reflect the following equivalents, in terms of main courses: **Very Expensive** ($$$$) = $31 & up; **Expensive** ($$$) = $19 to $30; **Moderate** ($$) = $10 to $18; **Inexpensive** ($) = under $10.

1 Best Dining Bets

- **Best Běijīng Duck:** Běijīng's most famous dish is available at dozens of locations, but nowhere is it as crisp and fine as at **Běijīng Dàdǒng Kǎoyā Diàn,** just east of the Sān Lǐ Tún drinking district on the East Third Ring Road. See p. 97.

- **Best Sìchuān:** The use of fertilizer and hormones in Chinese produce has dulled the flavor of many raw ingredients, so locals have turned to the fiery food of Sìchuān to provide their culinary kicks. At **Málà Yòuhuò,** in the south of town, you'll have to wait for a table every night of the week; such is the draw of their heavenly spices. See p. 100.

- **Best Cantonese: Horizon,** inside the Kerry Centre Hotel, serves nicely executed upscale Cantonese food and high-quality dim sum in a luxurious setting at less-than-luxurious prices. The raucous **Otto's Restaurant** offers for-the-people southern dishes, rarely found outside Guǎngdōng, Hong Kong, and the largest of U.S. Chinatowns. See p. 93 and 87, respectively.

- **Best Hot Pot:** Searingly spicy Sìchuān-style hot pot in an unusually classy setting can be found at the immensely popular **Huángchéng Lǎo Mā.** Out of the way but well worth the trip, **Tàipó Tiānfǔ Shānzhēn** features a mouthwatering broth made from 32 kinds of mushrooms and a whole black-skinned chicken—the city's most delicious do-it-yourself dining experience. See p. 95 and 101, respectively.

- **Best Noodles:** Available in dozens of shapes and sauces, Shānxī-style noodles at the fashionable and aptly named **Noodle Loft** are among the most satisfying in Běijīng, and without the crimes of hygiene perpetrated by the more typical noodle joints. See p. 99.

- **Best Karma** (Vegetarian): A favorite among Buddhist monks, clean and bright **Bǎihé Sùshí** serves food to match its decor: mushrooms and tofu masquerading as meat, light and flavorful vegetables. No animals anywhere, but you won't miss them. No smoking either. See p. 103.

- **Best European: Aria** (p. 91) is one of the capital's most thoroughly satisfying dining experiences, from *amuse-bouche* to dessert. More than one visit may be necessary to do justice to a menu of thoroughly intelligent yet understated dishes, served with helpful suggestions for accompanying wines in very comfortable and relaxingly woody surroundings. The unassuming Belgian restaurant **Morel's** (p. 93), once considered the greatest Western eatery in Běijīng, is your best source of waffles, steak, beef stew, and beer.

- **Best Asian** (non-Chinese): Stylish decor and creative rolls make **Hatsune** (p. 92) the best Japanese option in Běijīng. Overpriced but superbly decorated, **Nuage** (p. 88) in the Back Lakes offers creative Vietnamese. **Cafe Sambal** (p. 87) is much the same for Malaysian cuisine. The gaudily decorated **Xīyù Shífǔ** (p. 104) provides Běijīng with its best Uighur food, including some divine lamb skewers.

- **Best Wine List:** High import duties and poor selection make life in Běijīng tough on wine drinkers. But **The CourtYard,** one of the city's most celebrated restaurants, both for its excellent menu and for its location in a courtyard house overlooking the Forbidden City moat, offers an astonishingly sophisticated wine selection you'd have to go to Hong Kong to equal, with many top wines available by the glass. See p. 86.

- **Best Quintessential Běijīng Setting:** Built inside the prayer hall of an old Daoist temple in a sea of crumbling residences near the Back Lakes, **Dào** eschews the polished gardens and pavilions of the city's other atmospheric restaurants in favor of something far more appropriate: the fast-fading intimacy of one of Běijīng's last *hútòng* neighborhoods. See p. 88.

- **Best Decor:** With its high ceiling, pleasing juxtaposition of black and white furnishings, and gracious owner, **Green T. House** is the most stylish restaurant in Běijīng. Flavorful and artfully arranged fusion dishes complete the visual package. See p. 92.

- **Best Breakfast:** Despite the appalling service, **Riverside Café** would be our first choice for breakfast, but it only offers a full breakfast menu on weekends. For a hearty American-style breakfast every day of the week, **Steak & Eggs,** run by a former navy chef, should be your first choice. They even have grits. See p. 191 and 97.

- **Best Coffee:** Despite the silly name, **Tasty Taste,** just west of the Worker's Stadium, is the city's best alternative to Starbucks. The cakes are excellent, and the Italian coffee hits the spot every time. See p. 191.

2 Restaurants by Cuisine

AMERICAN
Steak & Eggs (Xī Lái Zhōng) (Cháoyáng, $$, p. 97)

BĚIJĪNG
Běijīng Dàdŏng Kǎoyā Diàn ✿✿ (Cháoyáng, $, p. 97)

Dào Jiā Cháng ✿✿ (Cháoyáng, $, p. 98)

Fújiā Lóu (Dōng Chéng, $, p. 90)

Jiŭhuā Shān ✿ (Hǎidiàn, $, p. 103)

Made in China (CityCenter, $$$, p. 86)

Sìhéxuān (Cháoyáng, $, p. 100)

BELGIAN
Morel's (Mòláolóngxǐ Xīcāntīng) ✿✿ (Cháoyáng, $$$, p. 93)

CANTONESE
Horizon (Hǎitiān Gé) ✿ (Cháoyáng, $$$, p. 93)

Otto's Restaurant (Rìchāng Chá Cāntīng) ✿ (City Center, $, p. 87)

DAOIST
Dào ✿ (Back Lakes, $$$, p. 88)

EUROPEAN
Aria (Ālìyǎ) ✿✿✿ (Cháoyáng, $$$$, p. 91)

FRENCH
Flo (Fú Lóu) (Cháoyáng, $$$, p. 92)

FUSION
The CourtYard (Sìhéyuàn) ✿✿ (City Center, $$$, p. 86)

Green T. House (Zǐ Yún Xuān) ✿ (Cháoyáng, $$$$, p. 92)

My Humble House (Dōngfāng Hánshè) ✿✿ (City Center, $$$$, p. 85)

RBL ✿✿✿ (City Center, $$$$, p. 86)

GUÌZHŌU
Sǎn Gè Guìzhōurén (Cháoyáng, $$, p. 95)

HAKKA
Kèjiā Cài ✿✿✿ (Back Lakes, $, p. 90)

HOMESTYLE (JIĀCHÁNG CÀI)
Ǎndiē Ǎnniáng (Cháoyáng, $, p. 97)

Gŏubùlǐ Bāozi Diàn (Běijīng South, $, p. 100)

Huājiā Yíyuán (Dōng Chéng, $, p. 89)

Xiàngyáng Tún (Hǎidiàn, $, p. 103)

Key to Abbreviations: $$$$ = Very Expensive $$$ = Expensive $$ = Moderate $ = Inexpensive

Tips **Green Dining**

- Don't let your culinary journey push rare species into extinction: avoid shark's fin and wild animal meats.
- Eat locally grown produce and support Běijīng's nascent organics industry where possible.
- Bring your own chopsticks and avoid disposable chopsticks—billions are discarded each year.

HONG KONG
Be There or Be Square (Bú Jiàn Bú Sàn) (City Center, $, p. 87)
Otto's Restaurant (Rìchāng Chá Cāntīng) ✿ (City Center, $, p. 87)

HOT POT
Dǐng Dǐng Xiāng (Cháoyáng, $, p. 98)
Huángchéng Lǎo Mā (Cháoyáng, $$, p. 95)
Tàipó Tiānfǔ Shānzhēn ✿✿ (Běijīng South, $, p. 101)

HUÁIYÁNG
Kǒng Yǐjǐ Jiǔlóu ✿ (Back Lakes, $, p. 91)
Zhāng Shēng Jì Jiǔdiàn, ✿✿ (Běijīng West, $$, p. 102)

INDIAN
Taj Pavilion (Tàijī Lóu Yìndù Cāntīng) (Cháoyáng, $$, p. 97)

ITALIAN
Annie's Café (Ānnī Yìdàlì Cāntīng) (Cháoyáng, $$, p. 93)
Le Café Igosso ✿✿ (Cháoyáng, $$, p. 95)

JAPANESE
Hatsune (Yǐn Quán) ✿✿ (Cháoyáng, $$$, p. 92)
Matsuko (Sōngzǐ) (Cháoyáng, $$, p. 95)

JIĀOZI
Tiānjīn Bǎi Jiǎo Yuán (Běijīng South, $, p. 101)

MALAYSIAN
Cafe Sambal ✿✿ (Back Lakes, $$$, p. 87)

NORTHEASTERN
Dōngběi Hǔ ✿ (Yàyùn Cūn, $, p. 103)
Xiàngyáng Tún (Hǎidiàn, $, p. 103)

NORTHWESTERN
Xībèi Yóumiàn Cūn ✿✿ (Yàyùn Cūn, $$, p. 102)

PIZZA
Hútòng Pizza (Back Lakes, $$, p. 89)

RUSSIAN
Traktirr (Lǎo Jǐng É'shì Cāntīng) (Dōng Chéng, $, p. 91)

SHÀNGHǍI
Hùjiāng Xiāng Mǎn Lóu (Dōng Chéng, $, p. 89)
Shànghǎi Fēngwèi Cāntīng ✿✿ (Cháoyáng, $$$$, p. 92)
Shànghǎi Lǎo Fàndiàn (Běijīng West, $$, p. 102)

SHĀNXI
Noodle Loft (Miàn Kù Shānxī Shíyì) (Cháoyáng, $, p. 99)

SHÂNXI

Sìhéxuān (Cháoyáng, $, p. 100)

Xībèi Yóumiàn Cūn ✷✷
(Yàyùn Cūn, $$, p. 102)

SÌCHUĀN

Chuān Jīng Bàn Cāntīng ✷
(Dōng Chéng, $, p. 89)

Málà Yòuhuò ✷✷ (Běijīng South, $, p. 100)

Yúxiāng Rénjiā ✷ (Běijīng South, $, p. 101)

TAIWANESE

Bellagio's (Lù Gǎng Xiǎozhèn) (Cháoyáng, $$, p. 94)

THAI

Serve the People (Wèi Rénmín Fúwù) (Cháoyáng, $$, p. 96)

TIBETAN

Makye Ame (Mǎjí Āmǐ) (Cháoyáng, $, p. 98)

UIGHUR

Pamer (Pàmǐ'ěr Shífǔ) ✷ (Běijīng South, $, p. 100)

Xīyù Shífǔ ✷✷ (Yàyùn Cūn, $$, p. 104)

VEGETARIAN

Bǎihé Sùshí (Lily Vegetarian Restaurant ✷✷ (Hǎidiàn, $, p. 103)

VIETNAMESE

Nuage (Qìng Yún Lóu) ✷
(Back Lakes, $$$, p. 88)

YÚNNÁN

Dà Jīnsī Hútòng 1 (Back Lakes, $$, p. 88)

Yúnnán Jīn Kǒngquè Déhóng Dǎiwèi Cānguǎn (Hǎidiàn, $, p. 104)

Yúnténg Bīnguǎn ✷ (Běijīng South, $, p. 101)

---

3 Běijīng City Center, Around Wángfǔjǐng Dàjiē
VERY EXPENSIVE

My Humble House (Dōngfāng Hánshè) 东方寒舍 ✷✷ FUSION There's nothing humble about this restaurant: The big players have come to town. The Singapore-based Tung Lok group made a low-key entry into the Chinese market, opening their first restaurant in Chéngdū, but by the time you arrive, they will have three outlets in Běijīng, all serving different cuisine in impressive settings. Perched above Oriental Plaza, the dramatic light-filled atrium sports a slightly sickly bamboo forest on the north side, and a rippling pond to the south, in line with *fēngshuǐ* principles. Staff is relaxed and confident, there is a vast amount of space between tables, and the background music complements the experience without becoming a distraction. The superb fare is a mixture of genuine fusion and Húnán-influenced seafood dishes. The menu changes constantly, but the juicy tenderloin Angus beef with black pepper is not to be missed. Those with a bottomless wallet may choose to order the abalone tuna. Priced at ¥ 3,000 ($375)—seriously; this is not a typo—this is one way to show off your wealth to your dining partner. If there are faults, it's the slim range of wine by the glass, and the inexperience of the bartenders, dumbfounded when asked for a dirty martini.

Dōng Cháng'ān Jiē 1 东长安街1号 (west side of Oriental Plaza, podium level); see map p. 106. ✆ 010/8518-8811. Main courses ¥38–¥375 ($5–$47) with one exception; see abaolone reference in review. AE, DC, MC, V. Daily 11am–3pm and 6–10:30pm. Metro: Wángfǔjǐng (118, exit A).

RBL ✦✦✦ FUSION   Handel Lee's latest venture is run by a team whose credits read like a food critic's naughty dream: Nobu, Megu, Sushi Yasuda, and Tetsuya's. RBL stands for Restaurant Bar Lounge, although the experience is LRB, a less catchy acronym, particularly to Australian ears. An unmarked opaque glass door opens into a stunning minimalist lounge, where Simon Wáng delivers impeccable cocktails, then on to the main event, the Japanese fusion restaurant. Two tasting menus are offered (¥450/$56 and ¥650/$81), with recommended wine pairings. New world wines dominate the wine list, with a respectable selection available by the glass. Few restaurants in Běijīng can claim to offer a dining adventure; RBL does. Not every creation hits the spot, but many are sublime, particularly the sakura smoked duck sushi, yukke marinated wagyu beef, and crème brûlée with orange marmalade. An anonymous, genuinely international dining experience is rounded off with live music in The Icehouse (reviewed in chapter 10, p. 186).

Dōng'ān Mén Dàjiē 53 东安门大街 53号 (west of Dōng'ān Mén night market); see map p. 106. ✆ 010/6522-1389. Main courses ¥160–¥375 ($20–$47). AE, DC, MC, V. Daily 5–11pm.

EXPENSIVE

The CourtYard (Sìhéyuàn) 四合苑 ✦✦ FUSION   If you read the food magazines, this may be the one Běijīng restaurant you know. Owned by a Chinese-American lawyer with family roots in Běijīng, the CourtYard serves admirable fare but wins the most accolades for its setting, in a restored courtyard-style house next to the Forbidden City. The house's gray brick exterior still blends with its old Běijīng surroundings, but inside is a different world: modernist white and glass, with tall art-hung walls and a beckoning staircase that leads to a contemporary art gallery in the basement. The fare isn't genuine fusion; dishes are recognizably Occidental or Oriental with only token mixing of styles, but they're delectable nonetheless. Fois gras brulée, cashew-crusted lamb chop, and black cod with tomato marmalade are longtime favorites. The tender grilled chicken breast in lemon grass and coconut curry is superb, justifying rave reviews almost by itself. The wine list is more comprehensive and well thought out than anything this side of Hong Kong, with a surprisingly large number available by the glass. An intimate cigar lounge upstairs, furnished with leather couches, looks out across the Forbidden City's eastern moat.

Dōnghuá Mén Dàjiē 95 东华门大街95号 (10-min. walk, on north side of street); see map p. 106. ✆ 010/6526-8883. Reservations essential. Main courses ¥145–¥245 ($18–$31). AE, DC, MC, V. Daily 6–10pm. Metro: Tiān'ān Mén East (117, exit B); east side of Forbidden City.

Made in China BĚIJĪNG   The Grand Hyatt's newest addition offers traditional northeastern and Běijīng dishes in a bustling open-kitchen restaurant. Made in China serves the capital's most palatable *dòu zhī* (fermented bean puree), excellent *má dòufu* (mashed soybean) and the ubiquitous *zhájiàng miàn* (wheat noodles with black bean mince), a dish that has spawned its own chain of restaurants. There's a lean Běijīng duck prepared in a manner reminiscent of Jiǔhuā Shān (p. 103). A whole duck is pricey at ¥198 ($25), though the presentation and flavors are impeccable. There's the odd fusion twist such as fois gras with sesame pancake, and there are excellent plain dishes such as tónghāo vegetable with rice vinegar and garlic sauce. Desserts are not the strong point of Běijīng cuisine; sensibly, only Western desserts are offered. Right next door you'll find the sleek **Red Moon Bar,** perfect for an apertif.

Dōng Cháng'ān Jiē 1 东长安街1号 (inside Grand Hyatt); see map p. 106. ✆ 010/8518-1234, ext. 3608. Reservations essential. Meal for 2 ¥250–¥350 ($31–$44). AE, DC, MC, V. Mon–Fri 7–10:30am; daily 11:30am–2:30pm and 5:30–10pm. Metro: Wángfǔjǐng (118, exit A).

⟨Overrated⟩ Imperial restaurants

Elaborately presented but seldom appetizing, dishes cooked in Běijīng's much-hyped imperial style are one of the city's biggest scams. Famous imperial restaurants **Fǎng Shàn Fànzhuāng** in Běi Hǎi Park and **Lì Jiā Cài (Lì Family Restaurant)** in the Back Lakes area are both set in picturesque surroundings but charge far too much for bad food and are therefore not included in this book. For a better dining experience in either location, pack a picnic. If you really want to drop a hundred bucks on camel paw and soup made from bird saliva, ask the concierge in your hotel to point the way. If you want to enjoy the cuisine of modern mandarins, we recommend **Chuān Jīng Bàn** (below) and the **Yúnténg Bīnguǎn** (p. 101), the restaurants of the Sìchuān and Yúnnán provincial governments, respectively.

INEXPENSIVE

Be There or Be Square (Bú Jiàn Bú Sàn) 不见不散 HONG KONG   This Hong Kong–style cafe chain, with its hip warehouse-style decor, is the city's most fashionable source of the Westernized Cantonese fare commonly found in the former British colony. All the classics are here: BBQ pork with rice, egg foo yung, beef with rice noodles, and strong milk tea made with condensed milk. There's also a selection of vaguely Western breakfast items, including peanut butter–stuffed French toast. Lines form at lunch, but the efficient staff, all equipped with SWAT-style headsets, make sure the wait is never long.

In basement of Oriental Plaza 东方广场 (at eastern end); see map p. 106. ℂ 010/8518-6518. Main courses ¥20–¥50 ($3–$6). No credit cards. Daily 24 hours. Metro: Dōng Dān (119, exit A). Another branch at Level B1 Capital Epoch Plaza. ℂ 010/8391-4078. Daily 9:30am–9:30pm. Metro: Xī Dān (115, exit E).

Otto's Restaurant (Rìchāng Chá Cāntīng) 日昌茶餐厅 ⚘ CANTONESE/HONG KONG   Otto's is authentic Hong Kong prole dining, down to the shouts, smoke, and indecipherable wall-mounted menu. The environment may be jarring and the staff too busy to care, but the food is tremendous. The restaurant specializes in *bāozǎi* (clay pot) rice dishes, best of which is the *làwèi huájī bǎozǎifàn*, a mix of rice, salty-sweet sausage, and chicken drizzled in soy. Also good, albeit messy, are the *suànxiāng jǐchì* (paper-wrapped garlic chicken wings). Thick glasses of iced coffee sweetened with condensed milk *(bīng kāfēi)* are the perfect remedy for midsummer malaise. New branches are sprouting all over town—notably a 24 *-hour branch just east of the north entrance to Běi Hǎi Park.

Dōng Dān Dàjiē 72 东单大街72号 (inside small alley past a movie theater on east side); see map p. 106. ℂ 010/6525-1783. Meal for 2 ¥60–¥80 ($8–$10). No credit cards. Daily 9am–4am. English menu. Metro: Dōng Dān (119, exit A); walk north several blocks.

4 Back Lakes & Dōng Chéng

EXPENSIVE

Cafe Sambal ⚘⚘ MALAYSIAN   Sambal embraces and surpasses all the clichés of a chic Běijīng eatery—a cozy courtyard house decorated with antique and modern furnishings, a sophisticated boss, relaxed service, and a well-balanced wine list. And then there's the food, prepared by a charming chef from Kuala Lumpur. You'll need to call a day in advance for the superb double-braised Australian lobster in *nyonya* sauce, or the incredibly fresh chili curry crab, served on a bed of curry leaves, dried shrimp, and chili paste. Try the fried four-sided bean with cashew nut sauce, or the yoghurt-based mutton curry. Don't miss the signature dish, Kapitan chicken, a mildly spicy dish with a nutty aftertaste, said to have been invented when Chinese migrants reached Penang during the Míng dynasty. The *kuih dadar*, shredded coconut fried with palm sugar and wrapped in a padang leaf roll, is delectable.

Dòufu Chí Hútòng 43豆腐池胡同43号 (walk south along Jiù Gǔlóu Dàjiē, it's near the corner of the 5th street on left, marked by a red lantern); see map p. 106. ℭ 010/6400-4875. Reservations recommended for dinner. Meal for 2 ¥250–¥400 ($31–$50). AE, DC, MC, V. Daily 12:30pm till late. Metro: Gǔ Lóu (217, exit B).

Dào 道 ⊛ DAOIST   Nestled in half of a defunct Daoist prayer hall at the back of a crum- bling residential cluster east of the Back Lakes, there's no sign in the *hútòng* outside, only an aged stone archway with the Míng-era temple's name (Guǎngfú Guàn) carved in faded characters at its apex. A narrow path leads from the arch past bemused neighbors to the hall, its beautifully crafted beams and murals brought back to life in early 2003. The manager, who was born in the building and recalls the false roof that hid it from Cultural Revolution vandals, has hired chefs from Qīng Chéng Shān in Sìchuān, where the Zhèngyī school of Daoism developed recipes for longevity and virility. The set meal includes fresh *jiǎozi*, accompanied by delicate side dishes like goose liver rolls with hoisin sauce (*é'gān juǎn*), deep-fried pork with medicinal herbs (*cùngū shāo*), and sweet gourd-shaped red bean rolls with mountain herbs (*shānyào húlu*). The drink menu features a bracing "immortal's abode" koumiss (*dòngtiān rǔjiǔ*), made with fermented milk, and the somewhat more appetizing Daoist medicinal tea (*gòng chá*).

Yāndài Xiéjiē 37 烟袋斜街37, next to the Lotus Bar (walking south from Drum Tower on Dì'ān Mén Wài Dàjiē, turn onto 1st hútòng on right; archway is on northeast side); see map p. 106. ℭ 010/6404-2778. Set meal ¥ 150 ($19). AE, DC, MC, V. Daily 10am–10pm.

Nuage (Qìng Yún Lóu) 庆云楼 ⊛ VIETNAMESE   Lake views from this restaurant's upstairs windows are matched only by its hallucinatory Hanoi-inspired interior. A long silver dragon snakes up the rear staircase to the main dining room, where the low light from red lanterns flickers on reed curtains and finely crafted wooden tables. The first floor has improbably stylish bathrooms, divided by an elaborate cut-glass pool, and the new rooftop section has breathtaking views of the Back Lakes. Food is not quite as impressive—portions are small and prices inflated—but there are some worthwhile gems. The grilled la lop leaf beef (*yè niúròu juǎn*) is exquisite; and the *phô* (Vietnamese beef noodles in soup) has a smooth, flavorful broth, but at a price 10 times higher than in Vietnam. This is the closest thing Běijīng has to a "hot" restaurant in the New York City sense, complete with a long-legged hostess who seems to take pleasure in turning people away. (Make reservations well in advance.) A dance club extends two floors underground.

Qián Hǎi Dōng Yán 22 前海东沿 22号 (east of the Yínding Bridge, at the intersection of Qián Hǎi and Hòu Hǎi); see map p. 106. ℭ 010/6401-9591. Reservations required. Meal for 2 ¥200–¥300 ($25–$38). AE, DC, MC, V. Daily 11am–2pm and 5:30–10pm.

MODERATE

Dà Jīnsī Hútòng 1 大金丝胡同1号 YÚNNÁN   The demolition of Bái Fēng's much-loved No Name Bar is inevitable, but his charming new restaurant has some of the spirit. Like the original, it lacks a name, and is known for now by the address.

There are smart touches: Mood lighting highlights the food; luminous inlaid stones, shimmering waterfalls, and maidenhair ferns create a soothing atmosphere; but the plastic chairs and tables on the rooftop smack of laziness. The minority-chic food is sublime, try the *nóngjiā shāo jiān jǐ* (spicy sautéed chicken fillet) which uses real bird's eye chili, or the delectable grilled lemon grass fish (*dǎizú xiāngmáo cǎo kǎo yú*), served wrapped in a lotus leaf. The finest dish is a juicy foil-wrapped beef marinated in mountain herbs (*sè shāo niúròu*). A range of fresh juices nicely complement the spicy fare, and they still make a mean gin and tonic.

Dà Jīnsī Hútòng 1号 (from Yíndǐng Qiáo head west and look for a narrow lane that soon forks right); see map p. 106. ✆ 010/6618-6061. Meal for 2 ¥120–¥200 ($15–$25). No credit cards. Daily 11am–2am (kitchen closes at 9pm).

Hútòng Pizza 胡同比萨 PIZZA   Silly name, great pizza. This hard-to-find pizzeria occupies the site of a former Buddhist nunnery and features untouched murals in the loft. There's no religious theme to the handmade thin-crust pizzas, but if you've arrived from the wilds of China, you may experience something akin to a spiritual experience. The only jarring touches are the unforgivable massage hotel carpet in the loft, and the presence of green pepper and black olives on an otherwise sublime three-cheese pizza.

Yíndǐng Qiáo Hútòng 9 银锭桥胡同9号 (from Yíndǐng Qiáo walk west, taking the left fork, and then right at T-junction); see map p. 106. ✆ 010/6617-5916. Main courses ¥25–¥109 ($3–$13). No credit cards. Daily noon–midnight.

INEXPENSIVE

Chuān Jīng Bàn Cāntīng 川京办餐厅 ✿ ⟨Value⟩ SÌCHUĀN   Anyone who has dealt with Chinese officials knows that there is one topic they are all experts on: food. This constantly crowded restaurant occupies the site of the Qīng Imperial examination hall (no traces remain). It is now the headquarters of the Sìchuān Provincial Government, and the masses can enjoy the fruits of their rulers' connoisseurship. The spicy *shuǐ zhǔ yú* is sublime, tender fish floating on a bed of crisp bean sprouts, and kids will appreciate the sweet pork with rice crust (*guōbā ròupiàn*). Sichuan standards, such as *mápó dòufu* (spicy tofu with chopped meat), are as authentic as the ingredients, which are flown in several times a week. The only evidence you're dining with cadres arrives later in the menu; two pages are dedicated to hard liquor and one to cigarettes.

Gòngyuàn Tóu Tiáo 5 贡院头条5号 (from metro, walk 1 block north along the second ring rd., turn left into Dōng Zǒngbù Hútòng, Dōng Chéng Qū); see map p. 106. ✆ 010/6512-2277. Meal for 2 ¥80–¥140 ($10–$16). No credit cards. Daily 10:30am–2:30pm and 4:30–10:30pm. English menu. Metro: Jiànguó Mén (211, exit A).

Huājiā Yíyuán 花家怡园 HOMESTYLE   The chef-owner behind this popular courtyard restaurant claims to have created a new Chinese supercuisine assembled from the best of the country's regional cooking styles. Whether Huācài (his name for the cuisine) will ever spread beyond Běijīng remains to be seen, but his long menu is one of the city's most impressive. The new restaurant is slightly less raucous than the recently demolished original, but locals still crowd around tables at night to devour heaped plates of spicy crayfish (*málà lóngxiā*) and drink green "good for health" beer. Try the *làròu dòuyá juǎnbǐng*, a mix of spicy bacon and bean sprouts rolled in pancakes roast duck–style.

Dōng Zhí Mén Nèi Dàjiē 235 东直门内大街235号; see map p. 106. ✆ 010/6403-0677. Meal for 2 ¥100–¥120 ($12–$15). AE, DC, MC, V. Daily 10:30am–6:30am. Metro: Dōng Zhí Mén (214, exit A).

Hùjiāng Xiāng Mǎn Lóu 沪江香满楼 SHÀNGHǍI   This large eating hall with somewhat cheesy mock-village decor has an extensive range of decently crafted Shàng-hǎi-style snacks, available in an easy point-to-choose format from a series of stalls that line the back. Both of Shànghǎi's famous pork-and-bread dumplings are here: *xiǎolóng bāozi* (steamed in water) and *shēngjiān bāozi* ("steamed" in oil).

Dōng Sì Shí Tiáo 34 东四十条甲34号 (long block west of metro stop); see map p. 106. © 010/6403-1368. Meal for 2 ¥60–¥100 ($8–$12). No credit cards. Daily 11am–2pm and 5–9pm. Metro: Dōng Sì Shí Tiáo (213, exit D).

Fújiā Lóu 福家楼 BĚIJĪNG   This Old Běijīng eatery is essentially a more stylized copy of the popular Dào Jiā Cháng branch that originally occupied the building. It provides a more pleasant atmosphere than its predecessor, with intricate lattice wood screens separating the dining rooms and dish names written on pieces of wood hung from the rafters. Food is high quality and comes quickly. Worth trying are the *zhá qiéhé* (two slices of eggplant deep-fried with pork in the middle), *kǎo yángròu* (thin-sliced roast mutton), and the *bǎnlì shāo chìzhōng* (soy chicken wings with chestnuts).

Dōng Sì Shí Tiáo 23 东四十条23号 (in gray brick building with fake tile-roof, west of metro stop); see map p. 106. © 010/ 8403-7831. Meal for 2 ¥40–¥80 ($5–$10). No credit cards. Daily 11am–2pm and 5–10pm. Metro: Dōng Sì Shí Tiáo (213, exit A).

Kèjiā Cài 客家菜 ✹✹✹ HAKKA   The Hakka, or "guest people" (Kèjiārén), are Hàn from central China who migrated southeast generations ago but never managed to integrate. Forced by discrimination to live in isolated communities in poor mountainous regions, they kept to their separate culture—and cooking traditions. A historically marginal cuisine, Hakka food has over the past 2 years become the center of epicurean fashion in Běijīng. The owner, a local artist, designed the space with a rustic motif: thick wood tables, stone floors, crinkled character-laden wallpaper next to patches of exposed brick, and waitresses in peasant garb. Enjoyable as the dining rooms are, it is the kitchen that keeps lines of customers winding out the door. The cooking style is hard to define vis-à-vis other cuisines available in the city, but ask regular patrons to explain the difference and most give a quick answer: It's better. The *yánjú xià* (shrimp skewers served in rock salt) and *lǎncài sìjìdòu* (diced green beans with ground pork) are both divine, as is the chicken with tea-mushroom soup *(cháshùgū bāo lǎojī).* The one dish you'll find on every table is *mìzhì zhǐbāo lúyú*, a "secret recipe paper-wrapped fish"—tender and nearly boneless, in a sweet sauce you'll want to drink.

Southeast bank of Qián Hǎi 前海南沿 (50m [165 ft.] north of Běi Hǎi Park north entrance); see map p. 106. © 010/6404-2259. Meal for 2 ¥80–¥100 ($10–$12). AE, DC, MC, V. Daily 11am–2pm and 5–10pm.

(Moments   Dinner on the Lakes, by Candlelight

For roughly ¥400 ($50) plus the cost of food, Běijīng's ancient roast-meat restaurant **Kǎoròu Jì** now arranges what may be the most charming dining experience in the city: a meal for up to eight people served aboard a narrow **canopied flat-bottom boat,** staffed by a lone oarsman who guides the craft in a gentle arc around the man-made serenity of Qián Hǎi and Hòu Hǎi. The entire trip takes roughly 2 hours. A little extra money buys live traditional music and the opportunity to float candles in the lakes after dark falls—a cliché in the making, but who cares? The restaurant is located next to Nuage (p. 88) at Qián Hǎi Dōng Yán 14 (meal for 2 ¥120–¥160/$15–$20; daily 11am–2pm and 5–9pm). To make boat arrangements, call © 010/6612-5717 or 010/6404-2554. *Note:* Boat-rental prices vary from season to season and will probably increase as time goes on.

Kǒng Yǐjǐ Jiǔlóu 孔乙己酒楼 ✦ HUÁIYÁNG   Named for the alcoholic scholar-bum protagonist of a short story by Lǔ Xùn, the father of modern Chinese literature, this popular restaurant offers an enjoyable dining experience, although it is somewhat weighed down by its own popularity. Service is not what it once was. A small bamboo forest leads to a traditional space outfitted with calligraphy scrolls, traditional bookshelves, and other trappings of Chinese scholarship. The menu, written vertically in the old style, features several hair-raising dishes, including the infamous *zuìxiā* (drunken shrimp), served still squirming in a small glass bowl filled with wine. Less shocking, and highly recommended, are the *mìzhì lúyú*, a whole fish deep-fried then broiled in tin foil with onions in a slightly sweet sauce; and the *yóutiáo niúròu*, savory slices of beef mixed with pieces of fried dough. Nearly everyone orders a small pot of *Dōngpō ròu*, extremely tender braised fatty pork swimming in savory juice, and a plate of *huíxiāng dòu*, aniseed-flavored beans. Fans of Lǔ's story will appreciate the wide selection of *huángjiǔ*, a sweet "yellow" rice wine aged for several years, served in silver pots, and sipped from a special ceramic warming cup. Less crowded branches have opened at Yàyùn Cūn (✆ **010/8480-3966**) and Dōng Sì Běi Dàjiē 322 (✆ **010/6404-0507**).

Déshèng Mén Nèi Dàjiē 德胜门内大街 (next to the octagonal Teahouse of Family Fù on the northwest bank of Hòu Hǎi); see map p. 106. ✆ **010/6618-4917**. No reservations. Meal for 2 ¥100–¥140 ($12–$18). AE, DC, MC, V. Daily 10:30am–2pm and 4:30–10:30pm.

Traktirr (Lǎo Jǐng É'shì Cāntīng) 老井俄式餐厅 ⓥⓐⓛⓤⓔ RUSSIAN   Běijīng boasts a substantial Russian community, many of them attached to the nearby embassy, which still refuses to employ Chinese staff, even for the cleaning jobs. The decor is more ski lodge than Russian, but there's no mistaking the hearty fare and the raucous clientele. Generous shots of Stolinichya vodka will get you warmed up for some borscht, the baked carp with cheese will put a lining on your stomach, and the salmon pancake is an excellent lighter dish. The show-stopping dish is the enormous salmon skewers. Most mains come with side dishes of salad and mashed potato, and everything is covered in parsley. A more expensive branch is set to open just to the south on Dōng Zhí Mén Nèi Dàjiē.

Xī Yángguān Hútòng 1A 西羊管胡同甲1号 (walk west to traffic lights; turn right and then take 1st left; marked by Christmas lights); see map p. 106. ✆ **010/6403-1896**. Main courses ¥18–¥60 ($2.20–$7.50). No credit cards. Daily 11:30am–11pm. Metro: Dōng Zhǐí Mén (214/1316, exit A).

5 Cháoyáng

VERY EXPENSIVE

Aria (Ā'lìyǎ) 阿丽雅 ✦✦✦ EUROPEAN   This is one of the most thoroughly satisfying dining experiences in Běijīng, from *amuse-bouche* to dessert. The dining room, reached by a spiral staircase from a bustling bar, has a comforting clubby atmosphere, full of woody alcoves and hung with green velvet curtains. All courses come with suggestions for accompanying wines, the bottles creatively stored in wooden slots that run the length of the staircase. Highly recommended specialties include a melt-in-the-mouth seafood tapas and pan-fried wild halibut served on pistou whipped potato, clam and fennel escabèche, and olive tapenade, perfectly paired with a nicely chilled Chateau Timberlay Bordeaux Superior Blanc. Don't skip dessert: "Rhubarb three ways" takes the humble laxative vegetable well beyond apple and rhubarb pie. An excellent selection of wines is offered by the glass, and under the new Australian management, requests to open a new bottle are not demurred. More than one visit may be necessary, and the business lunch for ¥128 ($16) is an unbeatable value.

Jiànguó Mén Wài Dàjiē 中国大饭店 (inside the China World Hotel); see map p. 111. ☎ 010/6505-2266, ext. 36. Reservations recommended on weekends. Main courses ¥145–¥255 ($18–$32). AE, DC, MC, V. Daily 11:30am–midnight. Metro: Guómào (122).

Green T. House (Zǐ Yún Xuān) 紫云轩 ☏ FUSION   If you're comfortable with the sentiment that "dining should be part of a lifestyle experience," you'll love this ultra-chic restaurant. If you think that sounds like pretentious twaddle, try Bellagio's, right next door. The name changes from purple to green in translation; dining at Green T. is a similarly psychedelic experience. The imaginatively prepared food is light, with tea-infused flavors, but the cuisine is beside the point. The minimalist decor and attentive service attracts a fashion-conscious crowd: Before the opening of RBL, this was *the* restaurant to be seen at. The stylish owner, a musician who exudes a Zen-like calm, is planning to open a new restaurant in the countryside, a half-hour drive to the east.

Gōngtǐ Xī Lù 6 工体西路6号 (a subtly marked door, on the east side of Bellagio's); see map p. 111. ☎ 010/6552-8310. Reservations essential. Main courses ¥86–¥260 ($11–$33). AE, DC, MC, V. Daily 11am–2:30pm and 6pm–midnight.

Shànghǎi Fēngwèi Cāntīng 上海风味餐厅 ☏☏ SHÀNGHǍI   When members of former president Jiāng Zémín's powerful Shànghǎi Clique come to Běijīng, this is where they dine. Set inside an elaborate and truly breathtaking fake forest, with rounded stone pathways that wind past misty waterfalls and plant-shielded private dining nooks, it may be Běijīng's most authentic Shànghǎi restaurant, and is certainly its most lavish. The central dining room is sumptuously furnished with Míng-style tables and chairs, dark polished wood floors, delicately latticed windows looking out onto the forest, and an elaborate gilded dragon set in the ceiling. The chef specializes in hairy crab (available July–Dec) and light, flavorful, stir-fried vegetables cooked with a spoonful of reduced soup. Dishes aren't really worth the prices, but the setting is. The gold and cream decor of the upstairs dining area is nice but not nearly as impressive.

Xīnyuán Nán Lù 2 新源南路2号 (inside the Kūnlún Hotel, block west of East Third Ring Rd.); see map p. 111. ☎ 010/6590-3388, ext. 5620. Reservations absolutely required. Meal for 2 ¥400–¥480 ($50–$60). AE, DC, MC, V. Daily 9am–2pm and 5:30–9:30pm.

EXPENSIVE

Flo (Fú Lóu) 福楼 ☏☏ FRENCH   This is a branch of the French restaurant empire described by some Paris foodies as the Starbucks of brasseries, but you can only be so picky in Běijīng. The restaurant occupies the front of a rather flashy building, all balustrades and staircases, with an (inaudible) nightclub at the rear. The menu is straightforward French favorites all done well. Recommended items include the smoked salmon salad with poached egg, pan-fried rib shortloin veal with mushrooms, and the chef's specialty, hot goose liver with apple. Reliability and good value may be why it's one of only a handful of free-standing Western restaurants to have survived more than a few years.

Dōng Sān Huán Běi Lù 12 福楼 (south of the Great Wall Sheraton); see map p. 111. ☎ 010/6595-5139. Main courses ¥90–¥230 ($11–$29); prix-fixe lunch ¥158 ($20). AE, DC, MC, V. Daily 11:30am–2:30pm and 6–11pm.

Hatsune (Yǐn Quán) 隐泉 ☏☏ JAPANESE   Hatsune is sushi sacrilege via Northern California, with a list of innovative rolls long and elaborate enough to drive serious raw fish traditionalists to ritual suicide. The unconventional attitude is also reflected in the stylish space, high-ceilinged and sleek, with a long glass-and-metal entryway and a rock garden path leading to the bathrooms. Nearly every item on the menu is among the best of its kind in the city, but the rolls are what make this place truly special. With the single exception of the Běijīng Roll, a roast duck and "special sauce" gimmick, you simply can't go wrong. The 119 Roll, with bright red tuna inside and out topped with a divine spicy-sweet sauce, absolutely should not be missed.

Guānghuá Dōng Lù, Héqiáo Dàshà C 光华东路和乔大厦C楼 (4 blocks east of Kerry Centre, opposite Petro China building); see map p. 111. ℂ 010/6581-3939. Meal for 2 ¥200–¥250 ($25–$31); Mon–Fri prix-fixe lunch ¥65 ($8); weekend lunch buffet ¥150 ($19). AE, DC, MC, V. Daily 11:30am–2pm and 5:30–10pm.

Horizon (Hǎitiān Gé) 海天阁 ★ Value CANTONESE

Shangri-La–managed Horizon is one of the finest and more sumptuously decorated Cantonese restaurants in Běijīng—and also one of its most reasonably priced. Cantonese is the subtlest of the Chinese cuisines, and this is the real thing, so don't expect the retina-straining colors or tooth-rotting sweet sauces you find at your neighborhood Chinese takeout joint. The menu features shark's fin, bird's-nest soup, and other classic indulgences designed to show off the fatness of your wallet. If instead you let your taste buds lead the way, then the stewed beef and dry bean curd with XO sauce, and the battered king prawns with mustard, should be among your choices. So should the Mandarin fish, deep-fried in the lightest of batters and prettily presented with a delicate sweet-and-sour sauce. The restaurant has also responded to the current obsession with Sìchuān food, and the sautéed crab with dried chili is a good choice if you're in the mood for more aggressive flavors. The weekend all-you-can-eat lunch, featuring a respectable selection of dim sum, costs only ¥128 ($16) for two.

Guānghuá Lù 1, inside Kerry Centre Mall 光华路嘉里中心 (near rear entrance of Kerry Centre Hotel); see map p. 111. ℂ 010/8529-6999. Meal for 2 ¥200–¥300 ($25–$38). AE, DC, MC, V. Daily 11:30am–2:30pm and 5:30–10pm. Metro: Guómào (122, exit A).

Morel's (Mòláolóngxǐ Xīcāntīng) 莫劳龙玺西餐厅 ★★ BELGIAN

Morel's reputation as the best Western restaurant in the city is a holdover from a less competitive era, but this is nevertheless a fine restaurant, with a rare, fanatic devotion to quality. Owned by Belgian Renaat Morel, one of China's most respected European chefs, and run with help from his wife, the restaurant has a casual and cozy feel, its yellow walls and green-and-white checked tablecloths reminiscent of someone's home. The food is simply presented and side dishes are somewhat limp, but main courses are supremely done, particularly the wonderful Flemish beef stew with tender chunks of meat cooked over many hours in a mix of Rodenbach beer, bay leaf, onion, and thyme. Soups change daily and sell out nightly. The restaurant also has an astounding array of Belgian beers; they now have their own range of purpose-brewed ales. Best of all, however, is the signature Morel's dessert: a near-perfect waffle—save room for it—made in a real waffle iron hand-carried on a plane from Belgium. Premature rumors of demolition forced Renaat to open a second outlet, and while the original restaurant has more charm, no one can say when the wrecking ball will hit. Call ahead to check.

Xīn Zhōng Jiē 5 新中街5号 (opposite Worker's Gymnasium north gate); see map p. 111. ℂ 010/6416-8802. Reservations recommended for dinner. Main courses ¥58–¥168 ($7–$21). AE, DC, MC, V. Tue–Sun 10:30am–2:30pm and 5:30–10:30pm. Another branch at Liàngmǎ Qiáo Lù 27 亮马桥路27号 (1 mile east of the Kempinski Hotel). ℂ 010/64373939.

MODERATE

Annie's Café (Ānnī Yìdàlì Cāntīng) 安妮意大利餐厅 Value ITALIAN   A casual, cozy, and tremendously welcoming Italian bistro tucked among the nightspots at the west gate of Cháoyáng Gōngyuán, Annie's is the hands-down favorite for affordable

Italian fare in Běijīng. Wood-fired pizzas are the most popular item, but try baked *gnocchi gratinate* with tomato and broccoli, or the chicken ravioli served with spinach and a fine tomato cream sauce. Appetizers and desserts are just average, the notable exception being the cannoli, a sinful blend of cottage cheese and dried fruit with a touch of brandy in a fresh shell of fried dough. Annie's staff is bend-over-backward friendly, happy to bring as many baskets of free bread (served with small jars of pesto) as you want.

Cháoyáng Gōngyuán Xī Mén 朝阳公园西门 (west gate of Cháoyáng Park); see map p. 111. (2) 010/6591-1931. Main courses ¥35–¥118 ($4.60–$15). AE, DC, MC, V. Daily 11am–11pm.

Bellagio's (Lù Gǎng Xiǎozhèn) 鹿港小镇 TAIWAINESE   Taiwanese food, characterized by sweet flavors and subtle use of ginger, is one of the most appealing to Western palates. While Bellagio's team of glam female waitstaff have an unjustified reputation for snooty service, the clientele of the Gōngtǐ branch, stumbling out from Babyface and Angel nightclubs, make for amusing people-watching. Both outlets are all sleek lines and shimmering beads. Don't miss the delicate *shāchá niúròu,* mustard greens combined perfectly with thinly sliced beef strips. *Táiwān dòfu bāo,* a tofu clay-pot seasoned with shallots, onion, chili, and black beans is also remarkable, as is the signature dish, *sānbēi jī* (chicken reduced in rice wine, sesame oil, and soy sauce). Běijīng's best pearl tea *(zhēnzhū nǎichá)* comes with the tapioca balls served separately. In summer, don't miss the enormous shaved-ice desserts: One serving is enough between four, but gobble it before it comes tumbling down!

Xiāoyún Lù 35 霄云路35号 (opposite Rennaisance Hotel); see map p. 111. *C* 010/8451-9988. Meal for 2 ¥120–¥200 ($15–$25). AE, DC, MC, V. Daily 11am–4am. Another branch at Gōngtǐ Xī Lù 6 工体西路6号 (south of Gōngtǐ 100 bowling center); see map p. ###. *C* 010/6551-3533.

Huángchéng Lǎo Mā 皇城老妈 HOT POT   Upmarket hot pot sounds like a contradiction in terms, but Huángchéng Lǎo Mā makes it work—and work well. Set inside a huge multi-storied building with a hyperbolic, tile-eave facade and relatively pleasant decor, the restaurant is almost constantly packed. The reason is their special ingredient, "Lǎo Mā's beef," a magical meat that stays tender no matter how long you boil it. Also popular are the large prawns, thrown live into the pot. The traditional broth is eye-watering spicy; order the split *yuānyang* pot with mild *wǔyútáng* (water world essence) broth in a separate compartment, or risk overheating your tongue.

Dàběiyáo Nán Qingfēng Zhá Hòu Jiē 39 大北窑南庆丰闸后街39 (south of China World Trade Center; south along East Third Ring, take left after crossing river); see map p. 111. *C* 010/6779-8801. Meal for 2 ¥180–¥200 ($22–$25). AE, DC, MC, V. Daily 11am–11pm. English menu.

Le Café Igosso *★★* ITALIAN   You'd never pick it, but a flight of stairs just north of an ugly flyover leads to Běijīng's finest Italian restaurant. Start with an apertif on the second-floor bar, which stocks an impressive range of spirits, before heading up to the small, intimate dining area, with dark wooden floors and furnishings. Service is unobtrusive; quite an achievement in such a small space. Both the chef and the owner are Japanese, so seafood dishes are compelling, particularly their appetizers. The sea-bream carpaccio marinated in seaweed has a liquid freshness, and the mustard roast duck is excellent. Move on to pasta for two: from the regular menu, the crab and olive spaghetti is competently delivered, or choose from the handwritten specials menu. Rosemary chicken, served with roast potatoes and fresh rosemary, is the pick of the main dishes. The wine list is simple but adventurous, although selection by the glass is limited. On the right night, this is Běijīng's most romantic dining experience.

Dōng Sān Huán Zhōng Lù 东三环中路 (360m [1,200 ft.] south of Guómào Bridge on East Third Ring Rd.); see map p. 111. *C* 010/8771-7013. Weekend reservations essential. Main courses ¥38–¥120 ($5–$12). AE, DC, MC, V. Daily 11:30am–2am. Metro: Guómào (122, exit C).

Matsuko (Sōngzǐ) 松子 *Value* JAPANESE   A surprising number of Japanese restaurants in Běijīng offer good lunch buffet deals, but Matsuko's stylish wasabi-green interior makes it a far more pleasant place to dine than its cafeteria-style competitors. The buffet (daily 11:30am–2pm; ¥68/$9) runs the gamut of Japanese favorites from sushi to udon, all with unlimited Asahi beer or soft drinks and a free plate of sashimi. The only complaint is with the tempura shrimp, so good they disappear as soon as they're brought out. Get there early to stake out one of the small tatami rooms, kept semi-separated from the throng by walls of wood and frosted glass. A la carte items are more expensive but nicely done.

In Báijiāzhuāng, on East Third Ring Rd. 东三环路 (across from T.G.I. Friday's); see map p. 111. *C* 010/6582-5208. Meal for 2 ¥160–¥180 ($20–23). AE, DC, MC, V. Daily 11:30am–2pm and 5–10:30pm.

Sǎn Gè Guìzhōurén 三个贵州人 GUÌZHŌU   Southern China's Guìzhōu Province is one of the country's poorest regions, which lends a certain irony to this restaurant's

hip minimalist setting and rich artist clientele. The menu offers a stylish take on the province's Miáo minority food with dishes that tend to be spicy, colorful, and slightly rough. Both table-top hot pots—the Miáo-style peppermint lamb and the cilantro-heavy dry beef—are highly recommended, as is the flavorsome but fatty *juébā chǎo làròu* (bacon stir-fried with brake leaves). ***Note:*** Items listed on the menu as "vegetarian" are not.

Guānghuá Xī Lù 3 光华西路3号 (walk north on Dōng Dà Qiáo Lù from Yǒng'ānlǐ metro [121], turn down alley north of Mexican Wave, look for blue sign); see map p. 111. (✆) **010/6507-4761.** Meal for 2 ¥80–¥120 ($10–$15). AE, DC, MC, V. Daily 11am–2:30pm and 5:30–10pm. Another branch at Building 7 Jiànwài SOHO 建外 SOHO 7楼 (south of Guómào metro [122, exit C]). (✆) **010/5869-0598.**

Serve The People (Wèi Rénmín Fúwù) 为人民服务 THAI   It's a sign of the times that Máo's best-known slogan can be used so frivolously by this chic Thai eatery, although Sanlitun Bar Street is now marked with a sign that reads SERVE THE PEOPLE'S ENTERTAINMENT NEEDS. In the heart of the Sān Lǐ Tún diplomatic quarter, you'll find Běijīng's finest Thai food at very reasonable prices. The grilled beef salad and green chicken curry are highly recommended, and the *pad thai* (rice

---

Value Chinese on the Cheap

Affordable Chinese food is everywhere in Běijīng, and not all of the places that provide it are an offense to Western hygiene standards. As with shopping in this city, high prices don't necessarily guarantee high quality in dining, and cheap restaurants often provide better food than expensive ones. Down-market dining also offers the best chance to connect with the average Běijīng resident.

Most convenient is a stable of adequately clean **Chinese fast-food** restaurants, many of which deliberately try to ape their Western counterparts. Menus typically offer simple noodles, baked goods, and stir-fries. Top chains include Yǒnghé Dàwáng 永和大王 (with KFC-style sign) and Mǎlán noodle outlets 马兰拉面 (marked with a Chicago Bulls–style graphic), both with locations throughout the city.

A better option is to visit one of the **point-to-choose food courts** on the top or bottom floor of almost every large shopping center. These typically feature a dozen or so stalls selling snacks, noodles, or simple pre-cooked selections from different regions. Prices are reasonable, making it easy to sample a wide range. Just point to what looks good. The food court in the basement of the Oriental Plaza, requiring purchase of a card you use to pay for food at each stall, is the most extensive. Others can be found in the China World Mall, the Yàxiù Clothing Market, and Xī Dān Bǎihuò Shāngchǎng north of the Xī Dān metro stop.

One of the most enjoyable local dining areas in Běijīng, the legendary 24-hour food street on Dōng Zhí Mén Nèi Dàjiē known to most as **Ghost Street (Guǐ Jiē 鬼街)**, took a hit from the wrecking ball but is still there in abbreviated form. From the Dōng Sì Běi Dàjiē intersection and running east, dozens of small eateries offer hot pot, *málà lóngxiā* (spicy crayfish), and homestyle fare through the lantern-lit night.

noodles with seafood in peanut sauce) is done to perfection. The small but interesting wine list has a limited by-the-glass selection. The temptation to use inappropriate local ingredients (such as cabbage!) plagues other Thai restaurants in the capital, but here the people are given their due.

Sān Lǐ Tún Xī Wǔ Jiē 1 三里屯西五街1号 (behind German embassy); see map p. 111. ☎ 010/8454-4580. Meal for 2 ¥150–¥200 ($19–$25). AE, DC, MC, V. Daily 10am–10:30pm. Metro: Dōng Zhí Mén (214/1316, exit B); 4 long blocks east, left at Xīn Dōng Lù, then 1st right.

Steak & Eggs (Xī Lái Zhōng) 喜来中 AMERICAN   A readers' poll in the expatriate magazine *City Weekend* voted this recently opened American diner as Běijīng's best restaurant. Given the variety of fare on offer in Běijīng, the poll is either an indictment of expatriate tastes or proof that friends of the owner voted early and voted often. But if it's home comforts you crave, servings are enormous, cups of coffee are bottomless, the ambience is authentically North American, and many of the cakes (particularly the carrot cake) are superb. The jumbo breakfast is an unbeatable value, and they even have grits.

Xiùshuǐ Nán Jiē 5 秀水南街5号 (behind Friendship Store); see map p. 111. ☎ 010/6592-8088. Reservations recommended on weekends. Main courses ¥35–¥99 ($4–$12). No credit cards. Mon–Fri 7:30am–10:30pm; Sat–Sun 7:30am–midnight. Metro: Jiànguó Mén (120/211, exit B); walk east 1 block, take 1st left, then right.

Taj Pavilion (Tàijī Lóu Yìndù Cāntīng) 泰姬楼印度餐厅 INDIAN   One of Běijīng's oldest Indian restaurants, this classy restaurant's small dining room holds only a few tables, nicely dressed in white linen, with subtle decor refreshingly free of camp. Food and service are both consistently high quality. Recommended dishes include vegetable *kofta* curry (deep-fried vegetables in tomato-based curry sauce), *palak paneer* (spinach curry), *rogan josh* (mutton in spicy tomato curry), and chicken *tikka masala* (marinated chicken in rich tomato sauce)—all authentic, thick, and deceptively filling. A second branch recently opened at the Holiday Inn Lido.

L1-28 West Wing of China World Trade Center, Jiànguó Mén Wài Dàjiē 1国贸中心; see map p. 111. ☎ 010/6505-5866. Meal for 2 ¥220–¥260 ($27–$33). AE, DC, MC, V. Daily 11:30am–2:30pm and 6:30–10:30pm. Metro: Guómào (122, exit A).

INEXPENSIVE

Ǎndiē Ǎnniáng 俺爹俺娘 HOMESTYLE   One local, eating here for the first time, described it as truly homestyle—the kind of place that recalled family meals in her parents' house. The atmosphere is casual, with diners on simple benches crowded around wooden tables in a clean, cozy space the size of a living room. The restaurant's immense *bāozi* (stuffed buns) are justifiably famous, best with the traditional *zhūròu báicài* (pork and cabbage) filling. Stuffed meat pies *(ròudǎng báicài xiànbǐng)* are also worth a try. Shelves line the walls, stacked year-round with jars of preserved garlic traditionally only available around Chinese New Year. Vinegar from the jars, known as *làbā cù*, makes a perfect dipping sauce for the *bāozi*. A small glass-enclosed kitchen in the corner provides entertainment while you wait.

Cháoyáng Gōngyuán Xī Mén 朝阳公园西门; see map p. 111. ☎ 010/6591-0231. Meal for 2 ¥25–¥50 ($3–$6). No credit cards. Daily 10am–4am.

Běijīng Dàdǒng Kǎoyā Diàn 北京大董烤鸭 ✹✹ BĚIJĪNG   No hundred years of history or obscure *hútòng* location here, just a crispy-skinned and pleasing roast duck that many say is the best in town. The restaurant claims to use a special method to reduce the amount of fat in its birds, although it seems unlikely that duck this flavorful could possibly be good for you. The birds come in either whole (¥98/$12) or half (¥49/$5) portions and are served in slices with a wide assortment of condiments (garlic, green onion, radish). Place the duck on a pancake with plum sauce and your choice of ingredients, and then roll and eat. An excellent plain broth soup, made from the rest of the duck, is included in the price. The English picture menu offers a wide range of other dishes, everything from mustard duck webs to duck tongue in aspic, plus a number of excellent *dòufu* (tofu) dishes with thick, tangy sauces. Every meal comes with a free fruit plate and walnut sago pudding for desert. This is one of the few restaurants in Běijīng with a nonsmoking room.

Tuánjié Hú Běi Kǒu 3 团结湖北口3号 (on east side of East Third Ring Rd., north of Tuánjié Hú Park); see map p. 111. ℂ 010/6582-2892. Reservations essential. Meal for 2 (including half-duck) ¥80–¥100 ($10–$12). No credit cards. Daily 11am–10pm.

Dào Jiā Cháng 到家尝 ☆☆ BĚIJĪNG
Chaos. The clanging dishes and shouting staff are too theatrical for this to be authentic Běijīng dining, but it's as close as you'll get. Decor is a cheap attempt to re-create the feel of Old Běijīng, with cut red paper substituting for real lanterns and eaves covered in cardboard tile, but cheapness is part of the atmosphere. Best by far are the servers, who rush about like madmen, pouring tea and clearing tables with a controlled, smiling fury. The kitchen produces a fine version of local favorite *jǐngjiàng ròusì* (shredded pork rolled in tofu skin with scallion) and slightly sweet *jiāoliū wánzi* (crisp-fried pork balls). They also serve some of the *real* stuff, traditional dishes only the oldest of natives still eat, like the pungent *yángròu mádòufu*, a mound of mashed tofu and whole soybeans drizzled in "lamb oil," and the simple *zhá guàn cháng* (taro chips with garlic sauce).

Guāngxī Mén Běilǐ 20, in Xībà Hé area northeast of the Chóngqìng Fàndiàn 光熙门北里20 (look for plaster Old Běijīng couple in window); see map p. 111. ℂ 010/6422-1078. Meal for 2 ¥40–¥60 ($5–$8). No credit cards. Daily 9am–9:30pm.

Dǐng Dǐng Xiāng 鼎鼎香 *finds* HOT POT
This Mongolian-style mutton hot pot restaurant is tremendously and justifiably popular for its signature dipping sauce (*jǐnpái tiáoliào*), a flavorful sesame sauce so thick they have to dish it out with ice cream scoops. Large plates of fresh sliced lamb (*yàngròu*) are surprisingly cheap; other options include beef (*niúròu*), spinach (*bōcài*), and sliced winter melon (*dōngguā piàn*). Decor is plain, and the place is clean for a local restaurant. You'll probably have to wait at the door.

Dōng Zhí Mén Wài Dōng Jiē 14 东直门外东街14号 (opposite Dōnghuán Guǎngchǎng, in alley across from Guǎngdōng Development Bank); see map p. 111. ℂ 010/6417-2546. Meal for 2 ¥80–¥100 ($10–$12). No credit cards. Daily 11am–11pm.

Makye Ame (Mǎjí Āmǐ) 玛吉阿米 TIBETAN
This ethnic theme restaurant combines a folk cabaret with decent but pricey food and surprisingly enjoyable decor. Paper lamps glow in the corners, grimacing wooden masks stare down from the beams, and traditional furniture lends color to the dimly lit room. Fare is "Tibetan"—yak and mutton with gourmet accents. Recommended dishes include *tashi-delek* (beef braised in brown sauce with carrots, cheese, and yak marrow) and the chicken with corn and juoma (a vegetable reminiscent of black bean from the Tibetan plateau). Tibetan-style *nan* is good for sopping up sauces. The English menu features several grain spirits, mixed with yogurt and served in silver goblets. Nightly shows start at 8pm.

Xiùshuǐ Nán Jiē Ā 2/F 秀水南街 (behind Friendship Store, next to Steak & Eggs); see map p. 111. ℂ 010/6506-9616. Meal for 2 ¥100–¥140 ($12–$18). AE, DC, MC, V. Daily noon–2am. Metro: Jiànguó Mén (120/211); walk east 1 block, turn left and then take 1st right.

Moments   Night Market Nosh

Late-night dining is a favorite Běijīng pastime, and the most convenient way to experience it is to visit one of several night markets scattered about the city. This is street food, government regulated but not guaranteed to be clean, so the weak in stomach or courage may want to pass. Gastrointestinal gamble aside, the markets are a vivid and often delicious way to spend an evening.

The markets are typically made up of stalls, jammed side by side, selling all manner of snacks that cost anywhere from ¥0.50 (6¢) to ¥5 (60¢). Most legendary are the little animals on sticks, a veritable zoo of skewers that includes baby birds and scorpions. There are popular markets on **Lóngfú Sì Jiē** 隆福寺街 (see chapter 8, p. 161) and **west of the Běijīng Zoo** (at the Dōngwùyuán Yèshì 动物园夜市), but the most celebrated is the **Dōnghuá Mén** night market 东华门夜市, just off Wángfǔjǐng Dàjiē opposite the Xīn Dōng Ān Plaza.

In a year of citywide cosmetic overhauls, even the Dōnghuá Mén has received a face-lift. With a history supposedly dating back to 1655, it was closed during the Cultural Revolution and finally reopened in 1984. Previously a charming mish-mash of independent operators each in their own battered tin shacks, it was "reorganized" in 2000. The stalls are all now a uniform red and white, each with identical twin gas burners. Prices have risen into the ¥10 ($1) range and the food has fallen a bit in quality. The payoff is an increase in revenues from foreign tourists.

Below are the most common items you'll find for sale at the stalls.

- **Bāozi** 包子: Steamed buns typically filled with mixtures of pork and vegetable, but occasionally available with just vegetables (around ¥3/40¢ for a basket of five).
- **Jiānbing** 煎饼: Large crepe with egg, folded around fried dough with cilantro and with plum and hot sauces (¥2/30¢).
- **Jiǎozi** 饺子: Pork and vegetable filling with doughy wrapper, commonly boiled (¥2–¥4/30¢–50¢ for 12).
- **Miàntiáo** 面条: Noodles, commonly stir-fried with vegetables or boiled in beef broth with cilantro (¥1–¥3/10¢–20¢).
- **Xiànbǐng** 馅饼: Stuffed pancakes, usually filled with meat or vegetables, fried golden brown (around ¥2/30¢).
- **Yángròu chuan** 羊肉串: Lamb skewers with cumin and chili powder, either fried or roasted; also available in chicken (*jīròu*) (¥1/10¢).

Noodle Loft (Miàn Kù Shānxī Shíyì) 面酷山西食艺 SHĀNXĪ   Unheard of outside China and rarely found in such stylish surroundings, Shānxī cuisine is noted for its vinegary flavors, liberal use of tomatoes, and large variety of interesting noodles. The Noodle Loft's interior is ultra-modern in orange and gray, with a large open kitchen featuring giant woks and steamers. An English menu makes ordering easy. Highlights include *yì bǎ zhuā* (fried wheat cakes with chives), *qiáo miàn māo ěrduo* (cat's ear–shaped pasta stir-fried with chopped meat), and *suāncài tǔdòu* (vinegared potato slices).

Xī Dàwàng Lù 20 西大望路20号 (from bus stop, walk back 90m [300 ft.]); see map p. 111. ✆ **010/6774-9950.** Meal for 2 ¥80–¥100 ($10–$12). No credit cards. Daily 11am–2:30pm and 5:30–10pm. Bus: 712 south for 2 stops from Dàwàng Lù metro stop (123, exit B).

Sìhéxuān 四合轩 BĚIJĪNG/SHĀNXĪ
A cluttered little restaurant with slightly more than token Old Bĕijīng interior, this longtime favorite is famous for its constantly changing range of typical Bĕijīng snacks. Some items are listed on the English menu, while others are rolled through dim sum–style on a cart. Shānxī staples are also offered. The best way to sample street food without fretting over hygiene.

Jiànguó Mén Wài Dàjiē 3 京伦饭店 (4th floor of Jīnglún Hotel); see map p. 111. ✆ **010/6500-2266,** ext. 8116. Meal for 2 ¥50–¥100 ($6–$12). AE, DC, MC, V. Daily 11:30am–2pm and 5:30–10pm. Metro: Yŏng'ānlĭ (121, exit B).

6 Bĕijīng South

INEXPENSIVE

Gŏubùlĭ Bāozi Diàn 狗不理包子店 HOMESTYLE
The most common explanation for *gŏubùlĭ bāozi* (dogs-won't-touch dumplings) is that they were named after their inventor, a man born when Chinese infant-mortality rates were still high and mothers named their children with a mind to protecting them from beasts and evil spirits. Other stories abound, but these addictive morsels of pork-stuffed bread remain popular, and are a cheap, satisfying way to refuel during a long day of shopping south of Qián Mén. A plaster empress dowager sits eating *bāozi* outside the entrance.

Dà Zhàlàn Jiē 21 大栅栏街21号 (west end of pedestrian mall); see map p. 114. ✆ **010/6315-2389.** Meal for 2 ¥20–¥35 ($3–$4). No credit cards. Daily 9am–10pm. Metro: Qián Mén (208, exit C).

Málà Yòuhuò 麻辣诱惑 ★★ *Finds* SÌCHUĀN
Bĕijīng's obsession with Sìchuān cuisine seems to have no end, and this restaurant, where locals queue down the street on a Monday night, currently enjoys the most fanatical following. Service is surprisingly friendly for such a busy restaurant, and the mock-village decor is cheesy but fun. The signature dish, *shuĭzhŭ yú* (boiled fish with chili and numbing hot peppers) comes in three different varieties, grass carp (*cǎoyú*), catfish (*niányú*), and blackfish (*hēiyú*). We still prefer the traditional grass carp, but the slightly firmer and less slippery blackfish makes a nice change. For a walk on the culinary wild side, try *málà tiánluó*, field snails stewed in chili and numbing hot pepper. Skewers are provided to extract the flesh from the sizable mollusks. Leave the innermost black part to the side, unless you want a serious tummy ache. A nice antidote to all the spice is a clear soup with seasonal leafy greens, *tŭtāng shícài*. A second branch recently opened northeast of Dà Zhōng Sì.

Guǎng'ān Mén Nèi Dàjiē 81, Xuānwŭ Qū 广安门内大街81号 (just south of Bàoguó Sì); see map p. 114. ✆ **010/6304-0426.** Meal for 2 ¥80–¥140 ($10–$17). AE, DC, MC, V. Daily 11:30am–10:30pm. Metro: Chángchūn Jiē (205, exit D1); walk south on Chángchūn Jiē then turn right (west) at 1st major road. Another branch at Dà Zhōng Sì Tàiyáng Yuán 帕米尔食府. ✆ **010/8211-9966.**

Pamer (Pàmĭ'ĕr Shífŭ) 帕米尔食府 ★ *Finds* UIGHUR
Pamer isn't much to look at, but it is clean, and the food it serves is cheaper and better than anything at the more famous Afunti, which is now overrun by tour groups. Cumin-spiced lamb skewers (*yángròu chuàn*) are immense and surprisingly low on fat. Also not to be missed are the *náng bāo ròu* (lamb and vegetable stew served on flat wheat bread) and *shŏubā fàn* (rice with lamb and raisins). They were renovating at press time; hopefully they'll match or even better the silly decor of Xīyù Shífŭ (see below).

Liánhuā Chí Dōng Lù 3莲花池东路3号 (north side of Báiyún Qiáo; large sign depicts dancing silhouettes); see map p. 114. ✆ **010/6326-3635.** Meal for 2 ¥60–¥100 ($8–$12). AE, DC, MC, V. Daily 10am–2:30pm and 5–9:30pm.

Tàipó Tiānfǔ Shānzhēn 太婆天府山珍 🌟🌟 HOT POT   To make the broth for their divine hot pot, this restaurant stews a whole black-skinned chicken with 32 different kinds of mushrooms and lets the mixture reduce for hours. The mushrooms are strained but the chicken stays, served with the by-now vibrant broth in a heavy clay pot kept boiling at your table. Already a fine meal on its own, it gets even better as you add ingredients—lamb *(yángròu)*, beef *(niúròu)*, lotus root *(ǒu piàn)*, spinach *(bōcài)*, or, best of all, more mushrooms *(shānjūn)*. Many of the mushrooms, shown in their uncooked form on a series of posters hung along the walls, are imported from the southern provinces. Good enough to make converts of fungus haters.

At south end of Èr Qī Jùchǎng Lù, behind east side of the Cháng'ān Shāngchǎng 二七剧场路长安商场东侧 (east of metro stop); see map p. 114. 📞 010/6801-9641. Meal for 2 ¥120–¥140 ($15–$18). No credit cards. Daily 11am–11pm. Metro: Mùxīdì (112, exit B1).

Tiānjīn Bǎi Jiǎo Yuán 天津百饺园 JIǍOZI   No restaurant has managed to fill the vacuum left by the inexplicable closing of Gold Cat, once Běijīng's most charming outlet for *jiǎozi* (ravioli-like dumplings), but Tiānjīn Bǎi Jiǎo Yuán comes closest. Staff are given to occasional catatonia, and the clichéd red-and-gold interior can't match Gold Cat's old courtyard setting, but the *jiǎozi* are just as delicious. The *xièsānxiān shuǐjiǎo* (dumplings with shrimp, crab, and mushroom filling) and *niúròu wán shuǐjiǎo* (beef ball dumplings) are treasures, best accompanied by a steaming pot of *chénpí lǎoyā shānzhēn bāo* (duck, mandarin peel, and mushroom potage). There's also a respectable range of Sìchuān dishes, pictured on the menu.

Xīn Wénhuà Jiē 12A 新文化街甲12号 (in alley opposite the Marco Polo); see map p. 114. 📞 010/6605-9371. Meal for 2 ¥30–¥60 ($4–$8). No credit cards. Daily 10am–2:30pm and 4:30–9:30pm.

Yúnténg Bīnguǎn 云腾宾馆 🌟 *(Finds)* YÚNNÁN   A low-key cadre restaurant with exceptionally fresh fare. Even though Yúnnán is one of the poorest provinces in China, the mandarins have their ingredients flown in several times each week. The decor exudes as much warmth as a hospital waiting room, but exceedingly friendly waitstaff more than compensate. The signature dish, *guòqiáo mǐxiàn* (crossing-the-bridge rice noodles) is worth the trip in itself, a delicious blend of ham, chicken, chrysanthemum, chives, tofu skin, and a tiny egg, all blended at your table with rice noodles in chicken broth. *Zhúsǔn qìguōjī* (mushroom and mountain herbs chicken soup) is ideal comfort food, and *zhútǒng páigǔ* (spicy stewed pork with mint), while not actually steamed in the bamboo tube it's served in, has hearty, complex flavors. Avoid choosing the enticing mushroom dishes on the picture menu without first checking the price; the Yúnténg stocks some fancy fungus.

Dōng Huáshì Běi Lǐ Dōng Qū 7, Chóngwén Qū 崇文区东花市北里东区 (follow Jiànguó Mén Nán Dàjiē south for 10 min.; on the south side of flyover); see map p. 114. 📞 010/6713-6439. Meal for 2 ¥80–¥140 ($10–$17). AE, DC, MC, V. Daily 11am–1:30pm and 5–10pm. Metro: Jiànguó Mén (120/211, exit C).

Yúxiāng Rénjiā 渝乡人家 🌟 SÌCHUĀN   Franchise food in the Chinese capital doesn't carry the same connotations of blandness it does in the United States. Yúxiāng Rénjiā, a constantly crowded chain of restaurants with bright mock-village decor and a talent for producing authentic Sìchuān fare, is a case in point. Dishes are slightly heavy on the oil but as flavorful as anything found outside Sìchuān itself. The spicy familiar *gōngbào jǐdīng* (diced chicken with peanuts and hot peppers) is superb, putting American versions of "kung pao chicken" to shame. They also produce several worthwhile signatures you aren't likely to have tried before, including an interesting smoked duck *(zhāngchá yā)* and the "stewed chicken with Grandma's sauce" *(lǎogānmā shāo jī)*. Waitstaff sometimes gets overwhelmed, and the impressive decor isn't matched by the hygiene.

Jiànwài SOHO Building 4 建外SOHO 4楼 (south of Guómào metro stop [122, exit C]); see map p. 114. © 010/5869-0653. Meal for 2 ¥80–¥120 ($10–$15). AE, DC, MC, V. Daily 11am–3pm and 5:30–10:30pm. Another branch at Cháoyáng Mén Wài Dàjiē 20, on 5th floor of Liánhé Dàshà, behind Foreign Ministry Building 联合大厦 (© 010/6588-3841; daily 11am–10:30pm).

7 Běijīng West, Hǎidiàn & Yàyùn Cūn

MODERATE

Shànghǎi Lǎo Fàndiàn 上海老饭店 SHÀNGHǍI   Shanghainese, thanks to ex-president Jiāng Zémín and his cronies, are now associated with shady real estate deals, and looking east you can view Běijīng's biggest real estate bubble: "Financial Street." While much of the menu promotes new Shànghǎi cuisine, the dishes labeled as traditional are superior. Inexpensive dim sum *(xiǎo chī)* is available all day, including delectable *luóbo sī sūbǐng* (shredded turnip shortcake) and *huángqiáo ròu sūbǐng* (shredded pork rolls). Huáiyáng appetizers such as *nánrǔ kòuròu* (braised pork in red fermented bean curd gravy) and *zuì jī* (chicken marinated in rice wine) are top notch, while *bābǎo làjiàng* (gingko, nuts, and pork in sweet chili sauce) and *xièfěn dòufu* (crab meat tofu) are also highly recommended. Stout is offered on tap, but green tea matches the delicate flavors better. Service and hygiene standards are impeccable: You may head for Shànghǎi after your meal.

Sānlǐ Hé Dōng Lù 5, Xī Chéng Qū 西城区三里河东路5号 (18F of Zhōngshāng Dàshà, 3 blocks west from metro, then turn right); see map p. 116. © 010/6858-7777. Meal for 2 ¥160–¥240 ($20–$30). AE, DC, MC, V. Daily 9am–9pm. Metro: Fùxīng Mén (114/204, exit A).

Zhāng Shēng Jì Jiǔdiàn 张生记酒店 ✮✮ HUÁIYÁNG   It may lack the ambience of Kǒng Yǐjǐ Jiǔlóu, but this branch of Hángzhōu's most successful restaurant delivers more consistent Huáiyáng fare. Service is no-fuss, there's a pleasing amount of space between tables with a high ceiling and plenty of light. For starters, try the flavorsome *jiǔxiāng yúgān* (dried fish in wine sauce). The recently added *mǎtí niúliǔ* (stir-fried beef with broccoli, water chestnuts, and tofu rolls) is excellent, and nearly every table carries the signature *sǔngān lǎoyā bāo* (stewed duck with dried bamboo shoots and ham) which has complex, hearty flavors. Explore the English picture menu without trepidation; Huáiyáng cuisine is delicately spiced, and largely eschews endangered species.

Běi Sān Huán, Zhèjiāng Dàshà 亚运村安慧北里与慧忠路街角 (west of Ānzhēn Qiáo on North Third Ring Rd.); see map p. 116. © 010/6442-0006. Meal for 2 ¥100–¥180 ($12-$22). AE, DC, MC, V. Daily 11am–2:30pm and 5–9pm.

Xīběi Yóumiàn Cūn 西贝莜面村 ✮✮ Kids NORTHWESTERN/SHǍNXĪ   This place is worth the trip out to Yàyùn Cūn in itself. Friendly staff, and bright, faux-rural decor make this the best "family restaurant" in Běijīng, and the cuisine (a hybrid of Mongolian and Shānxī fare) will have you looking through the picture menu to plan your next visit. The signature dish is *yóumiàn wōwo* (steamed oatmeal noodles) served with mushroom *(sùshíjūn rètāng)* or lamb *(yángròu rètāng)* broth, with coriander and chili on the side. Familiar *yángròu chuàn'r* (mutton skewers with cumin) and yogurt *(suānnǎi)* with honey make excellent side dishes, while the house salad *(Xīběi dà bàncài)* is a meal in itself, crammed with unusual ingredients such as wild greens, radish, purple cabbage, and topped with a delicious sesame dressing. The one dish you must try is *zhĭjĭcăo kăo niúpái* (lotus leaf–wrapped roast beef with mountain herbs). Roast beef will never be the same.

Yàyùn Cūn Ānyuán 8 Lóu 亚运村安慧北里与慧忠路街角 (corner of Ānhuì Bĕi Lĭ and Huìzhōng Bĕi Lù); see map p. 116. © 010/6489-0256. Meal for 2 ¥120–¥200 ($15-$25). AE, DC, MC, V. Daily 10am–1:50pm and 5–9pm.

INEXPENSIVE

Băihé Sùshí (Lily Vegetarian Restaurant) 百合素食 ★★ VEGETARIAN   My Bĕijīng friends howl in protest whenever I suggest dining vegetarian; this ultra-clean and friendly restaurant is the only one to win them over. Chinese vegetarian restaurants often get bogged down torturing meaty flavors out of gluten, but here you'll find delectable dishes with high-quality ingredients. Start with the hearty *shānyào gēng* (yam broth with mushrooms) and the slightly fruity *liángbàn zĭ lúsŭn* (purple asparagus salad), followed by *rúyì hăitái juăn* (vegetarian sushi rolls) and the excellent *huángdì sŭn shāo wánzi* (Imperial bamboo shoots and vegetarian meatballs). When in season, their vegetables are sourced from an organic farm west of Bĕijīng, so ask if they have any organic vegetables (*yŏujī shūcài*). Monks dine for free, so you're likely to meet a few from Guăngjĭ Sì in the evening. Mind your head in the bathroom.

Bĕi Sān Huán Jìmén Qiáo, Jìmén Fàndiàn 蓟门饭店南侧 (180m [600ft.] north of North Third Ring Rd., attached to Jìmén Hotel; walk east from metro on Zhīchūn Lù, turn right at Xuéyuàn Lù); see map p. 116. © 010/6202-5284. Meal for 2 ¥80–¥140 ($10–$17). No credit cards. Daily 11am–10pm. Metro: Zhīchūn Lù (1303).

Dōngbĕi Hŭ 东北虎 ★ NORTHEASTERN   Natives of Dōngbĕi (the Northeast) are famously direct, and few hestitate for more than a picosecond before nominating this raucous establishment as the source of Bĕijīng's best Dōngbĕi cuisine. Welcoming, florally dressed staff usher you upstairs past an open kitchen with whole cuts and huge jars of wine on show. Start with the refreshing cold noodle dish, *dà lāpí*, served in a sesame and vinegar sauce. Your table will groan under the weight of the signature dish, *shŏuzhuā yáng pái* (lamb chops roasted with cumin and chili). Filling snacks, such as *tiēbĭngzi* (corn pancakes cooked on a griddle) and *sānxiān làohé* (seafood and garlic chive buns), are delicious, as is the sweet and sour battered eggplant (cuìpí qiézi). So cheap, you won't begrudge the taxi fare out to Yàyùn Cūn.

Ānhuì Lĭ Èr Qū Yī Lóu, Yàyùn Cūn 安慧里二区一楼 (300m [984 ft.] east of intersection with Ānlì Lù); see map p. 116. © 010/6498-5015. Meal for 2 ¥50–¥80 ($6–$10). No credit cards. Daily 10am–10pm.

Jiŭhuā Shān 九花山烤鸭店 ★ BĔIJĪNG   Another fine roast duck eatery, Jiŭhuā Shān is larger and not quite as pleasant as the Bĕijīng Dàdŏng Kăoyā Diàn (see earlier), but it's more conveniently located for people staying on the west side of the city. Whole ducks, relatively low on fat and crispy, are reasonable at ¥88 ($11). Sesame buns make a nice alternative to traditional pancakes. They only roast 200 birds a day, so get there early. A new branch, with the same state-run ambience, is located inside the Worker's Stadium.

Zēngguāng Lù 55 增光路55号 (behind the Zĭyù Hotel); see map p. 116. © 010/6848-3481. Meal for 2 (including half duck) ¥100–¥140 ($12–$18). AE, DC, MC, V. Daily 11am–2pm and 5–9pm. Another branch at east side of the Worker's Stadium 工体东门; see map p. 116. © 010/6508-5830.

Xiàngyáng Tún 向阳屯 HOMESTYLE/NORTHEASTERN   Set in a new courtyard-style complex in northwestern Bĕijīng, this nostalgia restaurant is one of the only venues in the city for *èrrénzhuàn*, a raunchily entertaining style of opera rarely performed outside the frigid northeast. The opera stage sits at one end of the cavernous main hall, decorated in an exaggerated Cultural Revolution–era countryside theme

with bright red tables and propaganda-heavy newspapers from the 1960s plastered on the walls. Dishes are large and simple in the northeastern tradition. Good choices are the *Dōngběi fēngwèi dàpái* (northeast-style braised ribs) and the *nóngjiā xiǎochǎo,* an authentically rural combination of soybeans, green onion, Chinese chive, and bell peppers in a clay pot. Combine a stop here with an afternoon visit to the Summer Palace.

Wànquán Hé Lù 26 海淀区万泉河路26号 (in Hǎidiàn, across from the Zhōngyī Yīyuàn [Chinese Traditional Medicine Hospital]); see map p. 116. ☏ 010/6264-5522 or 010/6264-2907. Meal for 2 ¥40–¥80 ($5–$10). No credit cards. Daily 10:30am–11pm.

Xīyù Shífǔ 西域食府 ★★ UIGHUR Directly opposite Olympic Park you'll find the best Uighur food this side of Turfan. The decor (typical of Yàyùn Cūn) is a nouveau riche fantasy of arches, Romanesque gold light fittings, and pictures of desert scenes hanging from marble walls, but it's spotless and welcoming, with an imaginatively translated menu. Beyond intriguing dishes such as "nourishing your brain" and "pretty soup for gentleman," are authentic Xīnjiāng favorites. The *dà pán jī* (diced chicken, pepper, potatoes, and thick noodles in tomato sauce) is spicy, so when they ask if you like it hot, be honest. The piping-hot *nan* (flat bread) is perfect for sopping up the delicious sauce, and the *shǒu zhuā fàn* (rice with lamb and carrot), which often appears as a limp version of fried rice with raisins this far east, is as tasty as anything you'll find in Kashgar. Although spicy mutton skewers with cumin and chili (*yángròu chuàn*) ranks as Běijīng's most popular dish, too often the spices are heavy, usually to disguise less than fresh meat. Not here.

Corner of Běichén Dōng Lù and Dàtún Lù, Yàyùn Cūn 亚运村北辰路与大屯路街角; see map p. 116. ☏ 010/6486-2555. Meal for 2 ¥70–¥100 ($9–$12). No credit cards. Daily 7:30am–8:30pm.

Yúnnán Jīn Kǒngquè Déhóng Dǎiwèi Cānguǎn 云南金孔雀德宏傣族餐馆 *(Value* YÚNNÁN The street north of the Minorities University (Mínzú Dàxué) was once a claustrophobic *hútòng* packed with Uighur, Korean, and Dǎi restaurants. Chaps who addressed you as "Hashish" are gone, along with most of the restaurants. But this holy grail of Dǎi cuisine remains, offering a superb synthesis of Thai and Chinese fare. Mirrors, tiled floors, and predictable bamboo furnishings lend it a sterile feel, but the gracious waitstaff more than compensates. Must-devour dishes include crispy *tǔdòu qiú* (deep-fried potato balls with chili sauce), delectable *bōluó fàn* (pineapple rice), *zhútǒng zhūròu* (steamed pork with coriander), *zhútǒng jī* (chicken soup), and *zhá xiāngjiāo* (deep-fried banana) for dessert. Wash it all down with a cup of sweet rice wine (*mǐ jiǔ*), served in a bamboo cup.

Mínzú Dàxué Běi Lù 1 民族大学北路1号 (cross footbridge, head right, take the 1st street on your left); see map p. 116. ☏ 010/6893-2030. Meal for 2 ¥50–¥100 ($6–$12). No credit cards. Daily 11am–10pm. Bus: 808 to Wèigōng Cūn from Xī Zhí Mén metro (201, exit A).

Exploring Běijīng

This is an overwhelming prospect. No other city in China, and few other cities in the world, offer so many must-see attractions, or such a likelihood of missed opportunity. It is technically possible to see the big names—the **Forbidden City, Temple of Heaven, Summer Palace,** and **Great Wall**—in as little as 3 days, but you'll want at least a week to get any sort of feel for the city. People spend years here and still fail to see everything they should. For suggested itineraries to help you organize your time, see chapter 3. Sights outside of Běijīng require at least half a day. However, the Great Wall requires a full day. (See chapter 11 for details on side trips.) *Note:* Most major sights now charge different prices for admission in summer and winter. The summer high season officially runs from April 1 to October 31 and the winter low season from November 1 to March 31.

HOW TO SEE BĚIJĪNG

Běijīng's traffic is appalling. Do *not* plan to see too many sights that are far apart, unless you want your memories of the capital to consist of staring helplessly out of a taxicab window. Regardless of whether you choose to get around by taxi, metro, bus, bike, or foot, plan each day to see sights that are close together.

The best option for reaching sights within Běijīng is to take the metro to the stop nearest the attraction you plan on seeing, and duck into one of the many waiting taxis. As an example, the **Summer Palace** is a short ¥15 ($2) cab ride from the new light rail station at Wǔdàokǒu. Buses are slow but plentiful and relatively safe, especially if you choose the air-conditioned 800-series buses. Maximum freedom (and usually speed) is realized by hiring a bike for the day. More convenient still is to hire a normal taxi for the day (see section 2, "Getting Around," in chapter 4).

The standard of organized tours in Běijīng leaves much to be desired. But if this is your preference, most hotels have offices of Panda Tours and Dragon Tours, which offer overpriced tours to the major attractions (see section 11, "Organized Tours," in this chapter). The advantage is that transport and language barriers are removed, but the freedom to visit smaller attractions and meet locals is sacrificed. The pace of these tours can leave you giddy.

The last and least recommended option is to hire a car through your hotel. You will be charged up to five times what you should pay. Aside from convenience, the only conceivable plus is that if you are staying at a foreign-run, luxury hotel, they have a reputation for good service to protect. Organizations such as Panda Tours, which are run by the China International Travel Service, do not.

1 Tiān'ān Mén Square (Tiān'ān Mén Guǎngchǎng)

This is the world's largest public square, the size of 90 American football fields (40 hectares/99 acres), with standing room for 300,000 people. It is surrounded by the

Běijīng City Center

Legend:
- Bus Station
- ¥ Bank
- (i) Information
- ✉ Post Office
- Rail Station
- **PSB** Public-Security Visas

Metro & Station
— MUXIDI 112 Ⓜ

文慧园路 Wenhuiyuan Lu

北京北站 **Beijing North Railway Station**

Desheng Men ⑦

Desheng Men 德胜门

Xi Zhi Men Bei Dajie 西直门北大街

Gaoliang Qiao Xiejie 高梁桥斜街

XI ZHI MEN 1301

Xinjiekouwai Dajie 新街口外大街

JISHUITAN 218

Xi Hai 西海

鼓楼 Gulou ⑧

Hou Hai 后海 ⑥

Beijing Zoo 北京动物园 ②

①

XI ZHI MEN 201

Xi Zhi Men 西直门

XI ZHI MEN 西直门

Desheng Men Xi Dajie 德胜门西大街

西直门内大街 Xi Zhi Men Nei Dajie

Xinjiekou Bei Dajie 新街口北大街

④ ⑤

Hou Hai 后海 Liuyin

Xi Zhi Men Wai Dajie 西直门外大街

Xinjiekou Nan Dajie 新街口南大街

Desheng Men Nei Dajie 德胜门内大街

San Li He Lu 三里河路

Chegongzhuang Dajie 车公庄大街

Zhanlanguan Lu 展览馆路

Nan Dajie 南大街

Xizhimen 西直门

'Ping'anli Xi Dajie 平安道

Ping 'an Dadao

Di'an Men Xi Dajie 地安门西大街 / Xishiku Dajie 西什库大街

XI ZHI MEN 西直门

CHEGONGZHUANG 202

Zhaodengyu Lu 赵登禹路

Xisi Bei Dajie 西四北大街

XI SI 西四

Fucheng Men 阜成门

Fucheng Men Wai Dajie 阜成门外大街

⑨ ⑩

Fucheng Men Nei Dajie 阜成门内大街

⑪

西安门大街 Xi'an Men Dajie

Fuyoujie 府右街

FUCHENG MEN 203

San Li He Lu 三里河路

Tai Ping Qiao Dajie 太平桥大街

XI CHENG 西城

Xidan Bei Dajie 西单北大街

Yuetan Nan Jie 月坛南街

Picai Hutong 辟才胡同

XI DAN 西单

XI DAN 115

西长安街 Xi Chang'an Jie

Fuxing Men Wai Dajie 复兴门外大街

Fuxing Men

③①

Fuxing Men Nei Dajie 复兴门内大街

③②

Bei Xinhua Jie 北新华街

MUXIDI 112 Ⓜ

NAN LISHI LU 113

FUXING MEN 114/204

Naoshikou Dajie 闹市口大街

Xuanwu Men Nei Dajie 宣武门内大街

Bayun Lu 白云路

White Cloud Temple 白云观

CHANGCHUN JIE 205

Changchun Jie 长椿街

XUANWU MEN 206

Xuanwu Men Xi Dajie 宣武门西大街

Xuanwu Men Wai Dajie 宣武门外大街

Xuanwu Men Dong Dajie 宣武门东大街

HEPING MEN 207

0 ——— 1/2 Mi
0 ——— .5 Km

Key for Běijīng City Center

ACCOMMODATIONS ■

Bamboo Garden Hotel
(Zhú Yuán Bīnguǎn) 14
竹园宾馆

Běijīng Hotel
(Běijīng Fàndiàn) 59
北京饭店

Crowne Plaza Hotel
(Guójì Yìyuàn Huángguān Fàndiàn) 43
国际艺苑皇冠饭店

Cuìmíng Zhuāng Bīnguǎn 39
翠明庄宾馆

Grand Hotel
(Běijīng Guìbīnlóu Fàndiàn) 58
北京贵宾楼饭店

Grand Hyatt Běijīng
(Běijīng Dōngfāng Jūnyuè Dàjiǔdiàn) 61
北京东方君悦大酒店

Hǎoyuán Bīnguǎn 50
好园宾馆

Héjìng Fǔ Bīnguǎn 25
和敬府宾馆

Lǚsōng Yuán Bīnguǎn 24
吕松园宾馆

Novotel Peace Běijīng
(Běijīng Nuòfùtè Hépíng Bīnguǎn) 47
诺富特和平宾馆

The Peninsula Palace Běijīng
(Wángfǔ Fàndiàn) 48
王府饭店

Qílǔ Fàndiàn 13
齐鲁饭店

Red Capital Residence 54
东四六条9号

Saga Youth Hostel
(Shǐjiā Guójì Qīngnián Lǚshè) 51
史家国际青年旅社

Tiānlún Sōnghè Jiǔdiàn 44
天伦松鹤酒店

Wángfǔjīng Grand
(Wángfǔjīng Dàjiǔdiàn) 42
王府井大酒店

Zhōnggòng Běijīng Shì Wěi Bàn
Jīguān Zha[li]odàisuǒ 53
中共北京市委办机关招待所

DINING ◆

Be There or Be Square
(Bú Jiàn Bú Sàn) 64
不见不散

Cafe Sambal 15
豆腐池胡同43号

Chuān Jīng Bàn Cāntīng 65
川京办餐厅

The CourtYard (Sìhéyuàn) 38
四合苑

Dà Jīnsī Hútòng 1 16
大金丝胡同1号

Dào 18
道

Fújiā Lóu 56
福家楼

Huājiā Yíyuán 29
花家怡园

Hùjiāng Xiāng Mǎn Lóu 55
沪江香满楼

Hútòng Pizza 17
胡同比萨

Kèjiā Cài 20
客家菜

Kǒng Yǐjǐ Jiǔlóu 6
孔乙己酒楼

Made in China 62

My Humble House
(Dōngfāng Hánshè) 60
东方寒舍

Nuage
(Qìng Yún Lóu) 19
庆云楼

Otto's Restaurant
(Rìchāng Chácāntīng) 21, 49
日昌茶餐厅

RBL/Icehouse 40

Běijīng South

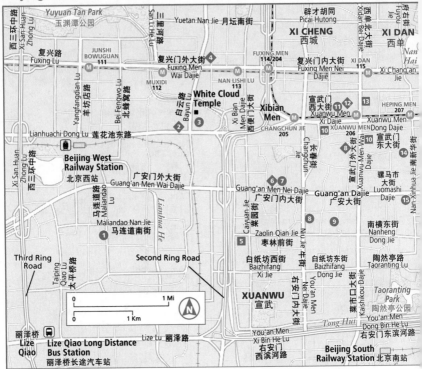

ACCOMMODATIONS ■

City Central Youth Hostel
(Chéngshì Qīngnián Jiǔdiàn) **27**

城市青年酒店

Far East Youth Hostel
(Yuǎn Dōng Qīngnián Lǚshè) **16**

远东青年旅社

Fēiyīng Bīnguǎn **10**

飞鹰宾馆

Harmony Hotel
(Huáměilún Jiǔdiàn) **26**

华美伦酒店

Holiday Inn Central Plaza
(Zhōnghuán Jiàrì Jiǔdiàn) **5**

中环假日酒店

The Marco Polo
(Mǎgē Bóluó Jiǔdiàn) **13**

马哥孛罗酒店

Qián Mén Chánggōng Fàndiàn **19**

前门长工饭店

Shǎnxī Xiàng Dì'èr Bīnguǎn **17**

陕西巷第二宾馆

DINING ◆

Gǒubùlǐ Bāozi Diàn **20**

狗不理包子店

Málà Yòuhuò **6**

麻辣诱惑

Pamer
(Pàmǐ'ěr Shífǔ) **2**

帕米尔食府

Tàipó Tiānfǔ Shānzhēn **4**

太婆天府山珍

Tiānjīn Bǎi Jiǎo Yuán **12**

天津百饺园

Yúnténg Bīnguǎn **29**

云腾宾馆

Yúxiāng Rénjiā **30**

渝乡人家

ATTRACTIONS AND SHOPPING ●

Běijīng West & Hǎidiàn

Metro & Station

MUXIDI
112

🚌	Bus Station
¥	Bank
ⓘ	Information
✉	Post Office
🚆	Rail Station
PSB	Public-Security Visas

0 ——— 1 Mi
0 ——— 1 Km

Yuanmingyuan Xi Lu 圆明园西路

Botanic Gardens

Xiangshan Lu 香山路

Wuhuan Lu 五环路

Yuquan Shan Lu 玉泉山路

Yuquan Shan Lu 玉泉山路

Summer Palace
6

Xiang Shan Nan Lu 香山南路

Bei Wucun Lu 北坞村路

Minzhuang Lu 闵庄路

Ba Da Chu Park
八大处公园

Badachu Lu 八大处路

Fourth Ring Road (Si Huan Lu)

Yuanda Lu 远大路

杏石口路
Xingshikou Lu

3

4

Tiancun Lu 田村路

阜成路
Fucheng Lu

PINGGUO YUAN
103

Fushi Lu 阜石路

八宝山
Ba Bao Shan

BAJIAO YULEYUAN
105

石景山路
Shijing Shan Lu

BA BAO SHAN
106

YUQUAN LU
107

WU KE SONG
108

GUCHENG LU
104

5

1

2

112

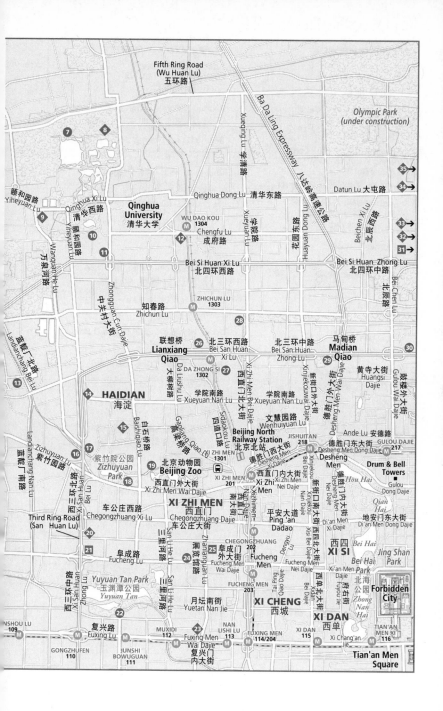

Fifth Ring Road
(Wu Huan Lu)
五环路

Olympic Park
(under construction)

Ba Da Ling Expressway 八达岭高速公路

7

8

35 →

Datun Lu 大屯路

34 →

颐和园路
Yiheyuan Lu

Qinghua Xi Lu
清华西路

Xueqing Lu 学清路

Qinghua Dong Lu 清华东路

Beichen Xi Lu 北辰西路

33 →

9

Qinghua University
清华大学

WU DAO KOU
M 1304
Chengfu Lu
成府路

32 →

Xueyuan Lu 学院路

Huayuan Dong Lu 花园东路

31 →

10

万泉河路 Wanquan He-lu

11

Bei Si Huan Xi Lu
北四环西路

Bei Si Huan Zhong Lu
北四环中路

Bei Chen Lu 北辰路

12

Zhongguan Cun Dajie 中关村大街

知春路
Zhichun Lu

ZHICHUN LU
M 1303

28

蓝靛厂北路 Landianchang Bei-lu

联想桥
Lianxiang Qiao
26

北三环西路
Bei San Huan
Xi Lu

北三环中路
Bei San Huan
Zhong Lu

马甸桥
Madian
Qiao

30

13

DA ZHONG SI
1302

27

29

黄寺大街
Huangsi
Dajie

Gulou Wai Dajie 鼓楼外大街

14

HAIDIAN
海淀

大柳树路 Da Liushu Lu

学院南路
Xueyuan Nan Lu

Xi Zhi Men Bei Dajie 西直门北大街

学院南路
Xueyuan Nan Lu

新街口外大街 Xinjiekouwai Dajie

德胜门外大街 Desheng Men Wai Dajie

Ande Lu 安德路

15

白石桥路 Baishiqiao-lu

高粱桥路 Gaoliang Qiao-lu

四道口路 Sidaokou Lu

文慧园路 Wenhuiyuan Lu

JISHUITAN
218

GULOU DAJIE
217

16

17

Zizhuyuan Lu 紫竹院路

Beijing North Railway Station
北京北站

德胜门东大街 Desheng Men Dong Dajie

Drum & Bell
Towers

紫竹院公园
Zizhuyuan
Park

ZHI CHUN
M 1301

Desheng
Men

Gulou
Dong Dajie

19

北京动物园
Beijing Zoo

XI ZHI MEN
201

西直门内大街
Xi Zhi Men
Nei Dajie

新街口南大街 Xinjiekou Nan Dajie

Hou Hai
后海

18

西直门外大街
Xi-Zhi Men Wai Dajie

西直门
Xi Zhi
Men

西直门内大街
Xizhimen
Nei Dajie

Qian
Hai
前海

地安门东大街 Di'an Men Dong Dajie

车公庄西路
Chegongzhuang Xi-Lu

XI ZHI MEN
西直门

平安大道
Ping 'an
Dadao

西四
XI SI

20

车公庄大街
Chegongzhuang Dajie

CHEGONGZHUANG
202

平安大道
Ping 'an
Dadao

Bei Hai
北海

Jing Shan
Park

21

阜成门
Fucheng
Men

阜成门内大街 Fucheng Men Nei Dajie

西单北大街 Xidan Bei Dajie

北海公园
Bei Hai
Park

Forbidden
City

24

25

展览馆路 Zhanlanguan Lu

阜成门
Fucheng Men

阜成门外大街
Fucheng Men
Wai Dajie

西单北大街 Xidan

府右街 Fu You Jie

中南海
Zhong
Nan Hai

Third Ring Road
(San Huan Lu)

阜成路
Fucheng Lu

FUCHENG MEN
203

月坛南街
Yuetan Nan Jie

XI CHENG
西城

西单
XI DAN
西单

Tian'an Men Xi
116

TIAN'AN
MEN XI
116

Yuyuan Tan Park
玉渊潭公园
Yuyuan
Tan

三里河路 San Li He-lu

XI DAN
115

22

109

复兴路
Fuxing Lu

MUXIDI
112

NAN
LISHI LU
113

FUXING MEN
114/204

Xi Chang'an
Xi Chang'an-jie

复兴门外大街
Fuxing Men
Wai Dajie

Tian'an Men
Square

GONGZHUFEN
110

JUNSHI
BOWUGUAN
111

复兴门内大街 Fuxing Men Nei Dajie

Key for Běijīng West & Hǎidiàn

ACCOMMODATIONS ■

Běijīng Marriott West
(Běijīng Jīnyù Wànháo Jiǔdiàn) **21**
北京金域万豪酒店

Crowne Plaza Park View Wǔzhōu
(Wu[av]zhōu Huángguān Jiǎrì Jiǔdiàn) **31**
五洲皇冠假日酒店

International Exchange Center
(Wàijiāo Xuéyuàn Guójì Jiāoliú
Zhōngxīn) **25**
外交学院国际交流中心

Shangri-La Běijīng Hotel
(Xiānggélǐlā Fàndiàn) **16**
香格里拉饭店

DINING ◆

Bǎihé Sùshí
(Lily Vegetarian Restaurant) **28**
百合素食

Dōngběi Hǔ **32**
东北虎

JiǔhuáShān **20**
九华山烤鸭店

Ko[av]ng Yǐjǐ Jiǔlóu **35**
孔乙己酒楼

Shànghǎi Lǎo Fàndiàn **23**
上海老饭店

Sculpting in Time
(Diāokè Shíguāng) **2, 12, 14**
雕刻时光

Xiàngyáng Tún **9**
向阳屯

Xīběi Yóumiàn Cūn **33**
西贝莜面村

Xīyù Shífǔ **34**
西域食府

Yúnnán Jīn Kǒngquè Déhóng Dǎiwèi
Cānguǎn **15**
云南金孔雀德宏傣味餐馆

Zhāng Shēng Jì Jiǔdiàn **30**
张生记酒店

Zuǒ Yòu Jiān (Mima Cafe) **8**
左右间

ATTRACTIONS AND SHOPPING ●

Altar to the Century
(Zhōnghuá Shìjì Tán) **22**
中华世纪坛

Bàoguó Sì Wénhuà Gōngyìpǐn Shìchǎng
报国寺文化工艺品市场

Běijīng Dàxué (Peking University) **9**
北京大学

Běijīng Shèyǐng Qìcái Chéng **5**
北京摄影器材城

Dà Zhōng Sì (Great Bell Temple) **26**
大钟寺

Fǎhǎi Sì **3**
法海寺

Jīn Wǔxīng Bǎihuò Pīfā Chéng **27**
金五星百货批发城

Lìmǎ Guāndì Miào **13**
立马关帝庙

Sānfū Hùwài Yòngpǐn (Sanfo Outdoors)
三夫户外用品

Summer Palace (Yíhé Yuán) **6**
颐和园

Tián Yì Mù **4**
田义墓

Tiānyì Xiǎoshāngpǐn Pīfā Shìchǎng **24**
天意小商品批发市场

Wànshòu Sì **17**
万寿寺

Wǔ Tǎ Sì (Five Pagoda Temple) **19**
五塔寺

Xiāng Shān Gōngyuán
(Fragrant Hills Park) **1**
香山公园

Yuán Míng Yuán (Old Summer Palace) **7**
圆明园

Zhōngguān Cūn **11**
中关村

Zǐzhúyuàn Gōngyuán **18**
紫竹院公园

Cháoyáng

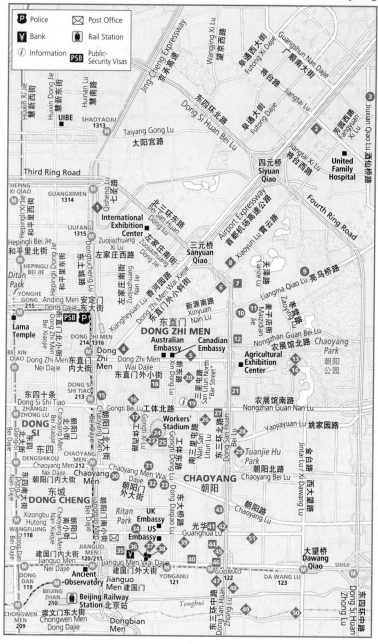

Key for Cháoyáng

Tiān'ān Mén Square

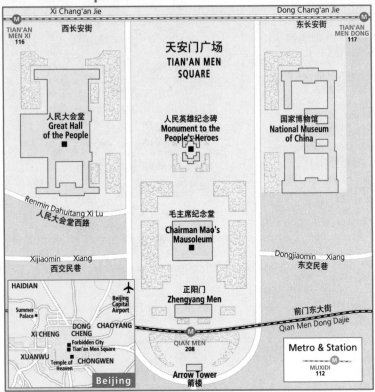

Tiān'ān Mén Square

Xi Chang'an Jie — 西长安街 — Dong Chang'an Jie — 东长安街

TIAN'AN MEN XI 116

TIAN'AN MEN DONG 117

天安门广场
TIAN'AN MEN SQUARE

人民大会堂
Great Hall of the People

人民英雄纪念碑
Monument to the People's Heroes

国家博物馆
National Museum of China

Renmin Dahuitang Xi Lu
人民大会堂西路

毛主席纪念堂
Chairman Mao's Mausoleum

Xijiaomin Xiang
西交民巷

Dongjiaomin Xiang
东交民巷

正阳门
Zhengyang Men

前门东大街
Qian Men Dong Dajie

QIAN MEN 208

Metro & Station

MUXIDI 112

Arrow Tower
箭楼

HAIDIAN

Beijing Capital Airport

Summer Palace

DONG CHAOYANG

XI CHENG CHENG

Forbidden City
Tian'an Men Square

XUANWU

CHONGWEN

Temple of Heaven

Beijing

Forbidden City in the north, the Great Hall of the People in the west, and the museums of Chinese History and Chinese Revolution in the east. In the center of the
square stands the Monument to the People's Heroes (Rénmín Yīngxióng Jìniàn Bēi),
a 37m (124-ft.) granite obelisk erected in 1958, engraved with scenes from famous
uprisings and bearing a central inscription (in Máo's handwriting): THE PEOPLE'S
HEROES ARE IMMORTAL. The twin-tiered dais is said to be an intentional contrast to the
imperial preference for three-tiered platforms; the *yīn* of the people's martyrs con-
trasted with the *yáng* of the emperors (see the "Lucky Numbers" box on p. 125).

The area on which the square stands was originally occupied by the **Imperial
Way**—a central road that stretched from inside the Forbidden City, through Tiān'ān
Mén, and south to Dà Qīng Mén (known as Zhōnghuá Mén during the Nationalist
era), which was demolished to make way for Máo's corpse in 1976 (see the review for
Chairman Máo's Mausoleum, below). This road, lined on either side with imperial
government ministries, was the site of the pivotal May Fourth movement (1919), in
which thousands of university students gathered to protest the weakness and corruption of China's then-Republican government. Máo ordered destruction of the old
ministries. The vast but largely empty **Great Hall of the People** rose from the rubble
to the west, and equally vast but unimpressive **museums** were erected to the east, as

part of a spate of construction to celebrate 10 years of Communist rule. But the site has remained a magnet for politically charged assemblies; the most famous was the gathering of **student protestors** in late spring of 1989. That movement, and the government's violent suppression of it, still defines Tiān'ān Mén Square in most minds. You'll search in vain for bullet holes and bloodstains. The killing took place elsewhere. Brutal scenes were witnessed near Fùxīng Mén and Xī Dān (west of the square), as workers and students were shot in the back as the regime showed its true colors, bringing a halt to a decade of intermittent political reform. Today, stiff-backed soldiers, video cameras, and plain-clothed police still keep a close watch on the square.

Other than flying a kite and playing "spot the plain-clothed policeman," there isn't much to do in the square, but early risers can line up in front of Tiān'ān Mén at dawn to watch the **flag-raising ceremony,** a unique suffocation-in-the-throng experience on National Day (Oct 1), when what seems like the entire Chinese population arrives to jostle for the best view.

Chairman Máo's Mausoleum (Máo Zhǔxí Jìniàn Guǎn)   This is one of the eeriest experiences in Běijīng. The decision to preserve Máo's body was made hours after his death in 1976. Panicked and inexperienced, his doctors reportedly pumped him so full of formaldehyde his face and body swelled almost beyond recognition. They drained the corpse and managed to get it back into acceptable shape, but they also created a wax model of the Great Helmsman just in case. There's no telling which version—the real or the waxen—is on display at any given time. The mausoleum itself was built in 1977, near the center of Tiān'ān Mén Square. However much Máo may be mocked outside his tomb (earnest arguments about whether he was 70% right or 60% right are perhaps the biggest joke), he still commands a terrifying sort of respect inside it. Not quite the kitsch experience some expect. The tour is free and fast, with no stopping, photos, or bags allowed inside.

South of Tiān'ān Mén Sq.; see map p. 118. Free admission. Mon–Sat 8–11:30am; sometimes also 2–4pm (usually Tues and Thurs). Bag storage in building across the street, directly west: ¥10 ($1) per piece. Metro: Qián Mén (208).

⁀*Fun Fact*   **National Theatrics**
_____

At a crowded restaurant, a group of Běijīng's Olympic planners gather for a lavish meal. "Bring me your finest, most expensive dish, and hang the cost!" bellows one, setting his manbag aside. The flamboyant meal eventually arrives, overshadowing the surrounding dishes. The diners are stunned into silence. The complaints begin, "How much did we pay for that?" "It's un-Chinese." "Can we get a discount?" "Who ordered this?" The official who ordered the dish is either keeping his silence, or has slipped away quietly. In essence, such has been the drama played out over Paul Andreu's controversial **National Theatre,** due to open west of the **Great Hall of the People** within the lifetime of this book. Andreu was awarded the project in 2000, and Beijingers have nicknamed it *jīdànké'r* (The Eggshell). Although the project has been downsized, it still features a dazzling titanium-and-glass dome perched on a lake and encasing three auditoriums. Patrons descend on escalators through the waters of the lake.

Qián Mén (Front Gate)   The phrase Qián Mén is actually a reference to two separate towers on the south side of the square which together formed the main entrance to the Tartar (or Inner) City. The southernmost Arrow Tower (Jiàn Lóu) is no longer open to the public. You can, however, still climb up inside the rear building, called the Zhèngyáng Mén, where an enjoyable photo exhibition depicts life in Běijīng's pre-1949 markets, temples, and *hútòng*.

South end of Tiān'ān Mén Sq.; see map p. 118. Admission ¥10 ($1.25). 8:30am–4pm. Metro: Qián Mén (208).

2 Forbidden City (Gù Gōng)

The universally accepted symbol for the length and grandeur of Chinese civilization is undoubtedly the Great Wall, but the Forbidden City is more immediately impressive. A 720,000-sq.-m (7,750,008-sq.-ft.) complex of red-walled buildings and pavilions topped by a sea of glazed vermilion tile, it dwarfs nearby Tiān'ān Mén Square and is by far the largest and most intricate imperial palace in China. The palace receives more visitors than any other attraction in the country (over seven million a year, the government says), and has been praised in Western travel literature ever since the first Europeans laid eyes on it in the late 1500s. Yet despite the flood of superlatives and exaggerated statistics that inevitably go into its description, it is impervious to an excess of hype, and it is large and compelling enough to draw repeat visits from even the most jaded travelers. Make more time for it than you think you'll need.

The palace, most commonly referred to in Chinese as Gù Gōng (Former Palace), is on the north side of Tiān'ān Mén Square across Cháng'ān Dàjiē (© **010/6513-2255; www.dpm.org.cn**). It is best approached on foot or via metro (Tiān'ān Mén Dōng, 117), as taxis are not allowed to stop in front. The palace is open daily from 8:30am to 5:30pm during summer and from 8:30am to 4:30pm in winter. Regular admission *(mén piào)* in summer costs ¥60 ($8), dropping to ¥40 ($5) in winter; last tickets are sold an hour before the doors close. Various exhibition halls and gardens inside the palace charge additional fees. All-inclusive tickets *(lián piào)* had been discontinued at press time, perhaps in an effort to increase revenues (see the box "The Big Makeover" below), but it's always possible these will be reinstated. *Tip:* If you have a little more time, it is highly recommended that you approach the entrance at **Wǔ Mén (Meridian Gate)** via **Tài Miào** (p. 134) to the east, and avoid the gauntlet of tiresome touts and tacky souvenir stalls.

Ticket counters are marked on either side as you approach. **Audio tours** in several languages (¥40/$5 plus ¥500/$63 deposit; the English version is narrated by Roger Moore) are available at the gate itself, through the door to the right. Those looking to spend more money can hire **"English"-speaking tour guides** on the other side of the gate (¥200–¥350/$25–$44 per person, depending on tour length). The tour guide booth also rents **wheelchairs** and **strollers** at reasonable rates. *Note:* Only the central route through the palace is wheelchair-accessible, and steeply so.

BACKGROUND & LAYOUT

Sourcing of materials for the original palace buildings began in 1406, during the reign of the Yǒnglè emperor, and construction was completed in 1420. Much of it was

Map of the Forbidden City
For a map of the palace, see the inside back cover of this book.

My, what an inefficient way to fish.

Ring toss, good. Horseshoes, bad.

Faster! Faster! Faster!

We take care of the fiddly bits, from providing over 43,000 customer reviews of hotels, to helping you find our best fares, to giving you 24/7 customer service. So you can focus on the only thing that matters. Goofing off.

travelocity
You'll never roam alone.℠

The Big Makeover

An immense **$75-million renovation of the Forbidden City,** the largest in 90 years, will be completed in two phases (the first by 2008, the second by 2020). Work started on halls and gardens in the closed western sections of the palace in 2002, with the most effort concentrated on opening the **Wǔyīng Diàn** (Hall of Valiance and Heroism) in the southwest corner of the palace, the **Jiànfú Gōng Huāyuán** (Garden of the Palace of Building Happiness) in the northwest, followed by **Cíníng Huāyuán** (Garden of Love and Tranquillity) next to the Tàihé Diàn. Wǔyīng Diàn, formerly the site of the Imperial printing press, should be open when you arrive, displaying a collection of Buddhist sutras, palace records, and calligraphy, as will Jiànfú Gōng Huāyuán, an ambitious restoration as the entire section was devastated by fire in 1923. Cíníng Huāyuán is said to be opening in 2008. Plans also call for the construction of new temperature-controlled buildings to house and exhibit what is claimed to be a collection of **930,000 Míng and Qīng imperial relics,** most now stored underground.

On the other side of the palace, within the northern section of the Níngshòu Gōng Huāyuán, a remarkable building is undergoing restoration with assistance from the World Cultural Heritage Foundation. Qiánlóng commissioned the European Jesuit painters in his employ to create large-scale *trompe l'oeil* paintings, which were used both in the Forbidden City as well as in the Yuán Míng Yuán (p. 137). **Juànqín Zhāi,** an elaborately constructed private opera house, houses the best remaining examples of these paintings, including a stunning image of a wisteria trellis, almost certainly painted by Italian master Castiglione. It is due to open in 2006.

designed by a eunuch from Annam (now Vietnam), Nguyen An, but without improvements to the Grand Canal, construction would have been impossible—timber came from as far away as Sìchuān, and logs took up to 4 years to reach the capital. The Yuán palace was demolished to make way for the Forbidden City, but the lakes created during the Jīn (1122–1215) were retained and expanded. Between 1420 and 1923, the palace was home to 24 emperors of the Míng and Qīng dynasties. The last of these was Aisin-Gioro Pǔyí, who was forced to abdicate in 1912 but remained in the palace until 1924.

The Forbidden City is arranged along a north-south meridian, aligned on the Pole Star. The Qīng court was unimpressed when the barbarians designated Greenwich Royal Observatory as the source of the prime meridian in 1885; they believed the Imperial Way marked the center of the temporal world. Major halls open to the south. Furthest south and in the center is the symmetrical **outer court,** dominated by immense ceremonial halls where the emperor conducted official business. Beyond the outer court and surrounding it on both sides is the **inner court,** a series of smaller buildings and gardens that served as living quarters. During the Míng, only eunuchs were allowed to pass between the two courts, enhancing their power.

The palace has been ransacked and parts destroyed by fire several times over the centuries, so most of the existing buildings date from the Qīng rather than the Míng.

The original complex was said to contain 9,999 rooms, testament to the Chinese love of the number nine (see the box "Lucky Numbers," p. 125), and also to an unusual counting method. The square space between columns is counted as a room *(jiān)*, so the largest building, **Tàihé Diàn,** counts as 55 rooms. Using the Western method of counting, there are now 980 rooms. Only half of the complex is open to visitors (expected to increase to 70% after repairs are completed in 2020; see the box, "The Big Makeover," above), but this still leaves plenty to see.

THE ENTRANCE GATES

Tiān'ān Mén (Gate of Heavenly Peace) ★★

This gate is the largest in what was once known as the Imperial City and the most emblematic of Chinese government grandeur. Above the central door, once reserved for the emperor, now hangs the famous **portrait of Máo,** flanked by inscriptions that read: LONG LIVE THE PEOPLE'S REPUBLIC OF CHINA (left) and LONG LIVE THE GREAT UNITY OF THE PEOPLES OF THE WORLD (right). Máo declared the founding of the People's Republic from atop the gate on October 1, 1949. There is no charge to walk through, but tickets are required if you want to ascend to the **upper platform** for worthwhile views of Tiān'ān Mén Square. Pretend to be the Great Helmsman addressing a sea of Red Guards, all struggling to understand your thick Húnán accent and waving your little red book. Note the pair of *huábiǎo* (ornamental columns) topped with lions, wreathed in dragons and clouds, and facing the square. In their original form, *huábiǎo* were wooden posts in the shapes of a battle-axes, upon which subjects would attach petitions or scrawl their grievances to the king. Over time, their function was reversed. Turned to stone and wreathed in the ultimate symbol of the emperor's mandate—the dragon—they became a warning to the ruled to keep out.

North of Tiān'ān Mén Sq.; ticket office to left as you enter. Admission ¥20 ($3) in summer, ¥15 ($2) in winter. 8am–4:30pm in summer; 8:30am–4pm in winter. Mandatory bag storage (¥2–¥6/30¢–75¢) behind and to left of ticket booth; cameras allowed.

Wǔ Mén (Meridian Gate)

The trees leading up to this gate are recent additions. Originally no trees were planted along the Imperial Way, stretching over 2km (1¼ miles) from **Dà Qīng Mén** (now demolished) to **Qiánqīng Mén (Gate of Heavenly Purity)** in the Inner Court, as according to the "five processes" *(wǔ xíng),* wood (green) subdues earth (yellow), the element associated with the emperor (hence the yellow glazed tiles). The **Outer Court** is also free of trees. Built in 1420 and last restored in 1801, Wǔ Mén is the actual entrance to the Forbidden City. The emperor would sit atop the gate to receive prisoners of war, flanked by a battalion of imperial guards clad in full battle armor. The prisoners, clad in chains and red cloth, kneeled in the courtyard while charges were read before the emperor confirmed they would be taken to the marketplace for execution. The order would be repeated first by two, then four, then eight officers, until the entire battalion was thundering the edict in unison. The watchtowers extending out either side of the gate *(què)* are an expression of imperial power. This style was prevalent during the Hàn dynasty (206 B.C.–A.D. 220); this is the only example from the Míng and Qīng.

Tàihé Mén (Gate of Great Harmony)

Immediately inside the Meridian Gate entrance is a wide courtyard with five marble bridges spanning the Jīn Hé (Golden River), followed by Tàihé Mén. Míng emperors came here to consult with their ministers; this function moved further inside under the Qīng.

THE OUTER COURT (QIÁN CHÁO)

Tàihé Diàn (Hall of Great Harmony) 🏛🏛 Located beyond Tàihé Mén, and across an even grander stone courtyard, is an imposing double-roofed structure mounted atop a three-tiered marble terrace with elaborately carved balustrades. This is the largest wooden hall in China, and the most elaborate and prestigious of the palaces' throne halls; it was therefore rarely used. Emperors came here to mark the New Year and winter solstice. Note the row of ceramic figurines on the roof, led by a man on a chicken (a despotic prince) fleeing a terrible dragon that heads a group of nine animal figures. The number of figures reflects the importance of the building.

Zhōnghé Diàn (Hall of Middle Harmony) The second great hall of the outer court houses a smaller imperial throne. The emperor would prepare for annual rites, such as sowing the fields at the Altar of Agriculture (Xiān Nóng Tán; see Gǔdài Jiànzhù Bówùguǎn, p. 138) in spring, by examining the appropriate manuals here.

Bǎohé Diàn (Hall of Preserving Harmony) This last hall, supported by only a few columns, is where the highest level of imperial examinations was held until the exams were suspended in 1901 and abolished in 1905. To the southwest, you can spy **Wényuān Gé** (the former Imperial Archive), easily recognized by its black-tiled roof with green trim. (Black is associated with water which, it was hoped, would protect the building from fire.) At the rear is an impressive carved marble slab weighing about 180 tons; during the reign of the Wànlì emperor (1573—1620) 20,000 men spent 28 days dragging it to this position from Fángshān, roughly 50km (31 miles) to the southwest.

THE INNER COURT (NÈI TÍNG)

During the Míng, only the emperor, his family, his concubines, and the palace eunuchs (who numbered 1,500 at the end of the Qīng dynasty) were allowed in this section. It begins with the **Qiánqīng Mén (Gate of Heavenly Purity)**, directly north of the Bǎohé Diàn, fronted by a magnificent pair of **bronze lions** 🏛 and flanked by a **Bā Zì Yǐngbì** (a screen wall in the shape of the character for "eight"), both warning non-royals not to stray inside. Beyond are three palaces designed to mirror the three halls of the Outer Court.

The first of these is the **Qiánqīng Gōng (Palace of Heavenly Purity)**, where the emperors lived until Yǒngzhèng decided to move to the western side of the palace in the 1720s. Beyond is **Jiāotài Diàn (Hall of Union)**, containing the throne of the empress and 25 boxes that once contained the Qīng imperial seals. A considerable expansion on eight seals used during the Qín dynasty, the number 25 was chosen because it is the sum of all single-digit odd numbers (see the box "Lucky Numbers," p. 125). Next is the more interesting **Kūnníng Gōng (Palace of Earthly Tranquility)**, a Manchu-style bedchamber where a nervous Pǔyí was expected to spend his wedding night before he fled to more comfortable rooms elsewhere.

At the rear of the inner court is the elaborate **Yù Huāyuán (Imperial Garden)** 🏛, a marvelous scattering of ancient conifers, rockeries, and pavilions, largely unchanged since it was built in the Míng dynasty. The crags allowed court ladies, who spent their lives inside the Inner Court, a glimpse of the world outside. Pǔyí's British tutor, Reginald Fleming Johnston, lived in the **Yǎngxīn Zhāi,** the first building on the west side of the garden (now a tea shop).

From behind the mountain, you can exit the palace through the **Shénwǔ Mén (Gate of Martial Spirit)** and continue on to Jǐng Shān and/or Běi Hǎi Park. Those with time to spare, however, should take the opportunity to explore less-visited sections on either side of the central path.

WESTERN AXIS

Most of this area is in a state of heavy disrepair, but a few buildings have been restored and are open to visitors. Most notable among these is the **Yǎngxīn Diàn (Hall of Mental Cultivation)**, southwest of the Imperial Garden. The reviled Empress Dowager Cíxǐ, who ruled China for much of the late Qīng period, made decisions on behalf of her infant nephew, the Guāngxù emperor, from behind a screen in the east room. This is also where emperors lived after Yōngzhèng moved out of the Qiánqīng Gōng.

EASTERN AXIS

This side tends to be peaceful and quiet even when other sections are teeming. Entrance costs ¥10 ($1.25) and requires purchase of useless over-shoe slippers which quickly disintegrate (¥2/30¢). The most convenient ticket booth is 5 minutes' walk southwest of the Qiánqīng Mén, opposite **Jiǔlóng Bì (Nine Dragon Screen)**, a 3.5m-high (11½-ft.) wall covered in striking glazed-tile dragons depicted frolicking above a frothing sea, built to protect the Qiánlóng emperor from prying eyes and malevolent spirits (that are only able to move in straight lines). The Qiánlóng emperor (reign 1736–1795) abdicated at the age of 85, and this section was built for his retirement, although he never really moved in, continuing to "mentor" his son while living in the Yǎngxīn Diàn, a practice later adopted by Empress Dowager Cíxǐ, who also partially took up residence here in 1894.

Zhēnbǎo Guǎn (Hall of Jewelry) ✿, just north of the ticket booth, has all 25 of the Qīng imperial seals, ornate swords, and bejeweled minipagodas—evidence that the Qīng emperors were devoted to Tibetan Buddhism. One of the highlights is the secluded **Níngshòu Gōng Huāyuán** ✿✿✿, where the Qiánlóng emperor was meant to spend his retirement. Water was directed along a snakelike trough carved in the floor of the main pavilion. A cup of wine would be floated down the miniature stream, and the person nearest wherever it stopped would have to compose a poem, or drink the wine. The Qiánlóng emperor, whose personal compendium of verse ran to a modest 50,000 poems, was seldom short of words.

East of the garden is the **Chàngyīn Gé**, sometimes called Cíxǐ's Theater, an elaborate green-tiled three-tiered structure with trap doors and hidden passageways to allow movement between stages. Further north is sumptuous **Lèshòu Táng** ✿✿, built entirely from sandalwood, where the Qiánlóng emperor would read, surrounded by poems and paintings composed by loyal ministers set into the walls and framed by blue cloisonné tablets. Cíxǐ slept in the room to the west. The following hall, **Yíhé Xuān,** is not a good place to bring friends from Mongolia or Xīnjiāng. The west wall has an essay justifying the Qiánlóng emperor's decision to colonize the latter, while the east wall has a poem celebrating the invasion of Mongolia. In the far northeastern corner is **Zhēn Fēi Jǐng (Well of the Pearl Concubine),** a surprisingly narrow hole covered by a large circle of stone. The Pearl Concubine, one of the Guāngxù emperor's favorites, was 25 when Cíxǐ had her stuffed down the well by a eunuch as they were fleeing in the aftermath of the Boxer Rebellion. According to most accounts, Cíxǐ was miffed at the girl's insistence that Guāngxù stay and take responsibility for the imperial family's support of the Boxers.

> **Fun Fact Lucky Numbers**
>
> The layout of imperial Běijīng is based on an ancient system of numerology that still resonates today. Odd numbers are seen as *yáng* (male, positive, light) and are more auspicious than even numbers, which are viewed as *yīn* (female, negative, dark). **Three** is a positive number, as seen in the three-tiered platforms that are reserved for Běijīng's most sacred structures—Tàihé Diàn in the Forbidden City; Tài Miào, the Hall of Prayer for Good Harvests at Tiān Tán; and Cháng Líng at the Míng Tombs. It's also the number chosen for China's latest political theory, the Three Represents, which explains how a Communist party can be staffed by capitalists. **Four** *(sì)*, as a *yīn* number, signifies submission. When the emperor carried out sacrifices at the Temple of Heaven, he would face north and bow four times. It's also faintly homophonous with death *(sǐ)*, and is the most inauspicious number. Many Chinese apartments lack a fourth floor. **Five** is revered as the center of the Luò Diagram (which allows single-digit numbers arranged in noughts-and-crosses formation to add up to 15), and for signifying the "five processes" *(wǔ xíng)*—metal, wood, water, fire, and earth, which also correspond to the five points of the Chinese compass and to the five colors. Significant imperial buildings are five rooms *(jiān)* deep; five openings welcome you into Tiān'ān Mén; and until Zhōnghuá Mén was razed to make way for Máo's corpse, the Imperial Way had five gates. **Eight** has gained popularity because it is homophonous with "get rich" in Cantonese: The Olympic Games are scheduled to open on August 8, 2008. **Nine,** situated at the top of the Luò Diagram and the largest single-digit odd number, was reserved for the imperial house, with grand buildings measuring nine rooms across.

Also worth seeing is the **Hall of Clocks (Zhōngbiǎo Guǎn),** a collection of timepieces, many of them gifts to the emperors from European envoys. Entrance to the exhibit costs ¥10 ($1.25).

3 Temple of Heaven (Tiān Tán Gōngyuán)

At the same time that the Yónglè emperor built the Forbidden City, he also oversaw construction of this enormous park and altar to Heaven directly to the south. Each winter solstice, the Míng and Qīng emperors would lead a procession here to perform rites and make sacrifices designed to promote the next year's crops and curry favor with Heaven for the general health of the empire. It was last used for this purpose by the president of the Republic, Yuán Shìkǎi, on the winter solstice of December 23, 1914, updated with photographers, electric lights (the height of modernity at the time), and a bulletproof car for the entrance of the increasingly unpopular president. This effectively announced his intent to promote himself as the new emperor, but few onlookers shared his enthusiasm. Formerly known as the Temple of Heaven and Earth, the park is square (symbolizing Earth) in the south and rounded (symbolizing

Heaven) in the north. ***Note:*** Qǐnián Diàn, the main reason for visiting, is closed until October 2006.

ESSENTIALS

Temple of Heaven Park (Tiān Tán Gōngyuán; ℂ **010/6702-8866**) is south of Tiān'ān Mén Square, on the east side of Qián Mén Dàjiē. It's open daily from 6am to 9pm (6am–8pm in winter), but the ticket offices and major sights are only open from 8:30am to 4:30pm. All-inclusive tickets *(lián piào)* cost ¥35 ($4.50) (¥30/$4 in winter); simple park admission costs ¥15 ($2). The east gate *(dōng mén)* is easily accessed by public transport; take the no. 807 or no. 812 bus from just north of the Chóng-wén Mén metro stop (209, exit B) to Fǎhuá Sì. However, the best approach is from the south gate *(nán mén),* the natural starting point for a walk that culminates in the magnificent Hall of Prayer for Good Harvests.

SEEING THE HIGHLIGHTS

During the Cultural Revolution, Tiān Tán lost its perfect symmetry as large bites were taken out of the southwest and southeast corners. There's no sign that the land will be returned, with massive apartment blocks ready to sprout on both corners, but it's still a vast park taking at least 2 hours to see in any depth. The west gate is convenient to the Altar of Agriculture (see Gǔdài Jiànzhù Bówùguǎn, p. 138) and Wànshèng Jùchǎng (see section 1, "Performing Arts," in chapter 10). At the northeast corner lie the shopping delights of Yuánlóng Silk Co. Ltd. (p. 179) and Hóng Qiáo Shìchǎng (see section 2, "Markets & Bazaars" in chapter 9).

Circular Altar (Yuán Qiū)   This three-tiered marble terrace is the first major structure you'll see if you enter from the south gate *(nán mén).* It was built in 1530 and enlarged in 1749, with all of its stones and balustrades organized in multiples of nine (see the box "Lucky Numbers," p. 125). Here, a slaughtered bull would be set ablaze, the culmination of an elaborate ceremonial entreaty to the gods.

Imperial Vault of Heaven (Huáng Qióng Yǔ)   Directly north of the Circular Altar, this smaller version of the Hall of Prayer (see below) was built to store ceremonial stone tablets. The vault is surrounded by the circular **Echo Wall (Huíyīn Bì).** In years past, when crowds were smaller and before the railing was installed, it was possible for two people on opposite sides of the enclosure to send whispered messages to each other along the wall with remarkable clarity. You can still experience this magical acoustic effect at the Western Qīng Tombs (see section 4 in chapter 11), but there's little hope of enjoying it here.

Hall of Prayer for Good Harvests (Qǐnián Diàn) ✸✸   Undoubtedly the most stunning building in Běijīng, this circular wooden hall, with its triple-eaved cylindrical blue-tiled roof, is perhaps the most recognizable emblem of Chinese imperial architecture outside of the Forbidden City. Completed in 1420, the original hall was struck by lightning and burned to the ground in 1889 (not a good omen for the dynasty), but a near-perfect replica was built the following year. Measuring 38m (125 ft.) high and 30m (98 ft.) in diameter, it was constructed without a single nail. The 28 massive pillars inside, made of fir imported from Oregon (China lacked timber of sufficient length), are arranged to symbolize divisions of time: The central four represent the seasons, the next 12 represent the months of the year, and the outer 12 represent traditional divisions of a single day. The hall's most striking feature is its ceiling, a kaleidoscope of painted brackets and gilded panels as intricate as anything in the

Bei Tian Men
北天门

Imperial Hall
of Heaven

神厨
Shen Chu

Chang Lang
长廊

Dong Men
东门

Hall of Prayer for
Good Harvests
(Qinian Dian)
祈年殿

百花园
Bai Hua Yuan

Rose
Garden
月季园

西天门
Xi Tian Men

东天门
Dong Tian Men

Bell Tower
钟楼

丹陛桥
Danbi
Qiao

Hall of
Abstinence
斋宫

皇穹宇
Imperial Vault
of Heaven

Echo Wall
回音壁

Triple Sound Stone
三音石

Shen Chu
神厨

圜丘
Circular Altar

HAIDIAN

Summer
Palace

Beijing
Capital
Airport

XI CHENG

DONG
CHENG

CHAOYANG

Forbidden City
Tian'an Men Square

XUANWU

CHONGWEN

Temple of
Heaven

Beijing

泰元门
Taiyuan Men

南天门
Nan Tian Men

country. Don't skip the **Imperial Hall of Heaven (Huángqián Diàn),** a smaller building to the north where the emperor would pray before the wooden tablets of his ancestors. Although Red Guards destroyed the tablets, the balustrades surrounding this prayer hall are elegantly carved.

Hall of Abstinence (Zhāi Gōng) Yuán Shìkǎi fasted for 3 days in his own residence rather than here, as tradition dictated. Perhaps this was his undoing (he died 1½ years later). Real emperors would fast and pray for 5 days, spending their final night in the **Living Hall (Qín Diàn)** at the rear of this compound. Note the rare swastika emblems, a symbol of longevity in China, on the door piers. This green-tiled double-moated compound faces east, the best side at which to enter. The grounds are agreeably dilapidated, and are on a more human scale than the rest of the compound.

4 Summer Palace (Yí Hé Yuán)

This expanse of elaborate Qīng-style pavilions, bridges, walkways, and gardens, scattered along the shores of immense Kūnmíng Lake, is the grandest imperial playground in China, constructed from 1749 to 1764. Between 1860 and 1903, it was twice leveled by foreign armies and rebuilt; hence it is often called the New Summer Palace, even though it pre-dates the ruined Old Summer Palace (Yuán Míng Yuán, p. 137). The palace is most often associated with the Empress Dowager Cíxǐ, who resided here for much of the year and even set up a photographic studio. The grounds were declared a public park in 1924 and spruced up in 1949.

ESSENTIALS

The **Summer Palace** (℘ 010/6288-1144) is located 12km (7 miles) northwest of the city center in Hǎidiàn. Take **bus no. 726** from just west of Wǔdàokǒu light rail station (1304, exit A); or take a 30- to 40-minute **taxi** ride (¥60/$8) from the center of town. A more pleasant option is to travel there by **boat** along the renovated canal system; slightly rusty "imperial yachts" leave from the Běizhǎn Hòuhú Mǎtóu (℘ 010/8836-3576), behind the Běijīng Exhibition Center just south of the Běijīng Aquarium (50-min. trip; ¥40/$5 one-way; ¥70/$9 round-trip; ¥100/$12 including entrance ticket), docking at Nán Rúyì Mén in the south of the park. The gates open daily at 6am; no tickets are sold after 6pm in summer and 4pm in winter. Admission is ¥30 ($4) for entry to the grounds or ¥50 ($6) for the all-inclusive *lián piào*, reduced to ¥20 ($2.50) and ¥40 ($5) respectively in winter (Nov–Mar). The most convenient entrance is Dōng Gōng Mén (East Gate). Go early and allow at least 4 hours for touring the major sites on your own. Overpriced **imperial-style food** in a pleasant setting is available at the Tīnglí Guǎn Restaurant, at the western end of the Long Corridor. Spots around the lake are perfect for picnics, and Kūnmíng Lake is ideal for skating in the depths of winter.

EXPLORING THE SUMMER PALACE

This park covers roughly 290 hectares (716 acres), with **Kūnmíng Lake** in the south and **Longevity Hill (Wànshòu Shān)** in the north. The lake's northern shore boasts most of the buildings and other attractions and is the most popular area for strolls, although walking around the smaller lakes (Hòu Hú) behind Longevity Hill is more pleasant. The hill itself has a number of temples as well as **Bǎoyún Gé (Precious Clouds Pavilion),** one of the few structures in the palace to escape destruction by foreign forces. There are literally dozens of pavilions and a number of bridges to be found on all sides of the lake, enough to make for a full day of exploration. Rather slow electric-powered boats may be rented; they are an appealing option on muggy summer days.

Rénshòu Diàn (Hall of Benevolence and Longevity)
Located directly across the courtyard from the east gate entrance, Rénshòu Diàn is the palace's main hall. This is where the Empress Dowager received members of the court, first from behind a screen and later, all pretenses dropped, from the Dragon Throne itself. North of the hall is Cíxǐ's private theater, now a museum that contains an old Mercedes-Benz—the first car imported into China.

Long Corridor (Cháng Láng) ⊛
Among the more memorable attractions in Běijīng, this covered wooden promenade stretches 700m (nearly half a mile) along the northern shore of Kūnmíng Lake. Each crossbeam, ceiling, and pillar is painted with

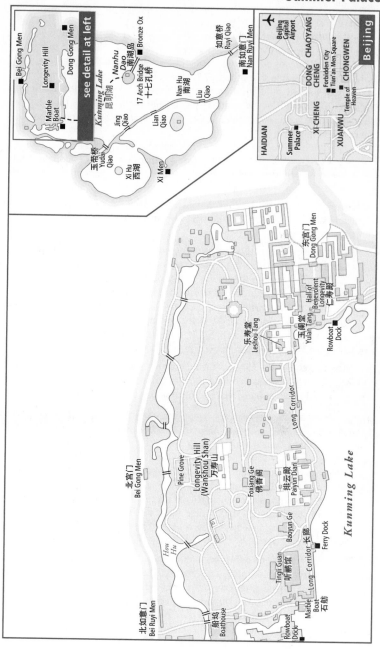

see detail at left

Bei Gong Men

Longevity Hill

Dong Gong Men 东宫门

Marble Boat

Kunming Lake 昆明湖

17 Arch Bridge 十七孔桥

Nanhu Dao 南湖岛

Bronze Ox

如意桥 Ruyi Qiao

南如意门 Nan Ruyi Men

Jing Qiao

Nan Hu 南湖

Liu Qiao

Lian Qiao

玉带桥 Yudai Qiao

Xi Hu 西湖

Xi Men

Beijing

✈ Beijing Capital Airport

CHAOYANG

DONG CHENG

Forbidden City

Tian'an Men Square

XI CHENG

CHONGWEN

Temple of Heaven

XUANWU

HAIDIAN

Summer Palace

东宫门 Dong Gong Men

Hall of Benevolent Longevity 仁寿殿

玉澜堂 Yulan Tang

乐寿堂 Leshou Tang

Rowboat Dock

Long Corridor

北宫门 Bei Gong Men

Longevity Hill (Wanshou Shan) 万寿山

Pine Grove

Foxiang Ge 佛香阁

排云殿 Paiyun Dian

Baoyun Ge

Ferry Dock

Hou Hu 后湖

Tingli Guan 听鹂馆

Long Corridor 长廊

北如意门 Bei Ruyi Men

船坞 Boathouse

Marble Boat

Long Corridor

Rowboat Dock

石舫

Kunming Lake

Impressions

"Most people hate the Old Buddha (Cíxǐ) for diverting the naval funds. How unjust! Any navy we built in those days would have been destroyed in the first battle. Which of our enemies would have helped us build a fleet capable of destroying a single ship of theirs? They would have sent our fleet to the bottom of the sea and then charged us with the costs of the action, as they always did! As it is, the Old Buddha's palace still stands—they say there is nothing equal to it in the world! Could anyone, Chinese or foreign, of our generation duplicate it?"

— Professor Ch'eng, quoted in John Blofeld,
City of Lingering Splendour, 1961

a different scene (roughly 10,000 in all) taken from Chinese history, literature, myth, or geography. Politely rebuff the "students" who offer to show you their "original art" at this spot.

Marble Boat (Shí Fǎng)   Docked at the end of the Long Corridor is an odd structure which is "neither marble nor a boat," as one novelist observed. Locals, keen to blame the Empress Dowager for China's decline during the Qīng dynasty, wring their hands and cite it as the symbol of China's demise. Cíxǐ funded a general restoration of the palace using money intended for the Chinese navy, and the (completely frivolous) boat is said to be Cíxǐ's backhanded reference to the source of the funds. Shortly after the restoration was completed in 1888, China's paltry fleet was destroyed in a skirmish with Japan, the loudest evidence yet of China's weakness in the modern era.

Seventeen-Arch Bridge (Shíqī Kǒng Qiáo) ✴   This marble bridge, 150m (490 ft.) long, connects South Lake Island (Nán Hú Dǎo) to the east shore of Kūnmíng Lake. There is a rather striking life-size bronze ox near the eastern foot of the bridge.

5 Temples, Mosques & Churches

While signs around Běijīng whip up indignation at the destruction of Chinese temples by foreign forces in 1860 and 1900, most destruction was carried out by the Chinese themselves, particularly after 1949. Medium-size houses of worship—Buddhist, Christian, Confucian, Daoist, and Muslim alike—fared badly; many were torn down straight away, while others were converted to factories, hospitals, schools, or police stations. With the realization by the Chinese authorities that tourists are willing to pay money to inspect them, some have been converted back to a semblance of their original form, if not function.

Bái Tǎ Sì (White Dagoba Temple)   Seemingly continuously under renovation, this Liáo dynasty temple features the largest Tibetan pagoda (also called *chorten, dagoba,* or *stupa*) in China, towering over the neighborhood at 51m (167 ft.) tall. A Nepali architect built it over 700 years ago (completed 1279) by order of Kublai Khan, one of the first Mongols to convert to Tibetan Buddhism. Originally known as Miào Yīng Sì, the temple has undergone numerous reconstructions, usually as a result of fire. The Dàjué Diàn (Hall of the Great Enlightened Ones), the first building, contains thousands of little Buddhas in glass cases, set into the columns. An earthquake in 1976 turned up numerous artifacts, some of which are now on display in the museum. You'll find Buddhist statuary demonstrating ritualistic hand positions *(mudra)* and vivid *thangka* (silk hangings depicting Buddhist images).

Fùchéng Mén Nèi Dàjiē 171, Xī Chéng Qū (a 10-min. walk east from the metro stop); see map p. 106. ✆ 010/6616-0211. Admission ¥20 ($2.50). 9am–4:30pm. Metro: Fùchéng Mén (203, exit B).

Báiyún Guàn 🛪🛪
If the incense here somehow smells more authentic, it's because this sprawling complex, said to have been built in 739, is the most active of Běijīng's Daoist temples. Chinese visitors seem intent on actual worship rather than smug tourism, and the blue-frocked monks wear their hair in the rarely seen traditional manner—long and tied in a bun at the top of the head. The temple acts as headquarters for the Chinese Daoist Association. Although the texts of Daoism (China's only native religion) decry the pursuit of wealth and honors as empty, the gods of wealth attract the most devotees. One notable structure is the Láolù Táng, a large cushion-filled hall in the third courtyard originally built in 1228, now used for teaching and ceremonies.

On Báiyún Guàn Lù, east of the intersection with Báiyún Lù, Hǎidiàn Qū (1st right north of Báiyún Qiáo, directly across from Báiyún Guàn bus stop); see map p. 110. ✆ 010/6346-3531. Admission ¥10 ($1.25). 8:30am–4:30pm. Bus: 727 from Mùxīdì metro (112, exit D2) to Báiyún Guàn.

Dōng Táng (East Church or St. Joseph's Cathedral)
This gray Gothic structure has endured a torrid history. Built on ground donated by the Shùnzhì emperor in 1655, this Jesuit church was toppled by an earthquake in 1720, then gutted by fire in 1812, after which it was leveled by an increasingly anti-foreign regime. It was rebuilt after foreigners forced their way into Běijīng in 1860, and was razed again during the Boxer Rebellion of 1900. Chinese Christians were the first targets of the xenophobic Boxers, who disparagingly referred to them as "lesser hairy ones." Local converts were slaughtered in the hundreds before the Boxers (who also murdered women with unbound feet) worked up the courage to kill a real foreigner. Yet they are usually portrayed as a "patriotic" movement in China's history books. After a major renovation in 2000, Dōng Táng is notable for its wide, tree-lined forecourt, a favorite spot for Běijīng's skateboarders. Its counterpart in the south of town, **Nán Táng (South Church)** is just northeast of the Xuānwǔ Mén metro stop, and has services in English. Call ✆ **010/6603-7139** to check times. *Note:* Catholic churches in Běijīng are not recognized by the Roman Catholic Church.

Wángfǔjǐng Dàjiē 74, Dōng Chéng Qū (walk north for 10 min.); see map p. 106. ✆ 010/6524-0634. Sunday services in Chinese and Latin at 6:15, 7, and 8am. Metro: Wángfǔjǐng (118, exit A).

Dōng Yuè Miào 🛪
Reopened to the public in 1999, one of Běijīng's most captivating Daoist temples stands largely disregarded. Founded in 1322 by the devotees of the Zhèngyī sect, the temple is dedicated to the god Dōng Yuè, who resides in the sacred mountain of Tài Shān. Aside from coping with the hordes of tourists who now visit his abode, Dōng Yuè is charged with supervising the 18 layers of Hell and the 76 departments *(sī).*

The garishly represented emissaries of these departments may be found in the 72 halls that ring the main courtyard of the temple. Worshipers present themselves at the relevant hall, with offerings of money, incense, and red tokens inscribed with their names *(fúpái).* With 76 departments (some are forced to share a cubicle), there are emissaries for every conceivable wish, and if viewed as a straw poll of China's preoccupations, the results are not encouraging. The Department for Accumulating Wealth ("justifiable" is added in the translation) is busy, while the Department of Pity and

Sympathy, depicting beggars, awaits its first petition, and there are an alarming number of donations for the Department for Implementing 15 Kinds of Violent Death. This may or may not be related to the ongoing popularity of the Department of Official Morality, which rails against corrupt government.

A glassed-in stele at the northeast corner of the courtyard is written in the fine hand of Zhào Mèngfǔ, recording the building of the temple and the life of its founder, Zhāng Liúsūn, who died soon after purchasing the land. At the north of the complex stands the two-story **Mínsú Bówùguǎn** (Folk Museum). This hosts exhibitions to remind Beijingers of their marvelous but largely forgotten traditions.

Cháoyáng Mén Wài Dàjiē 141, Cháoyáng Qū (10-min. walk east on the north side); see map p. 115. (C) **010/6551-0151**. Admission ¥10 ($1.25); free during festivals. Tues–Sun 8am–4:30pm. Metro: Cháoyáng Mén (212, exit B).

Fǎhǎi Sì Located in the far west of Běijīng, this early Míng temple, a must for those with an interest in Buddhist art, is easily combined with a visit to the cemetery for eunuchs, **Tián Yì Mù** (p. 142). The decoration of this temple in 1443 was funded by Lǐ Tóng, a wealthy eunuch who attracted artists from the Imperial court to produce stunning murals and statuary. The statues didn't survive the Cultural Revolution, but Red Guards failed to notice the exquisite **Buddhist murals** ✹✹ in the gloom of the main hall. These murals, miraculously preserved intact, were modeled on the art of the Táng, but show influences of Sòng dynasty landscape painting, and later Míng innovations in the use of perspective and depth in portraiture. The brushwork, particularly in the depiction of robes, clouds, and flowers, is extraordinarily fine.

Móshì Kǒu Dàjiē, Shíjǐng Shān Qū (from bus stop, continue up the rise and take a right after 5 min.; pass Tián Yì Mù, take a left turn, and continue uphill to a T-junction, take a right turn; the temple is a further 5 min. up the hill); see map p. 112. (C) **010/8871-5776**. Admission ¥20 ($2.50). 8:30am–4:30pm. Bus: 959 or 746 from left of Píngguǒ Yuán metro stop (103, exit D) to Shǒugāng Xiǎoqū.

Fǎyuán Sì (Source of Dharma Temple) *Finds* Despite guides droning on about a long and glorious history, most of Běijīng's sights are relatively new, dating from within the last 600 years. This temple, constructed in 645 in what was then the southeast corner of town, retains both an air of antiquity and the feel of a genuine Buddhist monastery. Orange-robed monks, housed in the adjacent Buddhist college, go about their business in earnest, and the visitors are asked to "respect religious ceremonies: do not interfere with religious activities." The ancient *hútòng* immediately surrounding the temple are "protected" and worth a wander. Lànmàn Hútòng, just to the east, was formerly a moat that marked the boundary of the old town during the Táng dynasty.

Fǎyuán Sì Qián Jiē 7, Xuānwǔ Qū; see map p. 110. Admission ¥5 (60¢). Thurs–Tues 8:30–11am and 1:30–4pm. Metro: Xuānwǔ Mén (206, exit D1).

Guó Zǐ Jiàn and Kǒng Miào ✹ Buried down a tree-shaded street west of the Lama Temple (see below), **Kǒng Miào**, China's second largest Confucian temple, is on the right, and **Guó Zǐ Jiàn (Directorate of Education)** is on the left; both were originally built in 1306. Two stelae at the front *(xià mǎ bēi)* instruct you to park your horse in six different languages. The front courtyard of the temple contains 198 stelae inscribed with the names of successful candidates in the *jìnshì* (highest level) imperial examinations during the Yuán, Míng, and Qīng dynasties. Staff admit they see few local visitors, except during the weekend before the university entrance examinations, when students and their parents descend in droves to ask for the Great Sage's assistance. The main hall, **Dàchéng Diàn,** is the focus for students, who must throw their incense on the shrine rather than burn it, because of fire regulations. Ancient musical instruments, which Confucius saw as essential to self-cultivation, are the main point of interest. Behind the hall and to the left are 189 stelae, which contain the 630,000 characters that make up the Thirteen Confucian Classics—incredibly, copied by one man over a 12-year period. The attendant enhances the mood of antiquity by earnestly reciting old texts.

Success in the imperial examination was the key to social advancement, so **Guó Zǐ Jiàn** wielded immense power. It was originally joined to Kǒng Miào by Chíjìng Mén, to the right as you enter. They will be reunited when the Ministry of Culture (housed in Guó Zǐ Jiàn) and the Ministry of Cultural Relics (housed in Kǒng Miào) can sort out their differences. A striking yellow glazed-tile *páilou* with elaborately carved stone arches leads to **Bì Yōng Dàdiàn** *⁀*, a square wooden hall encircled by a moat. The emperor would deliver a lecture on the classics here at the start of his reign, although the irrepressible Qiánlóng visited three times—after assuming the throne, after renovations were completed to mark the 50th anniversary of his reign, and when handing the throne over to his son, the Jiāqìng emperor. He even wrote poems to decorate the sandalwood screen behind the throne. Ministers and the royal family were permitted inside, while three criers (to the west, south, and east) would repeat the emperor's words to students and minor officials kneeling outside.

Kǒng Miào at Guó Zǐ Jiàn Jiē 13, Dōng Chéng Qū (walk south from station along west side of Lama Temple, turn right onto street marked with arch); see map p. 106. ℂ 010/8401-1977. Admission ¥10 ($1.25); Guó Zǐ Jiàn (next door) admission ¥6 (75¢). 8:30am–4:30pm; Guó Zǐ Jiàn 9am–5pm. Metro: Yōng Hé Gōng/Lama Temple (215, exit C).

Lìdài Dìwáng Miào (Temple of Past Emperors) *⁀* *(Finds)*

Built on the grounds of a former Buddhist temple (Bǎo'ān Sì), there's nary a Buddha in sight. Lìdài Dìwáng Miào is where Míng and Qīng emperors made sacrifices to the emperors of previous dynasties. Rulers didn't always come in person, but their representatives diligently carried out sacrifices in spring and autumn. The Yōngzhèng emperor, who killed his brother to usurp the throne, had more reason to pray than most, and made five appearances during his short reign. The layout is akin to Tài Miào in miniature, with an imposing spirit wall opposite the entrance, and two horse-dismounting tablets on either side of the entrance. There were originally three marble bridges and a spectacular wooden memorial arch *(páilóu)* outside the entrance; these feudal elements were demolished in 1953 and 1954. Curatorial standards are improving: Patches of the original ceiling have been left in their original state, touch screen displays in the exhibition halls roughly translate the captions, and there are plush carpets and piped music, and even an admission of past vandalism. The original wooden tablets, once housed in the impressive twin-eaved main hall, were smashed during the Cultural Revolution. Their replacements look inauthentic, but the original order has been preserved. Central position goes to the legendary ruler Fúxī and his successors are arranged outwards in order of venerability, one to the left, one to the right (*yī zuǒ yī yòu*), a seating arrangement still followed by China's rulers. The most striking feature is the intricately carved stelae (nearly 8m [26 ft.] tall) set to the east and west of the main hall.

Fùchéng Mén Dàjiē 131 (a 5 min. walk east from metro); see map p. 106. ℂ 010/6653-0060. Admission ¥20 ($2.50). 9am–4pm. Metro: Fùchéng Mén (203, exit B).

Niú Jiē Lǐbài Sì (Niú Jiē Mosque)

This is Běijīng's largest mosque and the spiritual center for the city's estimated 200,000 Muslims. Built in 996, the complex looks more Eastern than Middle Eastern, with sloping tile roofs similar to those found in

Buddhist temples. Halls are noticeably free of idols, however. A small courtyard on the south side contains the tombs and original gravestones of two Arab imams who lived here in the late 13th century. The main prayer hall is ghostly quiet except on Friday, the traditional day of worship.

Niú Jiē 88, Xuānwǔ Qū (on east side of street); see map p. 110. 𝄞 010/6353-2564. Admission ¥10 ($1.25) for non-Muslims. 8am–7pm. Bus: 61 to Lǐbài Sì from Chángchūn Jiē metro stop (205, exit D).

Tài Miào 𝄞𝄞 (finds) Sometimes the biggest surprises are under your nose. Just east of Tiān'ān Mén stands the only example of an imperial ancestral hall *(zǔ miào)* remaining in China; here are grand imperial edifices in a sleepy, atmospheric setting. Laid out in accordance with the ancient principle from the Rites of Zhōu, "Ancestors to the left, land to the right" *(zuǒ zǔ yòu shè)*, the wooden tablets *(páiwèi)* that represented the ancestors of the imperial house were housed to the left of the Forbidden City (the land was offered its due at the Altar of Land and Grain, housed in Zhōngshān Gōngyuán to the west). Beyond the Halberd Gate (Jǐ Mén), untouched since it was constructed in 1420, the three main buildings are lined up on a central axis. Sacrifices to the ancestors took place in the southernmost building (Xiǎng Diàn). This is one of only four buildings in Běijīng to stand on a three-tiered platform, a hint that it was the most sacred site in imperial Běijīng. Máo renamed it the Workers' Cultural Palace (Láodòng Rénmín Wénhuà Gōng), and the wooden tablets were pilfered during the Cultural Revolution. The workers have moved on, and the complex is largely deserted. Once you reach the moat at the northern end of the complex, turn left. Immediately opposite is **Zhōngshān Gōngyuán**; to the right stands **Wǔ Mén** and the Forbidden City. Infinitely preferable to running the souvenir vendor gauntlet north from Tiān'ān Mén, entering the Forbidden City from Tài Miào may be the best ¥2 you'll ever spend.

East of Tiān'ān Mén, Dōng Chéng Qū; see map p. 106. 𝄞 010/6525-2189. June–Sept 6am–10pm; Oct–May 7am–8:30pm. Admission ¥2 (25¢); admission to bell exhibit ¥10 ($1.25). Metro: Tiān'ān Mén Dōng (117, exit A).

Wànshòu Sì 𝄞 The Longevity Temple, now home to the **Běijīng Art Museum (Běijīng Yìshù Bówùguǎn),** was funded by a eunuch and was originally constructed in 1577. It later became a stopping point for the Qiánlóng emperor and his successors (particularly the Empress Dowager Cíxǐ) on their way to the Summer Palace by boat, a route now followed by tour boats departing from just north of the zoo. The long sequence of heavily restored but low-key halls now houses an odd set of exhibitions, featuring everything from early ceramics, iron, and copperware, to late and very intricate lacquerware and carved ivory. Puzzlingly, the museums most interesting exhibit, highly decorated and ancient seals *(zhuànzhāng)* wrought from a variety of precious and semiprecious materials are now kept in storage. At the rear of the complex is a rock garden from whose top Cíxǐ is supposed to have admired the surrounding countryside, now long built over. Also visible are the original east and west wings of the complex, now occupied by squatters and staff, although there are plans to renovate the west wing.

Xī Sān Huán Běi Lù 18, Hǎidiàn Qū (on north side of Cháng Hé, east side of the West Third Ring Rd.); see map p. 112. 𝄞 010/6841-3380. Admission ¥60 ($7), including guide. 9am–5pm. Bus: 811 from Gōngzhǔ Fén metro stop (110) to Wànshòu Sì.

Wǔ Tǎ Sì (Five Pagoda Temple) More correctly known as Zhēnjué Sì (Temple of True Awakening), the one ancient building remaining on this site is a massive stone block with magnificently preserved Indian Buddhist motifs carved out of the bare rock. Peacocks, elephants, and dharma wheels adorn the base, which is also decorated with sutras copied out in Sanskrit (the large script) and Tibetan (the small script). The central pagoda has an image of two feet, harking back to an age where artisans could only hint at the presence of Buddha through symbols. The circular pavilion was added by the Qiánlóng emperor to honor his mother, an act of architectural vandalism which ruined the original simplicity and symmetry of the pagoda. The surrounding courtyard is gradually filling up with stone tombstones, spirit-way figures, and stelae commemorating the construction or renovation of temples; most are refugees from construction and road-widening projects around the capital. The wonderfully curated **Shíkè Yìshù Bówùguǎn (Stone Carving Museum)** ✸✸ is at the rear of the complex. Běijīng Aquarium is a 15-minute walk to the northeast.

Wǔ Tǎ Sì Cūn 24, Hǎidiàn Qū (from Běijīng Túshūguǎn walk south and turn left at the Nánchāng Canal; the walk takes 10 min.); see map p. 112. ✆ 010/6217-3836. Admission ¥20 ($2.50). 9am–4:30pm. Bus: 808 from just east of Xī Zhí Mén metro stop (201, exit B) to Běijīng Túshūguǎn.

Yōnghé Gōng (Lama Temple) ✸✸✸

If you only visit one temple after the Temple of Heaven, this should be it. A complex of progressively larger buildings topped with ornate yellow-tiled roofs, Yōng Hé Gōng was built in 1694 and originally belonged to the Qīng prince who would become the Yōngzhèng emperor. As was the custom, the complex was converted to a temple after Yōngzhèng's move to the Forbidden City in 1744. The temple is home to several rather beautiful **incense burners,** including a particularly ornate one in the second courtyard that dates back to 1746. The Fǎlún Diàn (Hall of the Wheel of Law), second to last of the major buildings, contains a 6m (20-ft.) bronze statue of Tsongkapa (1357–1419), the founder of the reformist Yellow Hat (Geluk) sect of Tibetan Buddhism, which is now the dominant school of Tibetan Buddhism. He's easily recognized by his pointed cap with long earflaps. The last of the five central halls, the Wànfú Gé (Tower of Ten Thousand Happinesses), houses the temple's prize possession—an ominous Tibetan-style **statue of Maitreya** (the future Buddha), 18m (60 ft.) tall, carved from a single piece of white sandalwood. Once something of a circus, Yōng Hé Gōng is slowly starting to feel like a place of worship, as there are now many Chinese devotees of Tibetan Buddhism.

Yōnghé Gōng Dàjiē 12, south of the North Second Ring Rd. (entrance on the south end of the complex); see map p. 106. ✆ 010/6404-3769. 9am–4pm. Admission ¥25 ($3); audio tours in English additional ¥25 ($3). Metro: Yōng Hé Gōng/Lama Temple (215, exit C).

6 Parks & Gardens

Imperial parks, used either for sacrifices to the gods or for leisure activities, were off-limits to the common folk. Now they are overrun with them, particularly just after dawn, when the older generation turns out in force to practice *tàijíquán* and ballroom dancing, or to chat and show off their caged birds *(zǒu niǎo).*

Běi Hǎi Gōngyuán (Běi Hǎi Park) ✸

An imperial playground dating back to the Tartar Jīn dynasty (1115–1234), Běi Hǎi lies to the north of Zhōng Hǎi and Nán Hǎi, which were also opened to the public in 1925. In the best tradition of *Animal Farm,* the Communist leaders created a new Forbidden City and named it Zhōng Nán Hǎi. Běi Hǎi was left to the masses. Although it's a convenient way to combine a morning visit to the Forbidden City with a more relaxing afternoon in the Back Lakes area, most visitors have a quick peek at the southern half and then disappear. But the north side of the park is more interesting.

Entering from the south, you come to **Tuán Chéng (Round City),** a small citadel on a raised platform whose most notable structure, **Chéngguāng Diàn,** houses a 1.5m-tall (5-ft.) statue of a feminine-looking Buddha, crafted from Burmese white jade. Crossing the Yǒng'ān Bridge to **Qióng Dǎo (Qióng Islet),** you soon reach **Yǒng'ān Sì,** where the founder of the prominent Geluk sect, Tsongkapa, was the focus of devotion. He is now portrayed as a Chinese reformer of corrupt Tibetan Buddhism, on the grounds that he was born in Qīnghǎi rather than "autonomous" Tibet. From here, boats run to the north side of the park (¥5/60¢), or you can walk around the east side, passing calligraphers wielding enormous sponge-tipped brushes to compose rapidly evaporating poems on the flagstones.

Boats pull in to the east of **Wǔ Lóng Tíng (Five Dragon Pavilion),** where aspiring singers treat the public to revolutionary airs popular in the 1950s. Off to the left is an impressive green-tiled *páilou* (memorial arch; the green tiles signify a religious purpose, in contrast to the yellow imperial tiles of the Forbidden City and Guó Zǐ Jiàn). Continue on to the square-shaped **Jílè Shìjiè Diàn** ✿, encircled by a dry moat. Built by the Qiánlóng emperor to honor his mother, the sandalwood structure is exquisite, topped with a priceless gold dome (apparently too high for either foreign troops or local warlords to reach). The gaudy fiberglass statuary inside brings you back to the present. To the west stands an impressive **Nine Dragon Screen,** which guarded the entrance to a now-vanished temple. Further east is **Dàcí Zhēnrú Bǎo Diàn** ✿✿, an atmospheric Buddhist hall built during the late Míng from unpainted cedar; topped with a black roof (to protect the precious wood from fire), it has a cool slate floor. Continue east to the northern exit onto Píng'ān Dàdào, which marks the southern end of the Shíchà Hǎi (Back Lakes) area.

Wénjīn Jiē 1, Xī Chéng Qū (south entrance is just west of the north gate of the Forbidden City; east entrance is opposite the west entrance of Jǐng Shān Park); see map p. 106. ✆ 010/6404-0610. Admission summer ¥10 ($1.25); winter ¥5 (60¢); ¥10 ($1.25) extra for Yǒng'ān Sì; ¥1 (10¢) extra for Tuánchéng. 6am–9pm. Bus: 812 from Dōng Dān metro stop (119, exit A) to Běi Hǎi.

Jǐng Shān Gōngyuán (Jǐng Shān Park)

If you want a clear aerial view of the Forbidden City, you'll find it here. The park's central hill was created using earth left over from the digging of the imperial moat and was the highest point in the city during the Míng dynasty. It was designed to enhance the *fēngshuǐ* of the Forbidden City, by blocking the harsh northern wind and by burying a Mongol Yuán dynasty pavilion, the Yánchūn Gé. In something of a riposte to the Chinese Míng dynasty, the Manchu Qiánlóng emperor built a tower by the same name (albeit in a very different style) in the Jiànfú Gōng Huāyuán, within the Forbidden City. A tree on the east side of the hill marks the spot where the last Míng emperor, Chóngzhēn, supposedly hanged himself in 1644, just before Manchu and rebel armies overran the city. The original tree, derided as the "guilty sophora" during the Qīng, was hacked down by Red Guards who failed to recognize a fellow anti-imperialist.

Jǐng Shān Qián Jiē 1, Dōng Chéng Qū (opposite Forbidden City north gate); see map p. 106. ✆ 010/6404-4071. Admission ¥2 (20¢). Summer 6am–10pm; winter 6:30am–8pm. Bus: 812 from Dōng Dān metro stop (119, exit A) to Gù Gōng.

Míng Chéngqiáng Gōngyuán (Míng City Wall Park) ✿

The section of wall presented here, running a mile east-to-west from Dōngbiàn Mén to Chóngwén Mén, was originally built in the Yuán dynasty (1279–1368) and reconstructed in the mid-1500s by the Míng. Modern restoration work on the section began in 2002 and is still in progress, using bricks from the original Míng reconstruction collected from nearby residents (some of whom employed them to build toilets after the wall was demolished in the 1950s). A pleasant park runs east along the length of the wall to the dramatic Dōngnán Jiǎolóu (Southeast Corner Tower; daily 9am–5pm; ¥10/$1), with its dozens of arrow slots; a contemporary art gallery and interesting exhibition on the history of Chóngwén can be found inside.

East of metro stop; see map p. 111. ✆ 010/6527-0574. Open 24 hr. Metro: Chóngwén Mén (209, exit B).

Rì Tán Gōngyuán (Rì Tán Park)   The Temple of the Sun (Rì Tán) served as an altar where the emperor conducted annual rites. Built in 1530, Rì Tán is a pleasant park with a delightful outdoor **teahouse** ☞ and a **rock-climbing wall** at its heart. Fishponds, a pedal-powered monorail, kites, and a bonsai market also keep the locals amused.

The other imperial altars are located in similar city parks, roughly marking the five points of the Chinese compass. To the north is **Dì Tán Gōngyuán (Temple of Earth),** just north of the Lama Temple; to the west is **Yuè Tán Gōngyuán (Temple of the Moon);** the much grander **Tiān Tán Gōngyuán (Temple of Heaven)** marks the southern point. **Shè Jì Tán (Altar of Land and Grain)** in Zhōngshān Gōngyuán southwest of the Forbidden City, pre-dates them all by several centuries, and marks that peculiarly Chinese compass point, the center.

Rì Tán Lù 6, Cháoyáng Qū; see map p. 111. ✆ 010/8561-1389. Admission ¥1 (5¢). 6am–8:30pm (from 6:30am in winter). Metro: Yǒng'ān Lǐ (121, exit A).

Yuán Míng Yuán ☞ (Kids)   An amalgamation of three separate imperial gardens, these ruins create a ghostly and oddly enjoyable scene, beloved for years as a picnic spot. Established by the Kāngxī emperor in 1707, Yuán Míng Yuán is a more recent construction than the New Summer Palace to the west, but it is misleadingly called the Old Summer Palace because it was never rebuilt after French and British troops looted and burned it down during the Second Opium War of 1860. Ironically, some of the buildings were Western-style and filled with European furnishings and art. Two Jesuit priests, Italian painter Castiglione and French scientist Benoist, were commissioned by Qiánlóng to design the 75-acre **Xī Yáng Lóu (Western Mansions)** in the northeast section of the park. Perhaps the most remarkable structure was a zodiac water clock which spouted from 12 bronze heads, three of which (an ox, a monkey, and a tiger) are now housed in the otherwise unremarkable **Poly Art Museum,** immediately above Dōng Sì Shí Tiáo metro stop. Inaccurate models suggest that the structures were entirely European in style, but they were curious hybrids, featuring Imperial-style vermillion walls and yellow-tiled roofs. A few restorations have begun, starting with the **Wànhuā Zhèn (10,000 Flowers Maze),** a nicely reconstructed labyrinth in the **Chángchūn Yuán (Garden of Eternal Spring).** Recently, the park has been the center of environmental controversy. Park management and the district government decided to line the lakes (an integral part of Běijīng's water ecology and a magnet for bird life) with plastic sheeting to save on water bills and raise the water levels to allow for a duck-boat business.

Qīnghuá Xī Lù 28, Hǎidiàn Qū (north of Peking University); see map p. 116. ✆ 010/6262-8501. 7am–7pm (to 5:30pm in winter). Admission ¥10 ($1.25); ¥15 ($2) to enter Xī Yáng Lóu. Bus: 743 from east of Wǔdàokǒu metro stop (1304) to Yuán Míng Yuán.

7 Museums

In keeping with the Communist (and Confucian) passion for naming and quantification, Běijīng has a museum for everything—police, bees, even the humble watermelon. If you share this passion and plan on spending a week or more in the capital, invest in a *bówùguǎn tōng piào* (¥60/$7.50), which grants you free (or half price) admission to over 70 sites in and around Běijīng.

Dà Zhōng Sì (Great Bell Temple) An attraction to bring out the hunchback in anyone, this Qīng temple now houses the **Ancient Bell Museum (Gǔ Zhōng Bówùguǎn)**, best visited on the way to the **Summer Palace** or in conjunction with **Wànshòu Sì,** which lies to the southwest along the Third Ring Road. The temple was known as Juéshēng Sì (Awakened Life Temple), but clearly there wasn't enough awakening going on, so a 47-ton bell was transported here on ice sleds in 1743. The third hall on the right houses clangers garnered from around Běijīng. Some were donated by eunuchs wishing the relevant emperor long life, with hundreds of donors' names scrawled on their sides. But frustratingly, none of this is fleshed out. The main attraction is housed in the rear hall, carved inside and out with 230,000 Chinese and Sanskrit characters. The big bell tolls but once a year, on New Year's Eve. Visitors rub the handles of Qiánlóng's old washbasin, and scramble up narrow steps to make a wish while throwing coins through a hole in the top of the monster. But it is no longer the "King of Bells"—that honor now goes to the 50-ton bell housed in the **Altar to the Century (Zhōnghuá Shìjì Tán),** constructed in 1999 to prove that China could waste money on the millennium, too.

Běi Sān Huán Xī Lù 31A, Hǎidiàn Qū (west of metro stop, north of Liánxiǎng Qiáo on the northwest side of the Third Ring Rd.); see map p. 112. ✆ 010/6255-0819. Admission ¥10 ($1.25); ¥2 (15¢) extra to climb the Bell Tower. Tues–Sun 8:30am–4pm. Metro: Dà Zhōng Sì (1302, exit A).

Gǔdài Jiànzhù Bówùguǎn (Museum of Ancient Architecture) 𝒜𝒜 This exhibition, a mixture of models of China's most famous architecture and fragments of buildings long disappeared, is housed in halls as dramatic as those on the central axis of the Forbidden City. These were once part of the **Xiān Nóng Tán,** or Altar of Agriculture, now as obscure as its neighbor, Tiān Tán, the Temple (properly Altar) of Heaven, is famous. From about 1410, emperors came to this once-extensive site to perform rituals in which they started the agricultural cycle by playing farmer and plowing the first furrows. The site where they once toiled is now a basketball court.

The exhibition in the surviving halls is striking in its extensive English explanations of everything from the construction of the complicated bracket sets, which support temple roofs, to the role of geomancy in Chinese architectural thinking, and curiosities from now razed sites such as Lóngfú Sì. Models of significant buildings around Běijīng can help you select what to see in the capital during the remainder of your trip.

The rearmost **Tàisuì Diàn (Hall of Jupiter)** of 1532, with its vast, sweeping roof, is only exceeded in magnificence by the Forbidden City's Hall of Supreme Harmony.

Dōng Jīng Lù 21, Xuānwǔ Qū (from bus stop, take 1st right into Nán Wěi Lù and walk for 5 min., look out for an archway down a street on the left; see map p. 110. ✆ 010/6301-7620. Admission ¥15 ($2). 9am–4pm. Bus: 803 from just south of Wángfǔjīng (118) or Qián Mén (208) metro stops to Tiān Qiáo Shāngchǎng.

National Museum of China (Guójiā Bówùguǎn) 𝒜 The Museum of the Chinese Revolution and the Musuem of History have been united in a single building, but renovations won't be completed until 2008. Until then, a series of exhibits emphasizing the greatness of the Chinese civilization will be shown. Some effort has been made to spruce things up, and English captions have been added to a number of the displays, although they are conspicuously lacking from the hilarious wax figure hall. In the past, interest centered on who was omitted from Chinese history; now it focuses on who is included. Former unpersons such as Liú Shàoqí and Lín Biāo, Máo's ill-fated heirs apparent, are displayed alongside their tormentors. The Party line is scrupulously followed: The passive and obsequious Lín, whose death went unreported for nearly a year, is still said to have plotted to seize power from Máo.

East side of Tiān'ān Mén Sq., Dōng Chéng Qū; see map p. 106. (*C*) 010/6512-8901. www.nmch.gov.cn. Admission ¥30 ($4) for *tōng piào*, or ¥10–¥20 ($1–$3) for each exhibit; English audio tours ¥30 ($4). 9am–3:30pm. Metro: Tiān'ān Mén East (117, exit D).

Zhōngguó Gōngyì Měishùguǎn (National Arts & Crafts Museum)   Located on the fifth floor of Parkson Department Store (Bǎishèng Gòuwù Zhōngxīn), you'll find no ancient, dusty treasures here. This is a museum to prove that contemporary Chinese craftsmanship is every bit as good as it was during the Táng dynasty. Many items suggest otherwise, particularly large chunks of jade painstakingly carved into monuments to bad taste, and ceramic statues of arhats picking wax from their ears. But it's a good introduction to traditional crafts in their places of origin. Striking exhibits include clay figurines from Jiāngsū, cloisonné from Běijīng, lacquerware from Fújiàn, and ceramics from Jǐngdé Zhèn, which steal the show.

Fùxīng Mén Nèi Dàjiē 101, Xī Chéng Qū; see map p. 106. (*C*) 010/6605-3476. Admission ¥8 ($1). Tues–Sun 9:30am–4pm. Metro: Fùxīng Mén (114/204, exit B).

8 Former Residences & Other Curiosities

Constructing memorial halls to the heroes of past and present dynasties has a long history, and the Communists have adopted this tradition with élan. As before, historical accuracy matters little; cultivating patriotic subjects is the goal.

Ancient Observatory (Gǔ Guānxiàng Tái)   Most of the observatory's large bronze astronomical instruments—mystifying combinations of hoops, slides, and rulers stylishly embellished with dragons and clouds—were built by the Jesuits in the 17th and 18th centuries. You can play with reproductions of the Chinese-designed instruments they superseded (the originals were moved to Nánjīng in 1933 and, for unexplained reasons, haven't been returned) in the grassy courtyard below. At the back of the garden, there's a "we-invented-it-first" display outlining the achievements of Sòng dynasty astronomer Guō Shǒujìng, who also has his own memorial hall on the northern tip of Xī Hǎi. To the right of the entrance there's a more useful exhibition, which houses a photo of a bone from 1300 B.C. on which China's first astronomers etched a record of solar eclipses, details of which are still used in present-day astronomy.

Jiànguó Mén Dōng Biǎobèi 2, Dōng Chéng Qū (southwest side of Jiànguó Mén intersection, just south of metro); see map p. 106. (*C*) 010/6512-8923. Admission ¥10 ($1.25). 9am–4:30pm. Metro: Jiànguó Mén (120/211, exit C).

Dìxià Chéng (Underground City) ⊗ ⟨*Kids*⟩   A sign near the entrance proclaims this seldom-visited attraction a "human fairyland and underground paradise." Far from it. Aside from odd recent additions, such as a silk factory, these tunnels are dark, damp, and genuinely eerie. A portrait of Máo stands amid murals of ordinary folk "volunteering" to dig tunnels, and fading but catchy slogans (DIG THE TUNNELS DEEP, ACCUMULATE GRAIN, OPPOSE HEGEMONY, and FOR THE PEOPLE: PREPARE FOR WAR, PREPARE

FOR FAMINE). Unintentional humor is provided by propaganda posters from the era, which advise citizens to cover their mouth in the event of nuclear, chemical, or biological attack. Built during the 1960s, with border skirmishes with the USSR as the pretext, the tunnels could accommodate all of Běijīng's six million inhabitants upon its completion—or so it was boasted. Army engineers were said to have built a secret network of tunnels connecting the residences of Party leaders at Zhōng Nán Hǎi to the Great Hall of the People and the numerous military bases near Bā Dà Chù to the west of town. Suspicions were confirmed in 1976 and 1989 when large numbers of troops emerged from the Great Hall of the People to keep the people in check. The construction boom means that this is the only remaining entrance to the non-secret tunnels; it may disappear soon.

Xī Dǎmóchǎng Jiē 64, Chóngwén Qū (from metro stop, walk west; take the 1st left into Qián Mén Dōng Dàjiē, then the 2nd right; entrance is on south side, just past Qián Mén Xiǎoxué); see map p. 106. (*C*) 010/6702-2657. Admission ¥20 ($2.50). 8:30am–5pm. Metro: Chóngwén Mén (209, exit D).

Factory 798 (Qījiǔbā Gōngchǎng) ★★ Optimistically billed as Běijīng's Soho district, this Soviet-designed former weapons factory is a center for local modern art and fashion. 798's long-term survival is uncertain, with Běijīng's mayor musing that they would "look, regulate, and discuss" the use of the space, which the owners and the Cháoyáng municipal government hope will become a technology park. Purchase a map (¥2/25¢) on arrival. From entrance no. 2, you'll soon arrive at the **Hart Center of Arts** on the right, which holds regular screenings of alternative films (see chapter 10, p. 184) and also sells interesting hand-painted T-shirts. Further down on the right is the remarkable Bauhaus-inspired **798 Space,** still daubed with slogans offering praise to Máo. The most consistently interesting exhibitions are held by **798 Photo,** immediately opposite. Turn right and right again as you emerge from the building to find the first gallery to open in Factory 798, **Běijīng Tokyo Art Projects** (www.tokyo-gallery.com), which boasts a formidable stable of local and international artists. Turn left and duck down a narrow lane, to emerge at the Gāo Brothers' cuddly **Běijīng New Art Projects** (*C* 010/8456-6660). At Cafe (Àitè Kāfēi; *C* 010/6438-7264), just across the road, is the best of Dàshānzi's middling cafes. If a visit to 798 whets your appetite for more avant-garde Chinese art, many of 798's artists, faced with spiraling rents and an increasingly commercial atmosphere, have moved to **Sòng Zhuāng,** a village to the east of town (www.artistvillagegallery.com).

Jiǔxiān Qiáo Lù 4, Cháoyáng Qū (north of Dàshānzi Huándǎo); see map p. 115. www.798space.com. 10:30am–7pm (some galleries closed Mon). Bus: 813 east from Cháoyáng Mén metro (212, exit A) to Wángyé Fén.

Lǎo Shě Jìniànguǎn (Former Residence of Lǎo Shě) The courtyard home of one of Běijīng's best-loved writers, Lǎo Shě (1899–1966), is the most charming of many converted homes scattered around Běijīng's *hútòng*. Despite being granted this home by Zhōu Ēnlái in 1950, the writer refused to become a cheerleader for the regime, and his post-revolution years were remarkably quiet for such a prolific writer. He recently came in at no. 5 in an online survey of "China's leading cultural icons," ahead of pop diva Wang Faye but well behind the no. 1 choice, the iconoclastic writer Lǔ Xùn (who has a memorial hall in the west of town, see chapter 8, p. 162). Lǎo Shě is renowned for the novel *Rickshaw (Luòtuo Xiángzi),* a darkly humorous tale of a hardworking rickshaw puller, Happy Boy.

Start in Hall 3, to the right, which records his early years in London, the United States, and Shāndōng Province. Hall 2 is an attempt to re-create the mood of his original study and sitting room, with his personal library untouched and his desk calendar left open at the day of his disappearance—August 24, 1966. While the date of his death is certain, the details are murky. The official line has him committing a poetic suicide in nearby Tàipíng Hú (pictured in Hall 1) after enduring a "struggle session" at Kǒng Miào. It's possible that he was simply murdered by Red Guards.

Fēngfù Hútòng 19, Dōng Chéng Qū (from Wángfǔjǐng Dàjiē, turn left at the Crowne Plaza along Dēngshìkǒu Xī Jiē to the 2nd *hútòng* on your right); see map p. 106. ✆ 010/6514-2612. Admission ¥10 ($1.25). 9am–5pm. Metro: Wángfǔjǐng (118, exit A).

Prince Gōng's Mansion (Gōng Wáng Fǔ) This splendid imperial residence belonged to several people, including the sixth son of the Guāngxù emperor (Prince Gōng) who, at the age of 27, was left to sign the Convention of Peking in 1860, after the Qīng royal family took an early summer holiday when British and French forces advanced on the capital. The convention (which ratified the ill-enforced Treaty of Tiānjīn) is reproduced in an exhibition hall. But other than one picture, there's little information concerning the original owner, Héshēn (1750–1799), the infamously corrupt Manchu official. Thought to have been the Qiánlóng emperor's lover, he ruled China for his own gain when Qiánlóng abdicated in 1796, embezzling funds earmarked for suppressing the White Lotus rebellion. After Qiánlóng's death, his demise was swift. While he was mourning in the Forbidden City, officials were dispatched to this mansion. Though the extent of his graft was widely known, officials were shocked by the piles of gold and silver ingots uncovered. His remaining friends at court managed to persuade the Qiánlóng emperor's son to spare him from "death by a thousand cuts," but he was soon hanged. The labyrinthine combination of rockeries and pavilions here offers plenty to see, but you're only seeing half of the mansion (see below) and it's often overrun by tour groups. Short but sweet performances of opera and acrobatics are served up in the three-story "Grand Opera House."

Liǔyīn Jiē 17 (signposted in English at top of Qián Hǎi Xī Dàjiē running north off Píng'ān Dàdào opposite north gate of Běi Hǎi Park; turn left at sign and follow alley past large parking lot; entrance marked with huge red lanterns); see map p. 106. ✆ 010/6618-0573. Admission ¥20 ($2.50); ¥60 ($7.50) including guide and opera performance. 8:30am–4:30pm. Metro: Jīshuǐ Tán (218, exit C).

Fun Fact Going, going, Gōng?

Běijīng's most remarkable building, Héshēn's opulent pleasure house (constructed entirely from precious *nánmù*) is found in the southern half of Prince Gōng's Mansion. It should be a major tourist attraction, but the site is currently occupied by the China Arts Research Council and a high school. When ordinary Běijīngrén are served with an eviction notice, they often have as little as 24 hours to move out before the demolition crews arrive, but when government ministries are involved, the game is rather different. In the 1980s, offices occupying the site were allocated relocation funds and ordered to move. New headquarters were duly built, but 20 years on, the mandarins have yet to quit their imperial surroundings. They have now been instructed to "act in accordance with the Three Represents," and move out before 2008 to make way for a "Princes' Museum" (Wángfǔ Bówùguǎn).

Sòng Qìnglíng Gùjū (Former Residence of Soong Ching Ling)   Sòng Qìnglíng is as close as you'll get to a modern Chinese Communist saint—wealthy, obsessed with children, and a friend of Máo to boot. She married Sun Yat-sen, 30 years her senior, a diminutive man acknowledged as the "father of modern China" on both sides of the Táiwān Strait (even though he was in Denver during the 1911 Revolution). Qìnglíng showed some sympathy to the Communist cause only after her husband's death in 1925. Her younger sister married Chiang Kai-shek (leader of the Nationalist Party and China's public enemy no. 1 until his death in 1975), while Qìnglíng nearly died during the "white terror" of 1927 when the Nationalist Party was purged of Communist sympathizers. Máo rewarded Qìnglíng for her loyalty by granting her this mansion in 1963, and she lived here until her death in 1981, devoting much time to education. The grounds are well-kept, making them the most popular spot in Běijīng for soon-to-be-weds to be photographed. The exhibition on her life seems to contain nearly every article of clothing she wore and every letter she wrote. It's all a little too perfect.

Hòu Hǎi Běi Yán 46, Xī Chéng Qū (northeast shore of Hòu Hǎi); see map p. 106. © 010/6404-4205. Admission ¥20 ($2.50). 9am–5pm (to 4:30pm in winter). Metro: Jīshuǐ Tán (218, exit B).

Tián Yì Mù ⭐ *Finds*   The first Míng emperor had a dim view of eunuchs, noting "not one or two of these people out of thousands are good . . . These people can only be given sprinkling and sweeping jobs," but upon the accession of the Wànlì emperor (reign 1573–1620), the Imperial City housed nearly 20,000 eunuchs (*huànguān*, later *tàijiān*), from powerful bureaucrats enjoying their own mansions, down to junior eunuchs scraping by through petty graft. The cemetery was built in 1605 for Wànlì's favorite eunuch, Tián Yì, who served three emperors and acted as Wànlì's mentor and confidant. It has a spirit way, an underground tomb complex, and memorial stelae wreathed in dragons, an unprecedented honor for a eunuch. It's a way from the city center, best combined with a visit to Tánzhè Sì or Chuān Dǐ Xià (see chapter 11 for both) and Fǎhǎi Sì (p. 132), a 10-minute walk to the northeast. Unlike its occupants, the cemetery has survived almost intact, and provides insight into their fraught spirituality. Buddhist and Taoist motifs are carved onto their graves, along with images depicting morality tales.

A small exhibition hall is set to the left of the entrance, but all captions are in Chinese. China's last eunuch, Sūn Yàotíng (1902–1996) is pictured making a visit to the Forbidden City in 1993, his first since Pǔyí was driven out in 1924. He is said to have taken issue with the accuracy of the captions there. On the right a naïve letter describes his years in service. Castrated at the age of 8, he was devastated when the emperor abdicated months later, although he continued to serve Pǔyí. He earned enough money to adopt a son, but lost his "treasure" during the Cultural Revolution (see the box, "Eunuchs: The Unkindest Cut" below).

Cíxǐ is photographed with a large entourage of eunuchs at the Summer Palace, and the temples pictured were sponsored by eunuchs. Buddhism, with its emphasis on celibacy and renunciation, had more appeal for eunuchs than Confucianism. Wealthier eunuchs would adopt sons, but most relied on Buddhist monks to tend their graves. A second eunuch museum will be opening soon inside a late Qīng temple, **Lìmǎ Guāndì Miào.** Built for one of Cíxǐ's most trusted eunuchs, Liú Chéngyìn, the keeper of the imperial seals, it stands south of the Summer Palace in an area akin to a eunuch retirement village.

Móshì Kǒu Dàjiē 80, Shíjīng Shān Qū (from bus stop, continue up the rise; take a right after 5 min.; cemetery is on the left); see map p. 112. © 010/8872-4148. Admission ¥8 ($1). 9am–5pm. Bus: 959 or 746 from left of Píngguǒ Yuán metro stop (103, exit D) to Shǒugāng Xiǎoqū.

Eunuchs: The Unkindest Cut

The practice that created eunuchs is said to date back 4,000 years, when it was an alternative to the death penalty, often used in the case of political crimes. By the Míng dynasty, most eunuchs submitted to this operation voluntarily, usually as a way out of poverty. The eunuch's abdomen and upper thighs were bound tightly with coarse rope or bandages; his penis was anesthetized with hot pepper water. He was then seated in a semi-reclining chair, with waist and legs held down by three assistants. At this point, he was asked if he would have any regrets. Consent given, the small curved blade flashed and "fountains of red, white, and yellow liquid spouted from the wound" as both the testes and penis were removed. A goose quill would then quickly be inserted into the urethra to prevent it from closing, and the wound plugged with cloth previously dipped in wax, sesame oil, and pepper. The surplus organs (or "treasure") were plopped in a jar and jealously guarded, as they were necessary to establish a eunuch's credentials for promotions, and to pass into the next life as complete men. After the patient (often unconscious by this point) had endured 3 days without food or drink, the plug was removed. If urine gushed out, the operation was a success, and a lifetime in service waited. If not, a horrible, lingering death. A less violent alternative involved slitting the scrotum and removing the testicles. Both operations were preferable to criminal castration, where the testicles were beaten off with a club.

9 Hútòng & Sìhéyuàn (Lanes & Courtyard Compounds)

As distinct as Běijīng's palaces, temples, and parks may be, it is the *hútòng* that ultimately set the city apart. Prior to the 20th century, when cars and the Communist love of grandeur made them impracticable, these narrow and often winding lanes were the city's dominant passageways. Old maps of Běijīng show the city to be an immense and intricate maze composed almost entirely of *hútòng*, most no wider than 10m (30 ft.) and some as narrow as 50cm (20 in.).

Běijīng's other famous feature is the **sìhéyuàn** (courtyard house)—traditional dwellings typically composed of four single-story rectangular buildings arranged around a central courtyard with a door at one corner (ideally facing south). Originally designed to house a single family, they now house up to five or six. Máo brought the countryside to the city during the Cultural Revolution, and most of these squatters never left. Foreign visitors charmed by the quaintness of the old houses often assume migration into modern apartment buildings is forced, and it often is. But many move willingly, eager for central heating, indoor plumbing, and most importantly, security of ownership. Many locals will try to convince you that *hútòng* are inherently run-down, but why would you renovate a house that could be torn down next week?

The *hútòng* are being leveled so rapidly the term **"fast-disappearing"** is now a permanent part of their description. With the 2008 Olympics looming, destruction carries the imprimatur of modernization. Never mind that visitors prefer quiet lanes to endless blocks of identical flats. But the main driving force behind the destruction is

Our Favorite Hútòng Names

The names of *hútòng* are a link to the history and humor of the capital. **Sān Bù Lǎo Hútòng,** a couple of blocks west of Prince Gōng's Mansion, is named for its famous former resident, Admiral Zhèng Hé, whose nickname was Sān Bǎo (three treasures, possibly a reference to his eunuch status). As described in 1421: The Year China Discovered America, this Huí Muslim led a vast armada of ships to Southeast Asia, India, Ceylon, the Persian Gulf (where he was able to visit Mecca), and West Africa over seven voyages between 1405 and 1433. Detachments of his fleet probably reached Australia, but the central contention of the book is dubious. Other names hint at long-forgotten markets. **Yāndài Xié Jiē (Tobacco Pipe Lane),** east of Yíndìng Qiáo, now harbors the capital's hippest cafes, but it once provided smoking paraphernalia for the capital's numerous opium dens. The meaning of **Xiān Yú Kǒu Jiē (Fresh Fish Corner Street)** seems straightforward, but locals swear it's a corruption of *xiányú* (salty fish), a reference to a man who burned down half the street while preparing his favorite meal. **Shōushuǐ Hútòng (Gathering Water Lane),** where you'll find the Liú Rèn Papercut House (see below), was originally known by the less-saleable name of **Chòushuǐ Hútòng (Smelly Water Lane),** as it was a ditch which ran along the north side of the old city wall.

banal: tax. Municipal governments are desperately short of revenue (following reforms implemented by the oft-lauded Zhū Róngjī), and land is the one thing they can sell. Property developers, who now rely on evictees for one-third of their sales, are happy to oblige. Drunk from these one-off influxes of capital, municipal governments expand further. New departments are created, and new jobs are found for friends and relatives. So the next time round, the hit has to be bigger. The Dōng Chéng government in particular has a reputation for ordering brutal evictions and arranging unfavorable resettlement schemes.

Intriguing swathes of *hútòng* still stand south of **Hépíng Mén** and **Qián Mén,** as well as northwest of **Xī Sì,** surrounding **Bái Tǎ Sì.** Here you may hear strange humming sounds, produced by pigeons wheeling overhead with small whistles attached to their feathers. For now, the destitution of these areas makes them unattractive to property developers, but their long-term survival is improbable. See them now. The *hútòng* most likely to survive because of their popularity with tourists are in the **Back Lakes (Shíchà Hǎi)** area and in nearby **Dì'ān Mén.** Pedicab tour companies offer to bike you around this area and take you inside a couple of courtyards, but they all charge absurd rates. It's much cheaper, and far more enjoyable, to explore on your own by foot or bicycle (see chapter 8 for suggested routes). If you must, the **Běijīng Hútòng Tourist Agency** (© 010/6615-9097) offers tours in English (¥240/$30). *Tip:* However you travel, *never* enter a *sìhéyuàn* uninvited.

10 Especially for Kids

Competition for the disposable income of Běijīng's one-child families is intense—advertising ruthlessly targets children. Alas, few of Běijīng's just-for-kids attractions are of a standard that will appeal to Western children, and those few tend to be over-crowded. Some exceptions are noted below.

Běijīng Hǎiyángguǎn (Běijīng Aquarium) ✸ "The world's largest inland aquarium" attracted plenty of opposition from local environmental groups when it opened in 1999, and the logic of keeping countless marine animals so far from the sea is questionable. Efforts to compensate are obvious—the environmental message is laid on thickly in the Chinese captions. Introducing Chinese children to the concept that shrimp can exist somewhere other than in a sea of garlic sauce has to be commended, although descriptions of "horrible" sharks show there's a way to go in environmental efforts. **Dolphin shows** at 11am and 3pm pack in the one-child families. **Běijīng Zoo (Běijīng Dòngwùyuán)** lies to the south, and despite improvements to some areas—notably the **Panda House**—the zoo is more likely to traumatize your child than provide entertainment. It is possible to take a boat from the canal south of the aquarium to the Summer Palace (50-min. trip; ¥40/$5 one-way, ¥70/$8.70 round-trip).

Gāoliáng Qiáo Xié Jiē 18B, Hǎidiàn Qū (from Běifāng Jiāo Dà cross road and walk west; north gate of the Běijīng Zoo); see map p. 106. ✆ 010/6217-6655. Admission ¥110 ($14) includes admission to Běijīng Zoo; children ¥60 ($7.50); 2 children free with 1 paid adult ticket. 9am–4:30pm (to 10pm during summer holidays). Bus: 16 (zhī xiàn) from Xī Zhí Mén metro stop (201) to Běifāng Jiāo Dà.

Gǔdài Qiánbì Zhǎnlǎnguǎn (Ancient Coin Exhibition Hall)   If your child is at the collecting phase, this may or may not be a wise place to visit, although the vast range of shells, coins, and notes is as likely to bewilder as to fascinate. While the tour guides' chant of "5,000 years of history" rings hollow, "5,000 years of retail" rings true. Confucius and Máo both railed in vain against the mercantile spirit. The exhibition should also impress upon you how simple it is to mint coins; the stalls of the **Ancient Coin Market (Gǔdài Qiánbì Jiāoyì Shìchǎng)** outside are testament to how easy they are to duplicate—*don't* make large purchases. **Déshèng Mén Jiànlóu (Déshèng Mén Arrow Tower),** which houses the exhibition, is akin to an imposing castle, with many dark crannies to explore.

Déshèng Mén Jiànlóu, Běi Èr Huán Zhōng Lù, Xī Chéng Qū (north side of North Second Ring Rd., just east of metro stop); see map p. 106. ✆ 010/6201-8073. Admission ¥10 ($1.25). Tues–Sun 8:30am–3:30pm. Metro: Jīshuǐ Tán (218, exit A).

Liú Rèn Papercut House (Liú Rèn Jiǎnzhǐ Wū)   The art of paper cutting might not sound exciting, but self-taught artist Liú Rèn, who works out of a charming court-yard house, works up such a good spiel you may be converted. Papercuts *(jiǎnzhǐ)* were gifts in rural China, to be stuck on windows, doors, or lanterns. There's nothing subtle about the traditional papercuts—a baby with a large member marks the birth of a boy, and a baby surrounded by protective wolves is appropriate for a girl. Liú Rèn knows her craft, and is happy to provide instruction (¥200/$25 per hr.; ¥60/$7.50 if taught by her students). Call ahead to book.

Shòu Shuǐ Hé Hútòng 16, Xī Chéng Qū (walk south on Xuānwǔ Mén Wài Dàjiē, take the 2nd hútòng on the right, turn left down the 1st lane, then take the 1st right); see map p. 110. ✆ 010/6601-1946. Metro: Xī Dān (115, exit E).

Mílù Yuàn (Mílù Park) ✸✸ *(Finds)*   Located on the site of the Southern Marshes (Nán Hǎizi) where Yuán, Míng, and Qīng emperors would hunt deer, rabbit, and pheasant, and practice military exercises, this ecological research center is the most humane place to view animals in Běijīng. The main attraction is Père David's deer *(mílù),* a strange deerlike creature that became extinct in China toward the end of the Qīng dynasty. The *mílù* you see today are the descendants of 18 animals that were collected in 1898 by the far-sighted Lord Bedford from zoos around Europe. In 1985, a group of 20 *mílù* was reintroduced to China; they now number about 200, and over 400 animals have returned to the wild. The expansive marshlands attract migratory birds, and also house other endangered animals, a maze, plots of land where members can grow vegetables without pesticides, and the chillingly effective World Extinct Wildlife Cemetery, which illustrates the plight of endangered species.

Nán Hǎizi Mílù Yuàn, Dàxīng Qū. ☏ 010/8796-2105. www.milupark.org.cn. Admission ¥20 ($2.50). 8am–5:30pm. Bus: 729 from Qián Mén metro stop (208) to Jiù Gōng. Change for minibus no. 4, which will drop you at the sign-posted turnoff.

11 Organized Tours

During a visit to Běi Hǎi, writer John Blofeld chanced upon an elderly eunuch, and inquired as to how he was making a living. He touchily replied, "I manage well. I am a guide—not one of those so-called guides who live by inventing history for foreigners and by making commissions on things they purchase. I have not fallen that far yet . . ." Little has changed. In a country where children are taught that South Korea and their American allies started the Korean War when they invaded innocent North Korea, many modern inventions are unintentional. Many visitors assume locals have a unique insight into their own culture. In China, and Běijīng in particular, all-pervasive censorship and a general lack of curiosity ensures this is rarely the case. You *do not* need the services of a local guide.

Several companies offer guided group tours of Běijīng for English speakers, but these are almost always overpriced, often incomplete, and best thought of as an emergency measure when time is short. The most popular operators are **Dragon Bus** (☏ 010/8563-9959; www.dragontour.com.cn) and **Panda Tours** (☏ 010/6522-2991), both with offices scattered through the four- and five-star hotels. City highlight tours by air-conditioned bus typically cost around ¥300 ($38) per person for a half day and around ¥500 ($60) for a full day with a mediocre lunch. **China International Travel Service (CITS)** (☏ 010/6515-8566; www.cits.net), offers tours that are more customizable, but at a much higher fee. The options listed below are infinitely preferable.

The **Chinese Culture Club** (☏ 010/8462-2081; www.chinesecultureclub.org) organizes outings, lectures, and film screenings for expatriates with an interest in Chinese culture. There's usually a weekend half-day or full-day tour. Events are often led by prominent lecturers, discussions go well beyond the "5,000 years of history" palaver that CITS subject you to, they are constantly on the lookout for new attractions, and multi-day tours to sites as far afield as Xīnjiāng are now offered. A smaller operation with a similar philosophy is **Cycle China** (☏ 010/6424-5913; www.cycle china.com). Many sights around Běijīng, such as the Míng tombs, are more appealing on two wheels than on two feet. *Hútòng* cycle tours are a specialty.

Surrounded by mountains on three sides, the environs of Běijīng provide tremendous scope for 1- or 2-day walks taking in scenery, ancient villages, and, of course, the Great Wall. **Běijīng Hikers** (☏ 1370/100-3694; huilin@bjhikers.com) organize day hikes for ¥150 ($19) departing from the Lido Hotel. Though popular with North American expatriates, groups are often too large. A cheaper and more interesting alternative is to join a hike organized by **Sanfo Outdoors** (☏ 010/6201-5550; www. sanfo.com.cn). Originally a small club at Peking University, they now have at least four hikes every weekend advertised (in Chinese) on their website. Visit one of their shops (p. 178) to obtain information on the weekend's activities, but take the grading system seriously—difficult hikes are really tough, while outings with all luxuries provided are humorously referred to as "corrupt" *(fǔbài)*.

12 Staying Active

Foreign-run five-star hotels offer the cleanest and best-equipped fitness centers and swimming pools for those desperate to work out. Most locals can't afford this, and head for the parks early in the morning to practice *tàijíquán,* practice ballroom dancing, or walk the bird (walking the dog is prohibited during daylight hours). At night, Běijīng's undersize canines emerge, along with seniors dancing (waddling, really) and beating drums to the rhythm of rice-planting songs *(yāng ge).* However, if you know where to look, you can find other leisure experiences with a local flavor.

ACTIVITIES A TO Z

BOWLING (BǍOLÍNGQIÚ)   With bottles of Johnnie Walker Red Label and French perfume readily traced, and visits to "karaoke" clubs easily photographed, the favorite way to curry favor with a Chinese official is . . . bowling. During the 1990s, more than 15,000 alleys were built, many in Běijīng. The biggest and most fun place to bowl is 24-hour **Gōngtǐ Yībǎi** at Gōngtǐ Xī Lù 6 (just south of the west gate of the Worker's Stadium), with 100 lanes, thumping music, and flashing video games to bring in the kids (✆ **010/6552-2688;** daily noon–midnight ¥30/$3.70 per game; daily midnight–noon ¥20/$2.50 per game).

GOLF (GĀO'ĚRFÚQIÚ)   If playing golf in a region desperately short of land and water doesn't bother you, then try negotiating the water hazards of **Běijīng International Golf Club** (**Běijīng Guójì Gāo'ěrfū Jùlèbù;** ✆ **010/6076-2288**), northwest of town near the Míng Tombs. Eighteen holes cost ¥600 ($69) during the week, rising to ¥1,200 ($159) on weekends. Caddie fees are ¥150 ($19).

ICE-SKATING (LIŪBĪNG)   Běijīng has superb outdoor ice-skating in the winter at **Běi Hǎi Gōngyuán, Qián Hǎi,** and the **Summer Palace.** Skate rental outfits charge about ¥20 ($2.50), but you might not find boots that fit. Even more popular in winter are "ice cars" *(bīng chē),* box sleds propelled by ski poles. Caveats about the thickness of ice sheets apply—global warming makes for a shorter skating season each year. Běijīng's largest skate rink is **Le Cool,** Guómào Liūbīng Chǎng (✆ **010/6505-5776**), in the underground shopping center that connects Traders Hotel to China World Hotel. Open Sunday through Friday from 10am to 10pm and Saturday until midnight, this rink charges ¥30 ($3.70) for 90 minutes from 10am to 6pm, ¥40 ($5) from 6 to 10pm, and ¥50 ($6) after 6pm on Saturday and Sunday.

KITE-FLYING (FÀNG FĒNGZHENG)   Flying in China at least 2,000 years before they were seen in Europe, the humble kite has been used as a communication link in battlefields, a device to frighten enemy troops, and even in the sport of kite fighting. But most locals fly kites peacefully, particularly at **Tiān'ān Mén Square** (where you can rent kites) or in parks such as **Rì Tán Gōngyuán.** You can purchase kites at several markets; good selections are available at Guānyuán Shìchǎng and on the fourth floor of Yǎxiù Fúzhuāng Shìchǎng (see section 2, "Markets & Bazaars," in chapter 9).

TABLE TENNIS (PĪNG PĀNG QIÚ)   Every community center in Běijīng has a table tennis table with willing opponents: an excellent way to meet locals, but humiliating when your conqueror is a generation or two older than you. Běijīng now boasts a table tennis bar, **W Restaurant and Bar** (*C* 010/6595-8039) at Nán Sān Lǐ Tun Lù 120, opened by Swedish table tennis ace Jan-Ove Waldner whose cardboard effigy stands outside. There are also plans to open an English-speaking academy at Peking University in September 2006; for now you can contact the club at *C* **010/6261-1188.**

TÀIJÍQUÁN Tai Chi practitioners can visit any park at daybreak, and enjoy the thrill of practicing with hundreds of others. The **Chinese Culture Club** (see above) has a regular course in English.

YOGA (YÚJIĀ) If you need to stretch out, the Yoga Yard, Yōnghé Jiāyuán 4-108 (*C* **010/5102-6108;** www.yogayard.com) offers Hatha Yoga classes for all levels. From the Yōng Hé Gōng metro stop (215, exit A), walk north and take the first right to follow the canal. Yoga Yard is located inside the Yōnghé Jiāyuán compound.

SPECTATOR SPORTS

Gōngrén Tǐyùchǎng (Workers' Stadium) is the home of the capital's football (soccer) team, formerly known as Běijīng Guó Ān, now called **Běijīng Xiàndài** (named for the Hyundai car company). A fanatical green-and-white army of fans follows the team, which perennially wallows in mid-table mediocrity, well behind the Chelsea of the Chinese league, Dàlián. Referees are usually corrupt, and worth two goals to Běijīng, but fans still shower them with invective you won't find in any language textbook. Tickets can be purchased at the Workers' Stadium north gate, **Lìshēng Tǐyù Shāngshà,** Wángfǔjǐng Dàjiē 74A (*C* **010/6525-0581;** daily 9am–8:30pm), or **ClubFootball** (see chapter 10, p. 189). The season runs from April through November.

Winding Down

While Běijīng is fascinating, it is *not* a relaxing honeymoon destination. Your first choice for unwinding should be the **St. Regis Spa** (*C* 010/6460-6688, ext. 2745), currently the only genuine spa in Běijīng (Sheraton and Shangri-La will open soon). Treatments range from a quick scalp massage (¥125/$16) up to a 4½-hour "Healthy Indulgence Package" (¥1,950/$244). Thai massage and foot reflexology are the specialties of **Bodhi Therapeutic Retreat** (*C* 010/6417-9595; www.bodhi.com.cn) at Gōngtǐ Běi Lù 17 (opposite the north gate of the Workers' Stadium). A full-body massage costs as little as ¥78 ($10) per hour from Monday to Thursday, including complimentary food and beverages: an absolute steal. Open 11am till midnight. China's atheist leaders surround themselves with *Qì Gōng* masters, astrologers, and masseurs; enjoy the cadre treatment at newly opened **Dà Guó Shǒu** (*C* 010/6417-8135), 300m (984 ft.) north of Dōng Sì Shí Tiáo metro stop (exit B) on the east Second Ring Road, where staff are trained by ex-president Jiāng Zémín's personal masseur, Zhèng Zhìjiàn. Open 11am to 2am. Traditionally, massage was a profession reserved for the blind. Mángrén ànmó (blind massage) may be experienced at the friendly **Lèshēng Mángrén Bǎojiàn Ànmó Zhōngxīn,** Dēngshìkǒu Xī Jiē 32 (*C* 010/6525-7532, ext. 3201), on the second floor of the Dōnghuá Fàndiàn, a long block west of the Crowne Plaza in Wángfǔjǐng. A 1-hour massage costs ¥88 ($11). It's open from 11am to midnight.

Běijīng Strolls

Taking a stroll in Běijīng can be hard work. The main boulevard, Cháng'ān Dàjiē, is a soulless and windswept thoroughfare, and the rest of town seems to be a huge construction site choking on dust and car fumes. These strolls will show you a gentler Běijīng, where octogenarians push cane shopping carts through even more ancient tree-lined *hútòng,* where young lovers clasp hands nervously as they gaze across the Back Lakes, and where pot-bellied cab drivers quaff beer while enjoying boisterous games of poker or chess in the middle of the sidewalk.

You'll need your wits about you. No one in Běijīng seems capable of walking in a straight line. Pedestrian crossings are decorative, and newly installed crossings with traffic lights are often ignored by motorists. The car, particularly the four-wheel-drive, dominates both the road and the sidewalk. Cars are the main source of

the air pollution that blankets the capital. Běijīng already boasts the highest rate of car ownership in China, and more than a thousand new cars hit the road every day; a suicidal path, akin to turning New York into Los Angeles.

Renting or purchasing a bike moves you one rung up the traffic food chain and is a less tiring way to get around. Youth hostels rent out bikes for around ¥30 ($4) per day, bike parking stations next to metro stops are cheaper yet (¥10/$1.25 per day), but you'll need a native speaker to assist you. You can purchase a second-hand bike from a streetside repair stall for less than ¥100 ($12); new bikes start from ¥140 ($17). Bike traffic is orderly, and unlike Guǎngzhōu and Shànghǎi, the capital has yet to block off large numbers of streets to cyclists. Whether you walk or ride a bike, avoid sudden changes of direction, and go with the substantial flow around you.

WALKING TOUR 1   LIÚLICHÂNG & DÀ ZHÀLÁN

Start:	Zhèngyǐ Cí Xilóu, just south of the metro on Qián Mén Xiī Héyàn Jiē (metro: Hépíng Mén, 207).
Finish:	Qián Mén, south end of Tiān'ān Mén Guǎngchǎng (metro: Qián Mén, 208).
Time:	3 hours.
Best times:	Any weekday starting at about 9am or 2pm.
Worst times:	Weekends are crowded. Most shops close about 8:30pm.

This pleasant stroll takes in many of Běijīng's most famous shops. Even if you're not interested in buying anything, it makes an agreeable break from the fumes of the capital's constantly gridlocked streets. **Liúlichǎng,** named for a factory that once turned out the glazed roof tiles that clearly delineated the rank of Běijīng's buildings, was renovated in the 1980s to capture the look and atmosphere of the late Qīng dynasty.

Scholars and art connoisseurs once frequented Liúlichǎng, and it is still home to the most famous art-supplies store in China, **Róngbǎo Zhāi.** There is a cluster (at times it feels like a gauntlet) of shops selling art books, scrolls, rubbings, handmade paper, paintbrushes, ink sticks, "jade," and antiques (which are nearly all fakes). Liúlichǎng runs about 6 blocks east–west. Southeast of it is **Dà Zhàlán,** an ancient, but more plebeian, shopping street that has been converted into a cobblestoned pedestrian-only mall. There are many ancient shops on Dà Zhàlán, including tailors, shoe stores, and apothecaries selling traditional medicines. North of Dà Zhàlán, the market streets of **Lángfáng Èr Tiáo** and **Lángfáng Tóu Tiáo** wind their ways towards **Qián Mén (Front Gate)** overlooking **Tiān'ān Mén Square.**

Walk south from the Hépíng Mén metro station down Nán Xīnhuá Jiē, and take the first left onto Qián Mén Xī Héyàn Jiē, where you'll find:

❶ Zhèngyǐ Cí Xìlóu

Dating back more than 340 years, much of the history of Běijīng Opera is tied up with this delightful theater, which began life as a Buddhist temple during the Míng dynasty. It's fairly quiet these days, although there are occasional evening performances (call ✆ **010/6317-7354** to check). During the day, opera fans gather to practice their art, and for a fee of ¥5 (60¢), you will be allowed to view the magnificently restored interior.

Backtrack to the main road and continue south to Liúlichǎng Xī Jiē. On the right-hand side of the road is:

❷ Cathay Bookshop (No. 18)

One of several branches of China Books, this bookshop (south side of street; ✆ **010/6301-7678**) has a great range of art materials—paper, ink stones, chops, brushes, and frames—at far more reasonable prices than you'll find at . . .

❸ Róngbǎo Zhāi (No. 19)

The most renowned art shop in China (north side of street) greets you with what may be the world's largest ink stone. Róngbǎo Zhāi sells woodblock prints, copies of famous calligraphy, historic paintings (reproductions), and art supplies. The handful of workers who are more interested in doing their jobs than

in reading the paper are gold mines of information on Běijīng's art scene.

Directly opposite is:

❹ Fùshān Huácǎi (No. 36)

This shop sells a range of Western and traditional Chinese instruments. Upstairs, you'll find classical sheet music at very reasonable prices. The names of the composers are usually written above the scores.

Further west, the street is due to be demolished to make way for a patch of lawn that no one is allowed to sit on. So backtrack to Nán Xīnhuá Jiē and cross the footbridge to Liúlichǎng Dōng Jiē. On the north side is:

❺ Zhōngguó Shūdiàn (No. 115)

Although it's a sprawling, state-run mess, the largest branch of China Books offers a wide range of books on Chinese art, architecture, and literature without the markups that plague arty bookstores.

Continue east to:

❻ Sōngyún Gé (No. 106)

This tiny shop, founded in 1903, stocks a marvelous collection of antiquarian books.

❼ Curio Shops

Further east, the street peters out into in a series of bric-a-brac shops. The sea of credit card signs is fair warning of why the vendors are so friendly. But you'll find a fascinating jumble of Buddhist statuary, lacquerware, ceramics, cloisonné, and jewelry, alongside old pipes, clocks, snuff-boxes, and general bric-a-brac.

1 Zhèngyǐcí Xìlóu
正乙祠戏楼

2 Cathay Bookshop (No. 18)
来薰阁

3 Róngbaǎo Zhāi (No. 19)
荣宝斋

4 Fùshaīn Huácǎi (No. 36)
富山华彩

5 Zhōngguó Shūdiàn (No. 115)
中国书店

6 Sōngyúngé (No. 106)
松筠阁

7 Curio Shops

8 Dà Zhàlán
大栅栏

9 Nèi Lián Shēng Xiédiàn (No. 34)
内联升鞋店

10 Tóngréntáng (No. 24)
同仁堂

11 Ruìfúxiáng Chóubù Diàn (No. 5)
瑞蚨祥绸布店

12 Liùbìjū Jiàngyuán (No. 3)
六必居酱园

13 Bā Dà Hútòng (Eight Great Lanes)
八大胡同

14 Lángfáng Èr Tiáo
廊房二条

15 Qián Mén (Front Gate)
前门

Liúlichǎng Dōng Jiē ends at Yánshòu Jiē. Head south before turning onto the second street on your left (Yīngtáo Xié Jiē), which leads to:

⑧ Dà Zhàlán (Dàshílànr in Běijīng dialect)

Known as Lángfáng Sì Tiáo during the Míng dynasty, its name was changed to Dà Zhàlán after a large stockade was built, presumably to give peace of mind to the wealthy retailers who set up shop here. Now the proletarian answer to Wángfǔjǐng, it's a bustling pedestrian-only street boasting some of Běijīng's oldest retailers.

In the first block on the right side, you'll find:

⑨ Nèi Lián Shēng Xiédiàn (No. 34)

Established in 1853, this famous shoe store (☎ 010/6301-4863) still crafts cloth "happy shoes" (qiāncéng bùxié) and delicately embroidered women's shoes by hand. Using a little bit of charm, you may get a peek at the workshop out back.

Turn left at the next street, and at the end of the block on the right you'll find:

⑩ Tóngrén Táng (No. 24)

Established in 1669, Běijīng's most celebrated dispenser of traditional Chinese medicines (☎ 010/6303-1155) has been imitated from Shěnyáng to San Francisco. In the building to the west is a clinic where you can have your pulse read and receive a prescription for your deficiencies. Reassuringly, everyone is lacking something. The second floor stocks raw herbs, including a single ginseng root (said to boost male yáng energy) from Chángbái Shān in the northeast retailing for ¥380,000 ($47,500).

TAKE A BREAK
Now is a good time to stop for a cup of tea and a Chinese steamed pastry on the second floor of **Zhāng Yīyuán Cháyè Diàn**, Dà Zhàlán Jiē 22 (☎ 010/6303-1082; open daily 8am–7pm). The shop sells a bewildering range of teas at reasonable prices. If you're feeling peckish, there's a branch of the celebrated dumpling restaurant, **Gǒubùlǐ Bāozi Diàn** (p. 100), diagonally opposite.

You're nearly at the east end of Dà Zhàlán. Don't miss its most famous store, on the left (north) side:

⑪ Ruìfúxiáng Chóubù Diàn (No. 5)

Established in 1893 on the north side of Dà Zhàlán, this fabric store (open daily 9am–8pm) was once the prime outlet for Qīng dynasty royalty and rich merchants. Sadly, the rich, dark wood panels of the original shop have been replaced by chipboard. Expect to bargain 30% to 50% off the marked prices of the vast selection of silks. A tailor-made qípáo (cheongsam) will cost upwards of ¥500 ($60). Allow 1 week, with a couple of fittings.

Turn right down Liángshi Diàn Jiē, the last hútòng before Qián Mén Dàjiē. On the right, you'll find:

⑫ Liùbìjū Jiàngyuán (No. 3)

Pickles and sauces of every imaginable variety sit in glass-covered ceramic vats. Parts of this dimly lit store look like they've been untouched since they opened for business 400 years ago.

To the south lies Běijīng's old red-light district. If time permits, explore the quiet lanes of the area once known as:

⑬ Bā Dà Hútòng (Eight Great Lanes)

A 1906 survey found that the capital boasted 308 brothels (more than the number of hotels or restaurants), most of them in this district. While there are assuredly now many multiples of that number in Běijīng, the government is embarrassed by this area, and forbids local tour agents from visiting or even mentioning Bā Dà Hútòng. Lanes were once graded into three levels, from "lower area" (xià chù) streets such as Wángpí Hútòng, where prostitutes satisfied the needs of the masses, up to lanes such as Báishùn Hútòng, where "flower girls" versed in classical poetry and music awaited. Money was no guarantee of success; there were various manuals on the etiquette of wooing courtesans. The Tóngzhì emperor (reign 1862–1874) was notorious for creeping out at night to sample the delights of "clouds and rain." He died of syphilis. These days, hair salons in nearby alleys are unlikely to house courtesans skilled in the arts of conversation and playing the lute, but the basic requirements of the masses are provided for.

North of Dà Zhàlán the *hútòng* becomes Zhūbǎoshì Jiē, a jumble of stands, shops, and carts peddling cheap clothing and bric-a-brac. Take the first left into:

⓮ Lángfáng Èr Tiáo

During the Qīng dynasty, this *hútòng* was renowned for its jade and antiques vendors. Two- and three-story houses with beautifully carved wooden balconies hint at past wealth. To the south is Lángfáng Sān Tiáo, the heart of the former banking district.

Head right (north) along Méishi Jiē up to Lángfáng Tóu Tiáo, known as Lantern Street (Dēng Jiē) during the Qīng dynasty. Turn right (east). Ahead looms:

⓯ Qián Mén (Front Gate)

North of Zhūbǎoshì Jiē is the south end of Tiān'ān Mén Square. To the northeast you'll see the old Front Gate (Qián Mén or more correctly Zhèngyáng Mén), a towering remnant of the city wall through which the emperors passed on their annual procession from the Forbidden City to the Temple of Heaven. Ascend the tower for excellent views of Tiān'ān Mén Square to the north and Dà Zhàlán to the southwest. There's also a photographic exhibition of the streets and walls of old Běijīng.

WINDING DOWN
The world's largest **KFC** is a block west on the south side of Qián Mén Xī Dàjiē. Continuing west, you can take in the nightly performance of opera and acrobatics at **Lǎo Shě Teahouse (Lǎo Shě Cháguǎn)**. It's worth paying extra for a seat close to the front. Performances start at 7:50pm and usually run for about 90 minutes. Call to book a spot (☎ **010/6303-6830**). Tea and pastries are included.

WALKING TOUR 2   BACK LAKES RAMBLE

Start:	Huìtōng Cí (metro: Jīshuǐ Tán, 218, exit B).
Finish:	Méi Lánfāng Gùjū, west side of Qián Hǎi (metro: Jīshuǐ Tán, 218, exit C).
Time:	4 hours.
Best times:	Any time between 9am and noon.
Worst times:	Mondays, when some sites are closed. Weekends can also be crowded.

There is, quite simply, no finer place to walk in Běijīng. The Back Lakes area (Shíchà Hǎi) is composed of three idyllic lakes—Qián Hǎi (Front Lake), Hòu Hǎi (Back Lake), and Xī Hǎi (West Lake)—and the tree-shaded neighborhoods that surround them. Combined with other man-made pools to the south, these lakes were once part of a system used to transport grain by barge from the Grand Canal to the Forbidden City. Prior to 1911, this was an exclusive area, and only people with connections to the imperial family were permitted to maintain houses here (a situation that seems destined to return). A profusion of bars and cafes has sprung up around the lakes in recent years (see chapter 10, "Běijīng After Dark"), providing ample opportunities to take breaks from your walk.

Beyond the lakes, stretching out to the east and west is the city's best-maintained network of *hútòng*. Many families have lived in these lanes for generations, their insular communities a last link to Old Běijīng. The energetic (or those with bikes) may wish to combine this stroll with stroll no. 4, "Lìdài Dìwáng Miào and Hùguó Sì".

Begin at a park just outside the Jīshuǐ Tán metro station (exit B) along the south side of the busy Second Ring Road at:

❶ Huìtōng Cí
This ancestral hall cum Buddhist temple dates from the Míng, but little of antiquity remains. The point of visiting is to climb to the top for a view of the road ahead. The nearest lake is Xī Hǎi, followed by Hòu Hǎi and the spires of the Bell Tower (to the left) and Drum Tower.

Retrace your steps, turn left as you exit the park, and then left again to follow Bǎn Qiáo Tóu Tiáo as it snakes around the side of Xī Hǎi. Cross busy Déshèng Mén Nèi Dàjiē (set to be transformed into a 50m–wide [164-ft.] thoroughfare during the life of this book), and take the next left turn to follow the north side of Hòu Hǎi to:

❷ Former Residence of Soong Ching-ling (Sòng Qìnglíng Gùjū)
Located at Hòu Hǎi Běi Yàn 46, this former imperial palace is where Soong Ching-ling (1892–1981), middle daughter of famous Bible salesman Charlie Soong and wife of Sun Yat-sen, spent most of her later life. While her family became leading supporters of the Guómíndǎng (Nationalists), Soong Ching-ling steered a more neutral course, displaying some measure of sympathy for the Communists only after her husband's death in 1925. Máo later rewarded her with this house (admission ¥20/$2.50; open daily 9am–4:30pm). China's last emperor, Henry Pǔyí, is said to have been born on this site. On weekends, there's a risk of being trampled by soon-to-be-wed brides in their finery.

Turn left and continue southeast along Hòu Hǎi Běi Yàn to the:

❸ Exercise Yard
On the right-hand side of the road, stretch your limbs and meet some locals. There's table tennis on offer, and Běijīng's hardiest swimmers take the plunge from here—year-round! Joining the swimmers is not recommended: There's a reason they wash themselves so quickly when they get out. Just south of here is a picturesque former royal residence, **Chún Qīnwáng Fǔ.**

Continue along the lakeshore, take the second left, and immediately turn right into Yǎ'ér Hútòng. On your left is:

❹ Guǎnghuà Sì
A Buddhist temple dating back to the Yuán dynasty (1279–1368), this complex originally comprised over 20 buildings. Only a few of the buildings remain. In residence are at least 20 monks, many from southern China. China's last known eunuch, Sūn Yàotíng, was caretaker of the temple for 2 decades, and died here in 1996. Admission is allowed on the 1st and 15th days of the lunar month, when the temple is filled with locals praying for the success of their latest business ventures.

At this point you can make an optional detour eastward to the:

❺ Drum Tower (Gǔ Lóu)
This vaguely trapezoidal building (admission ¥20/$2.50; open daily 9am–4:30pm) with its bright yellow tile roof is the most conspicuous structure north of the old Imperial City. Skip the "free Tibetan Culture Exhibit" on the first floor (essentially an overpriced fake antiques market) and go around back to the steep set of stairs that leads to the upper chamber. From here you can survey the Back Lakes and take in tremendous views of the old Tartar City, set against the jagged-tooth backdrop of urban Běijīng.

Walk south on Dì'ān Mén Wài Dàjiē and take the first right onto Yāndài Xié Jiē, home to some of Běijīng's trendiest bars and cafes. Bear left until you reach:

❻ Yíndìng Qiáo (Silver Ingot Bridge)
This white marble bridge, which marks the boundary between Hòu Hǎi and

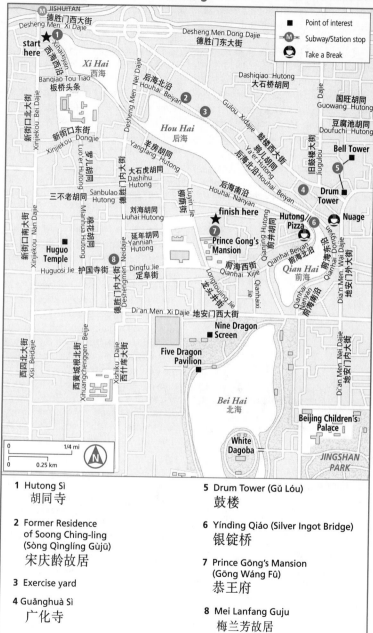

Legend:
- ■ Point of interest
- Ⓜ Subway/Station stop
- Take a Break

1 **Hutong Sì**
胡同寺

2 **Former Residence of Soong Ching-ling (Sòng Qìnglíng Gùjū)**
宋庆龄故居

3 **Exercise yard**

4 **Guǎnghuà Sì**
广化寺

5 **Drum Tower (Gǔ Lóu)**
鼓楼

6 **Yíndìng Qiáo (Silver Ingot Bridge)**
银锭桥

7 **Prince Gōng's Mansion (Gōng Wáng Fǔ)**
恭王府

8 **Mei Lanfang Guju**
梅兰芳故居

Qián Hǎi, has stood here for centuries, although the latest version is the work of modern masons (1984). Standing on this bridge in the 18th century, the Qiánlóng emperor could see as far as the Western Hills, and he deemed it one of the Eight Great Views of Běijīng. Air quality has dropped since, but there's plenty of entertainment below the bridge, where the rowboats of romantically minded oarsmen bump bows.

Cross the bridge and turn right. Take the winding road along the southwest shore of Hòu Hǎi past a jumble of cafes, bars, and shops, and stop for a bite or a paddle :

TAKE A BREAK
Turn left before you cross the bridge, immediately on your left is an impressive four-story structure. This is **Nuage,** which delivers pricey but heavenly Vietnamese cuisine amid delightful colonial ambience (p. 88). If the weather is fine, aim for a seat on the rooftop.

If you're not sufficiently rested, turn left as you exit and hire a rowboat or a "duck boat" (yāzi chuán) and go for a paddle around the lake for about ¥50 ($6) per hour. In winter, pull on a pair of ice skates for only ¥20 ($2.50).

❼ Prince Gōng's Mansion (Gōng Wáng Fǔ)

The most lavish of the courtyard residences in the Back Lakes is located at Liǔyīn Jiē 17 (admission ¥20/$2.50; open daily 8:30am–4:30pm). Inside is one of the city's most spectacular gardens, a combination of pavilions and rockeries perfectly arranged to make it all seem larger than it really is. You're only seeing part of the picture—the original complex, built by the corrupt eunuch Héshēn (said to have been Qiánlóng's catamite), was even larger. More extravagant buildings, built entirely from the rare *nánmù* (cedar), are housed in the National Arts Research Institute (Zhōngguó Yìshù Yánjiūyuàn) next door. See p. 141 for a more detailed description of Prince Gōng's Mansion.

Turn left as you exit, continue past the touts to turn right at a T-junction. On your right, you'll soon pass another prince's mansion, Qìng Wáng Fǔ. This spectacular residence is occupied by the army, so there's no chance of admission. Cross Déshèng Mén Nèi Dàjiē, and on your right is:

❽ Méi Lánfāng Gùjū

This is the superbly preserved courtyard residence of Běijīng opera's most eminent star, Méi Lánfāng. Much is made of Méi joining the CCP, but a meticulous portrait of Guān Yīn painted by the actor (displayed in Exhibition Hall 2), suggests he learned a new tune when the Communists came to power. Most intriguing is the exhibition of postures and hand gestures that Méi produced while at the height of his powers in 1935. Specific postures and hand gestures used to convey shyness, dozing, and mild surprise hint at the intricacies of the art form.

WINDING DOWN
Turn left as you exit, and continue straight to rejoin the lakes at Qián Hǎi. On your right is Lotus Lane, which sports **Starbucks, Kosmo,** and bars with silly names like Sex and Da City. We recommend you continue on to Yíndìng Qiáo, and follow the directions on p. 89 to find **Hútòng Pizza.**

WALKING TOUR 3   WÁNGFŬJĬNG

Start:	Wángfǔjǐng Palaeolithic Museum (metro: Wángfǔjǐng, 118, exit A).
Finish:	Dōng Sì Mosque (metro: Dōng Dān, 119, exit A).
Time:	3 to 4 hours.
Best times:	Weekday mornings or late afternoons.
Worst times:	Weekends when window shoppers run rampant. Lunchtime can also be crowded.

Wángfǔjǐng (Well of the Prince's Palace) is the commercial heart of Běijīng, the modern face that China's leaders desperately want the world to see. But, as you'll find on this tour, duck down alleyways in any direction and the facade melts away. Situated east of the Forbidden City, Wángfǔjǐng was the favorite residential neighborhood of royalty during the Míng and Qīng dynasties. At the end of the Qīng, when the princes fell on hard times, there was plenty of family silver to be sold. Pawnshops sprang up, and the street got its start as a commercial area. It also began catering to foreign tastes, not only for Chinese antiques but for imported luxuries. Unsurprisingly, it was one of the first targets of the Boxer Rebellion in 1900.

You wonder what the xenophobic Boxers would make of it now. There are only a handful of traditional Chinese stores left—most of them have been bulldozed to make way for huge mega-malls. The cathedral razed by the Boxers was soon rebuilt and was fully refurbished in 1999; its forecourt is a magnet for local skaters, talking a talk that owes nothing to the Confucian Classics. But continuing on, the Boxers might find solace in the small remnants of *hútòng* and the distinctly Chinese (and more affordable) fashions and street food on offer in the stalls of **Lóngfú Sì Jiē** and **Dōng Sì.**

Taking exit A from the metro, you'll find:

❶ Wángfǔjǐng Palaeolithic Museum

The owners of Oriental Plaza were unimpressed when they struck 24,000-year-old bone in the basement of the largest mall in Asia. However, the powers-that-be couldn't resist the urge to build yet another monument to the longevity of Chinese civilization, and forced the Hong Kong developers to build this museum to house their ancestors (admission ¥10/$1.25).

Ascend the escalator to find yourself in the basement of:

❷ Oriental Plaza (Dōngfāng Xīn Tiāndì)

If you don't get enough of this back home, have a poke around Asia's largest shopping center, which stretches east all the way to the next metro station at Dōng Dān. Upscale clothing stores, the Sony ExploraScience Museum, the fine restaurant South Beauty, and the 24-hour eatery Be There or Be Square (Bú Jiàn Bú Sàn; p. 87) are all here.

Emerging from the west side of the mall, stick to the right (east) side and head north up Wángfǔjǐng Dàjiē, passing the huge but chaotic Wángfǔjǐng Bookstore. Cross the road to:

❸ Gōngměi Dàshà (No. 200)

This is the most reliable shop in town at which to purchase jade rather than the colored glass you'll likely encounter elsewhere. Aim to pay about a third of the marked price. They also stock high-quality tea sets and calligraphy materials, alongside tacky souvenirs. On the fourth floor is a small but interesting craft exhibit (open daily 9am–9pm).

Continue along the right-hand side of Wángfǔjǐng Dàjiē to:

❹ Shèngxīfú (No. 196)

Established in 1912, this hat shop was one of the fortunate few to survive the remodeling of Wángfǔjǐng. A paean to the wisdom of the CCP on the first floor suggests they're not taking survival for granted. The modern hats are popular with locals, and the shop displays its revolutionary credentials on the second floor, which brims with sturdy Léi Fēng hats (earflaps, thick tops, shiny red stars) and proletarian Máo caps.

Return to Wángfǔjǐng Dàjiē, and continue north along the left (west) side to:

 TAKE A BREAK
Wángfǔjǐng Xiǎochī Jiē is about as spruced up as street food gets in Běijīng. Ordering is a cinch—everything is on display, and the vendors are well-versed in sign language. In the evening, **Dōnghuá Mén night market** (p. 99), further north, offers more choices, though hygiene can be a concern. Further on, behind an opaque glass door on the right hand side, is the superb **RBL** (p. 86), open 6pm to 2am, which serves the best coffee and cocktails in town. The fare and the ambience are so sublime that your evening stroll may well end here.

Return to the main street, and continue north. On the left (west) side is:

❺ Běijīng Shì Bǎihuò Dàlóu (No. 255)

Despite a recent merger with the fancy Sun Dong An Plaza, the upper floors of Běijīng's premier department store are still chaotic. A branch of **China Silk** on the third floor offers silk at economical prices.

The east side of the pedestrian mall is dominated by what was just a few years ago China's glitziest shopping center:

❻ Sun Dong An Plaza (Xīn Dōng'ān Shìchǎng) (No. 138)

Rising like a tombstone on the grave of shop-vendors past, this massive emporium holds designer clothing shops and the usual Western and Japanese food chains—Baskin-Robbins, Pizza Hut, McDonald's, KFC, Yoshinoya, UCC,

Starbucks, and Délifrance. There's also an excellent hot pot restaurant, **Dōng Lái Shùn,** which recently celebrated its 100th anniversary. The old shops that once stood here are mocked by **Old Běijīng Street,** a tacky re-creation found in the basement.

Directly across Wángfǔjǐng Dàjiē, on the west side, beyond the life-size bronze statues of a Qīng dynasty barber, a musician, and a rickshaw puller, is the:

❼ Foreign Language Bookstore (No. 235)

The Wàiwén Shūdiàn houses Běijīng's largest selection of English-language materials on the first and third floors. The second floor has a surprisingly wide range of CDs featuring local alternative bands, as well as Běijīng opera and soothing instrumental music.

Continue north. On the left side is:

❽ Lìshēng Tǐyù Shāngshà (No. 201)

A purveyor of sporting goods since 1921, the store has mountains of sporting clothes and shoes. The basement stocks everything from camping gear and skateboards to gyrating massage machines and shuffleboard tables. **Hóngshēng Musical Instruments,** a highbrow vendor of pianos (grand and otherwise), looks out of place on the third floor. Daily from 9am to 9pm.

Diagonally across the road, it's hard to miss:

❾ Dōng Táng (East Church)

Also known as St. Joseph's Cathedral, this gray Gothic structure has endured a torrid history. Built on ground donated by the Shùnzhì emperor in 1655, this Jesuit church was toppled by an earthquake in 1720, gutted by a fire in 1807, and completely razed during the Boxer Rebellion of 1900. Sunday services are held at 6:15, 7, and 8am. After a major renovation from 1999 to 2000, the church became notable for its wide, tree-lined forecourt, the favorite spot of Běijīng's skaters.

Walking Tour 3: Wángfǔjǐng

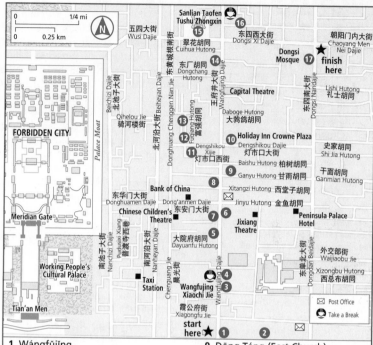

1 Wángfǔjǐng
   Palaeolithic Museum
   王府井古人类文化遗址博物馆

2 Oriental Plaza
      (Dōngfāng Xīn Tiāndì)
   东方新天地

3 Gōngměi Dàshà (No. 200)
   工美大厦

4 Shèngxǐfú (No. 196)
   盛锡福

5 Běijīng Shì
      Bǎihuò Dàlóu (No. 255)
   北京市百货大楼

6 Sun Dong An Plaza
      (Xīn Dōng'ān
      Shìchǎng) (No. 138)
   新东安商场

7 Foreign Language
      Bookstore (No. 235)
   外文书店

8 Lìshēng Tǐyù
      Shāngshà (No. 201)
   利生体育商厦

9 Dōng Táng (East Church)
   东堂

10 Běijīng Guójì
       Yìyuàn Měishùguǎn
   北京国际艺苑美术馆

11 Lèshēng Mángrén Bǎojiàn
       Ànmó Zhōngxīn (No. 32)
   乐生盲人保健按摩中心

12 Lǎo Shě
       Jìniànguǎn (No. 19)
   老舍纪念馆

13 Fùqiáng Hútòng
   富强胡同

14 Běijīng Kǎogǔ
       Shūdiàn (No. 27)
   北京考古书店

15 Zhōngguó Měishùguǎn
       (National Museum of Fine Art)
   中国美术馆

16 Lóngfú Sì Jiē
   隆福寺街

17 Dōngsì Qīngzhēn Sì
   东四清真寺

159

Continuing north up Wángfǔjǐng Dàjiē, you come to a second major intersection with Dēngshìkǒu Dàjiē. Cross over and enter the Crowne Plaza Běijīng. To the right-hand side of the lobby you'll find:

❿ Běijīng Guójì Yìyuàn Měishùguǎn

This art gallery ((C) **010/6513-3388;** open daily 9am–6pm) can be hit-and-miss, and is often clogged with flaccid depictions of rural and *hútòng* life. But their collection of Russian oil paintings, most from the early 1990s, contains some startling and innovative works. You can't go too far wrong—the works are not for sale, admission is free, and staff is friendly.

Cross over and follow Dēngshìkǒu Xī Jiē a long block west. If your feet are aching, look for the Dōnghuá Fàndiàn on the left-hand side and pop up to the second floor, where you'll find:

⓫ Lèshēng Mángrén Bǎojiàn Ànmó Zhōngxīn (No. 32)

"Loving Life Massage Center" (open daily 11am–midnight) can lift you up with a full-body blind massage *(quán shēn ànmó)* or a foot wash and rub *(zúdǐ ànmó)*. ¥88 ($11) buys an hour of bliss. "Hot pot" *(bá huǒ guàn)* won't fill your belly, but the heated glass bowls will leave red welts all over your back.

If you can still walk, there are two narrow lanes opposite. The lane to the left, Fēngfù Hútòng, is the site of:

⓬ Lǎo Shě Jìniànguǎn (No. 19)

The memorial hall to Lǎo Shě, one of China's best-loved writers, is located in a quiet and atmospheric courtyard residence (p. 140). Former premier Zhōu Ēnlái bestowed the house on the writer when he returned from overseas in 1950. While the regime hoped Lǎo Shě would become a cheerleader like fellow scribbler Guō Mòruò, his post-liberation years were relatively unproductive, and his final work (before he drowned himself in a Cultural Revolution–induced suicide) concerned his Manchu ancestors.

Retrace your steps back to the next narrow alleyway to the east, and turn left (north). You are now on:

⓭ Fùqiáng Hútòng

The immodestly named "Rich and Powerful" Hútòng still boasts some *sìhéyuàn* courtyard houses that hint at its wealthy past. Note the finely carved roof lintels with swastika motifs and the lotus-emblazoned door piers *(mén dūnr)* at no. 18. While the rectangular door pier indicates the residents weren't officials (whose houses were marked by circular door piers), they must have been well-off to be able to afford skilled stonemasons. The presence of soldiers is due to a more recent resident: Party General Secretary, Zhào Zǐyáng, who was ousted during the Tiān'ān Mén massacre (even though he prepared the documents for martial law). He lived under house arrest at no. 3 until his death in January 2005.

The *hútòng* ends at a T-junction. Turn right to Wángfǔjǐng Dàjiē. To the south you can see Shǒudū Jùchǎng (Capital Theater), but turn left and head north. On your left is:

⓮ Běijīng Kǎogǔ Shūdiàn (No. 27)

Most bookshops near the National Museum of Fine Art are fond of the "stick-up"—a sticker that elevates the price of the book by as much as a factor of eight. Not this shop (open daily 9am–8pm), which houses a staggering range of art and architecture folios. To the right as you enter, you'll find bronze reproductions of drinking vessels, cooking tripods, and the inevitable "flying horse" *(tóng bēn mǎ)*.

Continuing north, you reach the intersection with Wǔsì Dàjiē. Off to the left, it's impossible to miss:

⓯ Zhōngguó Měishùguǎn (National Museum of Fine Art)

Along with musicians and reformist politicians, avant-garde artists took much of the blame for "spiritually polluting" the minds of China's young folks in the 1980s. Once the place to see cutting-edge art, the National Museum of Fine Art ((C) **010/8403-3500;** open daily 9am–4pm; admission ¥20/$2.50) gained a conservative director and a reputation for lackluster exhibitions. After a recent makeover, the Cultural Bureau promises those days are over.

TAKE A BREAK
Just east of the National Museum of Fine Art is one of Běijīng's most interesting Chinese-language bookstores, **Sānlián Tāofèn Túshū Zhōngxīn**, at Měishùguǎn Dōng Jiē 22 (open daily 9am–9pm). The second floor houses gorgeous pictorials, a music store, and a tranquil cafe.

Backtrack south from the bookstore, and take the next street on your left:

⑯ Lóngfú Sì Jiē

Along with Hùguó Sì, Lóngfú Sì was one of the two main markets in old Běijīng. It's a tad down market these days, but is still a lively spot to hunt for cheap clothes, music, and street food, and it makes an interesting contrast to its main competitor, Wángfǔjǐng. Halfway down the street, on the south side, is a branch of Běijīng's most renowned vendor of wonton soup *(húntun)*, **Húntun Hóu,** looking much more at home here than the original store does on Wángfǔjǐng.

An archway marks the end of the mall. In front of you is Dōng Sì Běi Dàjiē. Turn right and head south to Dōng Sì Nán Dàjiē. On the right-hand side, you soon arrive at:

⑰ Dōng Sì Qīngzhēn Sì

This is one of Běijīng's earliest mosques (admission ¥10/$1.25 for non-Muslims; open daylight hours). It has enjoyed a peaceful history of worship since the 14th century. The second courtyard is serene, a wonderful break from the mercantile and traffic pandemonium.

You can either walk north (or take bus no. 807) to Yōng Hé Gōng and Kǒng Miào (20 min.), or you can head south towards the Dōng Dān metro station and the east end of Oriental Plaza (15 min.). In the basement, you'll find:

WINDING DOWN
Be There or Be Square (Bú Jiàn Bú Sàn; p. 87), in the basement of **Oriental Plaza,** offers Hong Kong–style food in a spacious, warehouse-like space. The pork buns, Singapore noodles, and congee are heavenly. If you're in need of a pick-up, try the caffeine-laden milk tea.

WALKING TOUR 4 LÌDÀI DÌWÁNG MIÀO & HÙGUÓ SÌ

Start:	Lǔ Xùn Bówùguǎn (metro: Fùchéng Mén, 203, exit B).
Finish:	Déshèng Mén Jiànlóu (metro: Jīshuǐ Tán, 218, exit A).
Time:	4 to 5 hours.
Best times:	Any time between 9am and noon.
Worst times:	Mondays, when some of the museums and sites are closed.

For the fourth edition, we've added a new stroll. With the Shíchà Hǎi area increasingly overrun with bar touts, "To the Hútòng" tours, and Běijīng's nouveau riche blocking the way with their Audis, we've added a new walking tour to let you rub shoulders with real *Běijīngrén*. You'll ramble along tree-lined quiescent lanes too narrow for automobiles, uncovering recently re-opened and long-forgotten temples; you'll explore the tranquil former residences of two of China's most influential artists and a lively local wet market; you'll meet bonsai and Peking opera aficionados and drink tea in a former concubine's residence. *Tips* **Take this tour soon:** Much of the area is threatening to disappear by way of the wrecking ball . . .

Taking exit B from the metro, turn left (east) along Fùchéng Mén Nèi Dàjiē, taking the first left (north) into Fùchéng Mén Nèi Běi Jiē. Ahead is:

❶ Lǔ Xùn Bówùguǎn

An online poll saw Lǔ Xùn (1881–1936), an acerbic essayist, outpoll pop divas and basketball stars as the most popular figure in China. Young visitors display something approaching reverence when they photograph the desk where the young Lǔ carved the character for early *(zǎo)* to remind him not to be late for school. Seek out a gruesome photo of a Japanese soldier beheading a Chinese national during the Russo-Japanese war of 1905. His Chinese compatriots look on with blank countenances. Lǔ, then a medical student in Japan, saw this as symptomatic of a national sickness, and credited the picture with changing the direction of his life towards literature. His charming residence (one of three in Běijīng), is set to the west side (Tues–Sun 8:30am–3:30pm, admission ¥5 (60¢).

Turning left as you emerge, your next destination is immediately visible. Pick your way southeast through unmarked lanes.

❷ Bái Tǎ Sì

This massive Nepali-designed stupa (p. 130) seems to be permanently under renovation. The last three times we visited, it was covered in scaffolding. A new exhibit in the western hall shows a chilling vision for "modernizing" the surrounding area. Open daily from 9am till 4:30pm; admission ¥20 ($2.50).

Turn left as you exit, and you'll soon reach:

❸ Lìdài Dìwáng Miào

This icon-free temple (p. 133), whose grounds were occupied by a school until recently, is where Míng and Qīng emperors would come to pay tribute to their predecessors. It boasts impressive stone carvings, and there are signs of improvements in local curatorial standards—some of the original roof murals have been left untouched; there are touch-screen displays; and there's even admission of past vandalism. Open daily 9am till 4pm; admission ¥20 ($2.50).

Turn left, and after a few minutes you'll find:

❹ Guǎngjì Sì

This is the closest thing Běijīng has to a real Buddhist temple. If you can arrange a visit on the first or 15th day of the lunar calendar, the impressive grounds are open to the public; otherwise, the monks will usually politely refuse entry. If you'd like to meet the monks, visit **Lily Vegetarian Restaurant** (p. 114) where they often dine.

Backtrack west in the direction of Lìdài Dìwáng Miào, taking the first right turn into a narrow lane that changes its name frequently as it jinks north to:

❺ Xīsì Běi Sān Tiáo

Formerly known as Bózǐ Hútòng, this is where bamboo screens for writing were produced. From this lane northwards, the original Yuán street grid remains intact, with east-west *hútòng* spaced exactly 79m (260 ft.) apart. Many of the original entrances and door piers *(mén dūn'r)* are in excellent condition, and this lane may be spared from development.

At no. 3, to the east of the *hútòng,* is a striking monastery gate, embellished with faded murals, which formerly marked the entrance to:

❻ Shèngzuò Lóngcháng Sì

A Buddhist temple dating from the Míng, this was the site of scripture reproduction, transcribed on the bamboo strips the street was famed for. It is possible to (discreetly) wander among the former halls; the original outlay of the temple is readily discerned. There are no plans for restoring these ancient halls.

Continue east to the busy Xī Sì Běi Dàjiē, turn left and continue north past electronics shops until you reach a Bank of China. At this point, carefully cross the road and duck into the unmarked lane, Zhōng Máo Jiā Wān. The south side of this street was the residence of Máo's ill-fated deputy, Marshal Lín Biāo. Appropriately, the residence is now occupied by the army. After

Walking Tour 4: Lìdài Dìwáng Miào & Hùguó Sì

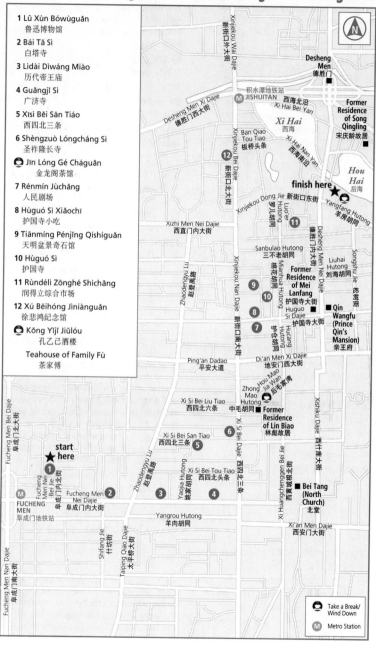

Take a Break/
Wind Down

Ⓜ Metro Station

60m (197 ft.), you reach a fork in the road. Follow it left to find:

TAKE A BREAK
Jīn Lóng Gé Cháguǎn occupies the two-story residence of a former imperial concubine. She sold the house in 2004, and lives nearby in a retirement home. Tea, served in traditional style on elaborate wood and bamboo sets, is affordable (¥50 – ¥180 [$6.25–$23] per pot), and homemade *jiǎozi* and *húntun* (ravioli soup) are also offered.

From the teahouse, turn right and continue up this winding *hútòng*. At the main road, turn left to continue north, crossing Píng'ān Dàdào into Hùcāng Hútòng. This area was formerly a prince's mansion, Zhuāng Qīn Wáng Fǔ. Turn left at a busy Hùguó Sì Dàjiē and you'll soon reach:

❼ Rénmín Jùchǎng

Built in honor of Méi Lánfāng (see stroll no. 2, p. 156) during the 1950s, this impressive wooden structure has been deemed too much of a fire hazard to host performances, although at the time of writing renovations were underway. It may eventually reopen as a Peking Opera museum. Next door is **Běijīng Yángguāng Yùnzhī Shūdiàn** (p. 176), which stocks Peking Opera DVDs, CDs, and instruments.

Immediately opposite is:

❽ Hùguó Sì Xiǎochī

From the late Yuán onwards, Hùguó Sì was the site of a huge temple fair (second only to Lóngfú Sì, see stroll no. 3, p. 161), held on the seventh and eighth days of Chinese New Year. Běijīng's most renowned snack shop claims to be faithful to temple fairs of the past, and at lunchtime, it's as chaotic as one. Tasty dishes include *xìngrén dòufu* (chilled almond pudding), and *shāobǐng jiā ròu* (miniburgers inside sesame buns), *wāndòu huáng* (green pea pudding), and *sàqímǎ* (candied rice fritter). Open daily 5:30am till 9pm.

Turn left to head north along Hùguó Sì Xī Jiē, right next to the snack shop. You'll pass a neighborhood notice board on the right, and shortly on the left you'll find:

❾ Tiānmíng Pénjǐng Qíshíguǎn

While bonsai is normally associated with Japan, quite a number of elderly *Běijīngrén* are passionate about its antecedent, *pénjǐng*. The owner of this exhibit is a quietly fanatical collector and creator of stunted trees and bizarrely shaped rocks.

Continue north, bear right and then right again to head south in the direction of Hùguó Sì Dàjiē. You'll pass a karaoke bar, a coal brick-pressing plant, and a hotel, just south of which is:

❿ Hùguó Sì

Only one hall, **Jīngāng Diàn** (the second hall of the original nine halls) is left standing. A hall just to the west burnt down last year, a result of authorities renting it out to migrant workers who set up a clothing sweatshop inside it. The site of the main hall, just to the north, is occupied by the seedy karaoke parlor you just passed. The temple dates from 1264: This is evident in the size of joinery, which is less fiddly than comparable Míng structures.

Head east to return to Hùcāng Hútòng, turn left and continue north, passing old men playing chess and selling grasshoppers. Shortly, you'll arrive at a more densely forested section, and you'll notice people emerging from the lanes to your right with bags of fruit and vegetables. Follow them to the source to find:

⓫ Rùndélì Zōnghé Shìchǎng

Still widely known as Sì Huán Shìchǎng, this is one of the few large wet markets still located within the city. There are vast stalls hawking clothing and fabric, animals (not intended as pets), and colorful spices.

Duck back out to Hùcāng Hútòng and continue north until you reach a major intersection, just before a hospital gate. Turn left into bustling Xīnjiēkǒu Dōng Jiē. This soon runs into still livelier Xīnjiēkǒu Běi Dàjiē, crammed with clothing and music shops. Continue north. On the left (west) side you'll soon find:

⑫ Xú Bēihóng Jìniànguǎn

The work on display in this memorial hall at Xīnjiēkǒu Běi Dàjiē 53 (admission ¥5/60¢; open daily 9am–3:30pm) is instantly familiar—copies of the watercolors of Xú Bēihóng are on display at most tourist sites. Xú did much to revive a moribund art, combining traditional Chinese brushwork with Western techniques he assimilated while studying and traveling in Europe and Japan.

Head north along this bustling thoroughfare, pass a KFC, and turn right (east) onto Bǎn Qiáo Tóu Tiáo. At this point, you can join up with the "Walking Tour 2: Back Lakes Ramble," or when you spy the waters of Hòu Hǎi, keep to the right side and you'll reach:

WINDING DOWN
The restaurant **Kǒng Yǐjǐ Jiǔlóu** (p. 91), named for the drunken hero of one of Lǔ Xùn's best-known short stories, serves delicate Huáiyáng cuisine in a scholarly setting. Slightly further south is the tranquil **Teahouse of Family Fù** (p. 192).

9

Shopping

Writer Wáng Shuò once observed that there were still devout Communists to be found in China, all of them safely under lock and key in a mental asylum. Consumerism is the official ideology of China, and shopping is the national sport. Spend, spend, and spend some more is the message drummed into China's bewildered citizens at every turn.

Dusty, empty, and useless state-run department stores are thankfully a thing of the past, though the **Friendship Store** still stands as an amusing reminder of the old days. Mega-malls, shopping streets, and the few remaining open-air markets fight for a share of the spoils. Avoid shopping forays on weekends and evenings, when it can feel as if all of Běijīng's 15 million residents line up at the cash registers to do their bit for the economic miracle.

1 The Shopping Scene

Western-style shopping malls are flexing their muscles in Běijīng, replacing the traditional storefronts, Chinese department stores, and alley markets. Even the new, privately run stores on major shopping streets tend to be versions of the boutiques and specialty outlets familiar to shoppers in the West. But there are still plenty of open-air markets and street-side vendors offering more traditional arts and crafts, collectibles, and clothing, usually at prices far below those in the big plazas and modern stores.

BĚIJĪNG'S BEST BUYS

Stores and markets in Běijīng sell everything from cashmere and silk to knockoff designer-label clothing and athletic wear, antiques, traditional art, cloisonné, lacquerware, Míng furniture, Máo memorabilia, and enough miscellaneous Chinesey doodads to stuff Christmas stockings from now until eternity. Prices are reasonable (certainly lower than in the Asian goods boutiques back home), though increasingly less so. Cheap one-time-use luggage is widely available for hauling your booty if you get carried away.

Before you rush to the ATM, however, it is important to remember that not all that is green and gleams in Běijīng is jade. Indeed, the majority of it is colored glass. The same principle holds for pearls, famous-brand clothing, antiques, and just about everything else. If you plan to make big purchases, you should educate yourself about quality and price well beforehand.

BĚIJĪNG'S TOP SHOPPING AREAS

The grandest shopping area in Běijīng is **Wángfǔjǐng Dàjiē,** east of the Forbidden City. The street was overhauled in 1999, and the south section was turned into a pedestrian-only commercial avenue lined with clothing outlets, souvenir shops, fast-food

---

Warning   **"Hello, I'm an Art Student"**

Be leery of any English-speaking youngsters who claim to be **art students** and offer to take you to a special exhibit of their work. This is a **scam**. The art, which you will be compelled to buy, almost always consists of assembly-line reproductions of famous (or not so famous) paintings offered at prices several dozen times higher than their actual value. You are almost sure to encounter this nonsense in the **Wángfǔjǐng** and **Liúlichǎng** areas.

---

restaurants, and the city's top two malls—the Sun (Xīn) Dōng Ān Plaza and Oriental Plaza (Dōngfǎng Guǎngchǎng). **Dōng Dān Běi Dàjiē,** a long block east, is a strip of clothing boutiques and CD shops popular among fashionable Běijīng youth. On the western side of town is the mirror image of Dōng Dān, bustling **Xī Dān,** and further north, **Xīnjiēkǒu Dàjiē.**

Other major Westernized shopping areas include the section of **Jiànguó Mén Wài Dàjiē** between the Friendship Store and the China World Trade Center, and the neighborhood outside the **Northeast Third Ring Road North,** southeast of Sān Yuán Qiáo around the new embassy district.

Běijīng's liveliest shopping zone, beloved for its atmosphere and Chinese-style goods, is the centuries-old commercial district southwest of Qián Mén. **Liúlichǎng** is an almost too-quaint collection of art, book, tea, and antiques shops lined up side by side in a polished-for-tourists Old Běijīng–style *hútòng* running east–west 2 blocks south of the Hépíng Mén metro stop. The street is good for window-shopping strolls and small purchases—like the unavoidable **chop** (*túzhāng;* stone or jade stamp), carved with your name—but beware large purchases: Almost everything here is fake and overpriced. In a similar setting but more raucous, Dà Zhàlán (pronounced Dàshílànr in the Běijīng dialect) is the prole alternative to Wángfǔjīng Dàjiē. Located in a pedestrian-only *hútòng* 2 blocks south of Qián Mén, it is jammed on either side with cheap clothing outlets, restaurants, and luggage shops (see "Walking Tour 1: Liúlichǎng & Dà Zhàlán" in chapter 8).

2 Markets & Bazaars

Although malls and shopping centers are becoming more popular, the majority of Běijīng residents still shop in markets. Whether indoors or out, these markets are inexpensive, chaotic and, for the visitor, tremendously interesting. Payment is in cash, bargaining is essential, and pickpockets are plentiful. Perhaps the most common item you'll find in the markets these days is not silk, souvenirs, or crafts, but designer-label clothing, much of it knockoffs with the upscale labels sewn in, although some items are factory seconds or overruns (sometimes smuggled out of legitimate brand-name factories). Before you stock up on too many fake items, however, check the U.S. Customs website, www.customs.ustreas.gov, to see what you are allowed to bring home.

The most popular market is **Yǎxiù Fúzhuāng Shìchǎng;** the best for jewelry is **Hóng Qiáo Shìchǎng;** the most interesting is **Pānjiāyuán Jiùhuò Shìchǎng;** but there are others worth browsing.

SILK ALLEY (XIÙSHUǏ JIĒ)   Herded indoors in 2005, Běijīng's most famous market among foreign visitors is a crowded maze of stalls with a large selection of shoes and clothing (and very little silk). Vendors formerly enjoyed so much trade they could afford to be rude, but the knockoff boot is now firmly on the shopper's foot, as Silk Alley now sees only a fraction of the business of Yǎxiù (see below). Most of the original vendors are gone, unwilling (or unable) to pay the new steep rental fees. Good riddance. Under no circumstances pay more than ¥150 ($20) for a North Face (North Fake, the expats call it) jacket, ¥50 ($6) for a business shirt, or ¥100 ($12) for a pair of jeans. Stores which sport a red flag are purported to "subscribe to higher ethics." Spot the ethical pirates. Corner of Jiànguó Mén Wài Dàjiē and Xiùshuǐ Dōng Jiē, above the Yǒng'ān Lǐ metro stop (121, exit A). It's open daily from 9am to 9pm.

HÓNG QIÁO SHÌCHǍNG ⍟   Also called the **Pearl Market,** Hóng Qiáo Shìchǎng is located at Hóng Qiáo Lù 16 (🕿 010/6713-3354), just northeast of Tiān Tán Gōngyuán (Temple of Heaven Park) and north of Tǐyùguǎn Lù. Hóng Qiáo began life as a fascinating curio market outside Tiān Tán Gōngyuán, but like most outdoor markets it was forced indoors and now sits above a malodorous wet market. Popular purchases include reproductions of 1920s Shànghǎi advertisements for "cow soap." Also popular is Cultural Revolution kitsch: Look out for flamethrower-like cigarette lighters that play "The East is Red" *("Dōngfāng Hóng")* when you light up. Elsewhere in the store, you'll need to bargain hard for brand-name clothing, footwear, luggage, watches, and **pearls** (see below), which attract swarms of bottle-blonde Russian women. The **toy market** *(wánjù shìchǎng),* housed in a separate building at the back, is overlooked by visitors, so starting prices are more reasonable; there are candles, incense, and stationery. There's a post office on the fourth floor. From Chóngwén Mén metro (209, exit A) take bus no. 807 to Hóng Qiáo, and cross the footbridge. Open daily from 8:30am to 7pm.

PĀNJIĀYUÁN JIÙHUÒ SHÌCHǍNG ⍟⍟⍟   Eureka! This is the Chinese shopping experience of dreams: row upon crowded row of calligraphy, jewelry, ceramics, teapots, ethnic clothing, Buddha statues, paper lanterns, Cultural Revolution memorabilia, PLA belts, little wooden boxes, Míng- and Qīng-style furniture, old pipes, opium scales, and painted human skulls. The market is also known as the Dirt or Ghost Market. There are some real antiques scattered among the junk, but you'd have to be an expert to pick them out. Locals arrive Saturday and Sunday mornings at dawn

---

Tips **Buying Pearls**

Most of the pearls on sale at **Hóng Qiáo Shìchǎng** are genuine, although of too low quality to be sold in Western jewelry shops. However, some fakes are floating around. To test if the pearls you want to buy are real, try any one of the following:

- Nick the surface with a sharp blade (the color should be uniform within and without)
- Rub the pearl across your teeth (this should make a grating sound)
- Scrape the pearl on a piece of glass (real pearls leave a mark)
- Pass it through a flame (fake pearls turn black, real ones don't)

Oddly, vendors are generally willing to let you carry out these tests, and may even help, albeit with bemused faces. If you'd rather not bother (most don't), assume the worst, shop for fun, and spend modestly.

or shortly after (hence the "ghost" label) to find the best stuff; vendors start to leave around 4pm. Initial prices given to foreigners are always absurdly high—Máo clocks, for instance, should cost less than ¥40 ($5) rather than the ¥400 ($50) you'll likely be asked to pay. Handily located just south of Pānjiāyuán on the west side of Huáwēi Qiáo, **Curio City (Gǔwán Chéng;** ℂ **010/6774-7711)** boasts four floors of jewelry (including diamonds and jade), old clocks, cloisonné, furniture, and porcelain, as well as curios and the odd genuine antique. International shipping is provided. Curio City is open daily from 9:30am to 6:30pm. Pānjiāyuán market is located on the south side of Pānjiāyuán Lù, just inside the southeast corner of the Third Ring Road. It's open Saturday and Sunday from noon until about 4pm.

YǍXIÙ FÚZHUĀNG SHÌCHǍNG 🕸 Whatever you may think of their business practices, Běijīng's clothing vendors are nimble: Here you'll find refugees from two now-extinct outdoor markets, Yǎbǎo Lù and Sān Lǐ Tún. Opened in May 2002, the market occupies the old Kylin Plaza building (Qílín Dàshà) and retains at least one feature of the old Kylin—excellent tailors can be found on the third floor. The fourth floor is a fine hunting ground for souvenirs and gifts—there are kites from Wéifāng in Shāndōng, calligraphy materials, army surplus gear, tea sets, and farmer's paintings from Xī'ān (laughably claiming to be originals by Pān Xiǎolíng, the most frequently copied artist). You can even treat yourself to a ¥20 ($2.50) manicure. The basement and the first two floors house a predictable but comprehensive collection of imitation and pilfered brand-name clothing, shoes, and luggage. The market has been "discovered" by fashion-conscious locals, and starting prices are often ridiculous. The market is just west of Sān Lǐ Tún Jiǔbā Jiē, at Gōngtǐ Běi Lù 58 (ℂ **010/6415-1726)**, and is open daily from 9:30am to 8pm.

SHOPPING WITH THE LOCALS

These markets are unknown to visitors and most expatriates. Asking prices are more reasonable than the markets listed above, and the quality of goods is often superior. **Tiānyì Xiǎoshāngpǐn Pīfā Shìchǎng** is the ultimate "Made in China" shopping experience. You'll find it 4 blocks west of the Fùchéng Mén metro stop (203, exit A) at Fùchéng Mén Wài Dàjiē 259 (ℂ **010/6832-7529)**, on the north side of the road. It's all here, crammed into hundreds of stalls in a spanking-new five-story building tucked behind the old market. The range of toys, sporting equipment, electronic appliances, and luggage is eye-popping. Open daily from 7:30am to 5pm.

Jīn Wǔxīng Bǎihuò Pīfā Chéng (ℂ **010/6222-6827)**, a single-story wholesale market just south of Dà Zhōng Sì metro (1302), is more comprehensive and more chaotic. They have everything. Open 8:30am to 7pm. **Bàoguó Sì Wénhuà Gōngyìpǐn Shìchǎng** (ℂ **010/6303-0976)**, Pānjiāyuán in miniature, is more relaxing. This delightful market has been a site of commerce since the Qīng dynasty, and is set in the leafy grounds of a Liáo dynasty (930—1122) temple. It offers mostly bric-a-brac, but vendors aren't pushy, and asking prices are reasonable. Coins, antiquarian books, and Cultural Revolution memorabilia abound. The market is liveliest on Thursday and Saturday mornings. From Chángchūn Jiē metro (205, exit D1), walk south along Chángchūn Jiē and take the third right onto a tree-lined avenue that ends at the east gate of Xuānwǔ Yīyuàn. Turn left and follow your nose southwest through the *hútòng* to Bàoguó Sì. It's open daily from 8am to 4pm.

3 Shopping A to Z

ANTIQUES & CURIOS

The **Pānjiāyuán Jiùhuò Shìchǎng** market (see above) was once *the* place to look for antiques, and it still is for bric-a-brac and oddities. If you're not in town on the weekend, visit **Bàoguó Sì Wénhuà Gōngyìpǐn Shìchǎng** market (see above), which has similar curiosities in a more pleasant setting. Any cracked and dusty treasure you find is almost certainly fake, but you won't have trouble taking it home. Genuine antiques are not allowed out of the country without an official **red wax seal,** and pieces made prior to 1795 cannot be exported at all. "Certified" antiques are available at astronomical prices in the **Friendship Store** (p. 173), at a few hotel gift shops, and in some of the nicer malls. But determined antiques lovers should look elsewhere.

Guǎng Hàn Táng ⚐ Set in a delightful courtyard house constructed from the ruins of a derelict factory, all of Guǎng Hàn Táng's pieces could be described as partially restored, as they maintain a feeling of antiquity. Softwood furniture, such as fir *(shānmù)* and elm *(yúmù)*, is disparagingly referred to as "firewood" *(cháimù)* by the locals, though the sturdiness of the latter wood is recognized in the expression for a die-hard traditionalist, *yúmù nǎodai,* literally "elm brain." Hardwood furniture, such as rosewood *(zǐtán* or *hóngmù),* commands a higher price. Prices are serious, but so is the owner, Mr. Liáng. No fakes here. Open daily 9am to 6pm. Cǎochángdì. ☏ 010/8456-7943. www.guanghantang.com. Bus: 418 from Dōng Zhí Mén metro stop (214/1316, exit B) to Cǎochángdì. Take the Dà Shānzǐ exit off the airport expwy., follow Jīchǎng Fù Lù northeast, and take the 2nd right onto Nán Gāo Lù. After passing under the railway line, take the left fork in the road and follow the signs.

Lǔ Bān Gǔdiǎn Jiājù Chéng *(Finds* Just east of town, Gāobēidiàn—one of the largest antique furniture markets in China—is one of Běijīng's best-kept secrets. Lǔ Bān was the first shop to open at the location in 1991, but it's remarkable that over a decade later so few locals know of its existence. This outlet is the most reliable of the many furniture stores in Gāobēidiàn. But if you know what you're looking for, the real bargains can be found in small workshops opened by enterprising peasants from Shāndōng, Shānxī, and Ānhuī. At least half of the merchandise is bogus, and any furniture marked with a tag that says TIBETAN should be regarded as counterfeit until proven otherwise. Open daily 8:30am to 6pm. Gāobēidiàn 4 Duì (from Gāobēidiàn bus stop continue south for around 90m/295 ft.; turn left just before the railway tracks). ☏ 010/8575-6516. Bus: 363 from Sìhuì Dōng metro stop (125, exit B, cross road) to Gāobēidiàn.

ART SUPPLIES

Liúlichǎng (see "Walking Tour 1: Liúlichǎng & Dà Zhàlán" in chapter 8) has many small shops and stalls selling calligraphy brushes, brush racks, chops, fans, ink stones, paper, and other art supplies. The best bargains are found in the stalls toward the far west end. The most famous outlet is **Róngbǎo Zhāi,** Liúlichǎng Xī Jiē 19 (☏ 010/6303-6090), although its prices are pushed ever higher by tour groups. Even if you can't afford the prices, take a peek at the gallery on the second floor. It's open daily 9am to 5:30pm. Many art-supply shops cluster around the **National Gallery. Bǎihuā Měishù Yòngpǐn,** located diagonally across from the gallery at Wǔsì Dàjiē 12 (☏ 010/6513-1721), stocks a wide range of modern art supplies and also has a reliable framing service. It's open daily 9am to 6:30pm. The largest art store in Běijīng is

Gōngměi Dàshà at Wángfǔjǐng Dàjiē 200 (𝒞 **010/6528-8866**), although its prices are high. Open daily from 9am to 9pm.

BIKES

Qián Mén Zìxíngchē Shāngdiàn   One of Běijīng's largest bike stores is handily located a short walk south of Qián Mén. New brands, such as Giant and Strong, dominate. But there are still some old-style Forever *(Yǒngjiǔ)* bicycles. Sadly, there's not a Flying Pigeon in sight. Open daily 8:30am to 6:30pm. Qián Mén Dàjiē 97, Xuānwǔ Qū. 𝒞 010/6303-1014. Metro: Qián Mén (208, exit C).

BOARD GAMES

Xīng Qíyì Yuàn Shāngmào Zhōngxīn   Better known in the West by the Japanese name of *go,* the complex game of strategy, *wéiqí,* is undergoing a welcome resurgence in its native land, if the number of TV programs dedicated to its exposition are any guide (although it doesn't make for great television). This friendly shop outside the south gate of the National Sports Training Center, where many of China's *wéiqí* masters work, sells boards and the 361 black-and-white pieces that fill in the spaces. These start at ¥40 ($5) for metal pieces in a wicker basket, and rise to ¥3,600 ($450) for agate stones in a jade bowl. "Traditional" Chinese chess, or *xiàngqí,* is more commonly seen on the street. Elaborate *xiàngqí* sets are also sold. Open weekdays 9am to 5pm; weekends 9am to 4pm. Tiān Tán Dōng Lù 80. 𝒞 010/6711-4691. Metro: Chóngwén Mén (209), then bus 807 to Dōng Cè Lù; cross bridge and head south, then turn left onto Cháng Qīng Lù.

BOOKSTORES

The bookshop on the first floor of the **Friendship Store** (p. 173) offers a wide range of English-language magazines. **Maps** of anyplace in China can be found on the first floor of **Wángfǔjǐng Shūdiàn,** Wángfǔjǐng Dàjiē 218 (𝒞 **010/6513-2842;** open daily 9am–9:30pm). The finest library of English language books can be found at **The Bookworm** (p. 190).

China Bookstore (Zhōngguó Shūdiàn)   Liúlìchǎng is the place to buy Chinese art books that hotels, museums, and galleries are all fond of marking up. This is the largest of several branches. Open daily 9am to 6:30pm (until 6pm in winter). Liúlìchǎng Dōng Jiē 115, Xuānwǔ Qū (northeast side of the intersection with Nán Xīnhuá Jiē). 𝒞 010/6303-5759. Metro: Hépíng Mén (207, exit C).

Foreign Language Bookstore (Wàiwén Shūdiàn)   You'll find a wide selection of maps on the first floor and the largest collection of English-language books in Běijīng on the third floor. Open daily 9am to 8:30pm. Wángfǔjǐng Dàjiē 235, Dōngchéng Qū. 𝒞 010/6512-6903. Metro: Wángfǔjǐng (118, exit A).

Sānlián Tāofèn Túshū Zhōngxīn   Come here for the most interesting selection of Chinese-language books in Běijīng, although **Wànshèng Shūdiàn,** south of Qīnghuá University in Hǎidiàn, runs a close second. There's a quiet cafe on the second floor, but most patrons prefer the stairwell. Open daily 9am to 9pm. Měishùguǎn Dōng Jiē 22, Dōngchéng Qū. 𝒞 010/6400-2710. Bus: 803 from north of Wángfǔjǐng metro stop (118, exit A) to Měishùguǎn.

Sānwèi Shūwū   Public outrage spared Běijīng's original "dissident bookstore" from being converted into a patch of lawn in 2002. Downstairs is a small bookstore with a few English-language titles. Upstairs is a tranquil, traditional teahouse (p. 186), ideal for a quiet read during the day. Open daily 9:30am to 10:30pm. Fùxīng Mén Nèi Dàjiē 60,

Xīchéng Qū (west of the metro stop, opposite Mínzú Wénhuà Gōng, on the corner of Tónglíngé Lù). ✆ 010/6601-3204. Metro: Xīdān (115, exit E).

CAMERAS & FILM

Color film and processing are readily arranged, but you're probably better off waiting until you return home or pass through Hong Kong. For black-and-white processing (the only choice for depicting Běijīng in winter), try **Àitúměi Cǎisè Kuòyìn Zhōngxīn,** Xīnjiēkǒu Nán Dàjiē 87 (✆ 010/6616-0718), open daily 9am to 9pm. Běijīng is not the place to buy new cameras and accessories, but those looking for sec-ondhand parts for their ancient SLR camera, or wanting to experiment with ancient Russian swing lens cameras, have the two excellent markets listed in this section.

Běijīng Shèyǐng Qìcái Chéng (Finds)   Běijīng's largest camera market has a bewilder-ing array of equipment—one shop only sells lens filters! If you're looking for the old, obscure parts they just don't make any more, you'll find them here. Competition between vendors is fierce. Open daily 9am to 4:30pm. Xī Sì Huán Lù 40, Xīchéng Qū (a mile south of the metro stop on the west side). ✆ 010/8811-9797. Bus: 748 from south of Wǔkēsōng metro stop (108, exit D) to Zhèngcháng Zhuāng.

Mǎlián Dào Shèyǐng Qìcái Chéng   Located on the top floor of Mǎlián Dào Tea City is a cluster of secondhand camera shops. **Hóngshēng Shèyǐng Fúwù Zhōngxīn,** on the north side, has the widest range of gear and the best repair service. Open daily 9am to 7pm. Mǎlián Dào 11 (cross road and walk south for 5 min.). ✆ 010/6339-5250. Bus: 719 from Fùchéng Mén metro stop (203, exit A) to Wǎnzi.

CARPETS

Qián Mén Carpet Factory   Most modern Chinese carpets are testaments to what azo compounds are capable of if they fall into the wrong hands. Fortunately, the car-pets in this dusty basement emporium (which was once a bomb shelter) are largely antiques. Rugs from Gānsù and Níngxià in northwest China feature swastikas, drag-ons, phoenixes, and auspicious symbols, and are free of alarming pinks and oranges. Antiques include Tibetan prayer rugs, Xīnjiāng yurt rugs, and Mongolian saddle rugs, all handmade using natural dyes. The factory also makes antique "reproductions" and Hénán silk carpets. Cleaning and repair services are available. The factory is located at the back of the Chóngwén Worker's Cultural Palace; follow the ANTIQUE CARPETS signs. Open daily 9:30am to 5:30pm. Xìngfú Dàjiē 59, Chóngwén Qū (opposite the east side of Tiān Tán Fàndiàn). ✆ 010/6715-1687. Bus: 807 from Chóngwén Mén metro stop (209, exit A) to Běijīng Tǐyùguǎn.

Torana Gallery   Run by Englishman Chris Buckley, a guidebook writer turned entrepreneur, Torana sources its exquisite Tibetan and Chinese wool rugs from Gangchen Carpets and Michaelian and Kohlberg. Chris has a passion for Tibet, and often hosts photographic exhibitions. No bargains, but if you're looking for a genuine hand-woven rug, and lack the time or expertise to hunt one down, Torana should be your first choice. Open daily 10am to 10pm. Shop 8, in the lobby of the Kempinski Hotel. ✆ 010/6465-3388, ext. 5542. Bus: 701 from Dōngsì Shí Tiáo metro stop (213, exit C) to Yànshā.

COINS & STAMPS

Coin collectors and philatelists rub shoulders in Běijīng. The largest market is **Mǎlián Dào Yóu Bì Kǎ Shìchǎng** at Mǎlián Dào 15 (open daily 8:30am–5pm), tucked away behind the tea shops, just south of yet another Carrefour supermarket. Housed in a half-empty building that resembles an aircraft hangar, you'll find stamps and envelopes commemorating great moments in Chinese diplomacy (more than you'd expect), coins and notes of all imaginable vintages, phone cards (popular with locals—there's even a Phone Card Museum), and a large range of Cultural Revolution memorabilia. To get here, take bus no. 719 from the Fùchéng Mén metro stop (203, exit A) to Wānzi, cross the road, and walk south for 5 minutes. Larger post offices also have special sections offering limited-issue stamps. Coin collectors should make the trip to the **Ancient Coin Market (Gǔdài Qiánbì Jiāoyì Shìchǎng;** ✆ 010/6201-8073) at Déshèng Mén (p. 145).

COMPUTERS

In a recent local soap opera, **Zhōngguān Cūn** (touted as China's Silicon Valley), to the northwest of Běijīng, was depicted as innovative, dynamic, and even sexy. Alas, with an education system that stifles creativity and a legal system incapable of enforcing intellectual property laws, copying software remains China's forte. (And software engineers are seldom sexy.) Don't rely on pirated software, but computer games usually work and computer whizzes have been known to build a computer from scratch here. Take bus no. 808 from Xī Zhí Mén.

Bǎi Nǎo Huì   Less dodgy and easier to reach than Zhōngguān Cūn, this four-story amalgam of stores sells computers, digital cameras, and accessories. Software is not sold inside, but a gaggle of gentlemen from Ānhuī loitering outside greet you with a chorus of "Hello. CD-rom!" Open daily 9am to 8pm. Cháowài Dàjiē 10 (10-min. walk east, on the south side of the street). ✆ 010/6599-5947. Metro: Cháoyáng Mén (212, exit B).

DEPARTMENT STORES

Friendship Store (Yǒuyì Shāngdiàn)   Friendship Stores were once the only places where locals and foreigners alike could purchase imported goodies. You even needed "foreign exchange currency" to obtain the viciously overpriced merchandise. This is the largest store, and it was recently spared demolition when plans for a high-rise complex caused a stir among nearby embassies, but its days are numbered. You can bargain for their overpriced wares, but it's really not worth your while. Starbucks, Baskin-Robbins, Délifrance, and Pizza Hut are appended, and the first-floor bookshop stocks a wide range of English-language magazines. Open daily 9am to 8:30pm. Jiànguó Mén Wài Dàjiē 17, Cháoyáng Qū. ✆ 010/6500-3311. Metro: Jiànguó Mén (120/211, exit B).

Lándǎo Dàshà   Unlike the Friendship Store, Lándǎo is always heaving with locals. By no means Běijīng's newest department store, the sprawling twin-block layout lends Lándǎo a certain charm. While they stock almost every conceivable item, it's *not* the place to visit if you want to make a quick purchase. Local brands of clothing and footwear, often heavily discounted, are the best buys. People will pester you at the checkout; don't fret—they are asking you to make purchases using their discount cards. Open daily 9am to 9pm. Cháoyáng Mén Wài Dàjiē 8, Cháoyáng Qū (10-min. walk east from metro stop). ✆ 010/8563-4422. Metro: Cháoyáng Mén (212, exit A).

DRUGSTORES

Wángfǔjǐng Drugstore   This emporium has a small selection of Western cosmetics and health aids, along with a large selection of traditional Chinese medicines. Open daily 8:30am to 10pm. Wángfǔjǐng Dàjiē 267, Dōngchéng Qū. ✆ 010/6524-9932. Metro: Wángfǔjǐng (118, exit A).

Watson's Another pawn in the Li Ka-Hsing empire, Watson's promises to double the number of stores in China during 2006. This should be your first choice for Western cosmetics and toiletries, though the range of over-the-counter medicines is limited. Open daily 10am to 9pm (Holiday Inn Lido branch 9am–9pm). Full Link Plaza (see below). ✆ **010/6588-2145**. Another branch at Holiday Inn Lido. ✆ **010/6436-7653**. Metro: Cháoyáng Mén (212, exit B).

FASHION

You wouldn't travel to Běijīng for the fashion any more than you'd travel to Milan for the tea, although there are some interesting couture outlets emerging at Factory 798 (p. 140).

Rì Tán Shāngwù Lóu 🖈🖈 Not as cheap as Yǎxiù, but far less nasty. If you lack the patience to wade through cheap copies of designer clothing in search of the genuine (or near-genuine) item at the markets listed above, or simply wouldn't be seen dead wearing such clothes, then swan on down to Rì Tán Office Building. From outside, it looks like an uninspiring office building, inside is shopping nirvana: more than 70 shops stocking high-quality womens' clothing, footwear, and accessories. There is a smattering of shops for the chaps, too. Open daily 10am till 8pm. Guānghuá Lù 15A, Cháoyáng Qu1 (just east of the south gate of Ri4tán Park, next to Schindlers). ✆ **010/8561-9556**. Metro: Yǒng'ān Lǐ metro stop (121, exit A).

FOOD

Carrefours dot the city, but the most convenient supermarkets for travelers to stock up on snacks are above the metro stops, and include: **CRC** (Guómào [122, exit A] and Wángfǔjǐng [118, exit A]), **Parksons** (Fùxīng Mén [114/204, exit A]), **Oriental Kenzo** (Dōng Zhí Mén [214, exit C]), and **Sogo** (Xuānwǔ Mén [206, exit C2]).

April Gourmet This place carries excellent fresh fruits and vegetables, with decent cheese, bread, and wine selections. They will deliver to within 2.5km (1½ miles) for purchases over ¥50 ($6). There are branches in all expat ghettoes; the best-stocked one is opposite On/Off. Open daily 8am to midnight. Xìngfu2 Èrcu1n, Jiézuò Dàshà, Cháoyáng Qū. ✆ **010/6417-7970**. Metro: Dōngsì Shí Tiáo (213, exit B).

Jenny Lou's (Tiānshùn Chāoshì) Similar to April Gourmet, though with a less impressive cheese and bread selection, Jenny's empire continues to expand, with a recent outlet opening at Jiànwài Soho. Open daily 8am to 10pm. Rìtán Gōngyuán Běi Lù 4, Cháoyáng Qū (east of the northeast side of Rìtán Park). ✆ **010/6586-0626**. Metro: Yǒng'ān Lǐ (121, exit A).

JEWELRY

Hóng Qiáo Shìchǎng (see section 2 of this chapter), also known as the Pearl Market, has dozens of jewelry stalls (mostly pearls and jade) on its third and fourth floors. Unless you're an expert, this is not a place to make large purchases.

Běijīng Gōngměi Dàshà The third-floor stalls stock all varieties of jade, from green Khotanese nephrite to Burmese jadeite. They're terribly popular with Hong Kong visitors. Count on paying no more than a third of the marked price. Open daily 9:30am to 8pm. Wángfǔjǐng Dàjiē 200, Dōngchéng Qū. ✆ **010/6523-8747**. Metro: Wángfǔjǐng (118, exit A).

Shard Box Store (Shèndégé Gōngyìpǐn) The wall of JCB, Amex, and Visa credit-card stickers on the front door are fair warning—you aren't the first to discover this charming jewelry shop. The shard boxes—supposedly made from fragments of porcelain vessels smashed during the Cultural Revolution—are gorgeous. The rather more ordinary jewelry is a mixture of colorful curiosities gathered from Mongolian and Tibetan regions, and pieces crafted in nearby workshops. Jewelry can also be made to order. Open daily 9am to 7pm. Rìtán Běi Lù 1, Cháoyáng Qū (continue east from northeast corner of Rìtán Gōngyuán). ✆ 010/8561-3712. Metro: Yǒng'ān Lǐ (121, exit A).

Xīncāng Zhūbǎo Jewelry Street (Zhūbǎo Yī Tiáo Jiē) is another traditional market cleaned up and forced indoors. This is the largest of more than 20 shops. The first floor stocks a full range of gemstones, wedding rings, and necklaces. Have a peek at the second floor, which stocks Western antiques—Swiss gramophones, American bibles, old telephones, and a suit of plate armor. There's even some fine French chinoiserie, which has come full circle. Open daily 9am to 7pm. Yángròu Hútòng 2, Xīchéng Qū (cross over and continue north; Jewelry St. is marked by an archway). ✆ 010/6618-2888. Bus: 808 from north of Xīdān metro stop (115, exit A) to Xīsì.

MALLS & SHOPPING PLAZAS

China's new generation of leaders would love nothing better than to wake up and find a more populous version of Singapore outside the gates of Zhōng Nán Hǎi. This isn't going to happen, but window-shopping in modern shopping malls is all the rage with Beijingers.

China World Trade Center Shopping Center (Zhōngguó Guójí Màoyì Zhōngxīn) Usually simply called "Guómào," this three-level mall caters to foreign business travelers and expatriate families. The ground level of China World contains airline offices, American Express, a food court, and Běijīng's first (but now far from only) Starbucks. As well as chic clothing stores such as Louis Vuitton and Jack and Jones, there's a CRC Supermarket and a specialty wine shop. Open daily 10am to 9:30pm. Jiànguó Mén Wài Dàjiē 1, Cháoyáng Qū. ✆ 010/6505-2288. Metro: Guómào (122).

COFCO Plaza (Zhōngliáng Guǎngchǎng) Handy to the railway station, this mall has branches of HSBC (open Mon–Fri 9am–12:30pm and 1:30–5pm), CITS, Mondo Gelato, Starbucks, and McDonald's. Park 'N' Shop is in Basement One. An underground walkway connects to the north side of Cháng'ān Jiē. Open daily 9am to 9pm. Jiànguó Mén Nèi Dàjiē 8, Dōngchéng Qū. ✆ 010/6526-6666. Metro: Jiànguó Mén (120/211, exit C).

Full Link Plaza (Fēnglián Guǎngchǎng) This spacious mall is a collection of chic foreign and local chain stores. The first floor boasts a Watson's Drug Store, there's a Kenny Roger's Roasters Restaurant on the fourth floor, and Air France on the fifth floor. On the first floor is Běijīng's most lavish Starbucks. Park 'N' Shop in the basement has been replaced by a lively market, where you'll find last season's clothes at affordable prices. Open daily 10am to 9pm. Cháoyáng Mén Wài Dàjiē 18, Cháoyáng Qū. ✆ 010/6215-5511. Metro: Cháoyáng Mén (212, exit B).

Lufthansa Yǒuyì Shopping Center (Yānshā Yǒuyì Shāngchéng) Located on the east side of the Third Ring Road and connected to the Kempinski Hotel, the Lufthansa Center is the largest mall in northeast Běijīng. There's a range of specialty shops, boutiques, and arts-and-crafts outlets on the upper floors, and a well-hidden bookstore tucked away on the fourth floor. There's a currency exchange on the fifth floor, which you'll need if you plan on shopping at the overpriced supermarket and deli in the basement. Open daily 9am to 10pm. Liàngmǎ Qiáo Lù 52, Cháoyáng Qū. ✆ 010/6435-4930. Bus: 701 from Dōngsì Shí Tiáo metro stop (213) to Yānshā.

Oriental Plaza (Dōngfāng Xīn Tiāndì)   Asia's second-largest shopping complex stretches from Wángfǔjǐng to Dōng Dān (the largest is Golden Resources Mall, an empty shopping complex in the west of town). Supplanting the world's biggest McDonald's, the project was backed by Hong Kong billionaire Li Ka-Hsing. The two-story arcade houses Sony ExploraScience museum; hip clothing stores such as Art of Shirts and Kookai; Be There or Be Square (p. 87); the Wángfǔjǐng Palaeolithic Museum; and another CRC supermarket. The Grand Hyatt (p. 65) stands above all the consumption. In summer, it is open daily 9:30am to 10:30pm; winter daily 9:30am to 9:30pm. Dōng Cháng'ān Dàjiē 1, Dōngchéng Qū. ℂ **010-8518-6363**. www.oriental plaza.com. Metro: Wángfǔjǐng (118, exit A).

Sun Dong An Plaza (Xīn Dōng'ān Shìchǎng)   This huge mall surrounds twin atriums and is filled with designer clothing shops. Aside from the usual Western food chains—Baskin-Robbins, Pizza Hut, McDonald's, KFC, Starbucks, and Délifrance—there's an excellent hot pot restaurant, Dōng Lái Shùn, on the fifth floor. Chinese medicine outlets, tea shops, and tacky "Old Běijīng Street" await in the basement, which also holds a children's jungle gym. Bank of China has a branch on the first floor. Open daily 9:30am to 10pm. Wángfǔjǐng Dàjiē 138, Dōngchéng Qū. ℂ **010/6527-6688**. Metro: Wángfǔjǐng (118, exit A).

MODERN ART

Many branches of traditional Chinese art have been on the wane since the Táng dynasty (A.D. 618–907). So rather than encourage the 5,000-year-old tradition of regurgitation, look for something different. It's a much better investment.

East Gallery (Yìsēn Huàláng)   Although quality varies, the East Gallery is the best of the locally run modern art galleries. The backdrop is magnificent, as you clamber up the narrow stairwells of the Déshèng Mén arrow tower (p. 145). You can visit the Ancient Coin Exhibition Hall downstairs. Open daily 9am to 5:30pm. Běi Èr Huán Lù, Déshèng Mén Jiànlóu, Xīchéng Qū (just east of the metro stop). ℂ **010/8201-4962**. Metro: Jīshuǐtan (218, exit A).

Red Gate Gallery (Hóng Mén Huàláng) ⚘   Opened by the delightfully camp Brian Wallace in the early 1990s, Red Gate has regular exhibitions featuring the work of its dozen or so artists. The Dōngbiàn Mén watchtower (admission ¥5/60¢) provides an airy and atmospheric viewing space. Open daily 10am to 5pm. Chóngwén Mén Dōng Dàjiē, Dōngbiàn Mén Jiǎolóu, Dōngchéng Qū (10-min. walk south). ℂ **010/6525-1005**. www.redgategallery.com. Metro: Jiànguó Mén (120/211, exit C).

MUSIC

Despite numerous well-publicized and photogenic police crackdowns, pirated *(dàobǎn)* CDs and DVDs are readily available in Běijīng, and with the proliferation of illegal music download sites, even the pirates are doing it tough. If you want to support local music, it's best to go to a concert and buy the music directly from the band. The second floor of the **Foreign Language Bookstore** (p. 171) boasts a wide range of Chinese music. There's maddening cross-talk *(xiàngsheng)*, bland mando-pop, and even a small alternative *(fēi zhǔliú)* music section featuring local bands such as Thin Man and Second Hand Rose. The alternative philosophy doesn't extend to the Western music section, which relies heavily on Richard Clayderman, Kenny G, and Boyzone.

Běijīng Yángguāng Yùnzhī Shūdiàn   An essential stop for those looking to develop an appreciation (or at least an understanding) of Peking Opera. Located next to the People's Theater, this tiny shop is crammed with DVDs and CDs featuring Peking opera's leading man, Méi Lánfāng. Traditionally, only three instruments were essential—the ubiquitous two-stringed *èrhú;* its smaller cousin, the *jǐnghuú;* and the banjolike *yuèqín.* Elegant handmade versions of all three are found here. Lessons can be arranged. Open daily 8am to 8pm. Hùguó Si4 Dàjiē 74, Xīchéng Qu1 (next to Rénmín Jùchǎng). ✆ 010/6617-2931. Metro: Jīshuǐtán (218, exit C).

Běijīng Yīnyuè Shūdiàn   At this store, located just to the east of the north end of the Wángfǔjǐng pedestrian mall, the top floor has a large range of sheet music at prices far cheaper than in the West. Composers' names are in Chinese, of course, but names are transliterated (Beethoven becomes Bèiduōfēn, Liszt is rendered as Lǐsītè), so you may be able to make yourself understood. If not, names are often written in English above the scores. Open daily 9am to 10pm. Dōng'ān Mén Dàjiē 16. ✆ **010/6525-4458.** Metro: Wángfǔjǐng (118, exit A).

Pǔluó Chàngpiān Chāoshì (Polo Records)   This shop, whose entrance is marked by a wall of black-and-white photographs, was among the first to stock their shelves with real *(zhèngbǎn)* CDs. Imported CDs are ¥148 ($18)—more than 15 times the price of a pirated CD—while local CDs start at ¥18 ($2.20). Remember that it's tough enough being a musician in China without having to do it for free. Open daily 9:30am to 6:30pm. Xīzhí Mén Nèi Dàjiē 26, Xīchéng Qū (walk south to a large intersection and turn right; the store is across a footbridge on the south side). ✆ **010/6618-3891.** Metro: Jīshuǐtán (218, exit C).

ODDITIES

Gōng'ānbù Dìyī Yánjiūsuǒ *(Finds)*   More Get Smart than James Bond, the commercial outlet of the "No. 1 Police Research Unit" is a bizarre example of socialist marketization. Aside from a range of authentic Chinese police gear—bulletproof vests, sturdy boots—there's a full range of dated surveillance equipment, including nifty spy pens. Suspicious (often with good reason) wives are said to be their main clients. Open daily 9am to 5:30pm. Zhèngyì Lù, Dōngchéng Qū (walk east to 1st intersection and turn right, walk for a few minutes; opposite Běijīng City Government Headquarters). ✆ **010/6522-9312.** Metro: Tiān'ān Mén Dōng (117, exit C).

Pyongyang Art Studio   More disturbing than odd, this tiny shop, opened by a Brit who has been traveling to the DPRK since 1993, is crammed with North Korean goods and socialist realist art. Cultural Revolution kitsch, while in questionable taste, has some distance to it. This is more confronting. There are anti-U.S. tracts, and paeans to the Dear Leader, Kim Il-Sung, the only man to card a perfect 18 in a round of golf. His love of cinema is described in "Great Man and Cinema," while "A Great Mind" celebrates his father, Kim Jong-Il. There are propaganda posters (many handpainted), magazines, flags, T-shirts, cigarettes, and even North Korean hooch. Compelling. Open daily 9am to 9:30pm. Chūnxiù Lù 10, Cháoyáng Qū (inside the Red House). ✆ 010/6416-7810. www.pyongyangartstudio.com.

3501 PLA Surplus Store (3501 Gōngchǎng) *(Finds)*   The official disposal store of the world's largest army is a delightful mix of fur-lined boots, army greatcoats, and kitsch Communist memorabilia. Where else will you find Léi Fēng hats, sturdy compasses and binoculars, and waist watches commemorating the 50th anniversary of liberation? Open daily 9am to 5:30pm. Dōng Sān Huán 23, Dōngchéng Qū (just south of Jīng Guǎng Zhōngxīn). ✆ 010/6585-9312. Metro: Guómào (122, exit A).

OUTDOOR EQUIPMENT

Sānfū Hùwài Yòngpǐn (Sanfo Outdoors) *Value*   This shop began life as an outdoor club at Peking University, and has a dedicated following among students and young professionals. Unlike the knockoffs for sale at Hóng Qiáo and elsewhere, Sanfo only stocks the genuine article, and most products come with a warranty. They have their own line of sleeping bags, and still organize weekend trips to the wilderness around Běijīng (p. 146). There are branches in Jīn Zhì Qiáo Dàshà west of Guómào, and northwest of Peking University. Open daily 9am to 8pm. Mǎdiàn Nán Cūn 4 Lóu 5. *(C)* 010/8202-1113, ext. 12. www.sanfo.com.cn. Metro: Jīshuǐtán (218, exit A), then bus no. 919 to Běijiāo Shìchǎng.

SHOES

Lǎo Fān Jiē Fúzhuāng Shìchǎng (Alien's Street)   It's hard to imagine anything more chaotic than the original Yǎbǎo Lù Market, but this brushed-down version comes close. It is impossible not to get lost. The first floor houses shoes, shoes, and more shoes, which mercifully come in sizes suitable to Western feet. Cheap, expansive, and often nasty, this market is popular with Russian traders. Open daily 9:30am to 6pm. Yǎbǎo Lù, Cháoyáng Qū (head east and take the 2nd right; continue south, the market is on the left side). *(C)* 010/8561-4641. Metro: Cháoyáng Mén (212, exit A).

Nèi Lián Shēng Xiédiàn   Cloth-soled "thousand layer happy shoes" *(qiāncéng bùxié)*, loved by martial arts stars and aging Communist leaders alike, are hard to find. Cheaper plastic-soled shoes are taking their place. A workshop behind this shop, founded in 1853, still turns them out; these shoes are well stitched and very comfortable. There are also some gorgeous women's shoes, modeled on Qīng fashions. Fortunately, they are now available in larger sizes. Bargaining is fruitless. Open Sunday to Thursday 8:30am to 8pm; Friday and Saturday 8:30am to 8:30pm. Dàzhàlán Jiē 34. *(C)* 010/6301-4863. Metro: Qián Mén (208, exit C).

SILK, FABRIC & TAILORS

The third floor of **Yǎxiù Fúzhuāng Shìchǎng** is a fine place to look for a tailor (see section 2 of this chapter).

Běijīng Sīchóu Diàn (Běijīng Silk Store)   Tucked away in a narrow *hútòng* just west of and running parallel with Qián Mén Dàjiē, this bustling store is said to date from 1840. Prices for tailoring and raw materials are affordable. Open daily 9am to 7:30pm. Zhūbǎo Shì 5, Chóngwén Qū (just south of metro stop). *(C)* 010/6301-6658. Metro: Qián Mén (208, exit C).

Dàxīn Fǎngzhī Gōngsī *Value*   It might not be as prestigious as other tailors, but with hand-tailored *qípáo* typically costing less than ¥200 ($25), it's impossible to argue with the price. Right next door to Yoshinoya Dairy Queen. Open daily 8:30am to 8pm. Xīnjiēkǒu Nán Dàjiē 22, Xīchéng Qū (walk south for 10 min.; the shop is on the left side, just beyond the main intersection). *(C)* 010/6618-7843. Metro: Jīshuǐtán (218, exit C).

Ruìfúxiáng Chóubù Diàn *(F)*   You'll find piles of gorgeous silk brocade at this store, in the trade for 110 years. They specialize in *qípáo* (¥500/$60 and up), which take 1 week to tailor, with a couple of fittings. If you're pushed for time, they can complete it in 2 days for an additional charge. They also have an outlet at Wángfǔjīng Dàjiē 190 (*(C)* 010/6525-0764), just north of Gōngměi Dàshà. Aim to bargain 30% to 50% off the marked prices. Open daily 9am to 8pm. Dàzhàlán Jiē 5, west off Qián Mén Dàjiē, Chóngwén Qū. *(C)* 010/6303-5313. Metro: Qián Mén (208, exit C).

Yuánlóng Sīchóu Gǔfèn Yǒuxiàn Gōngsī (Yuánlóng Silk Co. Ltd.)   A huge range of silk fabric occupies the third floor; prices are clearly marked and surprisingly competitive. A *qípáo* or suit can be made in a couple of days, but it's best to allow at least a week. Exquisite (and expensive!) silk carpets from Hénán are sold on the first floor. Try not to visit at midday, when the third floor is overrun by tour groups. Open daily 9am to 6:30pm. Tiān Tán Lù 55, Chóngwén Qū (northeast side of Tiān Tán Gōngyuán). ℂ 010/6702-2288. Bus: 807 from Chóngwén Mén metro stop (209, exit B) to Hóng Qiáo.

SKATEWEAR

Yán Chéng Yǔ (Over Workshop) *Kids*   With acres of empty concrete, the capital is a skateboarder's paradise. The skating park in Tiān'ān Mén Square is a distant memory, but the owners of this shop can steer you in the right direction. Decks and wheels are imported, but local skate fashions feature striking designs. Danny Way, who skated over the Jūyōng Guān section of the Great Wall in 2005, figures prominently. Some designs can be viewed online at www.skatechina.com and www.shehuisk8.com. Open daily 10am to 8pm. Xīnjiēkǒu Xī Lǐ Yī Qu1 6-002, Xīchéng Qū (cross road, take 1st right after Xu2 Bēihòng Memorial Hall, inside a block of yellow apartments on left side). ℂ 010/6222-7003. Metro: Jīshuǐtán (218, exit C).

TEA

Gēng Xiāng   With a survey finding that more than half of Běijīng's teas have traces of pesticides or heavy metals, organic teas are a sensible choice. The largest retailer of organic tea in Běijīng, Gēng Xiāng, survived the scandal with their reputation enhanced. Their green tea *(lǜ chá)* is among the best in China. Open daily 8:30am to 9pm. Dì'ān Mén Wài Dàjiē 116, Xīchéng Qū (south of Drum Tower on east side of street). ℂ 010/6404-0846. Metro: Gú Lóu Dàjiē (217).

Mǎlián Dào *★★*   This might not be all the tea in China, but with over a mile of shops hawking tea leaves and tea paraphernalia, it feels like it. Shops are run by the families of tea growers from Fújiàn and Zhèjiāng, and many rate this friendly street as the highlight of their visit. The four-story Tea City *(Chá Chéng)*, halfway down the street, is a pleasant spot to start. Black tea *(hóng chá)* and Pǔ'ěr tea (sold in round briquettes, a tea that improves with age) are usually sold by the same vendors. The Běijīng outlet of **Měnghǎi Cháchǎng** (ext. 8165), at the south end of the first floor, stocks exquisite black tea. Oolong tea *(wūlóng chá)* is usually encountered in the West in substandard form: Here is the genuine article. There is such a wide range of flavors—from flowery *gāoshān* to caffeine-laden *tiě guānyīn*, from milky *jīnxuān* to the sweet aftertaste of *rénshēn* (ginseng)—that most shoppers find a brew to suit. Try **Táiwān Tiānbǎoyáng Míngchá** (ext. 8177), on the west side of Tea City's first floor. Ceramic and cloisonne tea sets are the other big draw. **Zǐyù Táofáng** (ℂ 010/6327-5268), on the east side of the second floor, sells fine pots and cups molded from Yíxīng clay. Bargain hunters should visit **Jīngmǐn Cháchéng,** an older wholesale market, further south on the same side of the street. Open daily 8:30am to 7pm. Mǎlián Dào Chá Chéng, Fengtai Qu1. ℂ 010/6328-1177.

Tiān Fú Jítuán (Ten Fu Tea)   Not quite the McDonald's of tea, but at last count there were 26 branches in Běijīng. This store is the largest. Their jasmine tea *(huā chá)* is excellent. Open daily 8:30am to 7:30pm. Wángfǔjǐng Dàjiē 176, Dōngchéng Qū. ℂ 010/6525-4722. Metro: Wángfǔjǐng (118, exit A).

TOYS

Mass-produced toys can be found at the **toy market** *(wánjù shìchǎng)* behind Hóng Qiáo Shìchǎng, or at **Alien's Street Market.** Check carefully before you purchase: There are no warranties or safety guarantees! We infinitely prefer:

Shèngtáng Xuān ⊛ A world away from the baubles produced in the sweatshops of Shēnzhèn, this tiny shop offers delightful handcrafted toys. Mr. Tàng, an octogenarian Manchu bannerman, with help from his team of geriatric artisans, turns out traditional wooden toys, tiny hairy monkeys made from cicada husks, and ceramic figures depicting scenes from old Běijīng—the street barber, the fortune teller, and old men playing chess. Běijīng opera figurines betray influences from Japanese *manga.* Open daily 9am to 7pm. Guò Zǐ Jiàn Jiē, Dōngchéng Qū (just west of Kǒng Miào, on the south side of the street). ✆ **010/8404-7179.** Metro: Yōnghé Gōng/Lama Temple (215, exit C).

10

Běijīng After Dark

If you measure a city's nightlife by the number of chances for debauchery it offers, then Běijīng has never held (and probably will never hold) a candle to such neon-lit Babylons as Shànghǎi and Hong Kong. If, instead, you measure nightlife by its diversity, the Chinese capital rivals any major city in Asia.

Such was not always the case. As recently as a decade ago, Běijīng's populace routinely tucked itself into bed under a blanket of Máo-inspired puritanism shortly after nightfall, leaving visitors with one of two tourist-approved options: Attend Běijīng opera and acrobatic performances in a sterile theater, or wander listlessly around the hotel in search of a drink to make sleep come faster.

Since then, the government has realized there is money to be made on both sides of the Earth's rotation. The resulting relaxation in nocturnal regulations, set against the backdrop of Běijīng residents' historical affinity for cultural diversions, has helped remake the city's nightlife. Opera and acrobatics are still available, but now in more interesting venues, and

to them have been added an impressive range of other worthwhile cultural events: teahouse theater, puppet shows, intimate traditional music concerts, live jazz, even the occasional subtitled film.

This diversity continues with Běijīng's drinking and dance establishments, of which there are scores. Although they don't quite match Shànghǎi's for style, they are generally cheaper and offer something for just about every mood. With the opening of a few modern dance clubs, the city's cheesy old discos are thankfully no longer the only dance option, although the latter can still be tremendously entertaining on the kitsch level. The same goes for karaoke, a favorite in China as it is in Japan. Foreign-Chinese interaction in bars hasn't progressed much beyond the sexual exploitation so rampant in the 1920s and 1930s, but this is by no means a necessary dynamic, and the traveler not afraid to bumble through language barriers can often make fruitful contact with local people over a bottle or two of beer.

1 Performing Arts

BĚIJĪNG OPERA

Běijīng opera (*jīngjù*) is described by some as the apogee of traditional Chinese culture and, at least according to one modest Chinese connoisseur, is "perhaps the most refined form of opera in the world." Many who have actually seen a performance might beg to differ with these claims, but few other Chinese artistic traditions can match it for sophistication and pure stylized spectacle.

The Běijīng tradition is young as Chinese opera styles go. Its origins are most commonly traced to 1790, when four opera troupes from Ānhuī Province arrived in

Běijīng to perform for the Qīng court and decided to stay, eventually absorbing elements of a popular opera tradition from Húběi Province. Initially performed exclusively for the royal family, the new blended style eventually trickled out to the public and was well received as a more accessible alternative to the elegant but stuffy operas dominant at the time.

How it could have ever been considered accessible is mystifying to most foreign audiences. The typical performance is loud and long, with archaic dialogue sung on a screeching pentatonic scale, accompanied by a cacophony of gongs, cymbals, drums, clappers, and strings. This leaves most first-timers exhausted, but the exquisite costumes and martial arts–inspired movements ultimately make it worthwhile. Probably the opera's most distinctive feature is its elaborate system of face paints, with each color representing a character's disposition: red for loyalty, blue for bravery, black for honesty, and white for cruelty.

Communist authorities outlawed the "feudalistic" classics after 1949 and replaced them with the Eight Model Plays—a series of propaganda-style operas based on 20th-century events that focus heavily on class struggle. Many of these are still performed and are worth viewing if only to watch reactions from audience members, some of whom have seen these plays dozens of times and loudly express their disgust when a mistake is made. But the older stories, allowed again after Máo's death, are more visually stunning. Among the most popular are *Farewell My Concubine,* made famous through Chén Kǎigē's film of the same name, and *Havoc in Heaven,* which follows the mischievous Monkey King character from the Chinese literary classic *Journey to the West.*

Several theaters now offer shortened programs more amenable to the foreign attention span, usually with English subtitles or plot summaries. Most people on tours are taken to the cinema-style **Líyuán Theater (Líyuán Jùchǎng)** inside the Qián Mén Hotel (nightly performances at 7:30pm; ¥30–¥200/$4–$25) or to one of several other modern venues. These are affordable but supremely boring. Your time and money are much better spent at one of the traditional theaters below.

Húguǎng Guild Hall (Húguǎng Huìguǎn Xìlóu)

This combination museum-theater, housed in a complex of traditional buildings with gray tile roofs and bright red gables, has a connection with Běijīng Opera dating back to 1830. To the right of the main entrance is a small museum filled with old opera robes and photos of famous performers (including the legendary Méi Lánfāng), probably interesting only to aficionados. On the left is the expertly restored theater, a riot of color with a beautifully adorned traditional stage, paper lanterns hung from the high ceilings, and gallery seating on all three sides. Subtitles are in Chinese only, but brochures contain brief plot explanations in English. Performances take place nightly at 7:30pm. Hǔfáng Lù 3 (at intersection with Luómǎshì Dàjiē; plaza out front contains colorful opera mask sculpture). ✆ 010/6351-8284. Tickets ¥150–¥580 ($19–$72). Metro: Hépíng Mén (207, exit D1); walk south 10 min.

Teahouse of Prince Gōng's Mansion (Gōng Wáng Fǔ Cháguǎn)

Not a traditional opera venue, Prince Gōng's teahouse is nevertheless picturesque, with a rare bamboo motif on the exterior beams and columns and an intimate interior outfitted with polished wood tables and pleasing tea paraphernalia. This is opera for tourists, kept short and sweet, with a guided tour of the surrounding gardens included in the price (see Prince Gōng's Mansion, p. 141). There are several performances daily until 4:30pm. Liǔyīn Jiē 17. (Signposted in English at top of Qián Hǎi Xī Dàjiē [running north off Píng'ān Dàdào opposite north gate of Běi Hǎi Park]; turn left at sign and follow alley past large parking lot. Entrance marked with huge red lanterns.) ✆ 010/6616-8149. Tickets ¥60 ($8).

Zhèngyǐcí Xílóu (Zhèngyǐcí Theater)   The 340-year-old Zhèngyǐcí is under constant threat of extinction but is the first choice for authentic Běijīng opera when it's open. A Míng dynasty temple converted into an opera theater in 1712, it fell to other uses after 1949 and was in danger of being torn down until a local businessman reopened it in 1995. Since then, funding problems and its position at the center of an urban reconstruction project have limited the number of performances. The theater itself is similar to the Húguǎng Guild Hall, with the same high ceilings and gallery seating, but it has a decidedly more local feel. Perhaps most unique, the staff themselves are connoisseurs, more interested in opera than in collecting tourist dollars. Pray it survives. Performances are held most nights at 7:30pm (call to check). Qián Mén Xī Héyán Jiē 220 (walk south of the Hépíng Mén Quánjùdé, take 1st left). © 010/8315-1650. Tickets ¥150–¥280 ($19–$35). Metro: Hépíng Měn (207, exit C2).

ACROBATICS

China's acrobats are justifiably famous, and probably just a little bit insane. This was the only traditional Chinese art form to receive Máo's explicit approval (back flips, apparently, don't count as counterrevolution). While not culturally stimulating, the combination of plate spinning, hoop jumping, bodily contortion, and seemingly suicidal balancing acts make for slack-jawed entertainment of the highest order. Shànghǎi is the traditional home of acrobatics and boasts its best troupes, but the capital has done a fair job of transplanting the tradition.

The city's best acrobatics (*zájì*) venue is the **Wànshèng Jùchǎng** on the north side of Běi Wěi Lù just off Qián Mén Dàjiē (west side of the Temple of Heaven); performances are by the famous Běijīng Acrobatics Troupe (© 010/6303-7449; nightly shows at 7:15pm; ¥100–¥200/$12–$25). The acrobats at the **Cháoyáng Jùchǎng** (© 010/ 6507-2421; Dōng Sān Huán Běi Lù 36, south of Tuánjié Hú Park; nightly shows at 7:15pm; ¥120–¥300/$15–$37) are clumsier but the theater is more conveniently located, a short taxi ride from the main bar district.

PUPPETS

Puppet shows (*mù ǒu xì*) have been performed in China since the Hàn dynasty (206 B.C.–A.D. 220). The art form has diversified somewhat over the past two millennia, coming to include everything from the traditional hand puppets to string and shadow varieties. Plot lines are simple, but the manipulations are deft and the craftsmanship is exquisite. Most performances, including weekend matinees, are held at the **China Puppet Art Theater (Zhōngguó Mù'ǒu Jùyuàn),** in Ānhuá Xī Lǐ near the North Third Ring Road (© 010/6425-4798); tickets cost ¥20 to ¥25 ($2–$3).

OTHER VENUES

Běijīng hosts a growing number of international music and theater events every year, and its own increasingly respectable outfits—including the Běijīng Symphony Orchestra—give frequent performances. Among the most popular venues for this sort of thing is the **Běijīng Concert Hall (Běijīng Yīnyuè Tīng;** © 010/6605-5812), at Běi Xīnhuá Jiē in Liùbùkǒu (Xuānwǔ). The **Poly Theater (Bǎolì Dàshà Guójì Jùyuàn;** © 010/6500-1188, ext. 5127), in the Poly Plaza complex on the East Third Ring Road (northeast exit of Dōng Sì Shí Tiáo metro station), also hosts many large-scale performances, including the occasional revolutionary ballet. For information on additional venues and the shows they're hosting, check one of the expatriate magazines.

2 Teahouse Theater

Traditional teahouse entertainment disappeared from Běijīng after 1949, but some semblance survives in a number of modern teahouses that have grown up with the tourism industry. Snippets of Běijīng opera, cross-talk (stand-up) comedy, acrobatics, traditional music, singing, and dancing flow across the stage as you sip tea and nibble snacks. If you don't have time to see these kinds of performances individually, the teahouse is an adequate solution. If you're looking for a quiet place to enjoy a cup of jasmine and maybe do some reading, look to one of the real teahouses listed later in this chapter.

Lǎo Shě's Teahouse (Lǎo Shě Cháguǎn)   This somewhat garishly decorated teahouse is named for one of the most famous plays by celebrated Chinese writer Lǎo Shě (see Lǎo Shě Jìniànguǎn [Former Residence of Lǎo Shě], p. 140). Performances change nightly but always include opera and acrobatics. It pays to buy the more expensive tickets, as views from the rear seats are frequently obscured. Nightly shows at 7:50pm. Qiánmén Xī Dàjiē 3 (west of Qián Mén on south side of the street). ℂ 010/6303-6830. Tickets ¥40– ¥130 ($5–$16).

Tiānqiáo Happy Tea House (Tiānqiáo Lè Cháguǎn)   The Tiānqiáo puts on essentially the same show as Lǎo Shě's Teahouse, but in a gallery seating framed in dark lacquered wood and a less eye-straining color scheme. The quality of the performances has declined markedly, however: Many performers are well past their prime. There's a roast duck dinner option (reservations required) for those who want to kill two birds in a single venue. Performances take place nightly at 8pm (arrive at 6:30pm for dinner). Běi Wěi Lù (just west of intersection with Qián Mén Dàjiē, west side of Temple of Heaven). ℂ 010/ 6304-0617. Tickets ¥150 ($19), or ¥330 ($41) with dinner.

3 Cinemas

State limitations on freedom of expression, the profusion of black market DVDs, and ready access to illegal download sites have taken their toll on China's film industry, but Běijīng has enough film fanatics to support a handful of theaters. **Cherry Lane Movies** (ℂ 139/0113-4745; ¥50/$6), run by a long-tenured and long-winded American expatriate, shows older and some new Chinese films with English subtitles on the weekends; films are listed at www.cherrylanemovies.com.cn and are screened inside the Kent Centre, at Liàngmǎ Qiáo Lù 29. They also have summer screenings at the Sino-Swiss Hotel. **Box Cafe** (Hézi Kāfēiguǎn; Xī Wáng Zhuāng Xiǎoqū 5; ℂ 010/ 6279-1280), a smallish cafe near the east gate of Tsinghua University (Qīnghuá Dàxué), offers free screenings on Tuesday and Saturday of Chinese independent and experimental films and a few foreign films of the same nature. The **UME International Cineplex** (Huáxīng Guójì Yǐngchéng; Shuāngyúshù Xuéyuàn Nán Lù 44; ℂ 010/6255-5566; ¥50–¥80/$6–$10), a full-scale theater just north of the Third Ring Road and southeast of Rénmín University, occasionally shows undubbed Hollywood films and Chinese blockbusters with English subtitles, as does the more conveniently located **Oriental Plaza Multiplex,** right next to Be There or Be Square, on the east side of the mall.

When international film festival directors go looking for new, edgy films, they visit **Hart Center of Arts** (Hātè Shālóng; ℂ 010/6435-3570; www.hart.com.cn) in the Factory 798 complex (see chapter 7, p. 140) which hosts festivals with themes no one

Rainbow Sexuality under the Red Flag

Same-sex relationships between men have a history of acceptance in China dating as far back as the Zhōu period (1100–256 B.C.). In official records of the Hàn dynasty (206 B.C.–A.D. 220), 10 emperors are described as openly bisexual and are listed with the names of their lovers. In the centuries following the Hàn, homosexuality was generally accepted among men, so long as it didn't interfere with their Confucian duty to marry and perpetuate the family name. Partly due to the influence of Western missionaries, homosexuality was outlawed by official decree in 1740, but Judeo-Christian notions of shame never fully took root in China and the practice persisted. Under the Communists, however, homosexuality came to be seen as disruptive of the social order, and persecution of gays was sanctioned during the Cultural Revolution.

The situation has improved markedly over the past decade. In 2002, the government rescinded its 1989 edict describing homosexuality as a psychological disorder, but laws still prohibit expat magazines from talking about gay bars (described instead as bars "for the alternative set"). The general populace tends to ignore the existence of gay relationships, a mental trick made easier by the fact that it's considered normal for men to be physically affectionate regardless of sexual orientation. As in ancient times, many gay men still marry and have children to satisfy their parents.

The first openly gay club in Běijīng is the recently opened **Club 70** (② 010/6508-9799) at Cháoyáng Gōngyuán Xī Mén, ironically directly opposite the ultimate heterosexual meat market, Suzie Wong's (p. 190). The beats are about right, but it's still in search of a comfortable vibe, a problem you won't face at **Destination (Mùdìdì;** ② 010/6551-5138) at Gōngtǐ Xī Lù 7, south of the Worker's Stadium west gate, where the crowd revels. **On/Off (Shàng Xià Xiàn;** ② 010/6415-8083) at Xìngfú Yī Cūn Xī Lǐ 5, is one of Běijīng's longest standing "alternative" venues. Things have turned a tad seedy in recent times, but the crowds still flock to this venue, which now boasts a bar, a restaurant, and even an Internet cafe.

For lesbians, the scene is slightly grimmer. Women perceived as homosexual are often subject to harassment. In the context of Chinese patriarchy, lesbianism has never received much attention. Outside a brief appearance in the Chinese classic *Dream of the Red Mansion,* it is invisible in literature, and the pressures of China's skewed gender ratio—an excess of boys brought on by age-old prejudices in response to the one-child policy—has made many single Chinese men resentful of any reduction in the pool of potential wives.

Aside from Thursday nights at Destination, try the Fēng Bar, just east of the south gate of the Worker's Stadium, on Saturday nights. As the scene is still developing, try connecting online, through the newly established Běijīng's Other Attractions (boa_productions@yahoo.com), or more general websites for lesbians in Asia, such as www.fridae.com or www.utopia.asia.com.

else is game to touch, and regularly screens movies at 8pm on Saturday (call to check). Most of the work shown here has not passed the censors.

4 Live Music

Most of the bars on Sān Lǐ Tún North Bar Street offer nightly live "music" performances by cover bands, usually of scant talent and almost invariably Filipino in origin. But there are several small venues, most of them in Cháoyáng, which host an increasingly varied lineup of musical acts. Performers range from traditional folk instrumentalists to jazz ensembles and rock outfits, and are usually interesting, if not always good. (See Appendix A: "Běijīng in Depth" for more on the city's better bands.) Most venues are bars open nightly from around 5pm to 1 or 2am, although few offer live acts every night. There is usually a small cover charge on performance nights (¥5–¥50/$1–$6), depending on the number of acts and their prestige. *Time Out* and *that's Beijing* maintain somewhat accurate listings of what is playing where and when.

CD Jazz Cafe (Sēndì Juéshì)   After much upheaval, this amalgamation of CD Café and the short-lived Treelounge is the best place to see local jazz and blues acts in Běijīng. If it's a special act, get there early. Dōng Sān Huán, south of the Agricultural Exhibition Center (Nóngzhǎn Guǎn) main gate (down small path behind trees that line sidewalk). ℂ 010/6506-8288. Cover ¥30 ($4).

The Icehouse (Kù Bīng)   Set in a warehouse that once stored the ice for the Forbidden City, Icehouse is the "B" in RBL (p. 86). Currently, a respectable blues band from Australia headlines, and the proprietors are hoping to attract top international acts. Open 6pm till 2am. Dōng'ān Mén Dàjiē Xīpèi Lóu 53 (connected to RBL by an underground passageway). ℂ 010/6522-1389.

New Get Lucky Bar (Xīn Háoyùn Jiǔbā)   This odd bar is the best venue to take in one of Běijīng's much-documented **punk** shows, often featuring the talents of Brain Failure and Hanging on the Box. A Chinese version of heavy metal played on a five-note scale sometimes substitutes for punk. If you value your eardrums, don't get too close to the speakers. In Nǚrén Jiē area, inside Oriental Qīcǎi World. ℂ 010/8448-3335. Shows ¥20–¥30 ($3–$4).

Sānwèi Bookstore (Sānwèi Shūwū)   The tiny Sānwèi has a well-worn teahouse upstairs that hosts intimate concerts on the weekends. Fridays it's jazz and Saturdays it's classical Chinese, usually with a minority twist. This is the city's finest venue for Chinese traditional music, if only because you sit close enough to really experience it. Tea and snacks are included in the price. Friday and Saturday performances take place at 8:30pm. Fùxīng Mén Nèi Dàjiē 60 (opposite the Minorities Palace [Mínzú Gōng]). ℂ 010/6601-3204. Cover ¥30 ($4).

Yú Gōng Yí Shān   This wonderful performance space is the best live music venue in Běijīng, period. The sound isn't perfect, it can get plenty stuffy in summer, and its location in the middle of a car park cum bus depot lends it a certain seediness, but the owners have a knack for turning up the best local acts. Run by the owners of the now defunct Loup Chante, the diverse line up—from punk to Mongolian mouth music, and everything in-between—means you can visit night after night. Daily 2pm to 2am. Gōngtǐ Běi Lù 1 (just north of the Bus Bar). ℂ 010/6415-0687. Cover varies for performances.

5 Clubs & Discos

The average Chinese will lump all dancing establishments into a single category—*tiàowǔdiàn* (dancing place), or, if they try it in English, "dee-si-ko." But while the distinction between a Běijīng disco and a Běijīng dance club is lost on most locals, it is readily apparent to any foreigner. Discos are typically old and cavernous, with exaggerated decor, horrible music, and a wholly Chinese clientele whose attempts to imitate Western modes of style and dance will send shivers down your spine. Clubs, by contrast, are newer, smaller, and more stylish, with a DJ-dominated atmosphere closer in feel to what you'd find in the United States or Europe. The club clientele is wealthier, more diverse (featuring both Chinese and foreigners), and not quite as clueless.

Both discos and dance clubs charge high covers (anywhere from ¥50–¥150/$6–$19). Both tend to get crowded on weekends around 10pm and empty around 3am, although a few clubs will host special parties that last until dawn. There is some activity on Thursday nights, but the rest of the week is slow. Discos pre-date the days of the drinking district and hence are scattered randomly around the city. Clubs tend to be situated next to bars, in foreigner-heavy areas like Sān Lǐ Tún and Cháoyáng Park.

Babyface   Definitely not a place to come for a quiet chat, Babyface serves it up for the wealthy young elite of the capital. If you think shows like "The OC" only have an impact in the West, Babyface will make you think again. The Valley Girl is on the march. Dance floors are small and much of the clientele has an air of studied boredom, but it's near impossible to fault the music (often supplied by Ministry of Sound DJs) and the stylish metal-and-glass decor. Try not to scratch the paint on anyone's Mercedes when you stumble back outside, disoriented by the thumping bass and the potent shooters. Gōngtǐ Xī Lù 6 (just south of the Workers' Stadium west gate). ℂ 010/6551-9081. Cover ¥50 ($6).

Banana (Bānànà)   Banana is one of Běijīng's oldest and most popular discos. This new, larger location is a classic bit of 1990s Miami Beach postmodernism with fake palm trees and white Doric columns. The crowd is mostly black-clad men and skinny women who wear sunglasses at night. The sound system produces enough bass to loosen tooth fillings. Jiànguó Mén Wài Dàjiē 22 (in front of Scitech Hotel). ℂ 010/6528-3636. Cover ¥30 ($4).

The Den (Dūnhuáng)   The Den is Běijīng's longest-standing meat market and an institution among youthful travelers. There's a vague opium den theme downstairs, with low light and lots of quasi-ornate wood embellishments, but the main draw is the sweaty, no-frills dance floor upstairs, crowded until the wee hours. Music is mostly 1990s pop dance hits and half-hearted R & B. There's an authentic Western brunch here, with eggs Benedict and bagels, from 9am to 1pm. The half-price happy hour, which runs for 5 hours (5–10pm), is unbeatable. Intersection of Gōngtǐ Dōng Lù 4A, next to the City Hotel (Chéngshì Bīnguǎn). ℂ 010/6592-6290. Cover ¥30 ($4).

Destination (Mùdìdi)   Jokingly renamed "Desperation" by locals, Běijīng's most successful (almost openly) gay club is indeed a fine spot to meet locals of the same sex, without the rent boy seediness that now afflicts On/Off. Bare grey concrete walls, dark lounges, and odd subtitled video footage that never quite seems to match the tunes doesn't sound like a successful formula, but somehow it works. The music isn't so loud that you can't duck into a corner for a chat, and is slightly camp without being cliché. Insanely crowded on weekends. Gōngtǐ Xī Lù 7 (south of the west gate of the Workers' Stadium, opposite Bellagio's). ℂ 010/6551-5138.

(*Moments* **Karaoke: Down that Drink and Pop in Those Ear Plugs, Ma, It's Time to Sing**

No one knows why Asian cultures have embraced karaoke (pronounced "*kǎlā* okay" in Mandarin) with such red-faced gusto, or why so many foreigners adopt the enthusiasm once they're on Eastern soil. Maybe the food lacks some amino acid crucial to the brain's shame function. Or maybe it's just fun to get soused and pretend you have talent thousands of miles from anyone who cares. It doesn't matter either way. Spend enough time in Běijīng and sooner or later you'll find yourself standing before a TV screen, beer and microphone in hand, with a crowd of drunkards insisting you sing to the Muzak version of a Beatles hit. Refuse and your Chinese host loses face; comply and you receive applause. Resistance is futile. Most karaoke venues in Běijīng are seedy and given over to less-than-legal side entertainment, so if you have any choice in the matter head to Party World, also known as the **Cash Box (Qián Guì; ℂ 010/6588-3333;** open 24 hr.), the city's classiest and best-equipped do-it-yourself concert venue. Located southeast of the Full Link Plaza, at the corner of Cháowài Shìchǎng Jiē and Cháowài Nán Jiē, Cash Box boasts a hotel-like lobby, pleasantly decorated private rooms, and a wide selection of Western songs, some even released in the last decade. Prices range from ¥39 to ¥365 ($5–$46) per hour, depending on size of the room and night of the week. There's usually a line, so you'll have to give them your name early. You wouldn't want to embarrass yourself anywhere else.

6 Bars

Although most average Chinese still prefer to get drunk at dinner, the Western pub tradition has gained ground among younger locals, and the city boasts a large, ever-growing population of establishments devoted exclusively to alcohol.

Drinking in Běijīng occurs in one of several districts, each with its own atmosphere and social connotations. The city's oldest and still most popular drinking district is **Sān Lǐ Tún,** located between the east second and third ring roads around the Workers' Stadium (Gōngrén Tǐyùchǎng). The area's name comes from Sān Lǐ Tún Lù, a north-south strip of drinking establishments a long block east of the Workers' Stadium that at one time contained practically all of the city's bars. Now known as North Bar Street (Sān Lǐ Tún Jiǔbā Jiē), it has been overshadowed by other clusters of bars in the Xìngfú Cūn area north of the stadium, and scattered around the stadium itself. Bars here are rowdy and raunchy, and packed to overflowing on weekends. Similar watering holes surround the south and west gates of **Cháoyáng Gōngyuán** (park) to the east, an area the government has tried to promote as the new drinking district because it has fewer residential buildings. The development of **Nǚrén Jiē,** northeast of the Kempinski Hotel, followed a similar logic. Bars and clubs in **Hǎidiàn,** the city's university district to the northwest, congregate around the gates of several universities and cater to a crowd of local English majors and foreign students.

The fastest-growing spot for late-night drinking is the **Back Lakes** (**Shíchà Hǎi** or **Hòu Hǎi**), a previously serene spot with a few discreetly fashionable bars north of Běi Hǎi Park which has exploded into a riot of neon, capped by the ghastly Lotus Lane. **Nǎn Luógǔ Xiàng,** to the east of the Back Lakes area, was previously home to only one cafe; now they are wall-to-wall. Perhaps the most notable trend is the resurgence of hotel bars, which are the most appealing and stylish drinking options in Běijīng, most notably **Centro** (Kerry Center), **Red Moon** (Grand Hyatt), and **Cloud Nine** (Shangri-La).

Běijīng bars generally open around 5 or 6pm and stay open until the last patrons leave or until the staff decides it wants to go home, usually by 2am on Friday and Saturday nights. Several of the Back Lakes bars double as cafes and open as early as 11am.

Bed Tapas & Bar (Chuáng Bā)
The risqué decor of this courtyard bar is the work of a New York designer. All bare concrete, gauze, four-poster beds, and antique furnishings, Bed pushes the boundaries of what constitutes an acceptable leisure space for wholesome socialist citizens. The olive tapenade is ideal finger food; the caipirinha and mojita are suitably refreshing. Bed is a block north of its sister establishment, Cafe Sambal, and attracts a similar crowd of design professionals. The rear courtyard is sublime on a warm summer evening. Zhāngwàng Hútòng 17 (from Gǔlóu Dàjiē metro station head south along Jiǔ Gǔlóu Dàjiē, take the 4th lane on your left). 🕿 010/8400-1554.

ClubFootball (Wànguó Qúnxīng Zúqiú)
Běijīng has several sports bars, but ClubFootball is the genuine article. TVs hang from every corner, tables are wobbly, brick walls bear the appropriate mix of action stills and team banners, and there's foosball to one side. Grab a stool at the wood bar and note the crescent-moon dents left by overzealous bottle-wielding patrons. The emphasis is on soccer, with occasional rugby, baseball, and American football. Beer is cheap, there's decent local wine, and the chili is fantastic. Chūnxiù Lù 10 (near Sān Lǐ Tún; attached to the Red House). 🕿 010/6417-0497.

First Cafe (Dìyī Kāfēi)
The best cocktails this side of Shànghǎi. While the main qualification of most of Běijīng's bartenders is a willingness to work for less than $1 per hour, the First Cafe houses a couple of bartenders who take their craft very, very seriously. The intimate, softly lit bar is becoming so popular the owner may soon be forced to decorate the downstairs lounge properly. For now, appreciate the jazz soundtrack and dark wood paneling of the upstairs section. Poaching of staff is rife; those who appreciate a dirty martini pray that George stays put. Open 7pm till 2am. Nán Sān Lǐ Tún Lù (100m/328 ft. south of the giant beer mug, on the east side of the street). 🕿 010/6501-8812.

Lotus Bar (Liánhuā Jiǔbā)
Set inside a narrow 70-year-old two-story house east of the Back Lakes, Lotus's small, artsy interior appeals to the city's shyer hipsters. The best reason to come is the pair of couches next to the upstairs window, with bird's-eye views of reconstructed Yāndài Xié Jiē, a quainter-than-quaint *hútòng* running east from the intersection of Hòu Hǎi and Qián Hǎi. Pleasant outdoor seating on the next-door roof is available in summer. If the bar is too crowded, head across the street to Ǒu, a similarly decorated Thai restaurant under the same management. Yāndài Xiéjiē 29 (Back Lakes; in 1st *hútòng* on right walking south from Drum Tower; look for a circular window above a bamboo and glass doorway). 🕿 010/6407-7857.

Palace View Bar (Guān Jǐng Jiǔbā)
The best panorama in Běijīng. If you can bear Celine Dion on continuous rotation, do not miss this largely undiscovered rooftop bar. With nothing but air between yourself and the Imperial City, you probably won't be perturbed by banal music or by drink portions that put the teeny back

in martini. Open May through September. Rooftop of Grand Hotel (see chapter 5, p. 64). ✆ 010/6513-7788, ext. 458.

Pass-by Bar (Guòkè Jiŭbā) Relocated in a restored courtyard house down a *hútòng* east of Qián Hǎi in 2002, Tibetan-themed Pass-by is more gathering place than nightspot, with an extensive English-language library, a useful message board, rotating photo exhibits on the walls, and a good mix of Chinese and foreign regulars. There's great Italian food by a chef stolen from Annie's (p. 93) and a separate nonsmoking section—almost unheard-of in a Běijīng bar. The courtyard is idyllic in summer with outdoor seating. Internet access is available (¥10/$1 per hr.). Nán Luógǔ Xiàng 108 (Back Lakes; alley is to left/west of a Muslim restaurant on the north side of Píng'ān Dàdào—walk north 150m/492 ft.). ✆ 010/8403-8004.

Press Club Bar (Jìzhě Jùlèbù) The nearby Běijīng International Club, renowned in a previous bye-gone era as the meeting spot for foreign correspondents, inspired this upscale bar inside the St. Regis Hotel. The elegant space, with leather-bound tomes, marble fireplace, leather armchairs, and brocade sofas, seats just 55. Old prints and vintage photos of Běijīng pundits and reporters from days past line the long bar. The place closes at midnight. Jiànguómén Wài Dàjiē 21 (at rear of St. Regis's main building). ✆ 010/6460-6688.

The Tree (Yǐnbì de Shù) Uprooted from South Bar street, the former Hidden Tree sports a new tree but is slightly more tranquil than its former incarnation. It still boasts an unmatched selection of Belgian beer: Trappist and abbey ales, lighter wild-fermented lambics, and several wheat (white) beers. The stock changes, but there's always bottled Chimay and draft Hoegaarden. Passable single-malts, cigars, thin-crust pizzas, and a pleasant but unpretentious brick and wood interior complete the picture. West of Sān Lǐ Tún North Bar St. (behind Poachers Inn). ✆ 010/6415-1954.

World of Suzie Wong (Sūxī Huáng) Named for the fictional Hong Kong hooker who falls for a much older William Holden (ironic given the current dynamic of the bar), this is the see-and-be-seen venue for nouveau-riche Chinese and newly arrived expatriates. DJs so cool it hurts play music for head-bobbers in the main room, and there's a Míng-style canopy bed next to the bar where the exhibitionists sit. Get there early to stake out one of the row of semi-private alcoves to the side, luridly lit and luxuriously outfitted with plush couches covered in brocaded pillows. West gate of Cháoyáng Park. ✆ 010/6593-6049.

7 Cafes & Other Drinks Spots

Just like the Manchurian hordes did 3½ centuries earlier, **Starbucks** swept into Běijīng in the 1990s and quickly conquered it. Branches are everywhere, including the China World complex, the Oriental Plaza, the Pacific Century Plaza near Sān Lǐ Tún, and, yes, the inner court of the Forbidden City. By far the city's most popular coffee chain, it is particularly beloved of young local women in search of eligible expatriates. But there are other options (see below), many of which offer a better brew.

Despite the coffee invasion, Běijīng is still ultimately tea territory, and many of the most pleasant sipping experiences are to be had in the small teahouses that lie scattered about the city.

The Bookworm (Lǎo Shū Chóng) The best spot in Běijīng for a quiet read, and better yet, there's no need to bring your own book. This Sān Lǐ Tún fixture, recently forced to move by developers, boasts a library of 6,000 English-language titles, including most of the works recommended in chapter 2. The new venue, which was undergoing the finishing touches at press time, will have three separate sections: a European restaurant which will house the library; a cafe; and a kids' corner which should also house a new bookshop. Open 9am till midnight. Nán Sān Lǐ Tún Lù Sì Lóu (behind Pacific Century shopping center, near The Loft). ℂ 010/6586-9507.

Cafe de Niro (Nílóu Kāfēi)

This would be the finest cafe in Běijīng, if only they would pay more attention to the coffee, which is overpriced, and has no detectable trace of caffeine. Tranquil music and the warm, airy, sleek-lined interior draw the deliberately tousled hair set like an Armani end-of-season sale. You'll enjoy the inexpensive set lunches and complimentary wireless Internet, but whatever you do, avoid the "House Health Drinks": hot chocolate and Japanese green tea were never meant to share a glass. Open 10am till midnight. Sān Lǐ Tún Jiǔbā Běi Jiē Tónglǐ Yī Céng (just west of Sān Lǐ Tún N. Bar St., 1st floor of Tónglǐ Studios, just north of Aperitivo). ℂ 010/6416-9400.

Purple Vine Tea House (Zǐténg Lú Cháguǎn)

This tiny teahouse next to the Forbidden City is one of the most peaceful in Běijīng, with private rooms separated by wood lattice screens and a small fountain in front that fills it with the sound of water. Order one of the more expensive oolong teas (¥200–¥400/$25–$50) and you'll be treated to the Chinese version of a tea ceremony, less aesthetically pleasing than the Japanese version but with a better-tasting end product. The menu is in English. Open daily noon to 2am. Nán Cháng Jiē 1, at the intersection with Xī Huá Mén (just outside west gate of the Forbidden City). ℂ 010/6606-6614.

Riverside Café (Hépàn Kāfēi)

The best continental breakfast in Běijīng is, alas, only served up on the weekend. It's not really by the riverside (and you wouldn't want it to be), but the outdoor seating is pleasant. The same can't be said of the service: Rarely have so few been ignored by so many. Australians will be delighted to find Vegemite on the menu, the sourdough toast and the poached eggs are both perfect and there's a tempting selection of pastries in the deli. Open 8am to 11pm. Sān Lǐ Tún Běi Xiǎojiē 10 (close to intersection with Liàngmǎ Hé Nán Lù). ℂ 010/6466-1241.

Sculpting in Time (Diāokè Shíguāng)

This was once Běijīng's most famous film cafe, but it lost that niche to Box Cafe (see section 3 of this chapter) when it moved from its location in a charming (now demolished) hútòng east of Peking University. Now at the Běijīng Institute of Technology, it seldom shows films but is still popular with students, foreign and Chinese both. A second branch south of the main entrance to Fragrant Hills Park (ℂ 010/8529-0040), has a pleasant remoteness and a large outdoor deck with views of the park, while the largest branch, just west of Wǔdàokǒu metro stop (ℂ 010/8286-7025), has less charm but is handy to the university district. All serve adequate coffee and Western snacks, and have wireless Internet. Open daily from 9am to 12:30am. Wēigōngcūn Xī Kǒu 7 (Lǐgōng Dà Nán Mén), just to left of the university's south gate. ℂ 010/6894-6825.

Tasty Taste (Tàidí Dàisī)

Don't be deterred by the asinine name, or the half-hearted decor, for here is the best coffee in Běijīng. In a town where innumerable crimes are committed against the bean, it's a relief to find Italian espresso coffee without any bitter aftertaste from poorly cleaned machines, milk frothed just so rather than tortured to produce enormous bubbles, and even cocoa powder and cinnamon served on the side with your cappuccino. The cheesecakes are divine too. Open 9am to 11pm. Gōngtǐ Běi Mén (on the southwest corner of Gōngtǐ Běi Lù and Gōngtǐ Xī Lù). ℂ 010/6551-1822.

The Teahouse of Family Fù (Chá Jiā Fù) Located in a unique octagonal building on the south bank of Hòu Hǎi, the Fù family's teahouse is among the city's most charming, furnished throughout with a pleasantly haphazard assortment of Míng reproduction furniture. Owned by a former mechanics professor and run with help from his friendly English-speaking mother, it sometimes plays host to poetry readings, lectures, and classical Chinese music performances. Teas are reasonably priced (¥50–¥152/$6–$20 for pot with unlimited refills) and presented on a fan. Semi-private rooms branch off to all sides. Free snacks. Open from 10:30am to midnight. Hòu Hǎi Xīběi Àn (northwest side of Hòu Hǎi, next to Kǒng Yǐjǐ). ✆ 010/6616-0725.

Zuǒ Yòu Jiān (Mima Cafe) The coffee and cuisine are just passable, but if you need a touch of serenity, visit Mima on a weekday afternoon or a summer evening. Located just north of the east gate of Yuán Míng Yuán (p. 137), outdoor courtyard seating is covered over by rice paper domes, set around clusters of bamboo. The washroom is the most stunning I have ever encountered, and worth the trek in itself. Open daily from 10am to midnight. Yuán Míng Yuán Dōng Mén Nèi Běi Liù Jiān Yuàn. ✆ 010/8268-8003.

11

The Great Wall & Other Side Trips

The hills around Běijīng are dotted with fascinating sights, the foremost, of course, being the **Great Wall.** Many of the sights listed in this chapter can be seen in a single excursion, which can include other sights just on the outskirts of the city. Nearly all organized tours include a stop at the **Míng Tombs** on the way to the Great Wall at **Bā Dá Lǐng** and **Jūyōng Guān.** **Tánzhè Sì** and **Jiètái Sì** are readily combined as an agreeable day trip, and the intriguing **Tián Yì Mù** (p. 142), a cemetery for eunuchs on the western outskirts of town, is on the road to the quiet courtyard houses of **Chuān Dǐ Xià.**

Surprisingly, the most enjoyable way to reach many of these sights is by public transportation. Although slower than an organized tour, public bus or train travel is flexible, doesn't drag you to dubious attractions, and costs a fraction of the overpriced tours offered by hotels. If you're short on time, an option is to hire a taxi for the day (see section 2, "Getting Around," in chapter 4). An entertaining (if slightly rushed) choice is to join a Chinese bus tour. Air-conditioned buses for these tours leave when full early in the morning from various metro stations, and make stops at two or three sites. Your last resort should be hiring a car through your hotel or a tour agency for a ludicrous fee.

When heading out of town, avoid weekend mornings when traffic can be gridlocked. Attempting to return on Sunday afternoon is also frustrating. Even on weekdays, allow at least half a day, and usually a full day, to explore the sights listed in this chapter. Take a picnic and take your time.

1 The Great Wall (Wànlǐ Chángchéng) ✵✵✵

Even after you dispense with the myths that it is a single continuous structure and that it can be seen from space (it can't, any more than a fishing line can be seen from the other side of a river), China's best-known attraction is still mind-boggling. The world's largest historical site is referred to in Mandarin as **Wànlǐ Chángchéng** ("10,000-Lǐ Long Wall" or simply "Very Long Wall"). The Great Wall begins at Shānhǎi Guān on the Bó Hǎi Sea and snakes west to a fort at Jiāyù Guān in the Gobi Desert. Its origins date back to the Warring States Period (453–221 B.C.), when rival kingdoms began building defensive walls to thwart each other's armies. The king of Qín, who eventually conquered the other states to become the first emperor of a unified China, engaged in large-scale wall building toward the end of his reign, although tales of 300,000 conscripted laborers are embellishments of subsequent dynasties. During the Hàn dynasty (206 B.C.–A.D. 220), the Wall was extended west, and additions were made in completely different locations, according to the military needs of the day.

Side Trips from Běijīng

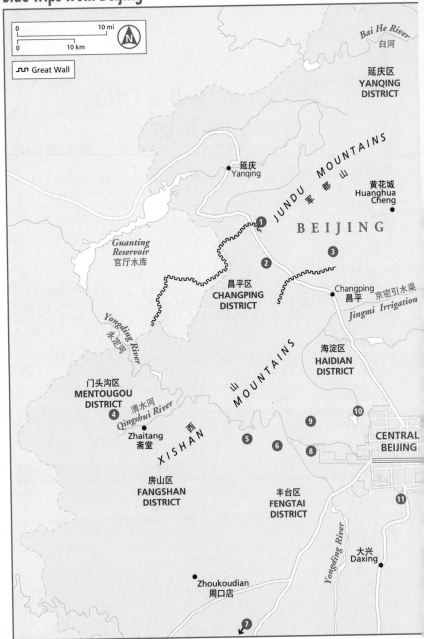

密云区
MIYUN DISTRICT

To Chengde

Gubeikou
古北口 ⑮ ⑯

Miyun Reservoir
密云水库

⑭

三渡河
San Du He

密云
Miyun

M U N I C I P A L I T Y

⑰

Huairou Reservoir
怀柔水库

怀柔
Huairou

Canal

顺义区
SHUNYI DISTRICT

平谷区
PINGGU DISTRICT

蓟县
Jixian

Běijīng Capital Airport (Shǒudū Guójì Jīchǎng) **13** 首都国际机场	Jiètái Sì (Temple of the Ordination Platform) **6** 戒台寺
Chuān Dǐ Xià **4** 川底下	Mílù Yuán (Mílù Park) **11** 麋鹿园
Eastern Qīng Tombs (Qīng Dōng Líng) **17** 清东陵	Míng Tombs (Shísān Líng) **3** 十三陵
Gāo Bēi Diàn **12** 高碑店	Summer Palace (Yíhé Yuán) **10** 颐和园
Great Wall at Bā Dá Lǐng **1** 八达岭长城	Tánzhè Sì (Temple of the Pool and Wild Mulberry) **5** 潭柘寺
Great Wall at Jīn Shān Lǐng **15** 金山岭长城	Tiányì Mù **8** 田义墓
Great Wall at Jūyōng Guān **2** 居庸关长城	Western Qīng Tombs (Qīng Xī Líng) **7** 清西陵
Great Wall at Mùtiányù **14** 慕田峪长城	Xiāng Shān Gōngyuán (Fragrant Hills Park) **9** 香山公园
Great Wall at Sīmǎtái **16** 司马台长城	

✈ ⑬

朝阳区
CHAOYANG DISTRICT

Wenyu River
温榆河

⑫
Tongzhou
通州

通州区
TONGZHOU DISTRICT

大兴区
DAXING DISTRICT

Beijing-Tianjin Highway
京津塘高速公路

Although many tour guides will try to persuade you otherwise, the Míng Wall you see today is unrelated to the Qín Wall, which lays far to the north. The Míng even went to the trouble of calling their wall Biān Qiáng (Frontier Wall) to avoid comparisons with the tyrannical first emperor of China, Qín Shǐ Huángdì. The original Wall was built almost entirely from tamped earth, and often crumbled away within decades of being constructed. Talk of satellite mapping the current Wall is fanciful—for most of its length, the structure is barely visible from the ground. This, and the fact that there is no single "Great Wall," makes it impossible to pin down the Wall's precise length.

Those with an interest in exaggerating Chinese xenophobia portray Wall building as an essential part of the national psyche, but after the Hàn, few dynasties bothered with Wall construction, and relied mostly on trade, diplomacy, and the odd punitive expedition to keep the peace. Even during the inward-looking Míng dynasty, the Wall was viewed by many at court as an ancient version of the Star Wars missile-defense idea—ineffective, absurdly expensive, and successful only in antagonizing China's neighbors. With the Míng wracked by internal rebellion, the Qīng armies simply bribed the demoralized sentries. The Qīng left the Wall as a monument to folly, and while early Western visitors were awed, it became a source of national pride only recently. Sun Yat-sen was among the first to view it as a symbol of national strength, an idea the Communists adopted, including it in the National Anthem.

The Wall's most easily visited sections are **Bā Dá Lǐng** and **Jūyōng Guān,** while **Mùtiányù, Jīn Shān Lǐng,** and the vertiginous **Sīmǎtái** require a full day's outing. Appealing options for overnight stays are **The Red Capital Ranch** at Mùtiányù and the more basic **Sīmǎtái YHA.**

THE GREAT WALL AT BĀ DÁ LÍNG
70km (43 miles) NW of Běijīng

The first section of the Great Wall opened to tourists, the portion at **Bā Dá Lǐng** remains the most popular. In 1957 it was fully restored to its original Míng appearance—although the reconstruction was sloppier than subsequent efforts at Mùtiányù, Jīn Shān Lǐng, and Sīmǎtái, where efforts were taken to preserve a sense of antiquity. A cable car was added at Bā Dá Lǐng in the 1980s, followed later by a museum, a Circle Vision Theater, several restaurants, a large number of souvenir stands, and a KFC. Although it is one of the most dramatic sections of the Great Wall, the sheer number of visitors is overwhelming: You might not be able to see Bā Dá Lǐng from space, but there's some chance of smelling the toilets.

Construction of this section of the Great Wall began in 1368 and continued for over 200 years. The sides are covered in stone, the top in layers of brick. The interior is a mixture of soil and rubble, painstakingly tamped into place. In unrestored sections, where the masonry has crumbled away, you can spy the striations. Set in a steep,

---

Tips Travelers with Disabilities

Exploring the Great Wall is tough enough for people in good shape. For those with disabilities, the Wall is a nightmare. At **Bā Dá Lǐng** a cable car provides access, but there are still steps to negotiate up to the cable car, and steep steps up to the Wall. There are no elevators or wheelchair assists at any of the sections.

Tips **On the Wild Wall**

Travelers with time and the inclination to explore beyond the typical tourist haunts are strongly encouraged to join a trip to the crumbling **"unofficial" sections of the Wall** that snake through more remote areas north of Běijīng. William Lindesay, a Briton who has been walking along and writing about the Great Wall since the mid-1980s, organizes excursions for the company **Wild Wall**. Joining one of his tours is the best way to learn about the Wall's construction and destruction, both by human and natural forces, from a knowledgeable source.

Wild Wall is based out of one of two modernized farmhouses, the first and more fully outfitted just north of Běijīng, and the second somewhat more primitive (but still comfortable) in Héběi. Wild Wall's most common weekend trips run 3 days (Fri–Sun) and cost $200 (prices are quoted in U.S. dollars), including guided hikes, accommodation in a farmhouse, and excellent home cooking (transportation to the farmhouse is an extra $65). Although a little pricey, these weekend trips are highly recommended and typically happen twice or three times a month. Day hikes and strenuous "Extreme Treks" are also available. For details see **www.wildwall.com**.

forested mountain range, Bā Dá Lǐng offers superb views and, for those willing to travel beyond the restored sections, worthwhile hiking.

ESSENTIALS

VISITOR INFORMATION   The ticket office at Bā Dá Lǐng is open from 6:30am to 7pm. Admission is ¥45 ($6) in summer, ¥40 ($5) in winter. A round-trip ride on the cable car costs ¥50 ($6) per person.

GETTING THERE   The cheapest way to get to Bā Dá Lǐng is on the red-and-yellow striped (air-conditioned) **bus no. 919** (daily 6am–6pm, about every 30 min.; 1-hr. trip; ¥10/$1), which leaves from the east side of Déshèng Mén. A comfortable option is to take one of the air-conditioned city-sponsored **tourist (*yóu*) buses** (© **010/6779-7546**): *Yóu* no. 1 leaves from the northeast side of Qián Mén (daily 6am–noon, every 20 min.; ¥50/$6), and *yóu* no. 2 leaves from Dōng Zhí Mén and the Běijīng Railway Station (daily 6:30–10am, every 30 min.; ¥50/$6); the price includes Jūyōng Guān (below) and one of the Míng Tombs (usually Dìng Líng, p. 200). A round-trip **taxi** should cost less than ¥300 ($38). **Group tours** are typically combined with a trip to the Míng Tombs and cost around ¥400 ($50) per person.

THE GREAT WALL AT JŪYŌNG GUĀN

59km (37 miles) NW of Běijīng

The most conveniently accessed section of the Wall is also the most historically significant. Guarding one of the two crucial passes to Běijīng (the other is to the northeast, at Gǔ Běi Kǒu) and the vast North China Plain, **Jūyōng Guān (Dwelling in Harmony Pass)** was the site of pitched battles, involving Jurchen, Mongol, and, more recently, Japanese invaders. There may have been fortifications here as early as the 6th century, before Běijīng existed. Climbing the steep section to the left offers marvelous views of Bā Dá Lǐng, snaking up the mountains to the north, and south toward Běijīng (in the event of a clear day). Restorations from 1993 to 1997 created over 4km (2½ miles) of wall, but railings mar the effect; there's little feeling of antiquity. All the construction must have eaten into the advertising budget, as crowds are thinner here than at Bā Dá Lǐng.

It's worth stopping at Jūyōng Guān to view the ancient and remarkable **Yún Tái (Cloud Platform)** ✸✸✸, which once stood astride the old road running northwest into Mongol territories. Dating from 1342, it was the base for three Tibetan-style stupas, which were toppled by an earthquake and replaced during the Míng dynasty by a Chinese-style Buddhist temple, also destroyed (by fire) during the early Qīng. The central tunnel is carved with elephants, Buddha figures demonstrating different *mudra* (hand positions), the four heavenly kings, and six different scripts. Facing north, the languages on the right-hand wall are Chinese, Xī Xià (the script of a vanished Tibetan race, decimated by Genghis Khan's armies during the 14th century), Uighur, and Mongolian. The top script is Sanskrit, with Tibetan below.

ESSENTIALS
VISITOR INFORMATION   The ticket office at Jūyōng Guān (✆ **010/6977-0394**) is open daily from 8am to 4pm. Admission is ¥40 ($5) in summer, ¥35 ($4.40) in winter.

GETTING THERE   For public transport information, see "Getting There" for Bā Dá Lǐng, above. A round-trip **taxi** should cost less than ¥200 ($25).

THE GREAT WALL AT MÙTIÁNYÙ ✸
90km (56 miles) NE of Běijīng

The Great Wall at Bā Dá Lǐng proved so popular that authorities restored a second section of the Wall to the east in 1986. **Mùtiányù** is slightly less crowded than Bā Dá Lǐng, but it does have its own traffic jams in summer. Located in a heavily forested area, it's especially photogenic in rainy, misty weather. You can hop over a fence to see more tempting, unrestored sections, but those planning to survey the entire length of restored wall will find themselves with little energy remaining. As at Bā Dá Lǐng, there is a cable car to help those who need it.

ESSENTIALS
VISITOR INFORMATION   The ticket office (✆ **010/6162-6873**) is open 24 hours. Admission is ¥35 ($4); the cable car costs ¥50 ($6) round-trip.

GETTING THERE   Mùtiányù is not as easy to reach as Bā Dá Lǐng. Most hotels can arrange **guided group tours** for around ¥250 ($31). The *yóu* **no. 6** combines a trip to Mùtiányù with visits to a temple and a lake; it leaves from the northeast side of the Xuānwǔ Mén (206) metro stop (Sat–Sun 6:30–8am, every 30 min.; ¥50/$6). The bus stops at Mùtiányù for about 3 hours. A **taxi** will cost between ¥200 and ¥400 ($25–$50).

WHERE TO STAY   Běijīng's most appealing Great Wall resort lies in a quiet river valley close to Mùtiányù at the **Red Capital Ranch** ✸✸ (✆ **010/8401-8886**; $190 including breakfast, plus 15% service charge; Apr–Nov). Similar to the Red Capital Residence (p. 68), all 10 rooms are thoughtfully decorated with antique furnishings. The oddly shaped Yán'ān room has considerable charm and a *very* firm bed. Fishing, bike riding, hiking on the Wall, and even a Tibetan essential oil massage are offered. A twice-daily shuttle bus connects with the Red Capital Residence.

THE GREAT WALL AT JĪN SHĀN LĬNG
130km (81 miles) NE of Běijīng, 90km (56 miles) SW of Chéngdé

Located in Héběi Province, this is the least visited and least spoiled of the Wall sections listed in this chapter. **Jīn Shān Lǐng** is 10km (6¼ miles) east of Gǔ Běi Kǒu (Old Northern Pass), through which Qīng royalty passed on the way to their summer retreat at Chéngdé (Jehol). The Wall here is in good condition, as it was a recent (after 1570) rebuild of an existing Míng wall, and construction was overseen by the outstanding general, Qī Jìguāng. The defensible pass, whose heart lies to the west at Gǔ Běi Kǒu, was 27km (17 miles), stretching all the way to Sīmǎtái in the east. Bricks are smaller, reflecting advances in wall-building technique. The Wall features unusual circular towers and elaborate defensive walls leading up to towers. Management dreams of tourist hordes—a cable car has been built, along with gradually rusting amusements—but the remoteness of the site makes large-scale tourism unlikely. The walk to **Sīmǎtái** (see below) is reason enough to visit.

ESSENTIALS
VISITOR INFORMATION   The ticket office (© **0314/883-8378**) is open 24 hours. Admission is ¥30 ($3.70).

GETTING THERE   Appealingly, Jīn Shān Lǐng can be reached by **train** from the Běijīng Běi Zhàn (North Railway Station), just north of the Xī Zhí Mén metro stop (201, exit A). A special tourist train for Gǔ Běi Kǒu, the L671 departs daily from mid-April to October at 7:25am (2½-hr. trip; ¥20/$2.50). The rest of the year, the slower L815, departing at 8am, will take you there (4-hr. trip; ¥10/$1.25). Returning trains depart at 3:05pm and 4:15pm, respectively. Walking down from the station, you can either find lodgings in the village of Gǔ Běi Kǒu Héxī Cūn, or take a minivan directly to the Wall (25-min. trip, ¥20/$2.50). From Xī Zhí Mén bus station, some **buses** to Chéngdé (daily 6am–5:30pm, about every 20 min.; 2½-hr. trip; ¥46/$5.75 for an Iveco or similar) also pass the turnoff, where you face either a 6km (4-mile) hike or haggling for a minivan (¥10/$1.25).

WHERE TO STAY   Standard rooms start at ¥140 ($17) in the dull but clean **Jīn Shān Lǐng Bīnguǎn**, to the right just inside the entrance of the wall. Staying at one of the simple courtyard houses in **Gǔ Běi Kǒu Héxī Cūn**, just below the railway station, is a cheaper and more appealing option; accommodations are usually ¥10 ($1.25) per person, and home-cooked meals are similarly priced.

THE GREAT WALL AT SĪMǍTÁI 𝄐𝄐
124km (77 miles) NE of Běijīng

Somewhat tamed after a series of deaths led to the closing of its most dangerous stretch, Sīmǎtái nevertheless remains one of the best options for those who want more of a challenge from the Great Wall. The most harrowing portion, steep and unrestored, is on the east (right) side of the Mìyún Reservoir. Several gravel-strewn spots require all four limbs to navigate. The endpoint is the **Wàngjīng Tǎ**, the 12th watchtower. Beyond this is the appropriately named **Tiān Qiáo (Heavenly Bridge),** a thin, tilted ridge where the Wall narrows to only a few feet—the section that is now off-limits. Despite the danger, Sīmǎtái can get rather crowded on weekends, especially since a cable car was installed, and souvenir vendors can be a nuisance. Those who speak Chinese would do well to pretend otherwise, or risk listening to hard-luck stories ("I've walked all the way from Mongolia."). The round-trip hike to Tiān Qiáo takes 3 hours at a moderate pace. The section of Sīmǎtái west of the reservoir is initially better restored and connects to another section of the Great Wall, Jīn Shān Lǐng, in Héběi Province (see the box "Jīn Shān Lǐng to Sīmǎtái" below).

ESSENTIALS

VISITOR INFORMATION The ticket office (© 010/6903-1051), a 10-minute walk away in a village south of the reservoir, is open 8am to 10pm in summer and 8am to 6pm in winter. Admission is ¥30 ($4). The cable car runs from April to November; a round-trip ride to the no. 8 Tower costs ¥50 ($6), or ¥30 ($3.60) one-way. Those walking west to Jīn Shān Lǐng will be charged ¥5 (60¢) to cross a bridge.

GETTING THERE The best no-hassle option is to visit with one of the **Youth Hostelling International tours** (© 010/8188-9323); these leave the YHAs daily between 7 and 8am and cost ¥90 ($11) for simple transportation. The *yóu* no. 12 travels to Sīmǎtái from northeast of the Xuānwǔ Mén (206) metro stop (Apr to mid-Oct Sat–Sun 6:30–8:30am, every 30 min; ¥70/$9); you get about 3 hours at the site. A round-trip **taxi** ride should cost less than ¥400 ($50).

WHERE TO STAY Responding to the popularity of the Jīn Shān Lǐng to Sīmǎtái hike (see below), Sīmǎtái YHA (© 010/8188-9323; standard room ¥260/$33) opened in 2004. Courtyard-style rooms are basic, but the coffee is world-class, and the view of the Wall from the patio is wonderful.

2 Míng Tombs (Shísān Líng)

48km (31 miles) NW of Běijīng

Of the 16 emperors who ruled China during the Míng dynasty (1368–1644), 13 are buried in a box canyon at the southern foot of Tiānshòu Shān (hence the Chinese name Shísān Líng, the 13 Tombs). The first emperor of the Míng, Hóngwǔ, is entombed in Xiào Líng, near Nánjīng. The location of the second emperor's tomb is uncertain, while the unfilial seventh emperor, who usurped the throne after his brother was taken by the Mongols, was buried near the Summer Palace among the graves of concubines. Despite these omissions, this is the most extensive burial complex of any Chinese dynasty. A red gate sealed off the valley, guards were posted, and no one, not even the emperor, could ride a horse on these grounds. The site was chosen by the Yǒnglè emperor, who also oversaw the construction of the Forbidden City. Protected from the bitter northern winds by a mountain range, the tombs are constructed in conventional fashion, with memorial halls at the front and burial chambers to the rear.

The entrance to the **Míng Tombs,** a long and celebrated **shén dào (spirit way)** is lined with statues of guardian animals and officials. Only three of the Míng Tombs— **Dìng Líng, Cháng Líng,** and **Zhāo Líng**—have been restored, and only one (Dìng Líng) has been fully excavated. Many of the buildings mirror Míng palaces found in the city. Because of this, the sight can be boring to people who've had their fill of imperial architecture. The Míng Tombs are at their most charming along the **shén dào** and on the grounds of **unrestored tombs** (free admission). In contrast, the restored tombs are dank, overcrowded, and uninspiring. The Míng Tombs are so unpopular with foreign tourists that they are often excluded from tour-group itineraries.

ESSENTIALS

GETTING THERE   The valley is just off the freeway that goes to Bā Dá Lǐng. Many **Chinese bus tours** to Bā Dá Lǐng also come here, visiting the spirit way and one of the tombs at blinding speed, but if you want time to explore some unrestored tombs (highly recommended), you'll have to make a separate trip. The most comfortable means of public transport is air-conditioned **bus no. 845** from the Chēgōng Zhuāng (202) metro stop (a 5-min. walk north of exit B) to Zhèngfǎ Dàxué in Chāngpíng (daily, about every 15 min.; 1½-hr. trip; ¥9/$1), then cross the street and take **bus no. 314** to the Nán Xīn Cūn stop (daily, about every 20 min.; 15-min. trip; ¥1/15¢), which is adjacent to the entrance to the spirit way. From there, you can continue north to either Dìng Líng Dàokǒu to visit Dìng Líng, a further 2km (1¼-mile) walk to the west, or on to the terminus at Cháng Líng. It is also possible to take the green-and-white *zhí* (express) version of **bus no. 919** to Zhèngfǎ Dàxué from Déshèng Mén (daily, about every 30 min.; 1-hr. trip; ¥9/$1). A **taxi** hired in Běijīng should cost less than ¥400 ($50).

EXPLORING THE AREA

The **spirit way (shén dào)** ☞ (admission Apr–Nov ¥30/$3.70, Dec–Mar ¥20/$2.50; daily 8am till dusk) is not to be missed. The main entrance to the valley is the **Dà Hóng Mén (Great Red Gate),** beyond which is a pavilion housing China's largest memorial stele, and beyond that the spirit way. The path, slightly curved to fool malevolent spirits, is lined on either side with willows and remarkable **carved stone animals** and human figures, considered among the best in China. The statuary includes pairs of camels, lions, elephants, and mythical beasts, such as the *qílín,* a creature of immense virtue referred to as the "Chinese unicorn" even though it has two horns.

The largest and best preserved of the 13 tombs is 4km (2½ miles) ahead: **Cháng Líng** (admission ¥45/$5.60 summer, ¥30/$3.70 winter; daily 7am–4:30pm), the tomb of the Yǒnglè emperor (reign 1403–1424). The layout is identical to the tomb of the first Míng emperor in Nánjīng. It feels like the Forbidden City in miniature, and is perhaps disappointing if you've seen the palace already. Most striking is **Líng'ēn Diàn** ☞, an immense hall in which the interior columns and brackets have been left unpainted, creating an eye-catching contrast with the green ceiling panels. Slightly wider than the Hall of Supreme Harmony, Líng'ēn Diàn contains a three-tiered platform and building materials that are superior to those of the Forbidden City.

The 4,000-sq.-m (13,000-sq.-ft.) **Underground Palace** at **Dìng Líng** (admission ¥60/$7.50 summer, ¥40/$5 winter; 8:30am–5pm), rediscovered in 1956, was the burial place of the Wànlì emperor (reign 1572–1620), his wife, and his favorite concubine. Construction of the burial chamber commenced before the emperor was 20 years old, making him "the living ancestor" in the words of Ray Huang, author of *1587, A Year of No Significance.* The "palace" is a vast marble vault, buried 27m (88 ft.) underground and divided into five large chambers. It's all a bit disappointing. The corpses have been removed, their red coffins replaced with cheap replicas, and burial objects moved to aboveground display rooms. The original marble thrones are still there, now covered in a small fortune of *rénmínbì* notes tossed by Chinese visitors hoping to bribe the emperor's ghost. Outside, behind the ticket office, is the respectable **Shísān Líng Bówùguǎn (Míng Tombs Museum),** with short biographies of all the entombed emperors; several reproduced artifacts; a detailed, wood reproduction of the Líng'ēn Diàn; and a 1954 photo of Máo reclining and reading a newspaper on a half-buried marble incense burner at Cháng Líng.

3 Eastern Qīng Tombs (Qīng Dōng Líng) ⟨★⟨★

125km (78 miles) E of Běijīng

The **Qīng Dōng Líng** have been open for more than 20 years but are still little visited despite offering considerably more to visitors than tombs of the Míng. Altogether 5 emperors, 15 empresses, 136 concubines, 3 princes, and 2 princesses are buried in 15 tombs here. The first to be buried was Shùnzhì—the first Qīng emperor to reign from Běijīng—in 1663, and the last was an imperial concubine in 1935. The tomb chambers of four imperial tombs, the **Xiào Líng** (the Shùnzhì emperor), **Jǐng Líng** (Kāngxī), **Yù Líng** (Qiánlóng), and **Dìng Líng** (Xiánfēng), are open as well as the twin **Dìng Dōng Líng** tombs (Dowager Empress Cíxǐ and Empress Cí'ān). Others of interest include a group site for the Qiánlóng emperor's concubines.

ESSENTIALS

VISITOR INFORMATION   The tombs are in Zūnhuà County, Héběi Province (daily 8am–5:30pm summer, 9am–4:30pm winter). The *tōng piào,* which offers access to all the tombs, costs ¥90 ($11).

GETTING THERE   A special Qīng Dōng Líng *yóu* bus departs from northeast of the Xuānwǔ Mén (206) metro stop (summer only, daily 7:30am; 3-hr. trip; ¥80/$10); this gives you about 3 hours at the site. If you want to explore at your own pace, you'll have to hire a cab or take a rickety local bus (daily 6:30am–4:30pm; 3½-hr. trip; ¥24/$3) to Zūnhuà from just east of the Dàwàng Lù metro stop (123, exit C). Alight just before Zūnhuà at Shí Mén Zhèn then hire a *miàndī* (minivan) to take you the rest of the way (about ¥20/$3). An assortment of three-wheelers will offer to take you around the site with a first asking price of ¥10 ($1.25).

WHERE TO STAY AND DINE   The **Yùyuàn Shānzhuāng** (Imperial Gardens Mountain Villa; ℂ 0315/694-5348) is a battered three-star set to the east of the tombs where the asking price for a twin room is ¥288 ($36), about twice what it's worth. Its best feature is the attached Manchurian restaurant, **Qīng Yàn Lóu** (daily 11am–noon and 5–9pm), which offers inexpensive game meats, and delicious green bean flour noodles, *cùliū làozhá.*

EXPLORING THE AREA

Although few others are as elaborate, the **Xiào Líng** was the first tomb on the site, and a model for others both here and at the Western Qīng Tombs. As here, usually an approach road or **spirit way** may have guardian figures, and the entrance to the tomb itself is usually preceded by a large stele pavilion and marble bridges over a stream. To the right, the buildings used for preparation of sacrifices are now usually the residences of the staff, and hung with washing. Inside the gate, halls to the left and right were for enrobing and other preparations, and now house exhibitions, as usually does each **Hall of Eminent Favor,** at the rear, where ceremonies in honor of the deceased took place. Behind, if open, a doorway allows access past a stone altar to a steep ramp leading to the base of the **Soul Tower.** Through a passageway beneath, stairs to either side lead to a walkway encircling the mound, giving views across the countryside. If the tomb chamber is open, a ramp from beneath the Soul Tower leads down to a series of chambers.

The twin **Dìng Dōng Líng** ⟨★⟨★ tombs have nearly identical exteriors, but Cíxǐ had hers rebuilt in 1895, 14 years after Cí'ān's death (in which she is suspected of having had a hand), using far more expensive materials. The main hall contains reproductions of pictures produced in 1903 by Cíxǐ's photo studio within the Summer Palace. Everywhere there are reminders of the Forbidden City, such as the terrace-corner spouts carved as water-loving dragons (chē). The interior has motifs strikingly painted in gold on dark wood, recalling the buildings where she spent her last years. There are walls of carved and gilded brick, and superbly fearsome wooden dragons writhe down the columns. After this, the other tombs seem gaudy.

The enclosure of the **Yù Fēi Yuán Qǐn (Garden of Rest)** contains moss-covered tumuli for 35 of the Qiánlóng emperor's concubines. Another is buried in a proper tomb chamber, along with an empress whom Qiánlóng had grown to dislike.

The **Jǐng Líng** is the tomb of Qiánlóng's grandfather, the Kāngxī emperor, and is surprisingly modest given that he was possibly the greatest emperor the Chinese ever had, but that's in keeping with what is known of his character. The spirit way leading to the tomb has an elegant five-arch bridge; the guardian figures are placed on an unusual curve quite close to the tomb itself, and are more decorated than those at earlier tombs. The **Yù Líng** ✦✦✦ has the finest tomb chamber, a series of rooms separated by solid marble doors, with its walls and arched ceilings engraved with Buddha figures and more than 30,000 words of Tibetan scripture. The 3-ton doors themselves have reliefs of bodhisattvas (beings on the road to enlightenment) and the four protective kings usually found at temple entrances. This tomb is worth the trip in its own right.

4 Western Qīng Tombs (Qīng Xī Líng) ✦
140km (87 miles) SW of Běijīng

The Yōngzhèng emperor broke with tradition and ordered his tomb to be constructed here, away from his father (the Kāngxī emperor). His son, the Qiánlóng emperor, decided to be buried near his grandfather and that thereafter burials should alternate between the eastern (see above) and western sites, although this was not followed consistently. The first tomb, the **Tài Líng,** was completed in 1737, 2 years after the Yōngzhèng reign. The last imperial interment was in 1998, when the ashes of Aisin Gioro Henry Pǔyí, the last emperor, were moved to a commercial cemetery here. He and 2 consorts were added to 4 emperors, 4 empresses, 4 princes, 2 princesses, and 57 concubines. The site is rural, more densely forested than the Qīng Dōng Líng, overlapped by orchards and agriculture, and with chickens, goats, and the odd rabbit to be encountered.

The **Cháng Líng** (tomb of the Jiāqìng emperor) and **Chóng Líng** (tomb of the Guāngxù emperor) are also open, as well as the **Cháng Xī Líng** with the extraordinary sonic effects of its **Huíyīn Bì**—an echo wall where, as the only visitor, you can try out the special effects available only in theory at the Temple of Heaven (p. 125).

ESSENTIALS
VISITOR INFORMATION   The ticket office is open from 8am to 5pm; a *tōng piào* (for access to all the tombs) costs ¥90 ($10) and is good for 2 days. There's no access by tourist bus—part of the appeal for most visitors.

GETTING THERE   Take a **bus** to Yìxiàn from the Lízé Qiáo long-distance bus station (daily 6:50am–5pm, every 15 min.; 3-hr. trip; ¥20/$2.50; last bus returns at 4pm), then switch to a minivan *(miàndī)* for the 15km (9¼-mile) ride to the tombs (around ¥20/$3; ¥100/$12 to visit all the tombs), or turn right as you exit the bus station to find bus no. 9 waiting on the first corner (every hour; ¥3/60¢). By **taxi** it's a reasonable day-trip down the Jīngshí Freeway from the Southwest Third Ring Road to the turnoff for Gāo Bēi Diàn to the west, and beyond to Yì Xiàn. It's possible to visit **Marco Polo Bridge (Lú Gōu Qiáo)** on the way.

WHERE TO STAY The modest, Manchu-themed **Bā Jiǎo Lóu Mǎnzú Zhuāngyuán,** just east of Tài Líng (*(C)* **0312/826-0828;** ¥100/$12 standard room). **Xíng Gōng Bīnguǎn,** near Yǒngfú Sì on the eastern side of the tomb complex (*(C)* **0312/471-0038;** standard room ¥150/$19 after discount), was where Manchu rulers stayed when they came to pay their respects, and the room constructed in 1748 to house the Qiánlóng emperor is now rented out as two suites (¥660/$82 after discount), although the 1980s decor is criminal.

EXPLORING THE AREA

The **Dà Bēi Lóu,** a pavilion containing two vast stelae, is on the curved route to the **Tài Líng.** The general plan of the major tombs follows that of the eastern tombs and, in fact, the **Chāng Líng,** slightly to the west, is almost identical, brick for brick, to the Tài Líng, with the addition of a purple-tinged marble floor. The Jiāqìng empress is buried just to the west on a far smaller scale in the **Chāng Xī Líng,** the tomb mound a brick drum. But the perfectly semicircular rear wall offers the whispering gallery effects found at some domed European cathedrals, and clapping while standing on various marked stones in the center of the site produces a variety of multiple echoes, while speech is amazingly amplified. The empress can't get much peace.

Jiāqìng's son, the Dàoguāng emperor, was meant to be buried at Qīng Dōng Líng, but his tomb there was flooded. The relocated **Mù Líng** appears much more modest than those of his predecessors. No stele pavilion or spirit way, largely unpainted, and the tomb mound is a modest brick-wall drum, but this is the most expensive tomb: Wood used to construct the exquisite main hall is fragrant *nanmu,* sourced from as far away as Myanmar. The Guǎngxù emperor was the last to complete his reign (although Cíxǐ, who died the next day, is again suspected of shortening it), and his **Chóng Líng,** which has the only tomb chamber that is open, uses more modern materials than other tombs. It wasn't completed until 1915, well after the last emperor's abdication.

Several other rather battered tombs are open, and more are being opened, including the **Tài Líng Fēi Yuán Qǐn,** a group of concubine tumuli, individually labeled with the years in which the concubines entered the Yōngzhèng emperor's service and their grades in the complex harem hierarchy.

The ashes of **Pǔyí** (properly known as the Xuāntǒng emperor) lie buried on the eastern end of the site, up a slope behind a brand-new Qīng-style memorial arch *(páilou),* and behind a shoddy, modern carved balustrade. Neighboring plots are available for the right price.

5 Tánzhè Sì & Jiètái Sì ⭑

Tánzhè Sì 48km (30 miles) W of Běijīng; Jiètái Sì 35km (22 miles) W of Běijīng

Buried in the hills west of Běijīng, **Tánzhè Sì (Temple of the Pool and Wild Mulberry)** and **Jiètái Sì (Temple of the Ordination Platform)** are the tranquil kinds of Chinese temples visitors imagine before they actually come to China. These temples were unusual because they received imperial support (Qīng rulers preferred Tibetan Buddhism), and both have long been popular with local pilgrims. They were also loved by early Western residents, who rented out halls inside the temples.

ESSENTIALS

VISITOR INFORMATION   Admission to Tánzhè Sì (© **010/6086-2505**) is ¥35 ($4), and the ticket office is open from 8am to 5:30pm in summer (8:30am–4:30pm in winter). Admission to Jiètái Sì (© **010/6980-6611**) is ¥35 ($4), and the ticket office is open from 8am to 6pm.

GETTING THERE   Both temples are easily accessible by taking **bus no. 931** from the Píngguǒ Yuán (103) metro stop to **Tánzhè Sì** (daily 7am–5:30pm, about every 30min.; 1-hr. trip; ¥2.50/40¢). At the far western end of Line 1 at the Píngguǒ Yuán metro stop (exit D), take a right and continue straight a few minutes to the bus station (be sure to take the plain red-and-beige, rather than the red-and-yellow *zhī* version of the bus). At Tánzhè Sì, the last stop on this line, hike up the stone path at the end of the parking lot. From there, take **bus no. 931** east 13km (8 miles) to **Jiètái Sì,** where you reach the site by walking uphill from the bus stop. On weekends, the *yóu* **no. 7** tourist bus runs from the northeast corner of Qián Mén (Sat–Sun 7–8:30am, every 30 min.; ¥60/$7.50), but it regrettably includes a stop at the garish Shíhuā Caves. Round-trip by **taxi** costs less than ¥300 ($37).

WHERE TO STAY   At both temples, basic but acceptable accommodations are available for those who want (or need) to spend more time in quietude.

EXPLORING THE AREA

Tánzhè Sì ✿✿, set in peaceful forested grounds, dates back to the Western Jìn dynasty (265–316), well before Běijīng was founded. In the main courtyard on the central axis is a pair of 30m (100-ft.) ginkgo trees, supposedly planted in the Táng dynasty (618–907), as well as several apricot trees, cypresses, peonies, and purple jade orchids. The complex is extensive, and is said to have provided a model for the layout of the Forbidden City. Above and to the right of the main courtyard lies a rare **stupa yard** *(tǎ yuán),* stone monuments built in different styles over a period of several centuries and housing the remains of eminent monks. The **Guānyīn Diàn,** at the top of the western axis, was favored by Princess Miào Yán, a daughter of Kublai Khan; she is said to have prayed so fervently here that she left footprints in one of the floor stones (now stored in a box to the left). The main object of interest to local visitors is the **stone fish** *(shí yú)* to the left and behind this hall. Rubbing the relevant part of the fish is said to cure the corresponding malady. Everyone seems to rub its stomach.

The **ordination platform** *(jiètái)* at **Jiètái Sì** ✿, China's largest, is a three-tiered structure with 113 statues of the God of Ordination placed in niches around the base; it's located in the **Jiè Tán Diàn (Hall of the Altar of Ordination)** in the far right (northwest) corner of the temple. It looks, as novelist Ann Bridge put it, "like a very high four-poster bed." Ceremonies conducted on this platform to commemorate the ascension of a devotee to full monkhood required permission from the emperor. Often referred to as the "Běidà [Peking University, nominally the best university in China] of Buddhism" for its ability to attract the most promising monastic scholars, along with temples in Quánzhōu and Hángzhōu, it has been the most significant site for the ordination of Buddhist monks for 900 years. Surrounding courtyards have ancient, twisted pines (as venerable as the temple itself) and fragrant peony gardens.

6 Chuān Dǐ Xià

100km (62 miles) W of Běijīng

Originally called **Cuàn Dǐ Xià (Under the Stove)**, this tiny village of around a hundred souls is an ideal 2-day trip for those with a passion for Chinese vernacular architecture or those keen for a glimpse of life in rural China. Set in a narrow valley off the old trade route to Shānxī, Chuān Dǐ Xià boasts the best-preserved *sìhéyuàn* (courtyard houses) in the Běijīng region. Opened to tourism in 1997, more than 70 dwellings are said to be here.

The impressive dwellings were designed by scholar-officials from the Míng who fled to this remote village toward the end of the dynasty. There they lived out one of the most pervasive legends in Chinese literature, that of the Peach Sanctuary (Táohuā Yuán), where inhabitants live peacefully in a hidden rural Arcadia, preserving the superior traditions of an earlier era. Corn dangles from the eaves of the ancient dwellings, donkeys plow the fields, and the hills are alive with wildflowers. The village faces south, nestled on the north side of the valley.

ESSENTIALS

VISITOR INFORMATION The ticket office (© **010/6981-9090**) is open from 9am to 4:30pm. Admission to the village costs ¥20 ($2.50).

GETTING THERE From the Píngguǒ Yuán (103) metro stop, turn right out of the southeast (D) exit and continue for a few minutes to the **bus no. 929 zhīxiàn stop** (the last sign) for the bus to Zhāitáng (daily 7am–5pm, every hour; 2½-hr. trip; ¥6/75¢). While traveling from the city, you'll leave behind the smokestacks of Shǒu Gāng (Capital Iron and Steel Works, Běijīng's number-one polluter). From Zhāitáng, **minivans** *(miàndī)* (¥10/$1.25) travel to Chuān Dǐ Xià. The last bus returns from Zhāitáng at 4:10pm. A *miàndī* from Píngguǒ Yuán costs ¥130 ($16) one-way. A **taxi** from Běijīng costs ¥400 ($50) round-trip.

WHERE TO STAY For those staying overnight, most lodgings offer basic accommodations (no shower) for ¥15 ($1.80). The friendly and freshly renovated **Lǎo Mèng Kèzhàn,** no. 23 in the lower part of the village (© **010/6981-9788**), is recommended. Their restaurant, which adjoins the rather quiet main road, is an agreeable spot for alfresco dining.

EXPLORING THE AREA

The area is a magnet for artists, poets, and period-drama camera crews; many local tourists are mystified by the lack of karaoke bars, duck boats, and "hairdressers" that any self-respecting resort should boast. One Beijinger asked in frustration, "Is there anything at all to do here?" A local, not much caring for his tone, deadpanned, "Absolutely nothing. You'd better go home." Wander through the narrow lanes, their walls still showing faded slogans from the 1966–76 Cultural Revolution, including LONG LIVE CHAIRMAN MÁO, WORKERS OF THE WORLD UNITE, and USE MÁO ZÉDŌNG THOUGHT TO ARM YOUR MINDS.

Beyond the village, the path continues to rise, passing an intriguing open-air grain mill before entering groves of peach trees. The next village, **Bǎiyù Cūn,** is around 6km (3¾ miles) to the northwest. The dwellings of this larger settlement are arranged in the more plebeian *píngfáng* (bungalow) style.

Appendix A:
Běijīng in Depth

1 Běijīng Today

As the English literary eccentric Osbert Sitwell remarked during a visit to Běijīng in the 1930s, "Restoration is often the favourite weapon of Siva the Destroyer, and can achieve more in a few weeks than can whole centuries of decay."

Some vengeful deity certainly seems to walk the streets of China's capital today, and he carries a brush with which he daubs on doors and walls the character *chāi*—"demolish." Within weeks, entire city blocks of historic housing vanish as the result of his attentions, their occupants driven away with compensation inadequate to replace their lost homes. Gossip among foreign journalists has it that by the time of the Běijīng Olympics in 2008, only 20 or so of the ancient *hútòng* (alleyways) will be left, and these will have been carefully refashioned in a dismaying Disneyfication to make them more appealing to visitors.

Once the ancient buildings come down to be replaced by shiny shops, the *chāi* character seems to reappear. But one little brush stroke is missing from the new version in shop windows—a *diǎn,* the smallest of all strokes, and little more than a dot. This tiny difference is enough to change the character's sound to *zhé,* and its meaning to something more constructive. Preceded by a number, *zhé* represents the number of tenths of its original price for which merchandise is now on sale. *Qī zhé,* seven-tenths, would appear in Western shop windows as *30% off.*

You may be impressed at first by all the shiny new buildings—but look closely and you'll spot incomplete projects and shuttered stores. And despite the supposedly explosive expansion of the Chinese economy, reported in unverifiable figures even the government doesn't believe, shops are *always* advertising sales.

Lazy Western journalism produces excitable reports of Cartier showrooms and shops with imported Italian designer baby clothes, and uncritically repeats impressive but unverifiable claims about growth. But the vast majority of the young and trendy are out in the suburbs buying fake versions or discovering real goods that somehow got separated from the rest of their consignment, going for a tenth of the price or less. In the temples to consumerism on the showcase shopping streets, you'll see that window-shoppers vastly outnumber those making purchases. In supermarkets, older people can be found puzzling over imported items whose prices they can't afford anyway. The reality is that however many glitzy new shopping malls open, the disposable income to support them is not there.

Western journalists aren't the only ones falling for the spin. A recent survey by the Chinese Academy of Social Sciences found that nearly half of the Chinese population believed they were middle class, even though less than 3% earned enough to qualify. A cup of Starbucks coffee is still a luxury, and those seen sipping a latte are in no way typical of Běijīng.

THE POLITICAL LIFE OF BĚIJĪNG Sitting at the heart of power,

Beijingers are supposedly the nation's most sensitive to subtle changes in the political winds, but these days there is ever-decreasing interest. Officials are almost universally deemed corrupt, and the leadership's gyrations in trying to demonstrate that the capitalism red in tooth and claw to which it now subjects its citizens is actually socialism "with Chinese characteristics" make the supposedly heroic leaders increasingly ridiculous. This is a pensionless "socialism," with no job security, no free medicine or free schooling, massive and growing unemployment (at least double the official figures), and bribes necessary at every turn to get things done. To most young people who missed the vast political movements of the second half of the 20th century, the Communist Party is an irrelevance—something that merely gets in the way on the road to a better life.

You'll find no free discussion of such issues in the government-controlled press, of which it is sometimes joked that the only true piece of information is the date. Constant announcements that production is up, that the minorities are happy, and that standards of one kind or another have been improved are usually fair indications that the opposite is true.

Television and print media, largely under government control, are stuck in a time warp. Instructions to study the latest political "theory," such as ex-president Jiāng Zémín's "Three Represents," an attempt to pass off the Party's U-turn to capitalism as a development of Marxism, is headline news. It's hardly surprising that the best-selling publication in China is a magazine dealing with soccer.

Even five-star-hotel access to the BBC or other foreign news channels (forbidden to ordinary domestic viewers) may suddenly "break down" around important political anniversaries, June 4 in particular. Once the anniversary is safely past, access is mysteriously restored. No view other than that sanctioned by the Party may be broadcast.

Not all foreign visitors to Běijīng are unhappy about this. International Olympic Committee Vice President Kevan Gosper, in a chilling interview on China Central Sports, told his shocked interviewer that the Australian press would just "make up stories." China, by contrast, was praised for its skill in "the management of information."

The loudest political voices are those of Běijīng's taxi drivers, at least within the confines of their vehicles. Theirs are the easiest opinions to canvass, and they are quoted with embarrassing frequency in Western newspaper articles as spokesmen for the ordinary Beijinger. In 2002 the government issued specific instructions forbidding the taxi drivers to talk about politics to foreigners, but because they are never named in articles, this injunction has been ignored, and they continue in their Western-appointed role of Everyman.

In the months leading up to the Olympic committee's decision in 2002, every foreign passenger who could understand enough Mandarin had to listen to bitter complaints that in support of Běijīng's bid the drivers were being forced to learn 100 simple English sentences. Examinations were pending. But as soon as Běijīng had won, the books and tapes they'd been forced to buy all quietly disappeared. Questions were greeted with laughter. "They've won the Games now. They're not bothered."

A CONSUMER SOCIETY   Until the 1980s it seemed that everyone was in uniform. The very rare young man wearing a pair of jeans might as well have been carrying a big banner saying "counterrevolutionary." Blue or green "Máo" suits *(Zhōngshān fú)* or uniforms provided by work units (employers) were the norm for both sexes.

But as soon as she was permitted to do so, Miss Běijīng gradually removed her peaked cap, shook down her tresses, and went wild. From the sighting of the first pair of high heels and the return of the skirt, hemlines crept up from calf to nearly waist level and stayed there. Colors went from khaki to clashing neons, simply because they could. Bus conductresses, now able to own more than just their uniforms, could be found selling tickets in spangled Lycra more suitable for the primitive discos that were sprouting up.

Things have now settled down, but anything goes, including dresses diaphanous enough to reveal more than a glimpse of stocking. The male, on the other hand, has remained dowdy, and seems to have swapped one uniform for another. Typically jacketless, Mr. Běijīng wears a short-sleeve shirt with a collar but no tie, and gray slacks. He parades his status through his shoes, watch, and belt, with the buckle, mobile phone, and of course, his manbag.

The genie of consumerism is permanently out of the bottle, and to stay in power by any means but brute force, the Party must feed an insatiable desire not just for the bare necessities of life, but for disposable goods with designer logos. Fakes will do, of course, and fakes are what most buy in back-street markets, but that tiny portion of the population who can buy a Mercedes will certainly do so, and will thank the Party for the opportunity rather than complain that it has held them back for so many decades. As late as the early 1990s foreign residents would coo with delight at the sight of milk and butter in the Friendship Stores, which only accepted hard-currency vouchers and which Chinese were not permitted to enter. Now most Western fashion labels have Běijīng outlets, as do supermarkets, fast-food chains, and luxury-car suppliers. Numerous foreign companies sucked in by the promise of fast growth are making a loss or a far from respectable return on their investment.

But they comfort each other in their farsightedness, and wait for the economic miracle repeatedly promised in the press.

EVERY MAN FOR HIMSELF   "What's the difference between your country and mine?" is a popular question from taxi drivers, and one that leaves the Mandarin-speaking foreign visitor floundering as to where to begin: An independent judiciary? Rule of law? Freedom to have as many children as you like? Freedom to live where you like? Freedom of the press? Fewer manbags?

Once, tired from a long flight, I was asked this question as we passed a crowd gathering around a bloody collision between a car and a cyclist, and I glumly answered, "When we see an accident, we run to help. When you see an accident, you run to look."

The driver nodded in agreement. "Yes," he said, "that's right. But there are *so many* of us." He drove on without stopping.

Beijingers expect to be cheated both by their rulers and by each other. They complain bitterly, but they have no hesitation in cheating others when they can wangle a university place for an academically unsuccessful child because of a favor owed, when they can get access to rail tickets at peak periods because an uncle works at the station, or when they barter their own access to some privilege for something else they want. When they need something, their first question is not "Where do I line up?" but "Who do I know?" The Chinese expression *xiān lái, xiān chī,* means "first to come, first to eat." This suggests not the idea of forming a fair lineup, but the necessity of barging to the front.

Complaints about government corruption and the privileges reserved for cadres are not usually based on a general moral principle, but on not getting a slice of the pie. Sympathy for others tends to extend no further than immediate family members, close friends, and those with whom the Chinese have *guānxi*—people who owe them or to whom they owe favors. Everyone else is just in the way and is often simply pushed out of it, as you will discover when you try to board a bus, line up to buy a ticket, or stand at any junction and observe the driving.

Běijīng may only represent Běijīng, but Beijingers, like everyone else in China, think themselves superior to Chinese from other regions. Finding themselves in difficulties away from home, they will appeal to other Beijingers for help. Faced with problems when overseas, they'll appeal for solidarity to anyone of Chinese descent—"We're Chinese: We should help each other." Back in Běijīng they'll use "peasant" as a term of abuse, and they are convinced that the several million migrant workers who now call the capital home are responsible for the rise in crime. But they'll complain loudly when street food stalls vanish, smaller restaurants close, and garbage services slow to a halt because those who do the menial labor they themselves despise have been temporarily driven out of town for some Party celebration or committee meeting.

Locals aren't unaware of these problems, and in recent years the neo-Confucian notion of *sùzhì* (roughly translated as "quality") has been popularized. Primary schools now teach *sùzhì* education, your taxi driver will tell you with a straight face, "my quality is very low," but the concept is mainly a handy way to gloss over the huge gap between rich and poor in this nominally socialist country. She earns $1 a day because her quality is low.

ROUND EYES & YELLOW HAIR

Foreigners are not relatives and do not understand *guānxi*. To some Beijingers they are figures of fun. To the few directly involved in commercial relationships with foreigners, they are strikingly naive and their extraordinarily deep pockets are to be dipped into as much as possible (the more apparently sweet-natured your tour guide, the more careful you should be).

Foreigners have an amazing tendency to smile and give away extra money even after being thoroughly fleeced. To stallholders, shopkeepers, and representatives of the tourism industry, they are therefore thoroughly welcome—in any society where most transactions involve bargaining, the ignorant outsider always will be. Shanghainese, Cantonese, and other outsiders will be taken for a ride whenever possible, but foreigners can be taken much more easily, and much further.

While central Běijīng is used to the sight of enormous people with big round eyes and yellow or red hair, many Chinese visitors to Běijīng are often catching their first sight of the rare and exotic foreign species. Most foreigners restrict themselves to the bigger attractions, the hotel complexes, the joint-venture office towers, and the bar areas, so a foreigner entering an ordinary department store elsewhere in the city can still have a traffic-stopping effect.

"*Lǎo wài,*" (Foreigner) the Chinese will observe without lowering their voices. They'll nudge each other and point you out, "Look! *Lǎo wài.*" And sometimes they'll shout at you, "*Lǎo wài!,*" with complete indifference to any offense taken.

The presence of everything foreign from McDonald's to Mercedes doesn't indicate the presence of a larger world picture, but rather an increasingly long checklist of which possessions indicate a degree of Westernization. Heaven, according to one recently popular Běijīng joke, is a German house, a Japanese wife, and an American salary. Heaven's only Chinese element is the cook. At the same time, it is taken as axiomatic that Chinese culture is superior.

The West is a place to live neither for democratic ideals nor to avoid the one-child policy (which anyone with cash or the right *guānxi* can get around), but largely for the chance to earn more money and gain a higher standard of living.

You'll likely pass through Běijīng completely unaware of all these undercurrents. Běijīng will open up just enough for you to pass through and close up again behind you, and you'll leave no more trace, in Pearl Buck's memorable phrase, "than a finger drawn through water."

2 Religion

Freedom to practice religion is enshrined in the Chinese constitution. In reality, of course, this right is subject to frequent and occasionally violent suspension—during times of political upheaval like the Cultural Revolution (1966–76) or, as in the case of Tibetan Buddhism and the banned spiritual movement Fǎlún Gōng, when specific groups are thought to pose a threat to Communist rule. Despite this, China has maintained what must rank among the world's most eclectic collection of religious traditions, encompassing not only native belief systems—Confucianism and Daoism—but Buddhism, Islam, and several strains of Christianity as well.

Those on tours of Chinese temples, churches, and mosques in the 1980s and early 1990s were wise to exercise a robust skepticism. The monks and nuns you encountered were invariably a specially selected bunch, likely to bombard foreigners with tales of how wonderfully supportive the government was. And the prettiest and best-restored temples were often barely more than showpieces, where it seemed incense was burned only to cover the sour smell of an Epcot-style cultural commodification.

But as faith in Communism wanes (to the point where some Chinese use the greeting *tóngzhì*, or comrade, with thinly veiled sarcasm), religious buildings are slowly recovering their vitality as places of genuine worship, sources of guidance in the moral vacuum of a new market-driven society.

Maps of pre-Communist Běijīng show an astoundingly large number of religious structures, from the grandest of glazed-tile complexes in the city's imperial quarter to hundreds of tiny shrines nestled in the maze of *hútòng*. Most were destroyed or converted to other uses immediately following the Communist victory in 1949 and during the Cultural Revolution. Several dozen more have been bulldozed as part of modern reconstruction efforts, and all but the most prestigious will probably disappear in the future.

China has always been a secular state, but as in European capitals prior to the 20th century, the line between religion and government in Míng- and Qīng-era Běijīng was usually blurred. The most

Dateline

- **930–1122** A provincial town roughly on the site of modern Běijīng becomes the southern capital of the Khitan Mongol Liáo dynasty, thousands of kilometers from the ancient centers of early Hàn Chinese empires.
- **1122–1215** The city is taken over by the Jurchen Tartar Jīn dynasty, first as Southern Capital, then Central Capital, as its empire expands.
- **1267–1367** The Mongol Yuán dynasty, having conquered most of Asia and eastern Europe, rebuilds the city on the modern site as the capital Khanbalik; Dà Dū (Great Capital) in Mandarin; Cambulac in Marco Polo's account of the city.
- **1273–1292** Marco Polo, his father, and his uncle are in China, much of the time in Khanbalik. Polo's ghostwritten account of the capital captures the imagination of European readers for several centuries afterward.
- **1368** The Míng dynasty, having driven out the Mongols, establishes its capital at Nánjīng. Dà Dū becomes Běipíng (The Pacified North).
- **1420** The Yǒnglè emperor, third of the Míng, returns

continues

direct example is the **Lama Temple (Yōnghé Gōng),** an immense imperial residence-turned-temple that houses a ritual urn used during the reign of the Qīng Qiánlóng emperor to determine reincarnations of the Dalai Lama, leader of the dominant Buddhist sect in distant Tibet.

The tradition continues today, with Communist leaders playing a controversial role in selecting the most recent Panchen Lama (second from the top in the Tibetan Buddhist hierarchy) and threatening to do the same after the death of the current Dalai Lama, the exiled Tenzin Gyatso.

CONFUCIANISM

The moral philosophy said to have originated with Kǒngzǐ—a 5th-century-B.C. figure also known as Kǒng Fūzǐ (Latinized to "Confucius" by Jesuit supporters enthusiastic about his "family values")—is not really a religion or even a well-defined thought system. Indeed, there is no word in Chinese for Confucianism but only *rú,* a rather vague term that connotes scholarship and refinement. The ideas about proper conduct and government as remembered by Kǒngzǐ's disciples in works like the *Lúnyǔ (Analects)* have nevertheless exerted more influence on China than either Buddhism or Daoism and have proven more resilient than anything written by Marx or Máo.

The *Analects* offer pithy observations on dozens of topics ("Those who make virtue their profession are the ruin of virtue," "The noble person is not a pot," and so on), but the three most important concepts are filial piety, proper execution of ritual, and humanity toward others. Confucius has little trust in Heaven or nature. The ultimate concern is with tangible human relationships: those of the son with the father, the subject with the emperor, and friends with each other. These relationships are rigidly defined, and acknowledgement of them is the highest virtue. Chinese rulers recognized early on that this philosophy was perfectly suited to governing their vast empire. Mastery of Confucian classics, proven through a series of increasingly difficult Imperial Examinations, was a prerequisite for all government officials up until the very end of the 19th century.

Confucian ideas were denounced as "feudal thought" after the Communists took over, but visitors to Běijīng need only go as far as a restaurant to realize how little this has meant. At any large table, diners will take seats according to their relationship with the host, toasts will be carried out with ritual precision, and forms of address will vary depending on who is speaking to whom. The Imperial Examinations, too, have been resurrected in the nationwide College Entrance Exam,

---

the city to capital status, the better to repel attacks by the Mongols from the north. He becomes the first Chinese emperor to reign from Běijīng, and the first to give it that name: "Northern Capital." Míng dynasty Běijīng is overlaid on the Yuán foundations, and the Forbidden City and Temple of Heaven are constructed.

- **1549** Mongol horsemen fire a message-bearing arrow into a Chinese general's camp saying that they will attack Běijīng the following year. Despite this advance announcement, they duly make their way up to the city walls as promised. So much for the Great Wall.

- **1550** In response to Mongol attacks, a lower southern extension to the city wall is begun, eventually enclosing the commercial district, the important ceremonial sites of the Temple (Altar) of Heaven and Altar of Agriculture, and a broad swath of countryside (which remains free of buildings well into the 20th century). The whole system of walls is clad in brick. Běijīng remains largely the same for the next 400 years, when casual and organized destruction begins with the Republic and is hastened under the People's Republic.

success in which is considered vital to any young person's future. Some students even study for the exam at **Guó Zǐ Jiàn** (the old Imperial College) in northeast Běijīng while their parents burn incense for them next door at the **Kǒng Miào**, the second largest Confucian temple after the one in Confucius's hometown of Qūfù in Shāndōng Province.

Although even the most modern Chinese display an attachment to family and ritual, cynical observers note that the emphasis on humanity seems to have disappeared. It is debatable, however, whether this was ever as forceful an idea in China as Confucius wanted it to be.

DAOISM

China's only native-born religion, Daoism (Taoism) began, like Confucianism, as a philosophical response to the chaos and bloodshed prevalent in China during the Warring States period (403–221 B.C.). It later split into several schools, certain of which absorbed elements of folk religion and concentrated on alchemy and other practices it was hoped would lead to immortality. With its emphasis on change and general distrust of authority, Daoism was the antithesis of Confucianism and remained largely on the fringes of Chinese civil society, more at home in the mountains than in the cities.

The oldest Daoist texts are the esoteric *Dào Dé Jīng* (or *Tao Te Ching*, "Classic of the Way and Virtue") and the *Zhuāngzǐ*, a prose book sometimes compared in its sly playfulness with the work of Nietzsche. Both deal with the Way *(Dào)*, a broad philosophical concept also mentioned by Confucius but described in a wholly different manner. In the *Dào Dé Jīng*, ostensibly written by a quasi-mythical figure named Laǒzǐ, the Way is more gestured at than defined, as in the famous opening line: "The way that can be spoken of/Is not the constant way."

The Daoists' dismissal of language, their habit of asking absurd questions, and their frequent self-contradictions are attempts to shake readers free of reason, which is said to obscure an understanding of the Way because it seeks to impose a rigid framework on a universe that is constantly changing.

Despite the *Dào Dé Jīng*'s remarkable global popularity as a deep source of mystical truths, one scholar, D. C. Lau, makes a convincing case that the book is best understood as a simple survival manual, its support for strength-in-supplication designed to help powerless Chinese avoid having their heads cut off at a time when such brutality was not at all uncommon.

There has been a revival of interest in both folk Daoism (particularly in the countryside) and the philosophical side of Daoism in recent years, but this

- **1601–1610** After years of campaigning, Italian Jesuit Matteo Ricci finally receives permission to reside in Běijīng and stays until his death, founding an influential Jesuit presence that survives well into the Qīng dynasty.

- **1644–1911** As peasant rebels overrun the capital, the last Míng emperor is driven to suicide by hanging himself from a tree in what is now Jǐng Shān Park,

behind the Forbidden City. Shortly afterward, the rebels are driven out by invading Manchu forces, whose Qīng dynasty transfers its capital from Manchuria to Běijīng, absorbing China into its own empire. Chinese are expelled from the northern section of the city, which becomes the home of Manchu military and courtiers. The southern section becomes the Chinese quarter of Běijīng.

- **1793–1794** George III's emissary to the Qiánlóng emperor visits China and passes through Běijīng, staying outside the city at a vast area of parks and palaces. His requests for increased trade and for a permanent trade representative in Běijīng are turned down in a patronizing edict written even before he arrives. China has no

continues

is largely invisible, and visitors who've read the *Tao of Pooh* and *Te of Piglet* are often disappointed by what they find at the few remaining active temples. Daoist complexes like Běijīng's immense **Báiyún Guàn** are garish and loud, reflecting the religious branch's fondness for magic potions and spells, with little of the contemplative feel most Westerners expect.

BUDDHISM

Buddhism traveled from India through Central Asia and along the Silk Routes to China sometime in the 1st century and began to flourish after a crisis of confidence in Confucianism caused by the fall of the Later Hàn dynasty (A.D. 25–220). But it would never achieve the same dominance as Confucianism, in large part because of the Buddhists' insistence that they exist beyond the power of the state, the monks' rejection of traditional family relationships, and the populace's xenophobic wariness of a foreign philosophy. Buddhism did become sufficiently pervasive during the Táng dynasty (618–907) to merit its own department in the government, but a neo-Confucian backlash under the succeeding Sòng dynasty (960–1279) saw it lose influence again. Although it never fully recovered the power it held under the Táng, Buddhism continued to have wide popular appeal and is still China's most prevalent organized religion.

All Buddhists believe human suffering can be stopped by eliminating attachment. But where the older Buddhism of India was a sparse atheistic tradition concerned with little more than the individual's achievement of Nirvana (enlightened detachment and extinction), Buddhism in China gradually absorbed elements of Daoism and local folk religion to become an incredibly complex belief system with various gods and demons, an intricately conceived heaven, several hells, and dozens of bodhisattvas (beings who have attained enlightenment but delay entry into Nirvana out of a desire to help others overcome suffering).

Among the various schools that eventually developed, the most popular was the Pure Land School, a faith-based tradition not unlike Christianity that believed the simple evocation of the name of Amitabha Buddha would result in the devotee's being reborn in the western paradise (the Pure Land), from which it would be easier to attain enlightenment. This tradition is still so popular in China that visitors will hear chants of Āmítuófó (the Mandarin transliteration of Amitabha) at several temples throughout Běijīng. A more revolutionary development was achieved by the Chán school (better known by its Japanese name,

inkling that Great Britain, and not itself, will soon be the superpower of the day. When the Qiánlóng emperor dies in 1799, the government is terminally corrupt and in decline.

■ **1858** The Second Opium War sees the Qīng and their Chinese subjects capitulating in the face of the superior military technology of "barbarians" (principally the British) for the second time

in 16 years. Under the terms of the Treaty of Nánjīng, China is forced to permit the permanent residence of foreign diplomats and trade representatives in the capital.

■ **1860** The Qīng imprison and murder foreign representatives sent for the treaty's ratification. British and French rescue forces occupy Běijīng and destroy a vast area of parks and palaces to the northwest, some of

the remnants of which form the modern Summer Palace. The Chinese loot what little the foreigners leave and put most of the area back under the plow. Foreign powers begin to construct diplomatic legation buildings just inside the Tartar City's wall east of the Qián Mén.

■ **1900** The Harmonious Fists, nicknamed the Boxers, a superstitious anti-foreign peasant movement, besieges

Zen), which held that even laypeople could achieve instantaneous enlightenment through a simplified but intense form of meditation.

Buddhist temples in Běijīng often contain large images of Mílefó (Maitreya, the Future Buddha) depicted in both Chinese (fat and jolly) and Tibetan (thinner and more somber) guises, and of Guānyīn (Avalokitesvara, the Bodhisattva of Compassion), a lithe woman in the Chinese style and a multi-armed, multi-headed man in the Tibetan pantheon, now incarnated as the Dalai Lama. The Manchu rulers of China's final dynasty, the Qīng (1644–1911), tried to maintain cultural ties with several ethnic groups on the fringes of the Chinese empire, which explains the unusual prevalence of Tibetan Buddhist architecture in Běijīng. Most noticeable are the two *dagobas* (Tibetan-style stupas), towering white structures like upside-down ice cream cones, at **Běi Hǎi Gōngyuán** and **Bái Tǎ Sì.**

ISLAM & CHRISTIANITY

Islam entered China through Central Asia in the 7th century, staying mostly in the northwestern corner of the empire, in what is now the Xīnjiāng Autonomous Region. It was introduced to more central regions through the occasional eastward migration of Xīnjiāng's Uighur people, and through the arrival of Arab trading vessels in southeastern ports like Quánzhōu during the Sòng dynasty (960–1270), but it failed to catch on with Hàn Chinese the way Buddhism did. Those Hàn who did convert are now lumped into a separate ethnic group, the Huí. Běijīng's Huí and Uighur populations don't mix as much as their shared religious beliefs might lead you to expect, the former dominating southeastern Běijīng around the **Niú Jiē Mosque** and the latter kept mostly in a series of constantly shifting ghettos. A visit to the mosque on Niú Jiē reveals Chinese Islam to be pretty much the same as Islam anywhere else; the glazed-tile roofs and basic layout resemble those of Buddhist or Daoist temples, but the main hall faces west (toward Mecca) rather than south, women and men pray separately, and there are absolutely no idols anywhere.

The first Christian missionary push to make much headway in China came in the 17th century, when Jesuits, led by Italian Matteo Ricci, sought to convert the country by first converting the imperial court. Ricci and his cohorts wowed the Qīng rulers with their knowledge of science, art, and architecture (see Jonathan Spence's *The Memory Palace of Matteo Ricci* for more about this) but ultimately failed to make Catholics of the Manchus. Subsequent missionaries, both

the foreign residents of the Legation Quarter, with the initially covert and finally open assistance of imperial troops. The siege begins on the 19th of June and is only lifted, after extensive destruction and many deaths, by the forces of Eight Allied Powers (several European nations, Japanese, and Americans) on August 14. Boxers, imperial troops, Chinese, foreign survivors, and allied soldiers take to looting the city. Payments on a vast indemnity take the Qīng a further 39 years to pay in full, although the British and Americans use much of the income to help found Yan-ching (now Peking) University and other institutions, and to pay for young Chinese to study overseas.

- **1911** The Qīng dynasty's downfall is brought about by an almost accidental revolution, and betrayal by Yuán Shìkǎi, the man the Qīng trusted to crush it. He negotiates with both sides and extracts an abdication agreement from the infant emperor's regent and an agreement from the rebels that he will become the first president of the new republic.

- **1915** Yuán Shìkǎi revives annual ceremonies at the Temple of Heaven, and

continues

Catholic and Protestant, continued the war on Chinese superstition and met with some success, but they were also seen as a nuisance. Christianity was linked with both major popular uprisings in the Qīng period—the Tàipíng Rebellion, led by a man named Hóng Xiùquán, who claimed to be Jesus's younger brother; and the Boxer Rebellion, a violent reaction to the aggressive tactics of missionaries in northern China which led to the siege of Běijīng's Legation Quarter.

Běijīng is particularly leery of Catholics, many of whom refused to join Protestants in pledging first allegiance to the state after 1949 and instead remained loyal to the Pope. Missionaries, it goes without saying, are not allowed in China anymore, but many sneak in as English teachers (a favorite tactic of the Mormons in particular). There are separate churches in Běijīng for foreigners, off-limits to Chinese, although foreigners are allowed to attend Chinese services. The Gothic-style church built in 1904 on the site of Ricci's house still stands near the Xuānwǔ Mén metro stop, and replicas of the Jesuits' bronze astronomical devices can be seen at the Ancient Observatory northeast of the main railway station.

Outside of monks and nuns, few Chinese people limit their devotion to a single tradition, instead choosing elements from each as they suit their particular circumstances. "Every Chinese," a popular saying goes, "is a Confucian when things are going well, a Daoist when things are going badly, and a Buddhist just before they die." But even this is a relatively rigid formulation—a Chinese person will often cross religious boundaries in the space of a single day if he thinks his problems merit the effort.

This pragmatic approach to beliefs allows not just individuals but also groups to create new religious systems with bits stolen from older traditions. Despite the government insistence that it is a cult, the Fǎlún Gōng's combination of Buddhism with qìgōng exercises and Daoist-like claims to impossible physical feats is very much in keeping with the Chinese tradition of religious collage. Unfortunately, its success has put Chinese leaders in mind of another tradition—the violent overthrow of dynasties by popular religious movements.

Despite the rise in religious participation, most visitors to Běijīng still complain of a made-for-tourists feel in most of the city's temples. Given the tidal wave of foreigners' cash that flows into places like the **Lama Temple,** this will probably never change, or at least not in Běijīng proper. For those willing to make the trip, however, the seldom-visited areas just outside Běijīng are home to several temples, such as **Tánzhè Sì** and **Jiètái Sì,**

---

prepares to install himself as first emperor of a new dynasty, but widespread demonstrations and the fomenting of a new rebellion in the south lead him to cancel his plans. He dies the following year.

■ **1917** In July a pro-monarchist warlord puts Pǔyí back on the throne, but he is driven out by another who drops three bombs on the Forbidden City, only one of

which actually explodes on target. The imperial restoration lasts exactly 12 days.

■ **1919** Students and citizens gather on May 4 in Tiān'ān Mén Square to protest the government's agreement that Chinese territory formerly under German control be handed to the Japanese.

■ **1924** The "Articles Providing for the Favourable Treatment of the Great Ch'ing [Qīng] Emperor after his Abdication"

provide for the emperor to continue to live in the Forbidden City pending an eventual move to the Summer Palace. But in November he is removed by a hostile warlord and put under house arrest, later escaping to the Legation Quarter with the help of his Scottish former tutor.

■ **1928** Despite fighting among warlords, many of whom are only nominally loyal to the Republic, the where tourism plays a secondary role to genuine religious practice. It is in places like these that you're most likely to witness the reawakening of China's older belief systems.

3 Film & Music

FILM

It is a source of frustration to some Chinese filmmakers that foreign audiences are easily duped. The most internationally successful films about China—Ang Lee's *Crouching Tiger, Hidden Dragon,* Zhāng Yìmóu's *Raise the Red Lantern,* Bernardo Bertolucci's *The Last Emperor*—wallow in marketable clichés. The China presented by these films exists almost solely in the simplified past tense, a mélange of incense, bound feet, and silk brocade designed to appeal to foreign notions of the country as unfathomably brutal and beautiful with an interminably long history.

Up until the late 1990s, much of the blame for this belonged to the government, which allowed the export of only those movies unlikely to provoke criticism of the present state of things, regardless of what they said about the past. Recently, however, films that deal with modern China, complex and often comic stories about everything from politics to relationships to harebrained attempts at money-making, have found their way to foreign viewers.

Běijīng sits at the center of the Chinese film world and serves as the setting for most of the best films now being produced in China. Many of these cannot be seen even in Běijīng itself except at small screenings unlikely to attract the attention of state censors. But those with access to a decent video rental shop will find a few.

Even Blockbuster carries copies of *Shower* (*Xǐzǎo,* 1999), Zhāng Yáng's at times sappy but ultimately enjoyable story of a Běijīng bathhouse owner and his two sons (one of them retarded) struggling to maintain a sense of family despite pressures of modernization. The film's depiction of a doomed *hútòng* neighborhood and the comic old characters who inhabit it won smatterings of praise in limited U.S. release and criticism from the Chinese authorities, who claimed it was anti-progress. Director Féng Xiǎogāng tried and failed to make it big in the U.S. with *Big Shot's Funeral* (*Dà Wàn,* 2001) featuring a (figuratively and literally) catatonic Donald Sutherland. But in a previous film set in and around Běijīng, *Sorry Baby* (*Méi Wán Méi Liǎo,* 1999), Féng displays a defter touch in a

Nationalist Party forces in the south declare Nánjīng the capital, and Běijīng reverts to the name of Běipíng. In the following years many ancient buildings are vandalized or covered in political slogans.

■ **1933** With Japanese armies seemingly poised to occupy Běipíng, the most important pieces of the imperial collection of antiquities in the Forbidden City are packed into 19,557 crates and moved to Shànghǎi. They move again when the Japanese take Shànghǎi in 1937, and after an incredible journey around the country in the thick of civil war, 13,484 crates end up with the Nationalist government in Táiwān in 1949.

■ **1937** Japanese forces, long in occupation of Manchuria and patrolling far beyond what the treaty permits them, pretend to have come under attack near the Marco Polo Bridge, occupy Běipíng, and stay until the end of World War II ("The War Against Japanese Aggression" to the Chinese).

■ **1949** Máo Zédōng proclaims the creation of the People's Republic of China from atop the Tiān'ān Mén on October 1. A vast flood of refugees from the countryside takes over the courtyard houses

continues

romantic comedy featuring bald-headed comic Gě Yōu at his brilliant best.

Among the earlier generation of films, two that deal specifically with Běijīng were big hits at Cannes, and you should have no trouble finding them. *Farewell My Concubine* (*Bà Wáng Bié Jī*, 1993), directed by Chén Kǎigē and starring the talented Gǒng Lì, is a long bit of lushness about a pair of Běijīng opera stars more dramatic in their alleged rivalry over a woman than they are on stage. Zhāng Yìmóu's unrelenting primer on modern Chinese history, *To Live* (*Huózhe*, 1994), also with Gǒng Lì, traces the unbelievable tragedies of a single Běijīng family as it bumbles through the upheavals of 20th-century China, from the civil war through the Great Leap Forward and Cultural Revolution and into the post-Máo reform period. More difficult to find (particularly with English subtitles), but very much worth the effort, are 1980s productions of Lǎo Shě's darkly satirical works, *The Teahouse* (*Chá Guǎn*, 1982) and *Rickshaw Boy* (*Luòtuo Xiángzǐ*, 1982).

Only specialty shops will carry *In the Heat of the Sun* (*Yángguāng Cànlàn de Rìzi*, 1995), a smart and deceptively nostalgic coming-of-age film about a pack of mischievous boys left to their own devices in Cultural Revolution–era Běijīng. Penned with help from celebrity rebel writer Wáng Shuò, it was one of the first pictures to break free of the ponderous melodrama that dominated Chinese cinema through most of the 1990s. Life for migrant workers on the margins of Běijīng is captured in the bleak but dryly witty *The World* (*Shìjiè*, 2004), set in The World Park in the southwestern suburbs of Běijīng. At times it borders on melodrama, and much of the subtlety is lost in translation, but Jiǎ Zhāngkē's film craft delivers a satisfying reverie on alienation, fantasy, and trust. If the film inspires you to "see the world without leaving Běijīng," take bus 744 from opposite Běijīng Railway Station to the terminus.

The documentary *Gate of Heavenly Peace* (1996) is obligatory viewing for anyone hoping to understand what transpired in 1989. If all you recall is a statue of liberty, a man with shopping bags, and talk of democracy, you're in for a shock.

MUSIC

The vapid, factory-produced syrup of **Mandopop** (think Celine Dion by way of Britney Spears sung in Mandarin) blares out of barber shops and retail stores in Běijīng, as elsewhere in China. But like Washington, D.C., and London, China's capital is ultimately a rock 'n' roll town.

Godfather of Chinese rock **Cuī Jiàn**, somewhat of a joke now as he clings to fading fame, got his start here in the early 1980s. A decade later, Chinese-American

commandeered from their owners, and those houses which once held a single family now house a dozen. Temples are turned into army barracks, storehouses, and light industrial units.

■ **1958–59** In a series of major projects to mark 10 years of Communist rule, the old ministries lining what will be Tiān'ān Mén Square and its surrounding walls are all flattened for the construction of the Great Hall of the People and the vast museums opposite. These and Běijīng Railway Station are built with Soviet help, which shows in the design. The city walls, which have survived for 400 years, are pulled down by "volunteers," to be replaced with a metro line and a ring road for an almost completely carless society. The stone from the walls goes to line a system of tunnels into which the entire city population can supposedly be evacuated in case of attack.

■ **1966–76** The destruction of old things reaches its peak as bands of Red Guards, fanatically loyal to Máo, roam around fighting each other, ransacking ancient buildings, burning books, and smashing art. Even the tree from which the last Míng emperor supposedly hung himself is cut down. Intellectuals are

Kaiser Kuo, front man for the no-longer-existent headbanger outfit **Tang Dynasty (Táng Cháo),** helped kick off a pretentious and fairly derivative heavy metal scene. But it wasn't until a shipment of Nirvana CDs found its way into local record shops in the late 1990s that Běijīng finally developed a genuine musical voice.

Like the Velvet Underground did in the U.S. 20 years earlier, Nirvana's *Nevermind* inspired nearly every Chinese kid who heard it to pick up a guitar and start a band. Investigations into Kurt Cobain's roots led to punk, which made its first major appearance in Běijīng in late 1997 at the Scream Club, a sweaty dive in the battered Wǔdàokǒu neighborhood. It was a natural response to Běijīng's swaths of urban decay and post–Tiān'ān Mén political disillusionment, and American pop culture magazines as big as *Details* quickly tapped the snarling, mohawked youth—most better at posing with their instruments than playing them—as easy symbols of China's new lost generation.

Běijīng's punks were probably never as concerned with political protest as they were made out to be, and are even less so now as they enjoy the fruits of small-scale fame (punks are among the few Chinese men able to attract Western women). But they continue to draw relatively large foreign audiences, and a handful have actually begun to produce music worthy of all the attention. The vulgar but talented **Brain Failure (Nǎo Zhuó)** and ska-influenced **Reflector (Fǎnguāng Jìng)**—both born at the now-defunct Scream Club—have each recorded listenable songs and evolved beyond just spitting beer in their live shows (though you can still expect the occasional shower). Also on Scream Records, the all-girl pop punk group **Hang on the Box (Guà Zài Hézi Shang),** with albums available at www.hangonthebox.net, sings in charmingly accented English.

Chinese musicians wanting to produce significant popular music suffer from the same dreadful self-consciousness of working in a foreign idiom as do artists in other imported media. Some try desperately (and without much success) to create "rock with Chinese characteristics," while others opt to simply lay Chinese lyrics over melodies lifted, sometimes note for note, from Western CDs. Even the most creative of efforts will sound suspiciously derivative, and those that don't usually appeal only to Mandarin-speaking foreigners who delight primarily in their ability to understand the lyrics. The other major barrier to the local music industry is piracy; particularly the ready availability of music downloads. Most band members still have day jobs.

---

bullied, imprisoned, tortured, and murdered, as is anyone with a history of links to foreigners. Scores are settled, and millions die. The education system largely comes to a halt. Many antiquities impounded from their owners are sold to foreign dealers by weight to provide funds for the government, which later decries foreign theft of Chinese antiquities.

■ **1976** The death of Zhōu Ēnlái, who is credited with mitigating some of the worst excesses of the Cultural Revolution, leads to over 100,000 demonstrating against the government in Tiān'ān Mén Square. The demonstrations are labeled counterrevolutionary, and hundreds are arrested. The death of Máo Zédōng, himself thought to be responsible for an estimated 38 million

deaths, effectively brings the Cultural Revolution to an end. Blame for the Cultural Revolution is put on the "Gang of Four"—Máo's wife and three other hard-line officials, who are arrested. The 450-year-old Dà Míng Mén in the center of Tiān'ān Mén Square is pulled down to make way for Máo's mausoleum. Leaders put

continues

Second Hand Rose (Èrshǒu Méiguī) have an eponymous full-length CD (available only in Běijīng), an excellent effort that stitches together Chili Peppers guitar, folk instrumentals, and sardonic *èrrénzhuàn* opera–influenced lyrics ("I'm a name brand cigarette/I've been stuffed in the mouth of a poor man") into one of the very few uniquely Chinese sounds you'd actually want to hear. The band's live performances, built around the raised-eyebrow theatricality of cross-dressing singer Liáng Lóng, are among the most entertaining musical experiences not just in China, but anywhere.

Folk rockers **Wild Children (Yě Háizi)** have their roots in the pared-down musical traditions of northwestern China, and play pleasantly repetitive chant-heavy acoustic songs likely to appeal more to the World Music set than to Dylan devotees. Information on the band's own recordings and its history, along with MP3s and videos, can be found at www. wildchildren.net.

For information on when and where the above bands might be playing, check music listings in either *that's Beijing* or *City Weekend,* both available free in hotels, bars, and cafes where foreigners gather. Currently, Yú Gōng Yí Shān (p. 186) is the best live music venue in Běijīng, hands down.

4 The Běijīng Menu

One of the best things about any visit to China is the food, at least for the independent traveler. Tour groups are often treated to a relentless series of cheap, bland dishes designed to cause no complaints and to keep the costs down for the Chinese operator, so do everything you can to escape and order some of the specialties we've described for you in chapter 6. Here they are again, in alphabetical order and with characters you can show to the waitress.

Widely available dishes and snacks are grouped in the first list; you can order most of them in any mainstream or *jiācháng cài* ("homestyle") restaurant. Some dishes recommended in this guidebook's reviews of individual restaurants are commonly available enough to be on this first list. Note that some of the specialty dishes in the second list are only available in the restaurants reviewed, or in restaurants offering a particular region's cuisine.

Supplement these lists with the bilingual menu from your local Chinese restaurant at home. The characters will not be quite the same as those used in Běijīng (more similar to those used in

their backing behind Dèng Xiǎopíng, who returns from disgrace to take power and launch a program of openness and economic reform. His own toleration for public criticism also turns out to be zero, however.

- **1989** The death of the moderate but disgraced official Hú Yàobāng causes public displays of mourning in Tiān'ān Mén Square, which turn into a mass occupation of the square protesting government corruption. Its hands initially tied by the presence on a state visit of the Soviet Union's Mikhail Gorbachev, the Party sends in the tanks live on TV on the night of June 3. Estimates of the number of deaths vary wildly, but the number is thought to run to several hundred unarmed students and their supporters.

- **2001** Běijīng is awarded the 2008 Summer Olympics, and as a result the destruction and complete redevelopment of the city accelerates, to the immense personal profit of the developers. That some are related to the top members of the administration is common knowledge.

Hong Kong and Macau), but they will be understood. Don't expect the dishes to be the same, however. Expect them to be *better*.

Any mainstream non-specialty restaurant can and will make any common Chinese dish, whether it's on the menu or not. But don't expect Běijīng cooks to manage the subtler flavors of Cantonese cooking, for instance, unless the restaurant advertises itself as a southern-food specialist.

A surprising number of restaurants now have English menus. In the past, this was a warning of inflated prices, but now an English menu is often used to brand a restaurant as "classy" in the eyes of the locals.

Dishes often arrive in haphazard order, but menus generally open with *liáng cài* (cold dishes). Except in top-class Sino-foreign joint-venture restaurants, you are strongly advised to avoid these for hygiene reasons. The restaurant's specialties also come early in the menu: They have significantly higher prices and if you dither, the waitress will recommend them, saying, "I hear this one's good." Waitresses always recommend ¥180 ($23) dishes, never ¥8 ($1) ones. Some of these dishes may occasionally be made from creatures you would regard as pets or zoo creatures (or best in the wild), and parts of them you may consider inedible or odd, like swallow saliva (the main ingredient of bird's nest soup, a rather bland Cantonese delicacy).

Main dishes come next; various meats and fish are followed by vegetables and *dòufu* (tofu). Drinks come at the end. You'll rarely find desserts outside of restaurants that largely cater to foreigners. A few watermelon slices may appear, but it's best to forgo them.

Soup is usually eaten last. Outside Guǎngdōng Province, Hong Kong, and Macau, rice also usually arrives at the end; if you want it with your meal, you must ask (point to the characters for rice, below, when the first dish arrives).

There is no tipping. Tea, chopsticks, and napkins should be free (although if a wrapped packet of tissues arrives you may pay a small fee); service charges do not exist outside of major hotels; and there are no cover charges or taxes. If asked what tea you would like, know that you are going to receive something above average and will be charged for it. Exercise caution—some varieties cost more than the meal!

Most Chinese food is not designed to be eaten solo, but if you do find yourself on your own, ask for small portions *(xiǎo pán, 小盘)*, usually about 70% of the size of a full dish and about 70% of the price. This allows you to sample the menu properly without too much waste.

WIDELY AVAILABLE DISHES & SNACKS

PĪNYĪN	ENGLISH	CHINESE
bābǎo zhōu	rice porridge with nuts and berries	八宝粥
bǎnlì shāo chìzhōng	soy chicken wings with chestnuts	板栗烧翅中
bāozi	stuffed steamed buns	包子
bīngqílín	ice cream	冰淇淋
chǎo fàn	fried rice	炒饭
chǎo miàn	fried noodles	炒面
cōng bào niúròu	quick-fried beef and onions	葱爆牛肉
dāndān miàn	noodles in spicy broth	担担面

PĪNYĪN	ENGLISH	CHINESE
diǎnxin	dim sum (snacks)	点心
dì sān xiān	braised eggplant with potatoes and spicy green peppers	地三鲜
gānbiān sìjìdòu	sautéed string beans	干煸四季豆
gōngbào jīdīng	spicy diced chicken with cashews	宫爆鸡丁
guōtiē	fried dumplings/potstickers	锅贴
hóngshāo fǔzhú	braised tofu	红烧腐竹
hóngshāo huángyú	braised yellow fish	红烧黄鱼
huíguō ròu	twice-cooked pork	回锅肉
huǒguō	hot pot	火锅
jiānbing	large crepe folded around fried dough with plum and hot sauces	煎饼
jiǎozi	dumplings/Chinese ravioli	饺子
jīngjiàng ròu sī	shredded pork in soya sauce	京酱肉丝
mápó dòufu	spicy tofu with chopped meat	麻婆豆腐
miàntiáo	noodles	面条
mǐfàn	rice	米饭
mù xū ròu	sliced pork with fungus (mushu pork)	木须肉
niúròu miàn	beef noodles	牛肉面
ròu chuàn	kebabs/kabobs	肉串
sānxiān	"three flavors" (usually prawn, mushroom, pork)	三鲜
shuǐjiǎo	boiled dumplings	水饺
suānlà báicài	hot and sour cabbage	酸辣白菜
suānlà tāng	hot and sour soup	酸辣汤
sù miàn	vegetarian noodles	素面
sù shíjǐn	mixed vegetables	素什锦
tángcù lǐji	sweet-and-sour pork tenderloin	糖醋里脊
tǔdòu dùn niúròu	stewed beef and potato	土豆炖牛肉
xiàn bǐng	pork- or vegetable-stuffed fried pancake	馅饼
xīhóngshì chǎo jīdàn	tomatoes with eggs	西红柿炒鸡蛋
yángròu chuàn	barbecued lamb skewers with round cumin and chili powder	羊肉串
yóutiáo	fried salty donut	油条
yúxiāng qiézi	eggplant in garlic sauce	鱼香茄子
yúxiāng ròu sī	shredded pork in garlic sauce	鱼香肉丝
zhēngjiǎo	steamed dumplings	蒸饺
zhōu	rice porridge	粥

SPECIALTY DISHES (FROM BĚIJĪNG & ELSEWHERE) RECOMMENDED IN RESTAURANT REVIEWS

PĪNYĪN	ENGLISH	CHINESE
bābǎo làjiàng	gingko, nuts, and pork in sweet chili sauce	八宝辣酱
bōluó fàn	pineapple rice	菠萝饭
cháshùgū bāo lǎojī	chicken with tea-mushroom soup	茶树菇煲老鸡
chénpí lǎoyā shānzhēn bāo	duck, mandarin peel, and mushroom potage	陈皮老鸭山珍煲
cuìpí qiézi	sweet and sour battered eggplant	脆皮茄子
cùngū shāo	deep-fried pork with medicinal herbs	寸骨烧
Dǎizú xiāngmáocǎo kǎo yú	Dǎi grilled lemon grass fish	傣族香茅草烤鱼
dà lāpí	cold noodles in sesame and vinegar sauce	大拉皮
dà pán jī	diced chicken and noodles in tomato sauce	大盘鸡
Dōngběi fēngwèi dàpái	northeast-style braised ribs	东北风味大排
Dōngpō ròu	braised fatty pork in small clay pot	东坡肉
é'gān juǎn	goose liver rolls with hoisin sauce	鹅肝卷
gǒubùlǐ bāozi	pork-stuffed bread dumplings	狗不里包子
guōbā ròu piān	pork with crispy fried rice	锅巴肉片
guòqiáo mǐxiàn	crossing-the-bridge rice noodles	过桥米线
huángdì sǔn shāo wánzi	Imperial bamboo shoots and vegetarian meatballs	皇帝笋烧丸子
huángqiáo ròu sūbǐng	shredded-pork rolls	黄桥肉酥饼
huíxiāng dòu	aniseed-flavored beans	茴香豆
jiāoliū wánzi	crisp-fried pork balls	焦熘丸子
jīngjiàng ròusī	shredded pork with green onion rolled in tofu skin	京酱肉丝
jīnpái tiáoliào	"gold label" sesame sauce (for Mongolian hot pot)	金牌调料
jīròu sèlā	deep-fried chicken pieces with herb dipping sauce	鸡肉色拉
jiǔxiāng yúgān	dried fish in wine sauce	酒香鱼干
juébā chǎo làròu	bacon stir-fried with brake leaves	蕨粑炒腊肉
kǎo yángròu	roast mutton	烤羊肉
làbā cù	garlic-infused vinegar	腊八醋
láncài sìjìdòu láncài sìj	green beans stir-fried with salty vegetable	榄菜四季豆
lǎogānmā shāojī	spicy diced chicken with bamboo and ginger	老干妈烧鸡

PĪNYĪN	ENGLISH	CHINESE
làròu dòuyá juǎnbǐng	spicy bacon and bean sprouts in pancakes	腊肉豆芽卷饼
làwèi huájī bāozǎi fàn	chicken and sweet sausage on rice in clay pot	腊味滑鸡煲仔饭
liángbàn zǐ lúsǔn	purple asparagus salad	凉拌紫芦笋
luóbo sī sūbǐng	shredded-turnip shortcake	萝卜丝酥饼
málà lóngxiā	spicy crayfish	麻辣龙虾
málà tiánluó	field snails stewed in chili and Sìchuān pepper	麻辣田螺
mǎtí niúliǔ	stir-fried beef with broccoli, water chestnuts, and tofu rolls	马蹄牛柳
mìzhì zhǐbāo lúyú	paper-wrapped perch and onions on sizzling iron plate	秘制纸包鲈鱼
náng bāo ròu	lamb and vegetable stew served on flat wheat bread	馕包肉
nánrǔ kòuròu	braised pork in red fermented bean curd gravy	南乳扣肉
niúròu wán shuǐjiǎo	beef ball dumplings	牛肉丸水饺
nóngjiā shāo jiān jī	spicy sautéed chicken fillet	农家烧煎鸡
nóngjiā xiǎochǎo	soybeans, green onion, Chinese chives, and green pepper in a clay pot	农家小炒
qiáo miàn māo ěrduo	"cat's ear" buckwheat pasta with chopped meat	荞面猫耳朵
ròudīng báicài xiànbǐng	meat cabbage pie	肉丁白菜馅饼
rúyì hǎitái juǎn	vegetarian sushi rolls	如意海苔卷
sān bēi jī	chicken reduced in rice wine, sesame oil, and soy sauce	三杯鸡
sānxiān làohé	seafood and garlic chive buns	三鲜烙合
sè shāo niúròu	foil-wrapped beef marinated in mountain herbs	色烧牛肉
shāchá niúròu	beef sautéed with Taiwanese BBQ sauce	沙茶牛肉
shānyao gēng	yam broth with mushrooms	山药羹
shānyao húlu	red bean rolls with mountain herbs	山药葫芦
shēngjiān bāozi	pork-stuffed fried bread dumplings	生煎包子
shǒuzhuā fàn	Uighur-style rice with carrot and mutton	手抓饭
shǒuzhuā yáng pái	lamb chops roasted with cumin and chili	手抓羊排
shuǐzhǔ yú	boiled fish in spicy broth with numbing peppercorns	水煮鱼
suànxiāng jīchì	garlic paper-wrapped chicken wings	蒜香鸡翅

PĪNYĪN	ENGLISH	CHINESE
sǔngān lǎoyā bāo	stewed duck with dried bamboo shoots	笋干老鸭煲
Táiwān dòfu bāo	Taiwanese tofu and vegetables clay pot	台湾豆腐煲
tiānfú shāokǎo yángtuǐ	roasted leg of mutton with cumin and chili powder	天福烧烤羊腿
tiēbǐngzi	corn pancakes cooked on a griddle	贴饼子
tǔdòu qiú	deep-fried potato balls with chili sauce	土豆球
tǔtāng shícài	clear soup with seasonal leafy greens	土汤时菜
xiāngcǎo cuìlà yú	whole fried fish with hot peppers and lemon grass	香草脆辣鱼
xiǎolóng bāozi	pork-stuffed steamed bread dumplings	小笼包子
Xībèi dà bàncài	Xībèi salad	西贝大拌菜
xièfěn dòufu	crab meat tofu	蟹粉豆腐
xièsānxiān shuǐjiǎo	boiled crab dumplings with shrimp and mushrooms	蟹三鲜水饺
yángròu chuàn	spicy mutton skewers with cumin	羊肉串
yángyóu má dòufu	mashed soybean with lamb oil	羊油麻豆腐
yán jú xiā	shrimp skewers in rock salt	盐局虾
yè niúròu juǎn	grilled la lop leaf beef	叶牛肉卷
yì bǎ zhuā	fried wheat cakes	一把抓
yóumiàn wōwo	steamed oatmeal noodles	莜面窝窝
yóutiáo niúròu	sliced beef with fried dough in savory sauce	油条牛肉
zhá guàncháng	taro chips with garlic sauce	炸灌肠
zhāngchá yā	crispy smoked duck with plum sauce	樟茶鸭
zhá qiéhé	pork-stuffed deep-fried eggplant	炸茄合
zhēnzhū nǎichá	pearl milk tea	珍珠奶茶
zhǐbāo lúyú	paper-wrapped perch in sweet sauce	纸包鲈鱼
zhījīcǎo kǎo niúpái	lotus leaf–wrapped roast beef with mountain herbs	枳机草烤牛排
zhūròu báicài bāozi	steamed bun stuffed with pork and cabbage	猪肉白菜包子
zhúsūn qìguō jī	mushroom and mountain herbs chicken soup	竹荪气锅鸡
zhútǒng jī	chicken soup in bamboo vessel	竹筒鸡
zhútǒng páigǔ	spicy stewed pork with mint	竹筒排骨
zhútǒng zhūròu	steamed pork with coriander	竹筒猪肉
zuì jī	chicken marinated in rice wine	醉鸡
zuì xiā	live shrimp in wine	醉虾

Appendix B:
The Chinese Language

Chinese is not as difficult a language to learn as it may first appear to be—at least not once you've decided what kind of Chinese to learn. There are six major languages called Chinese. Speakers of each are unintelligible to each other, and there are, in addition, a host of dialects. The Chinese you are likely to hear spoken in your local Chinatown or Chinese restaurant, or used by your friends of Chinese descent when they speak to their parents, is more than likely to be Cantonese, which is the version of Chinese used in Hong Kong and in much of southern China. But the official national language of China is **Mandarin** (**Pǔtoōnghuà**—"common speech"), sometimes called Modern Standard Chinese, and viewed in mainland China as the language of administration, of the classics, and of the educated. While throughout much of mainland China people speak their own local flavor of Chinese for everyday communication, they've all been educated in Mandarin which, in general terms, is the language of Beěijīng and the north. Mandarin is less well known in Hong Kong and Macau, but it is also spoken in Táiwān and Singapore, and among growing communities of recent immigrants to North America and Europe.

Chinese grammar is considerably more straightforward than those of English or other European languages, even Spanish or Italian. There are no genders, so there is no need to remember long lists of endings for adjectives and to make them agree, with variations according to case. There are no equivalents for the definite and indefinite articles ("the," "a," "an"), so there is no need to make those agree either. Singular and plural nouns are the same. Best of all, verbs cannot be declined. The verb "to be" is *shì*. The same sound also covers "am," "are," "is," "was," "will be," and so on, since there are also no tenses. Instead of past, present, and future, Chinese is more concerned with whether an action is continuing or has been completed, and with the order in which events take place. To make matters of time clear, Chinese depends on simple expressions such as "yesterday," "before," "originally," "next year," and the like. "Tomorrow I go New York," is clear enough, as is "Yesterday I go New York." It's a little more complicated than these brief notes can suggest, but not much.

There are a few sounds in Mandarin that are not used in English (see the rough pronunciation guide below), but the main difficulty for foreigners lies in tones. Most sounds in Mandarin begin with a consonant and end in a vowel (or -n, or -ng), which leaves the language with very few distinct noises compared to English. Originally, one sound equaled one idea and one word. Even now, each of these monosyllables is represented by a single character, but often words have been made by putting two characters together, sometimes both with the same meaning, thus reinforcing one another. The solution to this phonetic poverty is to multiply the available sounds by making them tonal—speaking them at different pitches, thereby giving them different meanings. *Mā* spoken on a high level tone (first tone) offers a set of possible meanings different from those of *má* spoken with a rising tone (second tone), *mǎ* with a dipping then rising tone (third tone), or *mà* with an abruptly falling tone (fourth tone). There's also a different meaning for the neutral, toneless *ma*.

In the average sentence, context is your friend (there are not many occasions in which the third-tone *mǎ* or "horse" might be mistaken for the fourth-tone *mà* or "grasshopper," for instance), but without tone, there is essentially no meaning. The novice best sing his or her Mandarin very clearly, as Chinese children do—a chanted sing-song can be heard emerging from the windows of primary schools across China. With experience, the student learns to give particular emphasis to the tones on words essential to a sentence's meaning, and to treat the others more lightly. Sadly, most books using modern Romanized Chinese, called *Hànyuǔ pīnyīn* ("Hàn language spell-the-sounds"), do not mark the tones, nor do these appear on **pīnyīn** signs in China. But in this book, the author, has added tones to every Mandarin expression, so you can have a go at saying them for yourself. Where tones do not appear, that's usually because the name of a person or place is already familiar to many readers in an older form of Romanized Chinese such as Wade-Giles or Post Office (in which Beĕijīng was written misleadingly as Peking); or because it is better known in Cantonese: Sun Yat-sen, or Canton, for instance.

Cantonese has *eight* tones plus the neutral, but its grammatical structure is largely the same, as is that of all versions of Chinese. Even Chinese people who can barely understand each other's speech can at least write to each other, since written forms are similar. Mainland China, with the aim of increasing literacy (or perhaps of distancing the supposedly now thoroughly modern and socialist population from its Confucian heritage), instituted a ham-fisted simplification program in the 1950s, which reduced some characters originally taking 14 strokes of the brush, for instance, to as few as three strokes. Hong Kong, separated from the mainland and under British control until 1997, went its own way, kept the original full-form characters, and invented lots of new ones, too. Nevertheless, many characters remain the same, and some of the simplified forms are merely familiar shorthands for the full-form ones. But however many different meanings for each tone of *ma* there may be, for each meaning there's a different character. This makes the written form a far more successful communication medium than the spoken one, which leads to misunderstandings even between native speakers, who can often be seen sketching characters on their palms during conversation to confirm which one is meant.

The thought of learning 3,000 to 5,000 individual characters (at least 2,500 are needed to read a newspaper) also daunts many beginners. But look carefully at the ones below, and you'll notice many common elements. In fact, a rather limited number of smaller shapes are combined in different ways, much as we combine letters to make words. Admittedly, the characters only offer general hints as to their pronunciation, and that's often misleading—the system is not a phonetic one, so each new Mandarin word has to be learned as both a sound and a shape (or a group of them). But soon it's the similarities among the characters, not their differences, which begin to bother the student. English, a far more subtle language with a far larger vocabulary, and with so many pointless inconsistencies and exceptions to what are laughingly called its rules, is much more of a struggle for the Chinese than Mandarin should be for us.

But no knowledge of the language is needed to get around China, and it's almost of assistance that Chinese take it for granted that outlandish foreigners (that's you and me unless of Chinese descent) can speak not a word (poor things) and must use whatever other limited means we have to communicate—this book and a phrase book, for instance. For help with navigation to sights, simply point to the characters in this book's map keys. When leaving your hotel, take one of its cards with you, and show it to the taxi driver when you want to return. In section 2, below, is a limited list of useful words and phrases that is best supplemented with a proper phrase book. If you have a Mandarin-speaking friend from the north (Cantonese speakers who know Mandarin as a second language tend to have fairly heavy accents), ask him or her to pronounce the greetings and words of thanks from the list below, so you can repeat after him and practice. While you are as much likely to be laughed *at* as *with* in China, such efforts are always appreciated.

1 A Guide to Pīnyīn Pronunciation

Letters in pīnyīn mostly have the values any English speaker would expect, with the following exceptions:

c *ts* as in bi*ts*

q *ch* as in *ch*in, but much harder and more forward, made with tongue and teeth

r has no true equivalent in English, but the *r* of *r*eed is close, although the tip of the tongue should be near the top of the mouth, and the teeth together

x also has no true equivalent, but is nearest to the *sh* of *sh*eep, although the tongue should be parallel to the roof of the mouth and the teeth together

zh is a soft j, like the *dge* in ju*dge*

The vowels are pronounced roughly as follows:

a as in f*a*ther

e as in *e*rr (*leng* is pronounced as English "lung")

i is pronounced *ee* after most consonants, but after c, ch, r, s, sh, z, and zh is a buzz at the front of the mouth behind closed teeth

o as in s*o*ng

u as in t*oo*

ü is the purer, lips-pursed u of French t*u* and German *ü*. Confusingly, **u** after j, x, q, and y is always ü, but in these cases the accent over "ü" does not appear.

ai sounds like *eye*

ao as in *ou*ch

ei as in h*ay*

ia as in *ya*k

ian sounds like *yen*

iang sounds like *yang*

iu sounds like *you*

ou as in t*oe*

ua as in g*ua*va

ui sounds like *way*

uo sounds like *or*, but is more abrupt

Note that when two or more third-tone "ˇ" sounds follow one another, they should all, except the last, be pronounced as second-tone "ˊ."

2 Mandarin Bare Essentials

ENGLISH	PĪNYĪN	CHINESE
Greetings & Introductions		
Hello	Nǐ hǎo	你好
How are you?	Nǐ hǎo ma?	你好吗？
Fine. And you?	Wǒ hēn hǎo. Nǐ ne?	我很好你呢？
I'm not too well/Things aren't going well	Bù hǎo	不好
What is your name? (very polite)	Nín guì xìng?	您贵姓
My (family) name is	Wǒ xìng	我姓。。。
I'm known as (family, then given name)	Wǒ jiào	我叫。。。
I'm from [America]	Wǒ shì cóng [Měiguó] lái de	我是从美国来的
I'm [American]	Wǒ shì [Měiguó] rén	我是美国人
[Australian]	[Àodàlìyà]	澳大利亚
[British]	[Yīngguó]	英国
[Canadian]	[Jiānádà]	加拿大
[Irish]	[Àiěrlán]	爱尔兰
[a New Zealander]	[Xīnxīlán]	新西兰
Excuse me/I'm sorry	Duìbùqī	对不起
I don't understand	Wǒ tīng bù dǒng	我听不懂
Thank you	Xièxie nī	谢谢你
Correct (yes)	Duì	对
Not correct	Bú duì	不对
No, I don't want	Wǒ de bú yào	我不要
Not acceptable	Bù xíng	不行

Basic Questions & Problems

Excuse me/I'd like to ask	Qǐng wènyíxià	请问一下
Where is . . . ?	. . . zài nǎr?	。。。在哪儿？
How much is . . . ?	. . . duōshǎo qián?	。。。多少钱？
. . . this one?	Zhèi/Zhè ge . . .	这个。。。
. . . that one?	Nèi/Nà ge . . .	那个。。。
Do you have . . . ?	Nǐ yǒu méi yǒu . . .	你有没有。。。？
What time does/is . . . ?	. . . jǐ diǎn?	。。。几点？
What time is it now?	Xiànzài jǐ diǎn?	现在几点？
When is . . . ?	. . . shénme shíhou?	。。。什么时候？
Why?	Wèishénme?	为什么？
Who?	Shéi?	谁？

ENGLISH	PĪNYĪN	CHINESE
Is that okay?	Xíng bù xíng?	行不行？
I'm feeling ill	Wǒ shěng bìng le	我生病了

Travel

luxury (bus, hotel rooms)	háohuá	豪华
high speed (buses, expressways)	gāosù	高速
air-conditioned	kōngtiáo	空调
When's the last bus?	mòbīnchē jǐdiǎn kāi?	末班车几点开？

NUMBERS

Note that more complicated forms of numbers are often used on official documents and receipts to prevent fraud—see how easily one can be changed to two, three, or even ten. Familiar Arabic numerals appear on bank notes, most signs, taxi meters, and other places. Be particularly careful with *four* and *ten,* which sound very alike in many regions—hold up fingers to make sure. Note, too, that *yī,* meaning "one," tends to change its tone all the time depending on what it precedes. Don't worry about this—once you've started talking about money, almost any kind of squeak for "one" will do. Finally note that "two" alters when being used with expressions of quantity.

zero	líng	零
one	yī	一
two	èr	二
two (of them)	liǎng ge	两个
three	sān	三
four	sì	四
five	wǔ	五
six	liù	六
seven	qī	七
eight	bā	八
nine	jiǔ	九
10	shí	十
11	shí yī	十一
12	shí èr	十二
21	èr shí yī	二十一
22	èr shí èr	二十二
51	wǔ shí yī	五十一
100	yì bǎi	一百
101	yì bǎi líng yī	一百零一
110	yì bǎi yī (shí)	一百一（十）
111	yì bǎi yī shí yī	一百一十一
1,000	yì qiān	一千
1,500	yì qiān wǔ (bǎi)	一千五百
5,678	wǔ qiān liù bǎi qī shí bāi	五千六百七十八
10,000	yí wàn	一万

MONEY

The word *yuán* (¥) is rarely spoken, nor is *jiǎo,* the written form for one-tenth of a *yuán,* equivalent to 10 *fān* (there are 100 *fēn* in a *yuán*). Instead, the Chinese speak of "pieces of money," *kuài qián,* usually abbreviated just to *kuài,* and they speak of *máo* for one-tenth of a *kuài. Fēn* have been overtaken by inflation and are almost useless. Often all zeros after the last whole number are simply omitted, along with *kuài qián,* which is taken as read, especially in direct reply to the question *duōshǎo qián*—"How much?"

¥1	yí kuài qián	一块钱
¥2	liǎng kuài qián	两块钱
¥.30	sān máo qián	三毛钱
¥5.05	wǔ kuài líng wǔ fēn	五块零五分
¥5.50	wǔ kuài wǔ	五块五
¥550	wǔ bǎi wǔ shí kuài	五百五十块
¥5,500	wǔ qiān wǔ bǎi kuài	五千五百块
small change	língqián	零钱

BANKING & SHOPPING

I want to change money (foreign exchange)	Wǒ xiǎng huàn qián	我想换钱
credit card	xìnyòng kǎ	信用卡
traveler's check	lǚxíng zhīpiào	旅行支票
department store	bǎihuò shāngdiàn	百货商店
or	gòuwù zhōngxīn	购物中心
convenience store	xiǎomàibù	小卖部
market	shìchǎng	市场
May I have a look?	Wǒ Kànyíxia, hǎo ma?	我看一下，好吗？
I want to buy	Wǒ xiǎng mǎi	我想买。。。
How many do you want?	Nǐ yào jǐ ge?	你要几个？
two of them	liǎng ge	两个
three of them	sān ge	三个
1 kilo (2¼ lb.)	yì gǒngjīn	一公斤
half a kilo	yì jīn	一斤
or	bàn gōngjīn	公斤
1 meter (3¼ ft.)	yì mǐ	一米
Too expensive!	Tài guì le!	太贵了
Do you have change?	Yǒu língqián ma?	有零钱吗

TIME

morning	shàngwǔ	上午
afternoon	xiàwǔ	下午
evening	wǎnshang	晚上
8:20am	shàngwǔ bā diǎn èr shí fēn	上午八点二十分

ENGLISH	PĪNYĪN	CHINESE
9:30am	shàngwǔ jiǔ diǎn bàn	上午九点半
noon	zhōngwǔ	中午
4:15pm	xiàwǔ sì diǎn yí kè	下午四点一刻
midnight	wǔ yè	午夜
1 hour	yí ge xiǎoshí	一个小时
8 hours	bā ge xiǎoshí	八个小时
today	jīntiān	今天
yesterday	zuótiān	昨天
tomorrow	míngtiān	明天
Monday	Xīngqī yī	星期一
Tuesday	Xīngqī èr	星期二
Wednesday	Xīngqī sān	星期三
Thursday	Xīngqī sì	星期四
Friday	Xīngqī wǔ	星期五
Saturday	Xīngqī liù	星期六
Sunday	Xīngqī tiān	星期天

TRANSPORT

I want to go to . . .	Wǒ xiǎng qù . . .	我想去。。。
plane	fēijī	飞机
train	huǒchē	火车
bus	gōnggòng qìchē	公共汽车
long-distance bus	chángtú qìchē	长途汽车
taxi	chūzū chē	出租车
airport	fēijīchǎng	飞机场
stop or station (bus or train)	zhàn	站
(plane/train/bus) ticket	piào	票

NAVIGATION

North	Běi	北
South	Nán	南
East	Dōng	东
West	Xī	西
Turn left	zuǒ guǎi	左拐
Turn right	yòu guǎi	右拐
Go straight on	yìzhí zǒu	一直走
crossroads	shízì lùkǒu	十字路口
10 kilometers	shí gōnglǐ	十公里
I'm lost	Wǒ diū le	我丢了

ENGLISH	PĪNYĪN	CHINESE
HOTEL		
How many days?	Zhù jǐ tiān?	住几天？
standard room (twin or double with private bathroom)	biāozhǔn jiān	标准间
passport	hùzhào	护照
deposit	yājǐn	押金
I want to check out	Wǎ tuì fáng	我退房
RESTAURANT		
How many people?	Jǐ wèi?	几位
waiter/waitress	fúwùyuán	服务员
menu	càidān	菜单
I'm vegetarian	Wǒ shì chī sù de	我是吃素的
Don't add MSG	qǐng bù fàng wèijīng	请不放味精
Do you have . . . ?	Yǒu méi yǒu . . .?	有没有...？
Please bring a portion of . . .	Qǐng lái yí fènr . . .	请来一份儿...。
I'm full	wǒ chībǎo le	我吃饱了
beer	píjiǔ	啤酒
coffee	kāfēi	咖啡
mineral water	kuàngquán shuǐ	矿泉水
tea	cháshuǐ	茶水
Bill, please	jiézhàng	结帐

SIGNS

Here's a list of common signs and notices to help you identify what you are looking for, from restaurants to condiments, and to help you choose the right door at the public toilets. These are the simplified characters in everyday use in China, but note that it's increasingly fashionable for larger businesses and for those with a long history to use more complicated traditional characters, so not all may match what's below. Also, very old restaurants and temples across China tend to write their signs from right to left.

hotel	bīnguǎn	宾馆
	dàjiǔdiàn	大酒店
	jiǔdiàn	酒店
	fàndiàn	饭店
restaurant	fànguǎn	饭馆
	jiǔdiàn	酒店
	jiǔjiā	酒家
vinegar	cù	醋
soya sauce	Jiàngyóu	酱油

ENGLISH	PĪNYĪN	CHINESE
bar	jiǔbā	酒吧
Internet bar	wǎngbā	网吧
cafe	kāfēiguǎn	咖啡馆
teahouse	cháguǎn	茶馆
department store	bǎihuò shāngdiàn	百货商店
	gòuwù zhōngxīn	购物中心
market	shìchǎng	市场
bookstore	shūdiàn	书店
police (Public Security Bureau)	gōng'ānjú	公安局
Bank of China	Zhōngguó Yínháng	中国银行
public telephone	gōngyòng diànhuà	公用电话
public toilet	gōngyòng cèsuǎ	公用厕所
male	nán	男
female	nǔ	女
entrance	rùkǒu	入口
exit	chūkǒu	出口
bus stop/station	qìchē zhàn	汽车站
long-distance bus station	chángtú qìchē zhàn	长途汽车站
luxury	háohuá	豪华
using highway	gāosù	高速
railway station	huǒchē zhàn	火车站
hard seat	yìng zuò	硬座
soft seat	ruǎn zuò	软座
hard sleeper	yìng wò	硬卧
soft sleeper	ruǎn wò	软卧
direct (through) train	zhídá	直达
express train	tèkuài	特快
metro/subway station	dìtiě zhàn	地铁站
airport	fēijīchǎng	飞机场
dock/wharf	mǎtóu	码头
passenger terminal (bus, boat, and so on)	kèyùn zhàn	客运站
up/get on	shàng	上
down/get off	xià	下
ticket hall	shòupiào tīng	售票厅
ticket office	shòupiào chù	售票处
left-luggage office	xíngli jìcún chù	行李寄存处
temple	sì	寺
	miào	庙

ENGLISH	PĪNYĪN	CHINESE
museum	bówùguǎn	博物馆
memorial hall	jìniànguǎn	纪念馆
park	gōngyuán	公园
hospital	yīyuàn	医院
clinic	zhěnsuǒ	诊所
pharmacy	yàofáng/yàodiàn	药房/药店
travel agency	lǚxíngshè	旅行社

Index

See also Accommodations and Restaurant indexes, below.

FROMMER'S® COMPLETE TRAVEL GUIDES

Alaska
Amalfi Coast
American Southwest
Amsterdam
Argentina & Chile
Arizona
Atlanta
Australia
Austria
Bahamas
Barcelona
Beijing
Belgium, Holland & Luxembourg
Belize
Bermuda
Boston
Brazil
British Columbia & the Canadian Rockies
Brussels & Bruges
Budapest & the Best of Hungary
Buenos Aires
Calgary
California
Canada
Cancún, Cozumel & the Yucatán
Cape Cod, Nantucket & Martha's Vineyard
Caribbean
Caribbean Ports of Call
Carolinas & Georgia
Chicago
China
Colorado
Costa Rica
Croatia
Cuba
Denmark
Denver, Boulder & Colorado Springs
Edinburgh & Glasgow
England
Europe
Europe by Rail

Florence, Tuscany & Umbria
Florida
France
Germany
Greece
Greek Islands
Hawaii
Hong Kong
Honolulu, Waikiki & Oahu
India
Ireland
Italy
Jamaica
Japan
Kauai
Las Vegas
London
Los Angeles
Los Cabos & Baja
Madrid
Maine Coast
Maryland & Delaware
Maui
Mexico
Montana & Wyoming
Montréal & Québec City
Moscow & St. Petersburg
Munich & the Bavarian Alps
Nashville & Memphis
New England
Newfoundland & Labrador
New Mexico
New Orleans
New York City
New York State
New Zealand
Northern Italy
Norway
Nova Scotia, New Brunswick & Prince Edward Island
Oregon
Paris
Peru

Philadelphia & the Amish Country
Portugal
Prague & the Best of the Czech Republic
Provence & the Riviera
Puerto Rico
Rome
San Antonio & Austin
San Diego
San Francisco
Santa Fe, Taos & Albuquerque
Scandinavia
Scotland
Seattle
Seville, Granada & the Best of Andalusia
Shanghai
Sicily
Singapore & Malaysia
South Africa
South America
South Florida
South Pacific
Southeast Asia
Spain
Sweden
Switzerland
Texas
Thailand
Tokyo
Toronto
Turkey
USA
Utah
Vancouver & Victoria
Vermont, New Hampshire & Maine
Vienna & the Danube Valley
Vietnam
Virgin Islands
Virginia
Walt Disney World® & Orlando
Washington, D.C.
Washington State

FROMMER'S® DOLLAR-A-DAY GUIDES

Australia from $60 a Day
California from $70 a Day
England from $75 a Day
Europe from $85 a Day
Florida from $70 a Day

Hawaii from $80 a Day
Ireland from $90 a Day
Italy from $90 a Day
London from $95 a Day

New York City from $90 a Day
Paris from $95 a Day
San Francisco from $70 a Day
Washington, D.C. from $80 a Day

FROMMER'S® PORTABLE GUIDES

Acapulco, Ixtapa & Zihuatanejo
Amsterdam
Aruba
Australia's Great Barrier Reef
Bahamas
Berlin
Big Island of Hawaii
Boston
California Wine Country
Cancún
Cayman Islands
Charleston
Chicago

Disneyland®
Dominican Republic
Dublin
Florence
Las Vegas
Las Vegas for Non-Gamblers
London
Los Angeles
Maui
Nantucket & Martha's Vineyard
New Orleans
New York City
Paris

Portland
Puerto Rico
Puerto Vallarta, Manzanillo & Guadalajara
Rio de Janeiro
San Diego
San Francisco
Savannah
Vancouver
Venice
Virgin Islands
Washington, D.C.
Whistler

FROMMER'S® CRUISE GUIDES

Alaska Cruises & Ports of Call

Cruises & Ports of Call

European Cruises & Ports of Call

FROMMER'S® DAY BY DAY GUIDES

Amsterdam
Chicago
Florence & Tuscany

London
New York City
Paris

Rome
San Francisco
Venice

FROMMER'S® NATIONAL PARK GUIDES

Algonquin Provincial Park
Banff & Jasper
Grand Canyon

National Parks of the American West
Rocky Mountain
Yellowstone & Grand Teton

Yosemite and Sequoia & Kings
  Canyon
Zion & Bryce Canyon

FROMMER'S® MEMORABLE WALKS

Chicago
London

New York
Paris

Rome
San Francisco

FROMMER'S® WITH KIDS GUIDES

Chicago
Hawaii
Las Vegas
London

National Parks
New York City
San Francisco

Toronto
Walt Disney World® & Orlando
Washington, D.C.

SUZY GERSHMAN'S BORN TO SHOP GUIDES

Born to Shop: France
Born to Shop: Hong Kong, Shanghai
  & Beijing

Born to Shop: Italy
Born to Shop: London

Born to Shop: New York
Born to Shop: Paris

FROMMER'S® IRREVERENT GUIDES

Amsterdam
Boston
Chicago
Las Vegas
London

Los Angeles
Manhattan
New Orleans
Paris

Rome
San Francisco
Walt Disney World®
Washington, D.C.

FROMMER'S® BEST-LOVED DRIVING TOURS

Austria
Britain
California
France

Germany
Ireland
Italy
New England

Northern Italy
Scotland
Spain
Tuscany & Umbria

THE UNOFFICIAL GUIDES®

Adventure Travel in Alaska
Beyond Disney
California with Kids
Central Italy
Chicago
Cruises
Disneyland®
England
Florida
Florida with Kids

Hawaii
Ireland
Las Vegas
London
Maui
Mexico's Best Beach Resorts
Mini Las Vegas
Mini Mickey
New Orleans
New York City

Paris
San Francisco
South Florida including Miami &
  the Keys
Walt Disney World®
Walt Disney World® for
  Grown-ups
Walt Disney World® with Kids
Washington, D.C.

SPECIAL-INTEREST TITLES

Athens Past & Present
Cities Ranked & Rated
Frommer's Best Day Trips from London
Frommer's Best RV & Tent Campgrounds
  in the U.S.A.

Frommer's Exploring America by RV
Frommer's NYC Free & Dirt Cheap
Frommer's Road Atlas Europe
Frommer's Road Atlas Ireland
Retirement Places Rated

FROMMER'S® PHRASEFINDER DICTIONARY GUIDES

French

Italian

Spanish

THE NEW TRAVELOCITY GUARANTEE

EVERYTHING YOU BOOK WILL BE RIGHT, OR WE'LL WORK WITH OUR TRAVEL PARTNERS TO MAKE IT RIGHT, RIGHT AWAY.

To drive home the point,
we're going to use the word "right" in every single sentence.

Let's get right to it. Right to the meat! Only Travelocity guarantees everything about your booking will be right, or we'll work with our travel partners to make it right, right away. Right on!

Here's a picture taken smack dab right in the middle of Antigua, where the guarantee also covers you.

The guarantee covers all but one of the items pictured to the right.

For example, what if the ocean view you booked actually looks out at a downright ugly parking lot? You'd be right to call – we're there for you. And no one in their right mind would be pleased to learn the rental car place has closed and left them stranded. Call Travelocity and we'll help get you back on the right track.

Now, you may be thinking, "Yeah, right, I'm so sure." That's OK; you have the right to remain skeptical. That is until we mention help is always right around the corner. Call us right off the bat, knowing that our customer service reps are there for you 24/7. Righting wrongs. Left and right.

Now if you're guessing there are some things we can't control, like the weather, well you're right. But we can help you with most things – to get all the details in righting,* visit **travelocity.com/guarantee**.

* Sorry, spelling things right is one of the few things not covered under the guarantee.

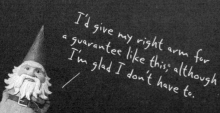

I'd give my right arm for a guarantee like this, although I'm glad I don't have to.

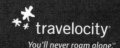

IF YOU BOOK IT, IT SHOULD BE THERE.

Only Travelocity guarantees it will be, or we'll work with our travel partners to make it right, right away. So if you're missing a balcony or anything else you booked, just call us 24/7. 1-888-TRAVELOCITY.

travelocity

You'll never roam alone